Innovative Professional Development Methods and Strategies for STEM Education

Kenan Dikilitaş
Hasan Kalyoncu University, Turkey

A volume in the Advances in Higher Education and Professional Development (AHEPD) Book Series

Information Science REFERENCE
An Imprint of IGI Global

Published in the United States of America by
Information Science Reference (an imprint of IGI Global)
701 E. Chocolate Avenue
Hershey PA, USA 17033
Tel: 717-533-8845
Fax: 717-533-8661
E-mail: cust@igi-global.com
Web site: http://www.igi-global.com

Copyright © 2016 by IGI Global. All rights reserved. No part of this publication may be reproduced, stored or distributed in any form or by any means, electronic or mechanical, including photocopying, without written permission from the publisher. Product or company names used in this set are for identification purposes only. Inclusion of the names of the products or companies does not indicate a claim of ownership by IGI Global of the trademark or registered trademark.
Library of Congress Cataloging-in-Publication Data

Names: Dikilitas, Kenen, 1973- editor.
Title: Innovative professional development methods and strategies for STEM
  education / Kenen Dikilitas, editor.
Description: Hershey PA : Information Science Reference, 2016. | Includes
  bibliographical references and index.
Identifiers: LCCN 2015031255 | 9781466694712 (hardcover) | 9781466694729 (ebook)
Subjects: LCSH: Science teachers--In-service training. | Mathematics
  teachers--In-service training. | Science--Study and teaching (Continuing
  education) | Mathematics--Study and teaching (Continuing education)
Classification: LCC Q181 .I48 2016 | DDC 507.1--dc23 LC record available at http://lccn.loc.gov/2015031255

This book is published in the IGI Global book series Advances in Higher Education and Professional Development (AHEPD) (ISSN: 2327-6983; eISSN: 2327-6991)

British Cataloguing in Publication Data
A Cataloguing in Publication record for this book is available from the British Library.

All work contributed to this book is new, previously-unpublished material. The views expressed in this book are those of the authors, but not necessarily of the publisher.

For electronic access to this publication, please contact: eresources@igi-global.com.

Advances in Higher Education and Professional Development (AHEPD) Book Series

Jared Keengwe
University of North Dakota, USA

ISSN: 2327-6983
EISSN: 2327-6991

Mission

As world economies continue to shift and change in response to global financial situations, job markets have begun to demand a more highly-skilled workforce. In many industries a college degree is the minimum requirement and further educational development is expected to advance. With these current trends in mind, the **Advances in Higher Education & Professional Development (AHEPD) Book Series** provides an outlet for researchers and academics to publish their research in these areas and to distribute these works to practitioners and other researchers.

AHEPD encompasses all research dealing with higher education pedagogy, development, and curriculum design, as well as all areas of professional development, regardless of focus.

Coverage

- Adult Education
- Assessment in Higher Education
- Career Training
- Coaching and Mentoring
- Continuing Professional Development
- Governance in Higher Education
- Higher Education Policy
- Pedagogy of Teaching Higher Education
- Vocational Education

IGI Global is currently accepting manuscripts for publication within this series. To submit a proposal for a volume in this series, please contact our Acquisition Editors at Acquisitions@igi-global.com or visit: http://www.igi-global.com/publish/.

The Advances in Higher Education and Professional Development (AHEPD) Book Series (ISSN 2327-6983) is published by IGI Global, 701 E. Chocolate Avenue, Hershey, PA 17033-1240, USA, www.igi-global.com. This series is composed of titles available for purchase individually; each title is edited to be contextually exclusive from any other title within the series. For pricing and ordering information please visit http://www.igi-global.com/book-series/advances-higher-education-professional-development/73681. Postmaster: Send all address changes to above address. Copyright © 2016 IGI Global. All rights, including translation in other languages reserved by the publisher. No part of this series may be reproduced or used in any form or by any means – graphics, electronic, or mechanical, including photocopying, recording, taping, or information and retrieval systems – without written permission from the publisher, except for non commercial, educational use, including classroom teaching purposes. The views expressed in this series are those of the authors, but not necessarily of IGI Global.

Titles in this Series

For a list of additional titles in this series, please visit: www.igi-global.com

Handbook of Research on Technology Tools for Real-World Skill Development
Yigal Rosen (Harvard University, USA) Steve Ferrara (Pearson, USA) and Maryam Mosharraf (Pearson, USA)
Information Science Reference • copyright 2016 • 913pp • H/C (ISBN: 9781466694415) • US $420.00 (our price)

Furthering Higher Education Possibilities through Massive Open Online Courses
Anabela Mesquita (CICE – ISCAP / Polytechnic of Porto, Portugal & Algoritmi RC, Minho University, Portugal) and Paula Peres (CICE – ISCAP / Polytechnic of Porto, Portugal)
Information Science Reference • copyright 2015 • 312pp • H/C (ISBN: 9781466682795) • US $175.00 (our price)

Handbook of Research on Teacher Education in the Digital Age
Margaret L. Niess (Oregon State University, USA) and Henry Gillow-Wiles (Oregon State University, USA)
Information Science Reference • copyright 2015 • 722pp • H/C (ISBN: 9781466684034) • US $415.00 (our price)

Handbook of Research on Enhancing Teacher Education with Advanced Instructional Technologies
Nwachukwu Prince Ololube (Ignatius Ajuru University of Education, Nigeria) Peter James Kpolovie (University of Port Harcourt, Nigeria) and Lazarus Ndiku Makewa (University of Eastern Africa, Kenya)
Information Science Reference • copyright 2015 • 485pp • H/C (ISBN: 9781466681620) • US $315.00 (our price)

Handbook of Research on Advancing Critical Thinking in Higher Education
Sherrie Wisdom (Lindenwood University, USA) and Lynda Leavitt (Lindenwood University, USA)
Information Science Reference • copyright 2015 • 568pp • H/C (ISBN: 9781466684119) • US $325.00 (our price)

Measuring and Analyzing Informal Learning in the Digital Age
Olutoyin Mejiuni (Obafemi Awolowo University, Nigeria) Patricia Cranton (University of New Brunswick, Canada) and Olúfẹ́mi Táíwò (Cornell University, USA)
Information Science Reference • copyright 2015 • 336pp • H/C (ISBN: 9781466682658) • US $185.00 (our price)

Transformative Curriculum Design in Health Sciences Education
Colleen Halupa (A.T. Still University, USA & LeTourneau University, USA)
Medical Information Science Reference • copyright 2015 • 388pp • H/C (ISBN: 9781466685710) • US $215.00 (our price)

Handbook of Research on Innovative Technology Integration in Higher Education
Fredrick Muyia Nafukho (Texas A&M University, USA) and Beverly J. Irby (Texas A&M University, USA)
Information Science Reference • copyright 2015 • 478pp • H/C (ISBN: 9781466681705) • US $310.00 (our price)

www.igi-global.com

701 E. Chocolate Ave., Hershey, PA 17033
Order online at www.igi-global.com or call 717-533-8845 x100
To place a standing order for titles released in this series, contact: cust@igi-global.com
Mon-Fri 8:00 am - 5:00 pm (est) or fax 24 hours a day 717-533-8661

Table of Contents

Preface xiv

Chapter 1
The Role of the Professional Doctorate in Developing Professional Practice in STEM Subjects 1
    Peter Smith, University of Sunderland, UK
    John Fulton, University of Sunderland, UK
    Alastair Irons, University of Sunderland, UK
    Gail Sanders, University of Sunderland, UK

Chapter 2
Mentoring Girls in Science: Eight Case Studies of a Science Camp Experience 17
    Donna Farland-Smith, The Ohio State University, USA

Chapter 3
Primary Grades Teachers' Fidelity of Teaching Practices during Mathematics Professional
Development 32
    Christie S. Martin, University of South Carolina at Columbia, USA
    Drew Polly, University of North Carolina at Charlotte, USA
    Chuang Wang, University of North Carolina at Charlotte, USA
    Richard G. Lambert, University of North Carolina at Charlotte, USA
    David Pugalee, University of North Carolina at Charlotte, USA

Chapter 4
A Paradigm Shift for Teachers' Professional Development Structure in Turkey: Moving from
Instruction to Learning 52
    Murat Günel, TED University, Turkey
    Melike Özer-Keskin, Gazi University, Turkey
    Nilay Keskin-Samancı, Gazi University, Turkey

Chapter 5
Systematic Support for STEM Pre-Service Teachers: An Authentic and Sustainable Four-Pillar
Professional Development Model 73
    Reenay R.H. Rogers, University of West Alabama, USA
    Jodie Winship, University of West Alabama, USA
    Yan Sun, University of West Alabama, USA

Chapter 6
The Role of Teacher Leadership for Promoting Professional Development Practices 91
    Patricia Dickenson, National University, USA
    Judith L. Montgomery, University of California Santa Cruz, USA

Chapter 7
Teachers' Professional Development in the Digitized World: A Sample Blended Learning
Environment for Educational Technology Training.. 115
    Emsal Ates Ozdemir, Istanbul Sehir University, Turkey
    Kenan Dikilitaş, Hasan Kalyoncu University, Turkey

Chapter 8
Introducing Educational Technology into the Higher Education Environment: A Professional
Development Framework.. 126
    Linda Van Ryneveld, University of Pretoria, South Africa

Chapter 9
Supporting the Enactment of Standards-based Mathematics Pedagogies: The Cases of the CoDE-I
and APLUS Projects 137
    Drew Polly, University of North Carolina at Charlotte, USA
    Christie Martin, University of South Carolina at Columbia, USA
    Chuang Wang, University of North Carolina at Charlotte, USA
    Richard Lambert, University of North Carolina at Charlotte, USA
    David Pugalee, University of North Carolina at Charlotte, USA

Chapter 10
Identifying the Target Needs of Non-Native Subject Teachers Related to the Use of English in
Their Professional Settings: A Case from Northern Iraq... 149
    Ece Zehir Topkaya, Çanakkale Onsekiz Mart University, Turkey
    İbrahim Nişancı, Ishik University, Iraq

Chapter 11
Impact of a Professional Development Programme on Trainee Teachers' Beliefs and Teaching
Practices 176
    Yasemin Kırkgöz, Cukurova University, Turkey

Chapter 12
Prospective EFL Teachers' Perceptions of Using CALL in the Classroom 195
    Anıl Rakicioglu-Soylemez, Abant Izzet Baysal University, Turkey
    Sedat Akayoglu, Abant Izzet Baysal University, Turkey

Chapter 13
The Impact of Pre-service Teachers' Reflection on their Instructional Practices.............................. 209
    Yesim Kesli Dollar, Bahcesehir University, Turkey
    Enisa Mede, Bahcesehir University, Turkey

Chapter 14
Exploring Prospective EFL Teachers' Beliefs about Teachers and Teaching through Metaphor
Analysis... 220
    Anil Rakicioglu-Soylemez, Abant Izzet Baysal University, Turkey
    Ayse Selmin Soylemez, Abant Izzet Baysal University, Turkey
    Amanda Yesilbursa, Uludag University, Turkey

Related References 238

Compilation of References 279

About the Contributors 305

Index 310

Detailed Table of Contents

Preface xiv

Chapter 1
The Role of the Professional Doctorate in Developing Professional Practice in STEM Subjects 1
    Peter Smith, University of Sunderland, UK
    John Fulton, University of Sunderland, UK
    Alastair Irons, University of Sunderland, UK
    Gail Sanders, University of Sunderland, UK

This chapter presents a study into the impact of the professional doctorate as a learning opportunity for STEM professionals including engineers, pharmacists, nurses, STEM teachers, healthcare professionals, and computing professionals. The professional doctorate is a relatively new approach to doctoral study, which has much to offer to STEM. This form of doctoral study encourages the candidate to undertake project work which is based in, and contributes to, their professional practice. The candidates are experienced practitioners, who wish to raise their practice to doctoral level. This chapter presents a mixed methods study, which has collected and analyzed quantitative data obtained from a survey, qualitative data obtained from focus group sessions, and in-depth narrative accounts. Analysis of these data revealed a number of themes including the importance of trans-professional working, reflection, and development of "authentic" professional voice.

Chapter 2
Mentoring Girls in Science: Eight Case Studies of a Science Camp Experience 17
    Donna Farland-Smith, The Ohio State University, USA

Content area specialists (scientists) are often recruited as mentors of students to address issues in science education. These scientists are frequently recruited to help with the teaching of science, however, quite often do not have the pedagogy skills needed to be role models for young children. Guidance in the selection appropriate mentors would help maximize the potential influence on students understanding of who does science, where science is done and what scientists do. This study illustrates six case studies of scientists as they worked with middle school girls and identifies five characteristics educators should look for in selecting science mentors successful in broadening students' perceptions of scientists. The data was collected during 'Side-by-Side' interaction with scientists/mentors during a summer camp experience and has implications for classroom practice as the use of mentors can be structured to support the infusion of Science as a Human Endeavor. As the students' experiences with mentor scientists helped to shape their perception of those who pursue careers in science and what it is that scientists do, careful consideration and preparation of mentors were critical to the success of the program, and so this paper also provides suggestions to help highly trained and highly educated scientists in these mentorship roles.

Chapter 3
Primary Grades Teachers' Fidelity of Teaching Practices during Mathematics Professional Development 32
Christie S. Martin, University of South Carolina at Columbia, USA
Drew Polly, University of North Carolina at Charlotte, USA
Chuang Wang, University of North Carolina at Charlotte, USA
Richard G. Lambert, University of North Carolina at Charlotte, USA
David Pugalee, University of North Carolina at Charlotte, USA

This chapter shares the findings from a study that examined primary grades teachers' fidelity of implementation during a year-long professional development program on formative assessment in mathematics. The project provided over 80 hours of professional development to elementary school teachers regarding their use of an internet-based formative assessment system for their students' mathematics achievement. This study examined teachers' online reflections and data in the internet-based assessment system to identify themes that lead to either a high fidelity or low fidelity of implementation. High fidelity teachers expressed beliefs that formative assessment supported their mathematics teaching, improved their students' learning, and was feasible to carry out in their classrooms. Low fidelity teachers' reflections were associated with numerous barriers to implementation as well as a lack of buy-in that the formative assessment system could benefit their teaching.

Chapter 4
A Paradigm Shift for Teachers' Professional Development Structure in Turkey: Moving from Instruction to Learning 52
Murat Günel, TED University, Turkey
Melike Özer-Keskin, Gazi University, Turkey
Nilay Keskin-Samancı, Gazi University, Turkey

This chapter concerns the importance of in-service training programmes for the professional development of science teachers. A description will be given of the general structure of in-service training activities in Turkey and the results will be presented of an in-service training project, which was conducted as part of a three-year longitudinal study. Within the scope of the project, an in-service training programme for science teachers was conducted based on the argument-based inquiry approach and the theoretical premises upon which it is built. The project aimed to direct science teachers towards student-centred teaching. The training activities focused on the scientific thinking underpinning the teachers' professional knowledge and practices, their perceptions on learning, and their pedagogical practices and epistemological beliefs. The extent to which these activities affected classroom applications and learning processes was investigated and the findings suggest that they had a statistically significant impact on the teachers' pedagogical development and on the students' academic performance and thinking skills.

Chapter 5
Systematic Support for STEM Pre-Service Teachers: An Authentic and Sustainable Four-Pillar
Professional Development Model 73
    Reenay R.H. Rogers, University of West Alabama, USA
    Jodie Winship, University of West Alabama, USA
    Yan Sun, University of West Alabama, USA

Developing a strong STEM teacher workforce is essential to improve K-12 (kindergarten to 12th grade) STEM education and to strengthen the STEM talent pipeline in the United States. Based on the successful experience in Project Engage, a grant funded by the U.S. Department of Education, this chapter proposes an authentic and sustainable four-pillar STEM professional development model. Grounded on social constructivist and interactive approaches, this professional development model is intended to cultivate STEM pre-service teachers' ability to provide K-12 students with authentic STEM learning experience as defined in the four types of authenticity (i.e., context authenticity, task authenticity, impact authenticity, and personal/value authenticity) identified by Strobel and his colleagues (Strobel, Wang, Weber, & Dyehouse, 2013).

Chapter 6
The Role of Teacher Leadership for Promoting Professional Development Practices 91
    Patricia Dickenson, National University, USA
    Judith L. Montgomery, University of California Santa Cruz, USA

This chapter examines the status of teacher professional development in mathematics and explores the role of teacher leadership to promote innovative professional development strategies that sustain the growth and development of an organization. Survey data was collected from teacher leader participants of one mathematics professional development organization to understand how participants' growth and development as a teacher leader not only shaped their mathematics instructional practices, but influenced their choices in leadership roles. Further the authors share how the learning environment and pedagogical choices of the project director supported a teacher-driven professional development approach. Recommendations as well as a model for developing a teacher-driven professional development organization are provided for replication.

Chapter 7
Teachers' Professional Development in the Digitized World: A Sample Blended Learning
Environment for Educational Technology Training.. 115
    Emsal Ates Ozdemir, Istanbul Sehir University, Turkey
    Kenan Dikilitaş, Hasan Kalyoncu University, Turkey

Professional development for in-service English language teachers has increasingly become a need in higher education not only in Turkey but across the world. Due to the limited time teachers have and the distance between the source of service and the potential participants, using digitized activities and materials have naturally become a necessity. The purpose of this research is to report the potential impact of the course described below and discuss the role of blended learning experience of professional development on the participating teachers. The theoretical background of the study is experiential learning initiated by Kolb and socio-constructivist learning theory by Vygotsky in that both theories highlight the role of experiencing the change and focus on personal meanings and learning with and from others in real and online environments.

Chapter 8
Introducing Educational Technology into the Higher Education Environment: A Professional Development Framework 126
> *Linda Van Ryneveld, University of Pretoria, South Africa*

Over the past decade or two advancements in educational technology have taken place so swiftly that it threatens to revolutionise the education system. This phenomena seem to drive higher education institutions to respond with costly roll out plans that bring state of the art computing hard- and software, together with other highly specialized educational technologies, to their campuses. The dilemma is that these investments in educational technology are often made in isolation, without consideration for imperative aspects such as professional development. To progress, educators need to acquire the skills, knowledge and attitudes necessary to make optimal use of the technology. This can be achieved, among other, by means of well-structured professional development programmes. In this chapter the author explores the role of educational technology in higher education and establishes the need for capacity building by means of carefully designed professional development programmes. It furthermore suggests an alternative professional development framework.

Chapter 9
Supporting the Enactment of Standards-based Mathematics Pedagogies: The Cases of the CoDE-I and APLUS Projects 137
> *Drew Polly, University of North Carolina at Charlotte, USA*
> *Christie Martin, University of South Carolina at Columbia, USA*
> *Chuang Wang, University of North Carolina at Charlotte, USA*
> *Richard Lambert, University of North Carolina at Charlotte, USA*
> *David Pugalee, University of North Carolina at Charlotte, USA*

In order for professional development in the STEM fields to be effective, teachers need worthwhile experiences to simultaneously develop their knowledge of content, pedagogy, and understanding of how students' learn the content. In this chapter we provide an overarching framework of learner-centered professional development and describe the implementation of two mathematics professional development projects designed to support elementary school teachers' mathematics teaching. We follow our description by highlighting some of the findings from our line of professional development research and provide implications for the design of learner-centered professional development programs in mathematics.

Chapter 10
Identifying the Target Needs of Non-Native Subject Teachers Related to the Use of English in Their Professional Settings: A Case from Northern Iraq 149
> *Ece Zehir Topkaya, Çanakkale Onsekiz Mart University, Turkey*
> *İbrahim Nişancı, Ishik University, Iraq*

This study primarily explores the target needs of subject teachers from various disciplines who are all non-native speakers of English and enrolled in a training program preparing them to teach their subjects in English. Secondarily, it looks into the key stakeholders' evaluation of the program to understand its effectiveness to meet the needs of the teachers. For the first question, key stakeholders were interviewed to identify the needs, wants, and lacks of the teachers based on Hutchinson and Water's (1987) needs analysis framework. Then, the pooled items were converted into a questionnaire which was administered to the teachers in the program. To investigate the second question, open-ended questions and semi-structured interviews were used. Findings revealed that participants were in need of developing productive language skills while they reported satisfaction over the program. It is concluded that a more specifically tailored course both in terms of content and practice is needed.

Chapter 11
Impact of a Professional Development Programme on Trainee Teachers' Beliefs and Teaching Practices 176
Yasemin Kırkgöz, Cukurova University, Turkey

This study emerged from the concerns experienced by the last-year English language trainee teachers during their school practicum. An increasing number of trainees complained that their existing beliefs conflicted, in many ways, with the school-based mentor's teaching practice. A collaborative action research (CAR) professional development programme (PDP) was established to help prospective teachers resolve many of the dilemmas and improve their classroom practices in a 10-week practicum course. It was found that CAR has a powerful impact upon teacher candidates as it solves many of the dilemmas and concerns. Belief changes of one trainee teacher are presented as an exemplary case. While such findings can improve our understandings of pre-service teachers' cognitive learning and problem solving skills at the practicum site, they also generate useful insights into designing a PDP to promote trainee teachers' school-based professional development in STEM (science, technology, engineering, and mathematic) education.

Chapter 12
Prospective EFL Teachers' Perceptions of Using CALL in the Classroom 195
Anıl Rakicioglu-Soylemez, Abant Izzet Baysal University, Turkey
Sedat Akayoglu, Abant Izzet Baysal University, Turkey

The study focuses on prospective English as a foreign language (EFL) teachers' perspectives on the use of Computer Assisted Language Learning (CALL) resources in teaching English as a foreign language context. In addition to examining prospective teachers' perceptions, the similarities and differences in their perceptions and factors affecting their beliefs about using CALL resources will be addressed. The study aimed to identify the prospective EFL teachers' perceptions of their existing skills to integrate CALL into their future professional practices. The perceived factors that will facilitate and inhibit their future teaching practices by using CALL resources and their expectations from the teacher education program in terms of providing the necessary training to use CALL resources in their teaching practices were examined. The perceived benefits and challenges of using CALL in EFL teaching contexts will be addressed from the participants' perspectives. Finally, the study provides implications for further research in addition to recommendations for EFL teacher education programs.

Chapter 13
The Impact of Pre-service Teachers' Reflection on their Instructional Practices 209
    Yesim Kesli Dollar, Bahcesehir University, Turkey
    Enisa Mede, Bahcesehir University, Turkey

This chapter aims to investigate the impact of reflection on freshmen pre-service English teachers' classroom practices. Specifically, it explores how the participating student teachers' perceptions influenced their instructional practices as a result of participation in reflection activities. The participants of the study were ten freshmen student teachers enrolled in the English Language Teaching undergraduate program at a foundation (non-profit private) university in Turkey. Data came from the reflections of the participating student teachers about their recently-completed 15-hour field-based experience at the pre-school level. As a part of this class reflection activity, the participants were prompted to keep a diary in one of their undergraduate courses and respond to a series of statements or questions related to their classroom observation tasks. They were also engaged in class discussions and were required to write their overall feedback based on their field-based experience. The findings of the study revealed that reflective activities helped the prospective student teachers identify their strengths and weaknesses related to classroom activities, use of materials (use of technology and visuals) and classroom management, leading to self-awareness about their understanding and application of teaching skills and strategies.

Chapter 14
Exploring Prospective EFL Teachers' Beliefs about Teachers and Teaching through Metaphor
Analysis...220
    Anil Rakicioglu-Soylemez, Abant Izzet Baysal University, Turkey
    Ayse Selmin Soylemez, Abant Izzet Baysal University, Turkey
    Amanda Yesilbursa, Uludag University, Turkey

This study aimed to explore prospective EFL teachers' metaphors of "teachers, teaching" and "being a prospective EFL teacher" at the beginning and end of a ten-week practicum course. A total of 110 Turkish prospective EFL teachers voluntarily participated in the study. Data were collected by means of semi-structured interviews and metaphor-elicitation forms. Results lead to three major conclusions. First, the participants' prior beliefs about the role of an EFL teacher and teaching were affected by their previous experiences as language learners. Second, although the content analysis of the metaphors revealed a limited change throughout the practicum experience, the analysis of the interviews showed the dynamic nature of beliefs held by the prospective teachers. Finally, data analysis of the interviews showed that the variation in beliefs and practices mainly derived from individual experiences with the mentoring practices of the cooperating teachers and the socio-professional context of the practicum school.

Related References 238

Compilation of References 279

About the Contributors 305

Index 310

Preface

Professional development (PD) is a growing area within the field of STEM. There is increasing need for STEM teachers' professional development activities in higher education across the world. Effective PD that serves for effective teacher learning in the long term requires cognitive, knowledge and practical development simultaneously. To this end, constructive, socio-constructive, and interactive approaches to PD are documented in this book in a way to show how teachers develop and are likely to change for better instruction and student learning. In this sense, the professional development strategies that teachers are involved in should reflect cognitive, constructive, interactive, thought-provoking and argumentative aspects of development. The major mission of this book is to bring together implementations of effective professional development strategies including those that are trainee-based and process-oriented, which extends the amounts of cognitive engagement and lead to concurrent cognitive and behavioral changes in teachers from the field of STEM education. However, the impact of various types of PD activities across the world needs more extensively documentation. The chapters in this book focus on the description, implementation and impact of PD strategies on the participating teachers and highlight several characteristics of trainees who are intrinsically motivated to develop and change personally and professionally.

Teachers' Professional Development and Learners

PD has been one of the critical areas in education sector in relation to teacher learning and development particularly at higher education level. The importance attached to PD increases as students profile is changing towards one that encompasses more in-depth capabilities enabled through multifaceted educational tools particularly thanks to the developing digital facilities connected through information exchange and sharing technology. This incremental and exponential change in student profiles necessitates developmental pedagogical growth in teachers who can address these shifted and increased students' learning potential. This book showcases these efforts for teachers' professional development across the world from a wide range of specific contexts.

In line with these development on the part of student profiles, the nature of PD is also changing from top down approach, which is externally governed to bottom up approach, which is internally initiated or individually managed over a course of period. The latter is introduced as a more contemporary approach in that it leads to more self-control over PD and more relevance to personal needs for own learning and development. These two basic approaches serve for different purposes. The former addresses short term

Preface

needs for discrete skill learning based on preset learning outcomes, while the latter addresses long term needs based on development personally identified which required cognitive processing of what is learnt. Knowledge generated in this way might lead to more permanent learning and developing ownership of self-constructed knowledge. Learners are the primary beneficiaries as opposed to actors and learning is the ultimate process that needs promoting through the impact of PD participation.

Professional Development Methods and Strategies

Several different methods and strategies are employed to promote teachers' knowledge, beliefs and skills which could play a key role in enhancing students' learning and promoting school development, which in turn contribute to socio-intellectual progress. In general there are two general paradigms to the concept of professional development. One is the top-down models which are planned, designed and delivered by those parties who are not going to benefit directly from the intervention namely decision makers such as administrators or coordinators. The other is bottom up models which prioritize those who will benefit from the interventions, namely the teachers. In the latter teachers are given the control of their own professional development with little or minimized interference from others such as trainers, supervisors or mentors. Teachers' own needs and ideas are centralized in these models, thus helping them sustain their professional development with an intrinsic motivation which includes a purpose to fulfil or a benefit to make at the end. On the other hand, the former may not be addressing and covering teachers own needs and understanding, thus leading to little or no positive impact at the end of the engagement in the activities.

Most PD models require principles of bottom-up paradigm, which is supported by top-down resources. This clarifies the role of each party. Teachers' role has shifted from the recipient of knowledge to constructor of it, which has also changed PD providers' role from source of knowledge to supporters of personal and social knowledge construction. However, it should be noted that top down models are not completely ignored but are changing in nature. When top down decisions are taken in relation to the needs of the teachers, and the guidance and control of the training process is shared democratically, where teachers also play key roles in learning new knowledge and skills, then top down models are not to be harshly criticized. Similarly, bottom up models may also bring about failure in creating efficient impact and results if the participants are totally given the control of the training process. First, it could be because trainees or teachers may not possess the skills and knowledge to decide properly on exact PD procedures to be followed. Second, general organization of PD can be evaluated and developed on the basis of the expert input and perspective without any relevance to the actually needs of the trainees. It is then clear that two models should go hand in hand to ensure quality of PD and clear and observable influence of the participants.

Scope of Professional Development

In the light of the discussion hitherto, it is necessary to consider a set of nine standards that all professional development should follow which were highlighted by The National Staff Development Council (2007): content knowledge and quality teaching, research-basis, collaboration, diverse learning needs, student learning environments, family involvement, evaluation, data-driven design, and teacher learning. This set of standards shows that professional development is a social activity that involves full participation and consideration of a wide range of parties from researchers to families of students. It is this integrity that could lead to greater learning on the part of the person who is doing professional development.

PD is no more an exception but a necessity. However, it should be well-resourced and supported in terms of money, time, incentive, and support. It is the institution that could provide all these conditions by offering finance and guidance. Therefore, the context where PD is carried out plays a major role in the continuation of professional learning opportunities. PD could empower and influence teachers, learners, and the schools positively when teachers' efforts are appreciated and considered in future decisions of curriculum, syllabus and appointment, which could lead to more motivation to do professional learning on the part of teachers.

Overview of Chapters

The future of PD seems brighter than it is today particularly because so many research studies are being carried out and disseminated which richly delineate and critically evaluate and insightfully synthesize the professional development activities in a wide range of disciplines. The chapters in this book are also adding to that increasing number of publication. This book is a collection of studies carried out in diverse contexts and contents including science, math, education, engineering, technology. It also encompasses theoretical research studies from pre-service and in-service levels, which helps see the status of professional development from different layers of education for professional community. Professional development of STEM teachers are also discussed and presented with special emphasis on theoretical perspectives underlying these PD initiatives.

In the first chapter, Smith, Fulton, Irons, and Sanders elaborate on the major role that practice-base doctorates, a new approach to promoting practice through project work, play in developing experienced practitioners' professional practice in STEM subjects. In the second chapter, Farland-Smith details how to mentor girls in science drawing on eight case studies which involve content specialists and middle school girls in order to provide implications for diverse roles of teachers and scientists in learning and teaching science. In the third chapter, Martin, Polly, Wang, Lambert, and Pugalee describe and discuss a mathematics professional development in order to report the potential impact of primary grades teachers' online reflections over the internet-based formative assessment system on their fidelity of implementation. In the next chapter, Günel, Özer-Keskin and Keskin-Samancı delineate a paradigm shift in the structure of in-service science and technology teachers' professional development in Turkey by explicitly focusing on how PD has been moving from instruction to learning through process-based approaches with a view to affecting teacher learning. In the fifth chapter, Rogers, Winship, and Sun draw on social constructivist and interactive approaches and describe an authentic and sustainable four-pillar professional development model which provides systematic support for STEM pre-service teachers to promote K-12 students' authentic STEM learning experience. In the following chapter, Dickenson and Montgomery describes the critical role of teacher professional development in mathematics in developing relevant instructional practices and teachers' leadership skills. In chapter 7, Ateş Özdemir and Dikilitaş describe a pedagogical technology-oriented professional development programme conducted with a group of in-service teachers from different subjects and report short and long term impact that the programme had on the participating teachers' integration of technology into their classrooms and institutions.

Preface

In the next chapter, Van Ryneveld describes a professional development programme that involves training educators to develop skills by which to use educational technologies especially for suggesting how technology can be integrated effectively in higher education. Chapter 9 by Polly, Martin, Wang, Lambert and Pugalee describes two learner-centered PD projects which aim to facilitate mathematics teaching practices of elementary school teachers with an emphasis on the implications for PD program designing, which is based on learner-centered PD in mathematics. Chapter 10 by Topkaya and Nişancı involves an ESP context and identifies the target needs of non-native science and mathematics teachers for the use of English in their professional /school settings. The data triangulated through interviews with stakeholders in the programme revealed a critical need for developing training aiming for productive skills. In the next chapter, Kırkgöz describes and discusses potential impact of a collaborative action research professional development programme on the change in the pre-service teachers' beliefs and teaching practices with special emphasis on implications for school-based professional development. In chapter 12, Rakıcıoğlu-Söylemez and Akay investigate prospective EFL teachers' perceptions of using CALL in the classroom to identify perceived benefits and challenges which facilitate and inhibit future teaching practices with reference to the implications for professional development and EFL teacher education programs. Chapter 13 written by Mede-Saban and Keşli-Dollar describes the possible effects of reflection-based teacher development activities such as diary keeping on pre-service teachers' perceived instructional practices, self-awareness and strategy implementation. In chapter 14 Rakıcıoğlu-Söylemez, Söylemez, and Yeşilbursa analyze pre-service EFL teachers' metaphors to explore their beliefs about teachers and teaching and the potential sources of impact in the prospective teachers' beliefs and practices in order to draw implications for identifying areas of improvement for professional development.

Overall, this edited volume brings together detailed descriptions and experiences of constructive, socio-constructive and interactive approaches to PD and offers a diverse collection of chapters from different STEM subjects including education and provides potential impact areas on trainees and implications drawn for trainees and trainers. It is my hope that academicians, researchers, advanced-level students (MA and Ph.D), and technology developers will find this book beneficial and contributing to their PD engagement in relevant topics in STEM subjects and education.

Kenan Dikilitaş
Hasan Kalyoncu University, Turkey

Chapter 1
The Role of the Professional Doctorate in Developing Professional Practice in STEM Subjects

Peter Smith
University of Sunderland, UK

Alastair Irons
University of Sunderland, UK

John Fulton
University of Sunderland, UK

Gail Sanders
University of Sunderland, UK

ABSTRACT

This chapter presents a study into the impact of the professional doctorate as a learning opportunity for STEM professionals including engineers, pharmacists, nurses, STEM teachers, healthcare professionals, and computing professionals. The professional doctorate is a relatively new approach to doctoral study, which has much to offer to STEM. This form of doctoral study encourages the candidate to undertake project work which is based in, and contributes to, their professional practice. The candidates are experienced practitioners, who wish to raise their practice to doctoral level. This chapter presents a mixed methods study, which has collected and analyzed quantitative data obtained from a survey, qualitative data obtained from focus group sessions, and in-depth narrative accounts. Analysis of these data revealed a number of themes including the importance of trans-professional working, reflection, and development of "authentic" professional voice.

INTRODUCTION

Recent years have seen the emergence of professional doctorate programmes in many subjects, including STEM subjects (UKCGE, 2010). A professional doctorate offers experienced candidates an alternative to the traditional PhD, which has been designed to meet the requirements of practitioners (Lester, 2004). Such doctorates offer the opportunity to study part-time on a work-based project, which applies research methodology and rigor to the solution of a problem which is of relevance to the candidate, their organisa-

DOI: 10.4018/978-1-4666-9471-2.ch001

tion and their community of practice. The programme will also often aim to develop within the candidate the skills of self-reflection, reflexivity and criticality. This form of doctorate satisfies the demand for programmes which equip graduates with high-level transferable skills which meet employer requirements and market demand (Guthrie, 2009). Those studying on professional doctorate programmes are senior professionals, and exposure to these individuals provides academics with welcome links to industry, creating important new opportunities for knowledge transfer and providing opportunities for students and their supervisors to engage in research projects which have demonstrable impact on professional practice as studied by Hadacek & Carpenter (1998), who examined the impact of nursing doctorates.

Previous studies by Lester (2004), Taylor (2007) and Costley & Stephenson (2005) explored the balance between the workplace and academia, the concept of the "researching professional" and the concept of the doctoral level practitioner. This chapter reports on the authors' experiences of running a professional doctorate and extends a previous study of student motivations for, and expectations of a professional doctorate programme (Smith, Curtis, Sanders, Kuit, & Fulton, 2011). The chapter presents a mixed research methods approach, including a questionnaire, focus groups and narrative accounts, which involved more than 50 students at different stages of doctoral study. This chapter outlines the key themes which have emerged from the authors' reflections on the study, and presents some lessons learned which the authors believe will be of use to those who are running, or considering running, professional doctorate programmes within STEM subjects.

BACKGROUND

This chapter presents a case study of one Professional Doctorate programme. The Professional Doctorate (DProf) scheme under study has been running since 2007, and currently has over 70 students drawn from a range of professional backgrounds (Smith et al., 2011). The scheme was designed to meet the growing demand for a doctoral level qualification which enables candidates from business, industry and the professions to build an individual research programme based upon work which they are undertaking within the workplace (Smith, Walker-Gleaves, Fulton, & Candlish, 2009a; Smith et al., 2011).

The scheme enables a student to build up a doctoral submission based on a study situated within their own workplace. The candidate is required to undertake formal assessed coursework in the areas of reflective practice, research methodology and contextualization and planning, and to ultimately produce a doctoral thesis which demonstrates the contribution made to knowledge and the impact which they have made on their profession.

Each student is supported by two internal supervisors. The students follow similar enrolment, registration and annual monitoring processes as are followed by MPhil and PhD students. The students on the programme came from a variety of professional backgrounds, covering several STEM subjects. They include:

- Senior pharmacists, working on a variety of projects relating to professional pharmacy practice,
- Senior engineering and computing staff working on projects involving the acceptance and application of technology, and,
- Senior managers from business and finance; working on projects which involve the management of significant change within their professional context.

The concept of a cohort has been integral to the operation and success of the programme (Smith et al., 2009a; Smith, Walker-Gleaves, Fulton, & Candlish, 2009b; Smith et al., 2011) and each cohort has come together with core staff from the programme every two months for formal learning sessions. These sessions have delivered key material on reflective practice, and research methodology. They have also given the candidates the opportunity to discuss their project work with their peers and to offer each other support.

Most of the current students are based in the UK, with some students coming from Ireland. All students meet current admissions requirements; at least an upper second class honours degree, Masters degree, or equivalent. All students are required to be working within their profession and, through their job; they must have the opportunity to make a contribution to their profession and to practice.

The programme aims are (Smith et al., 2011):

- Develop students as reflective practitioners to enhance their professional practice and enable them to innovate, and make informed judgements.
- Develop within students the ability to synthesize ideas, concepts and approaches from their profession with relevant theoretical frameworks to create solutions, drive change, innovate and make a difference within their workplace
- Develop within students the ability to select appropriate research approaches from a range of research methods and to apply these to issues and dilemmas which they encounter in their own professional practice, and hence by doing so making a contribution to the practice within their profession
- Provide opportunities for personal fulfilment, professional development and career enhancement.

METHODOLOGY

The authors have undertaken a series of studies of the students of the programme and have reflected upon their own experiences to date in running the programme (Smith et al., 2009a, 2009b, 2011; Sanders, Kuit, Smith, Fulton, & Curtis, 2011; Sanders, Kuit, Smith, & Fulton, 2012; Fulton, Kuit, Sanders, & Smith, 2012a; 2012b; Thompson, Smith, & Cooper, 2012). This chapter presents a mixed methods study incorporating a survey, student focus groups and narrative accounts from tutors and students. The aim of the study was to explore student and tutor perceptions of the doctoral programme, in order to better understand student motivation, the impact which the programme has on students, to identify common themes and to use these themes as a basis for future development. The evaluation framework was based on the use of mixed methods for expansion; to "increase the scope of inquiry by selecting the methods most appropriate for multiple inquiry components" (Greene, Caracelli, & Graham, 1989).

For the survey, an online questionnaire was set up and all students on the DProf programme were asked to complete it. The questions were designed to explore the perceptions and expectations that the students had of the doctoral programme. In this study, 54% of students choose to complete the survey. In addition to the questionnaire, four focus group sessions were held with 6-10 students in each group. These were used to further explore some of the themes which emerged from the questionnaire. Finally, students and tutors were asked to write narrative accounts of these experiences. The authors analyzed the data from the survey, the focus groups and the narrative accounts, identifying a number of themes, using the thematic analysis approach of Fereday & Muir-Cochrane (2008) which recommends a hybrid approach of inductive and deductive coding and theme development, taking themes both from the data and from the literature. The data were coded by two of the authors working individually; the results were then compared and discussed and the final themes agreed by all authors.

THE IMPACT OF PROFESSIONAL DOCTORATE STUDY ON STEM STUDENTS

Themes

The authors have identified the following themes through their analysis:

- Cohort experience.
- Structure and academic support.
- Personal impact.
- Mixed employer perceptions.
- Reflective practice.
- Personal and professional values
- Professional identity, authenticity and personal voice.
- Trans-professional working.

The Survey

In the quantitative survey students were asked as series of questions about why they chose to study on the doctoral programme. The students were given the following choices (and could choose as many as they wished): (a) for personal achievement, (b) to achieve the qualification, (c) for career development and (d) for professional / subject interest. The highest response to this question was (a) for personal achievement (80% of respondents), with the next most popular choice being (d) professional / subject interest (67%). The other options scored thus: (b) to achieve the qualification (37%) and (c) career development (40%).

The students were also asked about the impact that the programme had upon themselves, and were given the following choices: (a) do you think more critically? (b) Do you understand theory more deeply?; (c) do you understand professional issues more deeply?; (d) do you approach your practice differently?; and (e) do you use reflective practice in your work? 68% of students felt that they thought more critically as a direct result of studying on the programme, 71% felt that they understood relevant theory more deeply, and 50% felt that they understood professional issues more deeply. All of the students recognised that studying on the programme had made a difference in the way that they approached their professional practice. 93% stated that they had begun to use reflective practice within their work context. Full details of the survey, the questions asked and the results can be found in Smith et al. (2011).

Focus Groups

Qualitative responses were obtained from focus group discussion. What came of them was that students greatly valued the cohort experience, and the way in which they were able to interact in a safe environment with professionals from other backgrounds. They also welcomed the structured nature of the programme, and found the days away from work a welcome escape from their busy professional environments, in which they could think and discuss their professional issues with tutors and peers. The deadlines for coursework were also seen to be a positive aspect, and something which they were all used to working to within their own work context. The personal impact of the programme and the way in which it enabled them to explore, and hence better understand their own professional issues, also came out strongly from the responses. Finally the students clearly greatly valued their interaction within academic tutors, and the different lenses through which they could view their work issues.

Some quotations taken from the focus groups and from the survey are given below:

A Professional Doctorate best fits with my learning journey, and allows me to explore professional issues.

The Programme provides me with flexibility, and yet a structured programme.

It provides the opportunity to site my project within the workplace, the freedom to work at my own pace; experiencing alternative ways of studying.

I greatly appreciate the support provided by the academic staff, and meeting up with the other students in the cohort, as we spur each other on.

I enjoy the interaction with a cohort of people from different disciplines and seeing how common themes emerge even from quite disparate areas.

The programme recognizes that applied industrial based research is a valid as pure academic traditional PhD research.

This process has helped me to make sense of my working life. It gives me a sense of achievement and maintains my interest in the sector I work in.

It has improved my ability to think critically and raised my self-confidence to a very high degree. And I am still very excited about what I am doing. I am developing the ability to think more critically and deeply.

There is a consistent focus on the need for your thoughts and emerging work to make a contribution to your profession. This is really important as I feel strongly that what I am doing should and must have a real impact on my profession and this doctorate facilitates this. I am thoroughly enjoying the programme and really gaining a significant body of knowledge and personal professional development.

The Programme has made me review my career in a structured way; and has allowed me to see my career contribution in a new light.

Narrative Accounts

Tutors and students were asked to write narrative accounts, reflecting on the impact which the Professional Doctorate has had upon them. Three accounts are reproduced here, as they were provided by the respondents. These are:

- A Programme Leader,
- A health scientist reflecting on Professional Doctorates in health within the UK, and
- An engineering academic reflecting on undertaking a Professional Doctorate.

In addition a series of extracts from student narrative accounts are included at the end of this section.

Programme Leader's Reflections

One of the aims of the Professional Doctorate is to encourage candidates to adopt fresh approaches to work issues and consider the workplace through what we describe as a 'fresh lens'. We introduce them to the idea that often solutions to problems within a profession can be found outside the boundaries of that profession, and we encourage them to explore different disciplines and working environments. We are assisted in this by the fact that our candidates are from a wide range of backgrounds, and all have considerable experience within their particular profession, many having already made a significant contribution to their field. As such, they bring with them a wealth of knowledge and experience that we seek to utilize and share within each cohort. However, this fact also brings with it problems for the type of transformational learning that we are trying to achieve with our programme. Profession-specific training and education helps to prepare individuals for their chosen field by equipping them with the requisite knowledge and skills that make them competent to practice. Throughout our post compulsory educational system the focus is on discipline-specific knowledge, with little if any time devoted to interdisciplinary or trans-disciplinary working. The disadvantage of this level of expertise is the potential for what Baumard has termed 'territorialisation' (Baumard, 1999). That is, an individual's knowledge and therefore their strategic approach to their professional practice is bounded by the cognitive map that they have created within that context, which can be a barrier to the creation of new knowledge in different situations. In effect the learning cycle (Kolb, 1984) is orbited so many times that the patterns and processes of thought become fixed and can cause problems with the systematic acquisition of new knowledge which is required of a professional student.

This issue of territorialisation is perhaps a greater problem in the modern world than ever before; few professionals will escape the impact of change over the course of their career. This could happen gradually over time, for example in the case of engineering, which typically is associated with technical problem-solving and construction based on specialized knowledge, but is changing in nature due to the advancements in technology (Olesen, 2001); or radically through political intervention. A particular driver for change is the trend for interprofessional working, seen most powerfully in the public service professions. For example, since 2000 the National Health Service in the UK has been adopting a modernization agenda, which is demanding more interdisciplinary working and the development of new roles and initiatives demanding that staff cross traditional professional boundaries (Department of Health, 2000, 2001, 2004).

This has informed our approach to the Professional Doctorate. We have developed a model to facilitate the development of our candidates as reflective practitioners, who can work across territorial boundaries of knowledge and seek solutions to problems from outside their established professional field (Sanders, 2010; Sanders et al., 2011) using techniques such as storytelling, metaphor and critical incident technique to help them break free of the 'mental grooves' (Thera, 1997, cited in Weick & Sutcliffe, 2006) that can often constrain their development as professional learners. The programme is underpinned by a module of Reflective Practice through which we start the process of development of enhanced reflexivity through activities that engage candidates in interprofessional dialogues and critical enquiry.

One of the key problems that we have found since the programme started more than seven years ago is that many of our professionals have great difficulty in being properly reflective because lack an ability to see alternative perspectives; it seems that their strength is also their weakness; the depth of their knowledge about their own profession seems to form a barrier to understanding and empathizing with others, and creates a resistance to new learning. Atherton (1999) has found that such resistance to learning in professional learners is symptomatic of a situation where the learning is 'supplantive' rather than 'additive', i.e. where we are trying to change existing knowledge systems. The greater the emotional investment in beliefs or practices, the greater the disturbance caused by efforts to change them; it is not unreasonable to assume that our professional learners, because of their expertise and success, have a strong investment in the practices that have been successful for them, and our efforts to challenge these create a significant destabilization for them. The management of de-stabilization is the most difficult and most strongly-resisted stage of the whole process.

The extent of expert knowledge possessed by the candidates can also create tensions with supervisors. This reflects the work of Malfoy (2005) who has argued that tensions can in part be attributed to the retention of traditional supervisory practices that are largely unsuitable for professional doctorate students, suggesting that some of these tensions can be dissipated by 'opening up' supervisory practices into a more collaborative learning environment, creating a strong sense of community of researchers.

As with a traditional PhD student, one of the key areas where academic staff can most influence the candidate is in term of providing academic rigor and research design and there is an expectation from the professional candidates that is what the academic supervisor is supposed to be doing. Unlike a traditional PhD student, the advantage that the professional doctorate candidate has over the supervisor is that the subject expertise has already been acquired by the candidate and they are, in this respect, more knowledgeable than their supervisor (Taylor, 2007). The main role of the supervisor therefore becomes to advise on how to locate the practitioner knowledge in the academic literature and on how to develop it so that it becomes more 'transdisciplinary and transprofessional' (p21, Fell, Flint and Haines, 2011). The success of the supervisory relationship depends a great deal on managing what Atherton (1999) calls 'representation', i.e. what the supervisor represents to the student. This is focused on personal credibility - professional students may frequently question if supervisors have direct experience of what they are talking about, and whether they understand the real-life difficulties a practitioner faces on a day to day basis. Atherton argues that what the academic represents is more important than his or her technical competence as a tutor.

We have found that developing new ways of thinking and supporting candidates to view their professional world through a fresh lens can be a difficult and daunting process for many of our students, and for some academics the shift from a purely discipline-based model of delivery is equally daunting. Despite these issues the programme has been extremely successful – commended in an independent review of the university's postgraduate research degree programmes in 2012, with a recommendation that our more traditional PhDs adopt some of the principles upon which our Professional Doctorate is based.

A Health Scientist Reflects on Professional Doctorates in Health Subjects

Many people from health backgrounds are attracted to the concept of professional doctorates. The strong NHS (UK National Health Service) focus on the development of practice makes the professional doctorate very attractive to healthcare staff. The professional doctorate provides the opportunity to provide a rigorous structured approach to the development of practice and allows a contextualization against the academic literature. It also necessitates a methodological framework which ensures rigor and consistency in the development of practice. While interdisciplinary working is well established in the NHS, many health care professional still retain a strong professional identity. Interestingly, when they reflect on their work and its development they often see that the community of practice is actually a very different group. For example, one senior nurse with a high professional profile, on examination and reflection actually found her community of practice was an interdisciplinary group of quality assurance managers.

The professional doctorate attracts arrange of healthcare professions from all professions and from people at all stages in the career. However, in our experience there are three broad groups. This is similar to that as described by Costley and Lester (2010) in that there are three broad groups of candidates, and these groupings transcend any professional group.

The commonest and are therefore the largest group are and are developing a particular area of practice mid-career professionals who have undertaken a series of usually small scale projects, usually developing a specific area of practice and see the professional doctorate as a way of further developing their work. The particular challenges lies in identifying the particular theme which runs through what is often a series of disparate projects, and also to identify their community of practice.

An example of this is one candidate who is a senior nurse and had in the course of her career, undertaken a series of practice development projects. As her career progressed these projects became increasing sophisticated, the professional doctorate allowed the opportunity to reflect and examine this work and establish the clear themes which ran throughout. One clear issue which emerged was the need for a structured framework against which the practice developments could be assessed. This led her to establish further initiatives and thereby develop a model of practice development.

A less common scenario is the early career professional who comes with a project they wish to develop and in many ways this is not dissimilar to the PhD, although as it is a professional doctorate there must be strong practice focus present in the research. An example of one of our candidates who worked on such an approach was (again) a nurse working at strategic level, building on previous work, she explored models of work force planning and demonstrated the ways in which a rigorous and systematic approach could lead to better outcomes, in terms of the overall patient experience.

The last group are people who have retired or are at the end of their career, they have an impressive body of work which they put together in a portfolio accompanied by a commentary which indicates their contribution to practice. An example of this is one candidate who is a health professional, who although not at the end of her career had a well-established position at a national strategic level. She had both influenced and been involved in the formulation of national policies, and also in their evolution. Her work involved the compilation of a portfolio illustrating the variety of initiatives and demonstrating how her work had affected policy.

One thing which all of the approaches undertaken in the professional doctorate have in common was that they all had an effect on patient care and were about improving the patient experience. No matter how seemingly removed from patient care, without exemption there was a demonstrable impact on patient

The Role of the Professional Doctorate in Developing Professional Practice in STEM Subjects

care. Again, many of the initiatives are context specific but through the dissemination to the health community it allows people to examine the initiatives and reflect on the applicability to their practice. Many of our candidates have had acknowledgement of their work around the ways in which it has stimulated development across arrange of settings.

No account of the health service would be complete without acknowledgement of re-organisation which takes place with increasing frequency. In practice this means many people changing their jobs and while this neither may nor may not be positive experiences, it does have implications for the professional doctorate. It means many projects coming to an end and an interesting and well developed project coming to sudden and abrupt halt. Most respond well to the challenge and refocus, one lesson many learn is it is not the actual project which is the focus and centrality of the doctorate but the underlying theme which can be continued albeit in another form.

An Engineering Academic Reflects on Undertaking a Professional Doctorate

This section is a brief reflection on the impact on my career and on my professional practice as a result of completing my professional doctorate. In my doctorate I examined the ways in which formative feedback could be used to enhance student learning in the STEM subjects – particularly in computing. The professional doctorate has had a significant impact on my career, my academic practice in teaching STEM subjects, my academic practice in the way that I provide feedback and the ways that I assess, my standing in the academic community (both STEM community and Educational Development community) and directly in the ways that I undertake supervision of my own professional doctorate students.

The main contribution to the body of knowledge that I presented from my professional doctorate was a critical analysis of the Assessment for Learning (AfL) "movement" which had a strong momentum at the time and to present different priorities in assessment and feedback to those presented by AfL. The research undertaken in professional doctorate thesis showed that whilst students are concerned about the feedback that they get as part of their learning there are also a number of problematic issues with the provision of formative feedback in STEM learning environments. The evidence from my thesis suggested that the link between formative feedback and student achievement is not as conclusive as suggested in the AfL literature and is difficult to measure effectively.

Many of the issues associated with assessment and feedback have been raised in the wide body of literature on assessment and feedback, but the research in my professional doctorate provided evidence to suggest that the relationship between feedback and improved student learning was not straightforward. The results from my case studies were unique in that the case studies were set in the Computing subject area and very little of the AfL work up to that point had been done in Computing. The case studies provided evidence which was different from the majority of mainstream views on the impact of feedback. As a result my findings were of interest to practitioners in Higher Education, STEM practitioners, educational policy makers and students.

Output from my case studies suggested that students wanted generic skills feedback rather than subject specific feedback or feedback that corrected mistakes (a practice found to be common in STEM subjects). This finding contradicted one of the pillars from the AfL literature where it was suggested that feedback should be subject specific. The rationale for students wanting academic skills development feedback rather than subject specific feedback that came out of my professional doctorate was that this was learning that they could carry forward and apply to their future learning and future assessments. In adopting this model into my practice I have ensured that academic skills being developed through formative feedback were linked to the next formative and / or summative assessment so as to give students the opportunity to practice and develop their skills.

A number of dissemination opportunities have been undertaken in order to share the findings from my professional doctorate including; a staff development book, 2 academic journal papers, 6 conference presentations (including STEM conferences), a number of staff development workshops and 2 invitations to visit overseas institutions and give workshops at the University of Southern Denmark, Odense, and the University of Cape Town in South Africa. This has contributed to my academic standing and formed the backbone to my submission in the recent Research Evaluation Framework (REF) activity where I was submitted as part of the Education team in Unit 25. In addition the findings from my professional doctorate have been included as paper of the curriculum on assessment on the Post Graduate Certificate in Education (PG Cert) in my University and used as a series of case studies in the sessions that I deliver on the PG Cert on assessment and feedback.

I am now in the fortunate position to be supervising a group (currently 4) professional doctorate students and I am able to draw on my experience as a professional doctorate student to understand the issues from a participant point of view. My experiences as a professional doctorate student have helped shape the way that I supervise my students and the way that we (the "we" is used on purpose rather than "I") run their supervision sessions. I believe that I am more sympathetic, empathetic and understanding than I would have been had I not undertaken a professional doctorate and been on the other side of the supervisory relationship

I had a fairly "hairy" experience during my professional doctorate viva and I felt that the examiners were not "playing fair". The experience of my viva and subsequent discussion with the chair of the panel and my supervisor ensured that my outlook on the examination process of the professional doctorate focusses on being supportive. I always do everything I can in helping to prepare students for vivas, participating as examiner in mock vivas (normally for professional doctorate students other than my own), participating as internal examiner and when I am chairing professional doctorate viva examinations.

The professional doctorate has without doubt had a positive and significant impact on my career. Undertaking my professional doctorate has led to a number of changes in my professional practice. Academic aspects of my practice such as exam interventions, academic skills development and helping students to understand feedback have been incorporated into my teaching. The doctorate has also been good to have on my CV!

A further impact on my practice has been the opportunity to utilize the educational research principles developed on the doctorate and apply them in a number of different educational settings. The processes of evaluating activities and attempting to measure the impact of interventions have been adopted as part of my continuing and ongoing reflection on my teaching practice.

Undertaking and completing the professional doctorate has made a difference to my professional expectations of what I should be doing in the workplace and how I should be approaching and undertaking those tasks. In addition this has had a beneficial impact on my colleagues that I have been working with and as a result my department, faculty and university. As I have been clearer in my expectations and have been pushing myself to achieve my goals it has rubbed off on those around me and their performance, effectiveness, professionalism, and I think their job satisfaction, has improved.

Perhaps the most significant impact from a personal point of view is that the work undertaken for my professional doctorate contributed to me being awarded the recognition of a National Teaching Fellowship form the Higher Education Academy. This has enhanced my standing in the academic community, broadened my professional network (now a member of the Association of National Teaching Fellows) and given me the funds to undertake innovative activities with my students that I wouldn't normally have the finance to do.

Individual Student Reflections

Below are some student reflections on their doctoral journey, taken from individual narrative accounts.

This has been a difficult journey; juxtaposing a full-time senior management career and personal family commitments; whilst at the same time trying to mesh in a demanding academic and doctoral research project. My knowledge and understanding of the subject, however, would not have been anywhere as near developed had I not embarked on this programme of study. I feel a real sense of achievement in being able to juggle so many demands and at the same time still managing to deliver the required outcomes to timescale.

When I embarked on my part time PhD, I had no clear expectations other than I wanted to see if I could achieve at this level of academic work. I had already undertaken several taught postgraduate courses. However, reflecting on my journey in undertaking this research and the reading and theory that I have covered.....I now realise that to get high quality work that I can be proud of is really (really) hard work and that it isn't enough to skim the literature.

I can honestly say that if my work resulted in a fail that, whilst I would naturally be disappointed, I could walk away knowing that I have personally developed in a way that I never anticipated.

In practice, I feel it is important for you to know who you are and what drives you, and yet, it has only been over the past three years that I have seen such clarity.

I am a great believer in learning by doing. The action learning nature of my doctorate enabled me to gain a deep understanding of my subject.

I found the action research nature of my project to be particularly appropriate. I was exploring a topic which was of interest to me, and of use to my work colleagues. Indeed they became part of my project, which helped enormously in developing my skills of critical thinking, as they were always there ready to question what I was doing.

Researching and writing up my research has provided an additional dimension to my work as I have become more knowledgeable about past and current policy and I am able to relate it to theory and academic literature.

The opportunity to study for a doctorate presented itself when I had just returned to work full time after six months maternity leave and a year working part-time. On reflection, perhaps full time work, a demanding toddler and a part-time doctorate were not an ideal combination but my employer was willing to part-fund my doctoral studies and this was too good an opportunity to miss. On a personal level, becoming a researcher has illuminated and given an added degree of purpose to my professional role. It has provided me with the opportunity to reflect on my work with almost indecent introspection. At times it has felt like an indulgence but the additional critical reflection and knowledge has impacted crucially and I believe significantly on the continuing success of my work projects. Undertaking the doctorate, the processes of reflection, the need for rigor, the collection of evidence critically and the application of theory have all impacted directly upon my practice and delivered real benefits for my work and my employer.

Discussion of the Themes

Each of these themes is discussed below.

Cohort experience. In general the students were very positive about working with a cohort of students from different backgrounds, and felt that there was much to be gained from this experience. The STEM students gained much from working alongside others who were not from a STEM background and welcomed the different methodological and practitioner perspectives which this gave. They enjoyed discussing work-based issues within a safe, supportive environment and often gained new insights from fellow students who brought different theoretical models, and practices to bear on the issues which the students were exploring for their doctoral studies. An element of competition developed within the cohort, and the students motivated, supported and encouraged each other. When a student graduated there was feeling of success for all, and group celebration of individual success became a very important aspect of the programme.

Structure and academic support. A number of issues regarding the structure of the programme and of the final doctoral submission were raised by the students. Although as busy professionals the students required flexible delivery, they also welcomed some structure, looking forward to teaching sessions and managing to reserve space for them within their work schedules. They also welcomed programme deadlines, which encouraged them to develop sections of their doctoral submissions within specific timeframes, a discipline and rigor which is often missing within a traditional PhD programme. The students welcomed the regular, consistent and independent support from academic staff which they enjoyed; this being provided by a much wider group of tutors than the more traditional student-supervisor model on which a PhD is often based.

Personal impact. The students seemed to indicate that studying on the programme had made a big impact upon their professional practice. This was evident from a range of students, including those who were relatively new to the programme. The students reported that they saw quite significant changes within their practice at work. They also reported much wider benefits as they increasingly introduced new practices, models and theoretical perspectives to the workplace, having studied these within their doctoral programme, or having learnt of them from other student practitioners.

Mixed employer perceptions. The students indicated a mix of employer reactions to, and perceptions of, the programme. Some employers were very supportive, and provided tangible resources to the student, including paying the fees for their doctoral programme. Others were much less supportive; some students reported having to keep their studies almost secret, as their employers seem jealous and resentful of the academic work which they were doing.

Reflective practice. One of the important elements of many professional doctorate programmes, including the programme within this case study, is reflective practice. Students are required to reflect upon their own practice in a formal manner, writing reflective essays discussing their own work based issues. Students from some STEM disciplines such as nursing or teaching are used to applying the principles of reflective practice within their work context. Others, including engineers and computer scientists, find the subject very difficult and take some time to come to terms with thinking and writing about themselves and their own practice. Reflective practice is almost alien to their training. In all cases, however, the students ultimately see the benefits of reflective practice, and begin to apply it at work. One manufacturing engineering student, after studying reflective practice for some time, said "I now realise that reflective practice is just like engineering. As an engineer, I have been taught to reflect on what went well, and what went wrong, and to learn from that. That is what reflective practice is all about."

Personal and professional values. The programme and its focus and emphasis on reflection encourage the students to explore their own personal and professional values, and those of the organisations by whom they are employed. This gives the student a much deeper understanding of that which they hold important, what their profession expects of them, and what their employer expects of them. In many cases, there is clear congruence within this. In other cases, however, the students identify a mismatch or clash of values. In several instances this has led to the student questioning whether they can reconcile the difference between their own values and those of their employer, and in some cases students have, as a consequence, changed job.

Professional identity, authenticity and personal voice. The students strive to find their own "voice" and to be more authentic in the way in which they practice. For some this is very natural. For others, this can take some time to develop or emerge. By the end of the doctorate, the student will have a much deeper understanding of what drives them personally and professionally, and is able to write, present and discuss their work with their own "voice".

Transprofessional working. Many of the students in the study had quite complex career histories and had migrated away from their first disciplines to a greater or lesser extent. In their doctorates they made use of this, reflecting back on their learning journey and building their experience into their doctoral work. Their work was very practical and not simply confined to one discrete discipline as you would normally find with a more traditional STEM PhD. They crossed professional boundaries and made a contribution that was applicable to multi-professional working environments. It was this that gave many of the candidates their motivation to do the professional doctorate. Some had previously considered doing, or even tried to do, a PhD in a STEM discipline at some time in the past, but it was the opportunity to utilize their professional knowledge and develop it further to make a real practical contribution that made the professional doctorate a more appealing and ultimately successful option for them.

FUTURE RESEARCH DIRECTIONS

This chapter has presented a case study of one professional doctorate programme which includes STEM students. There is a need for further study of programmes and of the impact which those programmes have upon graduates and their practice. In particular, little evidence exists, in qualitative or quantitative terms, of the impact that professional doctorate graduates have upon their organisations and their wider communities of practice. Intuitively, one would expect graduates to drive change within the workplace, and to apply the methodological and theoretical perspectives which they have learnt within the doctorate. This should, in turn, provide useful results for their organisations. However, the evidence of this does not yet exist; or rather, data to allow the assemblage of such evidence have not yet been collected. This is to be expected, as professional doctorate programmes are a relatively new development. It is important that such evidence, and case studies of impact, are collected, particularly as governments across the world are now looking to fund research which provides real impact. Future research studies should focus on this aspect of the professional doctorate.

CONCLUSION

This chapter has presented the results of a mixed methods case study of a professional doctorate programme. Professional doctorate programmes are especially relevant to today's STEM practitioners, in that they equip graduates with methodological skills to use action research approaches to drive change within their own organisation and their wider community of practice. Our study has identified a number of themes which resonate with other similar studies (Costley & Stephenson, 2005; Lester, 2004), and hold lessons for the further development of professional doctorate programmes. These themes are: cohort experience, structure and academic support, personal transformation, employer perceptions, reflective practice, personal and professional values, professional identity, authenticity and personal voice, and transprofessional working.

REFERENCES

Alkin, M. C. (1976). Evaluation: Who needs it? Who cares? *Studies in Educational Evaluation*, *1*(3), 201–212. doi:10.1016/0191-491X(75)90023-1

Atherton, J. (1999). Resistance to Learning: A discussion based on participants in in-service professional training programmes. *Journal of Vocational Education and Training*, *51*(1), 77–90. doi:10.1080/13636829900200070

Baumard, P. (1999). *Tacit knowledge in organisations*. London: Sage.

Costley, C., & Lester, S. (2010). Work-based doctorates: Professional extension at the highest levels. *Studies in Higher Education*, *37*(3), 257–269. doi:10.1080/03075079.2010.503344

Costley, C. & Stephenson, J. (2005). The Impact of Workplace Doctorates – a review of 10 case studies at Middlesex University. Proceedings of *AERA conference*.

Department of Health. (2000). *The NHS Plan: A plan for investment. A plan for reforms*. London: The Stationery Office.

Department of Health. (2001). *Working Together, Learning Together: A framework for lifelong learning in the NHS*. London: The Stationery Office.

Department of Health. (2004). *The NHS Improvement Plan: putting people at the heart of public services*. London: The Stationery Office.

Fell, A., Flint, K., & Haines, I. (2011). *Professional Doctorates in the UK*. London: UK Council for Graduate Education.

Fereday, J., & Muir-Cochrane, E. (2008). Demonstrating rigor using thematic analysis: A hybrid approach of inductive and deductive coding and theme development. *International Journal of Qualitative Methods*, *5*(1), 80–92.

Fulton, J., Kuit, J., Sanders, G., & Smith, P. (2012a). The role of the Professional Doctorate in developing professional practice. *Journal of Nursing Management*, *20*(1), 130–139. doi:10.1111/j.1365-2834.2011.01345.x PMID:22229909

Fulton, J., Kuit, J., Sanders, G., & Smith, P. (2012b). *The Professional Doctorate: A Practical Guide for Students and Supervisors*. London: Palgrave.

Greene, J. C., Caracelli, V. J., & Graham, W. F. (1989). Toward a conceptual framework for mixed-method evaluation designs. *Educational Evaluation and Policy Analysis*, *11*(3), 255–274. doi:10.3102/01623737011003255

Guthrie, J. (2009). The Case for a Modern Doctorate of Education Degree (Ed.D): Multipurpose Education Doctorates No Longer Appropriate. Peabody Journal of Education, 84(1), 3-8.

Hadacek, S., & Carpenter, D. (1998). Student Perceptions of Nursing Doctorates: Similarities and Differences. *Journal of Professional Nursing*, *14*(1), 14–21. doi:10.1016/S8755-7223(98)80008-2 PMID:9473900

Kolb, D. A. (1984). *Experiential Learning: Experience as the Source of Learning and Development*. Englewood Cliffs, NJ: Prentice Hall.

Lester, S. (2004). Conceptualising the Practitioner Doctorate. *Studies in Higher Education*, *29*(6), 757–770. doi:10.1080/0307507042000287249

Malfroy, J. (2005). Doctoral Supervision, workplace research, and changing pedagogic practices. *Higher Education Research & Development*, *24*(2), 165–178. doi:10.1080/07294360500062961

Olesen, H. S. (2001). Professional Identity as Learning Processes in Life Histories. *Journal of Workplace Learning*, *13*(7/8), 290–297. doi:10.1108/13665620110411076

Sanders, G. (2010). Towards a Model of Multi-organisational Work-based Learning: Developmental networks as a mechanism for tacit knowledge transfer and exploration of professional identity. *Learning and Teaching in Higher Education*, *4*(1), 51–68.

Sanders, G., Kuit, J., Smith, P., & Fulton, J. (2012). Hidden Voices: Searching for Authenticity in Professional Doctorate Candidates. *Third International conference on Professional Doctorates*, UK Council for Graduate Education.

Sanders, G., Kuit, J., Smith, P., Fulton, J. & Curtis, H. (2011). Identity, reflection and developmental networks as processes in professional doctorate development. *Work Based Learning e-Journal, 2*(1), 113-134.

Smith, P., Curtis, H., Sanders, G., Kuit, J. & Fulton, J. (2011). Student perceptions of the professional doctorate. *Work Based Learning e-Journal, 2*(1), 135-154.

Smith, P., Walker-Gleaves, C., Fulton, J., & Candlish, C. (2009a). Developing Inter-Professional Communities of Practice within the context of a Professional Doctorate Programme. Proceedings of Higher Education Academy conference, Manchester.

Smith, P., Walker-Gleaves, C., Fulton, J., & Candlish, C. (2009b). The Professional Doctorate within the context of Leadership Development Strategies. *First International conference on Professional Doctorates*, UK Council for Graduate Education.

Taylor, A. (2007). Learning to Become Researching Professionals: The case of the Doctorate of Education. *International Journal of Teaching and Learning in Higher Education, 19*(2), 154–166.

Thompson, J., Smith, P. & Cooper, B. (2012). An autoethnographic study of the impact of reflection and doctoral study on practice. *Work Based Learning e-Journal, 2*(2), 1-12.

UKCGE. (2010). *Professional Doctorate Awards in the UK*. London: UK Council for Graduate Education.

Weick, K. E., & Sutcliffe, K. M. (2006). Mindfulness and the Quality of Organisational Attention. *Organization Science, 17*(4), 514–524. doi:10.1287/orsc.1060.0196

KEY TERMS AND DEFINITIONS

Action Research: A research approach which involves iterations of practical action, followed by reflection.
Doctorate: A higher degree obtained by research.
Professional Doctorate: A practice-based research degree.
Reflection: The action of thinking and analysing one's actions in order to learn for the future.

Chapter 2
Mentoring Girls in Science:
Eight Case Studies of a Science Camp Experience

Donna Farland-Smith
The Ohio State University, USA

ABSTRACT:

Content area specialists (scientists) are often recruited as mentors of students to address issues in science education. These scientists are frequently recruited to help with the teaching of science, however, quite often do not have the pedagogy skills needed to be role models for young children. Guidance in the selection appropriate mentors would help maximize the potential influence on students understanding of who does science, where science is done and what scientists do. This study illustrates six case studies of scientists as they worked with middle school girls and identifies five characteristics educators should look for in selecting science mentors successful in broadening students' perceptions of scientists. The data was collected during 'Side-by-Side' interaction with scientists/mentors during a summer camp experience and has implications for classroom practice as the use of mentors can be structured to support the infusion of Science as a Human Endeavor. As the students' experiences with mentor scientists helped to shape their perception of those who pursue careers in science and what it is that scientists do, careful consideration and preparation of mentors were critical to the success of the program, and so this paper also provides suggestions to help highly trained and highly educated scientists in these mentorship roles.

INTRODUCTION

Without clear boundaries or definitions of the characteristics of science content specialists who will likely be successful in the classroom, all scientists may be welcomed. Recently, President Barack Obama, in the National Math and Science Initiative, requested that scientists do their part in helping young students achieve better grades in science by occasionally visiting school classrooms. However, the indiscriminate use of visiting scientists should be cautioned, because all scientists don't necessarily make teachers.

Classroom teachers are limited by time and responsibility. They must attend to day-to-day issues while worrying about meeting instructional standards and the requirements of end-of-course tests. As a

DOI: 10.4018/978-1-4666-9471-2.ch002

result, classroom teachers need guidance in working with appropriate science content specialists for their students. As this will maximize the potential influence mentor scientists have on students' understanding of who does science, where science is done, and what scientists do. This paper explores the approaches of content specialists when working with middle school girls and suggests as to how scientists should be prepared to serve in these mentorship roles.

Literature Review

Reform in science education has always been a top priority for science educators and an interest of the Obama presidential administration. Recruitment and retention of students are the two main areas targeted for reform, because many students who initially display an interest in science do not remain in science fields. As more students choose to pursue interests unrelated to science, there is growing concern about attracting future scientists, especially females, in the United States. The lack of female scientists has been a concern in the science and science-education fields for some time, as women are under-represented in the profession (Buck et al., 2007). Professional scientists interacting with students in a formal, classroom setting is often suggested as a possible solution. Yet this approach remains under-researched from the perspective of the classroom teacher and the benefit students derive from interacting with a scientist.

The research on visiting-scientist programs is built on the assumption that a scientist in the classroom will benefit children's perceptions of who scientists are and the work they do. Bozdin and Gerhinger (2001) and Flick (1990) reported that visits from scientists in classrooms resulted in a decrease in many stereotypical beliefs about scientists, indicating that children's images of scientists can indeed be influenced by a visit from a scientist. However, it cannot be assumed that these relationships are successful in every classroom.

While much is known about mentoring new teachers in science, the research concerning scientist mentoring individual students remains unexamined. A science camp was selected as the context for this study, as it has been established that it is successful in establishing a transformative experience for young female students, broadening their perceptions about scientists (Author, 2009). The data collected over the last four years appears to be enough to start guiding educators towards selecting, preparing, and maintaining successful interactions between middle-school girls and working scientists.

The National Science Education Standards, used as a framework for this summer camp/"Side-by-Side" experience, advocate that Science as a Human Endeavor should be taught as early as the elementary grades, "in order to provide a foundation for the development of sophisticated ideas related to the history and nature of science that will be developed in later years" (NRC, 1996, p. 141). The narrow and erroneous impression of science held by many students has, in part, inspired science reformers to create The *National Science Education Standards* (NSES) (National Research Council [NRC], 1996). The standards recommend the teaching of specific science content and science processes, as well as emphasizing the human element of scientific enterprise. The new version of standards, *Next Generation of Science Standards* continues support this idea about learning about science and the human beings who have made significant contributions by identifying the goal for K-12 science education is to develop a scientifically literate person who can understand and the nature of the scientific knowledge. According to *NGSS Science and Engineering Practices* in the school setting have three interrelated aspects; a) asking questions and defining problems, b) developing and using models, and, c) planning and carrying out investigations.

Many students view scientists as being quite different from people working in other jobs. Additionally, they often hold highly stereotypical and inaccurate views of scientists and the work they do. In studies spanning five decades, it has been noted that students typically portray scientists as males confined to a laboratory, surrounded by dangerous chemicals, and conducting laborious experiments (Barman, 1997; Chambers, 1983; Finson, 2002; Fort & Varney, 1989; Mead & Metraux, 1957; Schibeci & Sorenson, 1983). These inaccurate views of scientists are widely held by students from elementary through secondary school (Barman, 1996; Chambers, 1983).

The *Standards* (1996) focus on the following four human dimensions of science:

1. Science and technology have been practiced by people for a long time.
2. Men and women have made a variety of contributions throughout the history of science and technology.
3. Science will never be finished. Although men and women using scientific inquiry have learned much about the objects, events and phenomena in nature, much more remains to be understood.
4. Many people choose science as a career and devote their entire lives to studying it. Many people derive great pleasure from doing science. (NRC, 1996, p.141).

These four aspects of "Science as a Human Endeavor" should be explicitly taught to children. The *NSES* recommend that students understand that science and technology have been practiced for a long time (NRC, 1996). Students also need to understand not only the key concepts and principles of science and how scientific knowledge is applied, but also the cultural and social contexts within which science is advanced (Kafai & Gilliland-Swetland, 2000).

Secondly, the *NSES* recommend that students become aware of the variety of contributions made by men *and* women scientists. Often, children's books and their pictures portray scientists as secretive and in pursuit of the "one answer to everything" (Chambers, 1983). For example, when children draw pictures of scientists, they often include captions such as, "I am going to blow up the world," or "Eureka, I've found the cure!" indicating the child's limited knowledge of scientists. Further, these captions suggest that scientists are always inventing or working on immense or dangerous projects, which is certainly not the case with most scientists.

Third, the *NSES* recommend that students grasp the idea that science will never be finished. Kuhn (1972) suggested that science textbooks may actually impede progress toward this aspect of scientific literacy. Science texts are beneficial in that they allow students to categorize an immense amount of factual information, but one of the negative effects of textbooks is that they give students the impression that everything they need to know is contained within the pages of the book. Knowledge contained in a book may suggest that science has been completed and the students' role is merely to study the contents of the book and regurgitate facts without considering additional possibilities (NRC, 2012).

Commonly held stereotypic images about scientists are often in direct opposition to what students are supposed to be able to understand about scientists. This is outlined by the fourth component of *NSES* (1996), which states "that many people derive great pleasure in doing science" (p.141). However, unless students have multiple interactions with scientists, they may never come to accept these four aspects of the human side of science. Thus, the summer-camp experience was designed around these four NSES tenets. The "Side-by-Side" experiences described in this paper provided a means for middle-school girls to experience first-hand these four dimensions of science. However, providing these four dimensions required careful thought and preparation by the mentors for them to be successful with the students.

In this paper, one key question was addressed in the examination of the eight scientists and their role with middle school girls: 1) How did the science content specialists approach their opportunity to teach middle-school girls? This question was asked in hopes of determining quality and effective future camp experiences. In addition, it was even more important in forming guidelines for classroom teachers that could be used in preparing, and maintaining successful personal and social interactions between middle-school girls and content specialists.

OVERVIEW OF THE RESEARCH CONTEXT

Eight professional scientists (six females and two males) were involved with 100 middle-school girls in a multi-year collaboration known as the "Side-by-Side" experience. The camp was held on the campus of a large Midwest regional university to take advantage of the university's resources, yet offer a more rural setting with a stream and wetlands for fieldwork.

Middle-School Girls

The girls attending the camp were drawn randomly from several public, private, and home-school populations. Unfortunately, the area where the girls live is now part of an economically depressed region whose economy was once based on one of three largest U. S. automakers. With the closing of a major auto plant, the area is now severely economically depressed. The unemployment rate is above the 10.5 percent national average, and the median family income is $37,541. "Side-by-Side with Scientists" camp was held each year for the past three years during the last two weeks of July. The girls were taught by five different scientists over the period of one week. During each week of camp up to 25 different girls participated for a total of 100 different campers over the three-year span. Some of the same girls returned to camp from year to year.

Selecting Science Content Specialists

Each scientist was a university professor and brought his/her own style of teaching and personality to the classroom. The professors wore name tags identifying them as a doctor (Ph.D), with their first name printed large and bold, followed by their last name in smaller print. The order in which the scientists presented their lessons was different each week to accommodate the scientists' individual work schedules. Table 1 is an example from year one. All scientists presented prepared, interactive laboratory or field work activities with the students.

Table 1. Sample schedule of year one

	Monday	Tuesday	Wednesday	Thursday	Friday
Week 1	Physics	Plant Ecology	Wetlands Ecology	Physical Anthropology	Chemistry
Week 2	Physical Anthropology	Chemistry	Wetlands Ecology	Plant Ecology	Physics

Mentoring Girls in Science

It is important to mention that all scientists were extremely interested in being involved with the summer camp, and were enthusiastic, willing participants. A description follows regarding the scientists' -content background, rank at their university, time associated with the camp, and how they presented and/or prepared their activities with the girls.

Mentor Scientist #1, Dr. Darlene

Darlene (participated two years) is an assistant professor of anthropology. She is a Caucasian female who grew up in the U.S., earning a doctorate in Ecology, Evolution, and Animal Behavior. She studies baboons in Botswana, and has performed surveys of primates in South Africa and Zanzibar. Dr. Darlene shared her work with the girls as a physical anthropologist. Both years, she began her lesson by showing many pictures and telling stories about her work in Africa studying the calls of various types of baboons. After her introduction the first year, students studied the behavior of three dogs by designing an investigation to see which type of treat the dogs liked best. In the second year, she led the girls to investigate sound using an inquiry-based method. The girls learned about sound in the forest and in the lab by utilizing Dr. Darlene's audio equipment.

Mentor Scientist #2, Dr. Juan

Juan (participated two years) is an assistant professor of earth science from Brazil. He holds a Ph.D in Coral Reef Ecology and Nutrient Biogeochemistry, and currently studies the hydrology and geochemistry of the Clear Fork River in Ohio. The first year, he introduced the girls to the age of the earth using his soil samples, and the girls learned about dinosaur fossils through a cookie paleontology activity. The second year, he did many different activities, each designed to broaden the girls' understanding of earth science. Some of these activities included examining the relative size and distance of the planets in the solar system, as well as studying the earth's atmosphere and clouds.

Mentor Scientist #3, Dr. James

James (participated four years) is a full professor with a Ph.D in Aquatic Zoology who studies invasive species of wetland grasses. He began his sessions with the girls by sharing his research. He always designs an investigation incorporating problem-based learning strategies. For example, to create a mock mystery, he asked the head of security at the university to come to class and tell the girls there had been a fish kill on campus. He said that he needed their help to solve the mystery of what had happened to the fish. A short time later, the officer returned to class with a suspect in hand cuffs. The officer asked the girls to figure out what the suspect had done to kill the fish. The girls were not initially told this was a mock fish kill, but they soon figured it out after finding paper fish scattered along a stream. The girls were very curious and determined to solve the mystery. While they were in the stream, they ran several tests and gathered evidence for their case against the suspect.

Mentor Scientist #4, Dr. Debbie

Debbie (participated two years) is an assistant professor with a Ph.D in Environmental Sciences, studying soils in local wetlands. In an effort to get the girls outside and investigating, she identified five different soil types within range of the camp, and led the girls to gather and analyze soil samples from each site.

Mentor Scientist #5, Dr. Francine

Dr. Francine (participated four years) is an Associate Professor of Chemistry. She is a Caucasian female who grew up in the U.S., and who studies the benefits of black raspberries to cancer patients. Due to the extensive activities she led in the class, Francine did not share much information about her work, nor did her fellow chemists who assisted with the lesson. On this day of camp, the girls were introduced to a mock crime-scene investigation in the chemistry lab. A "Dr. James" had been kidnapped, and the girls gathered evidence they then analyzed by performing six to nine chemical tests. Using the scenario provided by the instructors, the girls actively worked to solve the crime.

Mentor Scientist #6, Dr. Geraldine

Geraldine (participated three years) is an Assistant Professor of Physics who grew up in Romania. Her Ph.D is in physics, and she studies Nuclear Structure Theory. The activities Geraldine led were based on college labs, and included topics such as pinhole cameras, circuits, and electricity. With the help of the camp director, she designed age-appropriate activities for the girls using a scale and elevator for measuring weight and weightlessness. In addition, she led an inquiry-based session on the physics of a working carwash.

Mentor Scientist #7, Scientist Jane

Jane (participated two years) also introduced the girls to physics. The girls used motion detectors and computers to make graphs of the time and distance objects traveled. These activities were based on a college lab. Jane also shared her story of how she became interested in science and ultimately rose to the rank of a university teacher.

Mentor Scientist #8, Dr. Christy

Christy (participated one year) is a plant reproductive ecologist who began her lesson with pictures and stories about her travels to tropical places. To help the girls learn about plants, she guided the students through several plant dissections. Later in the day, the students conducted their own pollination field studies in the university's wetlands.

In addition to the eight scientists, two licensed teachers and the camp director/researcher were present each day of the camp. The teachers facilitated activities and transitions between activities. The researcher has an Ed.D in mathematics and science education, and was a science methods professor for the university. She took field notes and assisted with activities when needed. She also greeted the girls each morning as they were dropped off at camp, collected data, and oversaw all aspects of camp. In seasons two through four, two additional helpers (high-school students too old to attend the camp) participated as assistants.

Method

This investigation of the eight scientists into their role with the middle school girls was conducted over a four- year period. Data collection began several months before the first science camp with an initial meeting between the camp director and each scientist. All scientists worked with the camp director/researcher to develop lessons before each camp (year) experience. This usually involved the scientist suggesting a lesson idea to the camp director, then working with the director to ensure science content relevant to the standards, and age-appropriateness of the activity or activities. The director/researcher took notes on each visit with each scientist in an effort to build a repository of data. The proposed approach of each scientist was then examined.

Preparation: Initial Meetings with Scientists

The focus of the initial meetings was to answer the scientists' questions and assist them in lesson construction. The length of these meetings, the general discussion, and the individual scientist's overall enthusiasm were recorded. The director/researcher listened to each scientist's lesson idea and discussed the time he or she was planning to spend with the girls during a one-day, six-hour time span. The director/researcher, using models for classroom inquiry and instruction, attempted to guide the scientists to enhance their lessons by using the five "Es" of the Learning Cycle: engage, explore, explain, expand, and evaluate, (Karplus, 1970). The only requirement was that the scientists engage the girls in real-world science, similar to the work the scientists conducted in their particular field of study.

The scientists were specifically instructed to *engage* or set up motivations to initiate or sustain the girls' interest in inquiry. One way in which they could do this was to set up central questions for the girls to investigate and answer. Next, mentors were guided to *explore* with the girls, and how that concept might look in a middle-school classroom setting. These would be opportunities for students to investigate the central question through student-centered experiences. Scientists were then asked to use guided questioning in a way that would help students *explain* or uncover the standards-based concept or skill which the lesson was designed to teach. Fourthly, the scientists were guided to help students *expand* or conceptualize their ideas in an effort to deepen their understanding of the prescribed concepts and/or skills around which the lesson was constructed. Lastly, the scientists were asked to *evaluate* or assess the learning as the students conducted their inquiry experience.

Following this initial contact with the researcher/camp director, each scientist had different levels of follow-up contact. For example, before the first year's camp experience, Dr. Darlene required four meetings to conceptualize her idea of what she wanted to present to the students. Many emails and phone calls were made in preparing for the camp. Dr. Francine, on the other hand, did not initiate any additional contact other than to ask for materials. Dr. James, because he didn't want to offer the same experience to the girls more than once, required three meetings and discussions to form his ideas. Contact with Dr. Juan and Dr. Debbie only involved the initial meetings. Scientist Jane and Dr. Christy each required one initial meeting to conceptualize their ideas.

METHODS USED DURING THE CAMP

During the "Side-by-Side" experience with the girls (two consecutive weeks in July), the researcher recorded field notes/observations of the interactions between the mentor scientists and the students, adding it to the repository of data for each mentor scientist. The researcher observed classroom interactions between the girls and the scientists, focusing on interactions both personal (one-on-one) and in the social context of the entire camp (whole class), as a means of identifying the characteristics of the most successful content specialists. Things that the scientists did and did not do with the girls were also recorded.

Since the camp was designed to take place during two consecutive weeks, the researcher/director had a chance to follow-up with scientists after week one to see if what support might be needed for week two. This was also a time to reflect on week one's lesson and modify, if necessary, the lesson for week two. In the four years of summer camp, only two mentors took advantage of this reflection time with the director to completely change their lesson for the second week.

Following each camp experience, each scientist was interviewed while reflecting on and discussing his/her own experience. These interviews were recorded, coded, and analyzed for themes of qualities or traits. Each teacher or camp staff who worked at the science camp with individual scientists was interviewed following his/her experiences and notes were taken on particular scientists. That information was added to the repository of data for each mentor scientist. These methods were repeated for four consecutive summers. Data collection was triangulated through the different methods used in collection (e.g., field notes, interviews with camp staff and scientists, and notes from meetings with the director).

Defining Successful Recruits

The purpose of the camp was to allow young females to explore a variety of areas of science, with a different scientist, on each of the five days of the camp. The hope was that this interaction with scientists would encourage middle-school girls to sustain an interest in science. Successful mentorship was defined not only by the parameters of the four tenets of the Human Endeavor, as specified earlier in the *NSES*, but also by the general enjoyment of the class by the girls. This was demonstrated by their participation in class, journal records, conversations, and illustrations. While the camp previously demonstrated the improvement of the girls' appreciation of science (Author, 2009), the mentors who were deemed successful also helped the girls appreciate science as a discipline. The scientists were deemed unsuccessful if the girls were frustrated by the scientist's teaching, or if the girls wrote or commented on the difficulty of understanding a particular scientist.

Results: How Mentor Scientists Approached their Roles with Middle-School Girls

There seemed to be some consistencies in the ways the eight scientists approached the mentorship experience. For example, all the scientists were university professors, and all had a variety of experiences teaching undergraduate or graduate students. However, the scientists each had his/her own distinct style of approach to mentoring/teaching the girl's science. These approaches were different than those of classroom teachers, mainly because of the scientists' previous experiences in academia. Each scientist verbalized his/her strong desire to help the girls "like" science and see science as a real career choice, yet they all had very different approaches. Table 2 includes (or illustrates) this continuum.

Table 2. Mentor-approach-to-teaching continuum

Disseminator of Knowledge	Demonstrator of Procedures	Disseminator of Activities	Side-By-Side Expert
• Lecture based on Power Point • Video, or computer assisted instruction • Passive Learners • Unable to modify to meet the needs of students	• Lecture with demonstration by the scientist only • Small groups or large groups • Looks like hands-on investigation, but in reality students are collecting data from the demonstration	• Lecture with activities for students • Many activities with no central connection • Looks like hands-on investigation, but lacks probing inquiry experience in an attempt to answer a specific question	• Mentor poses question and students develop procedures to answer the question. • Hands-on inquiry with critical thinking and problem solving.

A *Disseminator of Knowledge* is defined as a scientist who approached the camp like a college classroom, the premise being that they (the scientist) have all the knowledge and the students are passive learners. Content Specialists who are *Disseminators of Knowledge* are unable to change their teaching style from the college level to the middle-school level, even with one-on-one help and guidance from the camp director for multiple years. Dr. Geraldine, for instance, the physicist, is an example of a *Disseminator of Knowledge (see Table 1)*.

By contrast, an innate teacher is described as one who interprets reactions from students, modifies her lessons based on those reactions, and, in turn, helps students achieve new learning.

But being a successful scientist/mentor involves more than the ability to be an innate teacher. Dr. Geraldine did not have the capacity to change, despite her attempts for three years to work one-on-one with the camp director. Of the eight scientists involved with the camp, no one wanted to participate more than Dr. Geraldine. This project was so important to her, that she agreed to meet and work with the camp director frequently. However, after year two, she finally admitted she was unable to be anything but a *Disseminator of Knowledge*. However, with the director assisting her through team-teaching, Dr. Geraldine agreed to participate in year three, but only during a half-day session.

A *Disseminator of Knowledge* presents information and gives directions as the students remain passive. The types of presentations that the *Disseminator of Knowledge* typically does well are often organized according to his/her ideas of logical order, not the student's. *Disseminators of Knowledge* rely on verbal presentations, but what is communicated by them is not always what is perceived in the same way by the students. These types of presentations are open to interpretation by the student, and limited by the student's attention span.

A *Demonstrator of Procedures* is defined as a scientist who approaches teaching as a watch-and-learn experience. In this case, the scientist is usually in front of the class doing a science demonstration, and the students are positioned at a distance, usually recording data. Dr. Debbie, the soil scientist, is an example of the *Demonstrator of Procedures* (see Table 1). The difference between the *Disseminator of Knowledge* and the *Demonstrator of Procedures* is the shift in thinking that the students will learn more by visual than by auditory means. However, the students are still passive learners when using this approach, and the focus is still on content.

Demonstrations do have their benefits in teaching science. For instance, they can protect students from dangerous conditions. Also, demonstrations can illustrate an important concept when there is not enough lab equipment for every learner to engage personally. Remember, this was not the explicit instructions given to the science content specialists prior to their participation at camp. In fact, the camp was called "Side-by-Side with Scientists" for the very purpose of these individuals was working *with* the girls. Demonstrations were supposed to be kept to a minimum. A discovery demonstration in which the scientist silently conducts an experiment and allows the students to determine why the demonstration worked the way it did would have been appropriate in this setting.

In her initial meeting with the director/researcher, Dr. Debbie discussed wanting to get the girls outside, collecting soil samples and analyzing data. When she sat down and discussed further details with the camp director, her lesson proposal seemed like a perfect way for the students to investigate and experience a variety of soils. As a result, the camp director purchased the needed equipment for the class, confident that the anticipated lesson would go well. Unfortunately, the lesson proved less than envisioned.

Dr. Debbie did not allow the girls to collect their own soil samples. Rather, they watched as she did all the work. Her need for control eliminated any discovery for the girls in the experience, and while the design of the lesson demonstrated that she was listening to the director, the outcome demonstrated her perceptions were quite different. Dr. Debbie was a *Demonstrator of Procedures* who began with the right intentions, yet failed to broaden the girls' experiences in science because of one important detail—she neglected to let them have the experience.

A *Disseminator of Activities* is defined as a sceitnist who also approaches mentorship like a college classroom. Knowledge is given first, then laboratory work follows, and there is little connection between the two. Dr. Juan, the earth-science professor, approached the camp in this manner (see Table 1). He seemed more focused on having the girls do "hands-on" activities, than engaging them in deep, meaningful investigation answering a particular question. When the camp director approached Dr. Juan to discuss this issue, he became frustrated, yet was willing to re-structure his lesson with the researcher's help. Even with this assistance, however, Dr. Juan had trouble comprehending children's misconceptions about science and revising his teaching methods to meet their needs.

For example, his daughter was one of the "Side-by-Side" campers, and he knew his daughter didn't get that opportunity in her school science class and so intent on having the girls engage in hands-on science activities. He provided many hands-on activities in several different content areas. One experiment was about clouds, the next about rocks, then paleontology, and the last about the atmosphere of the earth. All of this unconnected activity seemed to leave the girls puzzled, because they were not able to anticipate what was next and why. There was no logical progression to the lesson. Rather, it was a smorgasbord of Mr. Wizard–type activities, and for that reason Dr. Juan was termed a *Disseminator of Activities*.

The director spent much time discussing research with the scientists about students' misconceptions concerning science and the importance of prior-knowledge questions. In each meeting, the researcher reiterated the original goals of the camp to Dr. Juan. He was unwilling to accept that his lack of questioning had any relevance to what the students were learning. When the director asked him, "What do you think the girls learned from their experience with you?", his response indicated he thought the girls did learn a lot about content. The researcher/director asked him how he could be sure, since he didn't ask the girls any prior-knowledge questions before his activities. She informed him of several methods used for teaching conceptual change. Yet, he was unwilling to listen. The result was that during the next week of camp his involvement was the same lesson he had previously presented. His unwillingness to discuss the "big ideas" and inability to adjust to the girls' developmental levels kept him from becoming a "Side-by-Side" expert. His lack of appreciation for the knowledge the director had about children's misconceptions and science education as a discipline of research study made for difficult working conditions.

A *Side-by-Side Expert* approaches camp from the perspective of, "How can I get these girls involved in what I do?" These mentors begin with the kind of Backward Design, described by Wiggins and Mc-Tighe, (2005). They focus on what they want the girls to understand about what they do as scientists.

Mentoring Girls in Science

They also guide students and set up experiences for them to gain this new appreciation and understanding. In four years of the camp, three "Side-by-Side" mentors were observed: Dr. James, wetlands ecologist; Dr. Francine, chemist; and Dr. Christy, plant ecologist (see Table 1).

With the three scientists that fell into this category, students were given freedom to solve the problems presented to them in their own way. This enabled the students to use process skills in a genuine problem-solving situation, and actively be involved in first-hand learning. It was no coincidence that the girls reported their days with these three scientists as the most enjoyable for four consecutive years. These three scientists had achieved what the director/researcher had intended, reinforcing the idea that it was possible for middle-school girls to have an authentic "Side-by-Side" experience.

PERSPECTIVES FROM THE CAMP DIRECTOR AND IMPLICATIONS FOR CLASSROOM TEACHERS WORKING WITH SCIENCE MENTORS

The four years of research and practice in this domain demonstrated that it is more difficult to teach highly-trained, highly-skilled scientists to engage girls in science activities than it is to teach pre-service teachers or practicing teachers the same concepts. It is accepted that in order to be a "good science teacher" one must have pedagogical knowledge, science-content knowledge, and science-pedagogical knowledge. Yet, scientists who do not have pedagogy skills or science-pedagogical knowledge are frequently recruited to help with the teaching of science in the classroom. As this study shows, it cannot be assumed that all scientists will make good teachers or good science mentors. These "Side-by-Side" experiences of the camp director/researcher working with scientists reveal that unless the scientists value the field of education as a research field, they are not open to learning science-content pedagogy.

Scientists may perceive their roles inaccurately, and be unwilling or unable to change them. This can be a nightmare for a long-term commitment between a classroom teacher and a scientist. So how do science educators get professional scientists to best understand their role in the classroom? It was soon obvious in this unique camp setting that the scientists' perception of "teaching" and the camp director's perception of "teaching" were very different.

The scientists often assumed the girls had multiple, in-depth experiences in science prior to attending the camp. Also, an absence of prior-knowledge questions by the scientists during investigations did not allow the girls to make predictions before the experiments were conducted. This questioning had been a central topic in each of the scientist/director meetings prior to camp, but during actual class sessions an overall lack of questioning by the scientists led the researcher to ask, "What exactly are the girls learning?"

Several scientists spent too much class time discussing the specifics of their research instead of focusing on the overall "big idea" and where their research or content fit into the body of science knowledge as a whole. Scientists possess a wealth of knowledge about science content, but most lack an understanding of children's misconceptions concerning science, scientists, and the age-appropriateness of what they are attempting to teach. Three of the eight content specialists grasped the understanding of what it meant to work "Side-by-Side" with scientists, (e.g., giving girls responsibility for collecting data that is meaningful), but five did not. These realities led the researcher/director to create the chart of expectations below (Table 2) to share with future mentors as a means of addressing these inadequacies.

Dr. James, who the girls reported in their journals as being extremely successful in encouraging the girls to like science, needed debriefing about his experience with young girls each time he completed a session. And this went on for six consecutive interactions. While he enjoyed the "Side-by-Side" experience tremendously, his first comment following the experience was how exhausted he was after working with young girls. He was used to teaching college students, and noted the different needs of these young learners. He needed time to remind himself that middle-school girls weren't like college students, and that his approach to teaching "Side-by-Side" required so much more energy than the traditional lecture.

Knowing this, it was helpful in constructing a visual image of the director's expectations and what the scientists could expect. Many scientists found this useful in working with the girls. For example, Dr. James was not used to the girls chatting and discussing the lesson topic while he was teaching. More comfortable with the traditional teaching methods used in his college classes, he expected the girls to sit quietly while he talked. Because of the different approach with "Side-by-Side" teaching, it took James some time to get acclimated to this new environment. He worked hard to improve his lessons and offer the girls a unique experience from year to year. Although a favorite scientist among the students, another reason James may have had to make some adjustments in being a role model to girls is because he is the father of three boys.

On the other hand, it cannot assume that because the scientists had female children of their own they will be able to relate to female students in a meaningful way. Recall Dr. Geraldine, who the girls reported had the most difficulty relating to the middle school females was actually the mother of two girls.

This study examined eight scientists: five Caucasian females from the United States, one Caucasian male from the United States, and two scientists from foreign countries, one male and one female. It is worth noting that the speaking accents of the two foreign scientists were mentioned in a negative way by the girls in their general discussions. One thing teachers may want to consider if working with a foreign scientist is if their accent interferes with students' learning. Also, could the accent potentially influence student's perception of the scientist in a negative way?

Other questions teachers might ask scientists when considering them for their classroom might include, "Do you have children of your own? And if so, how do you communicate your science experiences with your children? Can you speak in a child-friendly, age-appropriate way concerning your particular science discipline?"

In addition, there may be cultural barriers to address. And how does the scientist plan to take his/her information or content and make it meaningful to students? And, finally, is the material age-appropriate for middle-school students?

Implications for Using Mentors

Scientists who are the ultimate content area specialists are often used as mentors for both teachers and students. However, when working with children, one of the reasons these relationships are not as successful as they could be is because not everyone can relate to children in an age-appropriate way. Some scientists, for example, may not be able to present their field of study in a positive light without reinforcing the common stereotypes about scientists.

In selecting a scientist for the classroom, asking the questions mentioned in this paper will help discern who would make a good science mentor for students. Teachers need some guidance in selecting appropriate mentors in order to maximize the mentors' potential influence he/she will have on students' understanding of who does science, where science is done, and what scientists do. A scientist's willingness to participate in a mentorship program or classroom situation is not sufficient in and of itself.

Second, teachers should make clear to the science mentor the goals and expectations of the proposed partnership. To do this, teacher could use *Table 2 Mentorship Expectations Guidelines* in this paper or make their own set of goals and expectations based on the needs of their classroom. And nothing should be taken for granted concerning scientists. Those scientists not in the field of education may need many discussions and reflections with the teacher to understand their role *before* entering the classroom.

Third, even when a scientist's roles have been clearly outlined, expect there will be a difference in what the scientist perceives and what the teacher perceives. Classroom teachers should use *Table 2.Mentor-Approach-to-Teaching Continuum* as a springboard for discussion with mentor scientists. As a result, it is hoped the scientists will then begin to ask themselves, "Am I a disseminator of knowledge or disseminator of activities?" It is important that the teacher help them understand the differences.

Lastly, a good scientist role model should help students see the connection between science in the classroom and the career of a professional scientist. While in this particular study six of the eight scientists were female, it is important for students to have a role model they can relate to in science, regardless of gender. Because the researcher/director hypothesized before the investigation how important it was to expose participants to gender-matched (female) science role models, the majority of scientists participating in the "Side-by-Side" camp experience were female. The results of another study by this Author (2010) demonstrate that while the gender of mentors does play a role, it was more important for girls to have a role model who possessed the five identified characteristics of a quality mentor. These five characteristics are: a connection to why mentors became a scientist in the first place, passion for their science-content area, the ability to be an innate teacher, the ability to discuss controversial issues sensitively with young students and not bias them, and The WOW Factor.

This author stresses that it is more important for a scientist to possess all five of these qualities than have the same gender as students, and recommends that when teachers look for effective mentors, they use these five characteristics as a starting point for selecting the best possible choice for a mentor or role model in science. It should be noted that none of the girls in the study mentioned the gender of the content specialist.

CONCLUSION

Perhaps what is most important is the flexibility of the scientists in adapting to a classroom teacher's needs. As demonstrated in this study, some scientists were unable to adapt in spite of their willingness to participate in the camp experience. Students' experiences with quality science mentors can be powerful. As teachers bring visiting scientists into the classroom, students' beliefs about science, scientists, and themselves lead to positive attitudes and less stereotypic views concerning the nature of science and the physical attributes of a scientist. The results of this research indicate that scientists can successfully provide dimensions of the Human Endeavor in classroom settings, if they are aware of the four teaching approaches as outlined, and are willing to value science educators' opinions about education, research, and their students.

Commonly held stereotypic images about scientists are in direct opposition to what students should understand about science. As identified by the National Science Education Standards (1996), learning about "Science as a Human Endeavor" begins as early as grades K-4, and is repeated in grades 5-8 and 9-12. This paper offers cautions, considerations, and guidance for educators seeking to bring science-content specialists into their classroom.

REFERENCES

Barman, C. (1996). How do students really view science and scientists? *Science and Children*, 30–33.

Barman, C. (1997). Students' views of scientists and science: Results from a national study. *Science and Children*, *35*(1), 18–23.

Bozdin, A., & Gehringer, M. (2001). Breaking science stereotypes: Can meeting actual scientists change students' perceptions of scientists? *Science and Children*, *38*, 24–27.

Buck, G., Plano, C. V., Leslie-Pelecky, D., Lu, Y., & Cerda-Lizarraga, P. (2007). Examining the cognitive processes used by adolescent girls and women scientists in identifying science role models: A feminist approach. *Science Education.*, *92*(4), 688–707. doi:10.1002/sce.20257

Chambers, D. W. (1983). Stereotypic images of the scientist: The Draw-a-Scientist Test. *Science Education*, *67*(2), 255–265. doi:10.1002/sce.3730670213

Evans, M. O. (1992). An estimate of race and gender role-model effects in teaching high school. *The Journal of Economic Education*, *23*(3), 209–217. doi:10.1080/00220485.1992.10844754

Finson, K. D. (2002). A multicultural comparison of draw-a-scientist test drawings of eighth graders. Paper presented at the Annual International Conference of the Association of Educators of Teachers of Science; Charlotte, NC.

Flick, L. (1990). Scientist in Residence program: Improving children's images of science and scientists. *School Science and Mathematics*, *90*(3), 204–214. doi:10.1111/j.1949-8594.1990.tb15536.x

Fort, D. C., & Varney, H. L. (1989). How students see scientists: Mostly male, mostly white, mostly benevolent. *Science and Children*, *26*(8), 8–13.

Kafai, Y. B., & Gilliland-Swetland, A. J. (2000). The use of historical materials in elementary science classrooms. *Science Education*, *85*(4), 349–367. doi:10.1002/sce.1014

Karplus, R. (1970). *Science curriculum improvement study-a program report*. Berkley: Educational Products Information Exchange Institute.

Kuhn, T. S. (1972). *The structure of scientific revolutions* (2nd ed.). Chicago: University Press.

Mead, M., & Metraux, R. (1957). The image of the scientist amongst high school students. In B. Barbar & W. Hirsch (Eds.), The Sociology of Science, 38-61. Lewes, England: Falmer Press.

National Research Council (NRC). (1996). *National science education standards*. Washington, DC: Academic Press.

National Research Council (NRC). (2012). *A Framework for K-12 science education. Practices, Cross-cutting Concepts, and core ideas*. Washington, D.C.: National Academy Press.

Schibeci, R. A., & Sorenson, I. (1983). Elementary school children's perceptions of scientists. *School Science and Mathematics*, *83*(1), 14–19. doi:10.1111/j.1949-8594.1983.tb10087.x

Wiggins, G., & McTighe, J. (2005). *Understanding by design* (2nd ed.). Alexandria, VA: Association for Supervision & Curriculum Development.

APPENDIX

Table 3. Results of Question One: How did the science mentors approach their opportunity to mentor middle-school girls?

	Disseminator of Knowledge	**Demonstrator of Procedures**	**Disseminator of Activities**	**Side-By-Side Expert**
Dr. James				X
Dr. Geraldine	X			
Dr. Darlene			X	
Dr. Francine				X
Scientist Joan			X	
Dr. Christy				X
Dr. Juan			X	
Dr. Debbie		X		

Table 4. Mentorship expectations guidelines

What We Expect	**What You Can Expect**
Question of the day? (Focus)	Girls will talk throughout the day
Girls will be asked to make predictions and follow a procedure or a variety of procedures and draw their own conclusions	Variety of academic abilities
Girls will be involved in collecting data as they spend the day Side-by-Side with you!	Girls will have misconceptions
You will ask the girls many questions and different levels of questions about what they know before giving content information and/or hands-on materials	We will have teachers to help you, they will most likely do this through questioning

Chapter 3
Primary Grades Teachers' Fidelity of Teaching Practices during Mathematics Professional Development

Christie S. Martin
University of South Carolina at Columbia, USA

Chuang Wang
University of North Carolina at Charlotte, USA

Drew Polly
University of North Carolina at Charlotte, USA

Richard G. Lambert
University of North Carolina at Charlotte, USA

David Pugalee
University of North Carolina at Charlotte, USA

ABSTRACT

This chapter shares the findings from a study that examined primary grades teachers' fidelity of implementation during a year-long professional development program on formative assessment in mathematics. The project provided over 80 hours of professional development to elementary school teachers regarding their use of an internet-based formative assessment system for their students' mathematics achievement. This study examined teachers' online reflections and data in the internet-based assessment system to identify themes that lead to either a high fidelity or low fidelity of implementation. High fidelity teachers expressed beliefs that formative assessment supported their mathematics teaching, improved their students' learning, and was feasible to carry out in their classrooms. Low fidelity teachers' reflections were associated with numerous barriers to implementation as well as a lack of buy-in that the formative assessment system could benefit their teaching.

DOI: 10.4018/978-1-4666-9471-2.ch003

EXPLORING PRIMARY GRADES TEACHERS' FIDELITY OF FORMATIVE ASSESSMENT PRACTICES DURING MATHEMATICS PROFESSIONAL DEVELOPMENT

Introduction

Research continues to document the struggles that United States elementary school teachers face related to teaching mathematics effectively (National Mathematics Advisory Panel, 2008). Barriers to effective mathematics teaching include teachers' beliefs in more traditional approaches (Clark et al., 2014; Stipek, Givvin, Salmon, & MacGyvers, 2001), a lack of knowledge related to the mathematics that they teach (Thames & Ball, 2010), insufficient curricula materials or a lack of knowledge on how to use them (Sherin & Drake, 2009), and pressure to teach a certain way in an effort to increase test scores (McGee, Wang, & Polly, 2013). In light of the research on mathematics teaching, it can clearly be stated as a complex process that requires specific skills and knowledge related to both pedagogy and content (Thames & Ball, 2010).

In an effort to support teachers' mathematics instruction, professional development programs are commonly viewed as a mechanism to positively support teachers and also improve student achievement. Mathematics professional development projects are most effective when they simultaneously can support teachers' development of knowledge related to content and pedagogy as well as how students develop an understanding of fundamental mathematics concepts. One, of the pedagogy-related processes, that has gained attention in the literature is formative assessment, specifically examining students' mathematical thinking, analyzing data, and then making sound instructional decisions based on that information (Wiliam, 2007a; Wiliam, 2007b). Teachers who are able to effectively carry out a formative assessment process have been empirically linked to gains in their students' mathematics achievement (Polly et al.., 2014; Wiliam & Thompson, 2007).

This chapter presents a study in which we analyzed participants who completed a professional development project designed to support primary school teachers' use of an internet-based mathematics formative assessment system to support their mathematics teaching. Teachers participated in an 80-hour learning experience and data was collected on their use of the assessment system, their responses to reflection prompts, and their students' scores in the formative assessment system.

BACKGROUND

Formative Assessment in Mathematics

The purpose of formative assessment is to elicit and collect data that directly impacts instruction for individual learners (Koellner, Colsman, & Risley, 2009). Further, when working on activities related to formative assessment, teachers must connect evidence with instruction, which in turn requires them to understand and apply their expertise of learning progressions and how students best learn (Wiliam, 2007a, 2010). To that end, research on formative assessment has noted that the process is only valuable to the teaching and learning when the data is closely examined to modify instructional goals, instructional activities, and instructional pedagogies (Black, Harrison, Lee, Marshall, & Wiliam, 2004; Heritage, 2007).

Formative assessment processes can positively impact student learning. Formative assessment has been empirically associated with gains in student learning, teachers' increased knowledge of their students' understanding, and an increase in the alignment of instructional activities to students' abilities (Polly et al., 2014; Black & Wiliam, 1998; Wiliam, 2007b). With students who are at-risk and performing below grade level expectations, formative assessment and data-based instructional decisions can improve students' learning in struggling areas (Fuchs & Fuchs, 1986).

While there is potential for formative assessment processes to transform teaching and learning, teachers report difficulty consistently and frequently using formative assessment in their classrooms (Polly et al., 2014, Wiliam, 2010). In Abrams' (2007) study, several teachers admitted that the time demands of simply teaching the standards prevented them from doing any types of formative assessment with their students. Cizek (2010) noted that while teachers may espouse the value of formative assessment, summative assessments at the end of units is the only types of assessments that teachers use. There is a need to examine ways to best support teachers' efforts to formatively assess their students' learning, analyze data, and use the data to make appropriate instructional decisions.

Learner-Centered Professional Development

Professional development continues to be highly regarded as a mechanism to provide teachers with support in terms of their adoption of new pedagogies and advance teachers' knowledge about the content related to what they teach (Borko, 2004; Loucks-Horsley et al., 2010). While teacher learning is important, many stakeholders posit that the primary reason for teacher professional development is to increase teaching effectiveness, therefore increasing student achievement (Polly & Hannafin, 2010; Borko, 2004). This study was grounded in the construct of learner-centered professional development ([LCPD]; National Partnership for Educational Accountability in Teaching, 2000; Polly & Hannafin, 2010), which aligns to the American Psychological Association's *Learner-centered Principles* (APA Work Group, 1997), as well as constructivist and socio-cultural views of teaching and learning (Alexander & Murphy, 1998). LCPD addresses student learning deficiencies, actively engages teachers in experiences that develop their knowledge of both content and pedagogy, gives teachers ownership and choice of some professional learning activities, provides collaborative opportunities, includes job-embedded activities, and promotes teachers' reflection of their experiences (Polly & Hannafin, 2010).

In specific relation to mathematics professional development, teachers need experiences to simultaneously deepen their understanding of mathematics content and pedagogies by exploring complex mathematical tasks (Polly, McGee, & Martin, 2010), analyzing concepts that are difficult for students to learn (Hawley & Valli, 1999), learning ways to address student learning deficiencies (Loucks-Horsley et al., 2010), as well as analyzing, modifying, and creating curricular resources to meet the needs of their students (Martin & Polly, 2015; Polly, 2010). Professional development should be ongoing and closely connected to classroom activities (Heck, Banilower, Weiss, & Rosenberg, 2008).

Purpose and Research Questions

The goal of the APLUS professional development program that was examined in this study was to support primary teachers (Grades Kindergarten through Grade 2) and their use a web-based formative assessment system focused on number sense. Based on prior research, teachers who effectively use formative assessment data to gather information about their students and make instructional data-based decisions have greatly improved their students' mathematical achievement (Polly, Martin, Wang, Lambert, & Pugalee, under review; Wiliam, 2007). Professional development focused on formative assessment can greatly influence teaching and learning (Polly et al., 2014; Wiliam & Black, 2007). This study intended to identify and examine the differences between teachers that were considered high fidelity and low fidelity. Fidelity was measured by the amount of participation in the professional development and how much the teachers used the internet-based formative assessment in their classroom.

To that end, this study was framed by the following research question:

1. What were the differences between high and low fidelity teachers in their use of the internet-based formative assessment system?
2. What were the differences between high and low fidelity teachers on a professional development survey?
3. What were the differences between high and low fidelity teachers in their professional development reflections?

METHOD

This inductive study included purposeful sampling in order to explicitly compare data for high fidelity and low fidelity teacher-participants in the professional development project. Moodle was the online platform used to deliver professional development. This site produces activity reports for each of the participants. AMC Anywhere allows those with administrator status to access reports of activities for each participant. Activity reports from Moodle and AMC Anywhere for all participants were analyzed simultaneously to identify a purposeful sample. The purposeful sample was selected based on high engagement and fidelity. Once the purposeful sample was generated the researchers analyzed the data to extract themes to further explain the experience of each participant.

Context and Setting

The professional development project, *Assessment Practices to Support Mathematics Learning and Understanding for Students (APLUS)*, was funded by the North Carolina Mathematics Science Partnership program in the United States. This grant program supports intensive professional development projects focused on developing teachers' knowledge of content and pedagogy. The APLUS project provided teachers with professional learning experiences focused on the use of the internet-based assessment system *Assessing Mathematics Concepts* (*AMC Anywhere* hereafter) (Richardson, 2012), and the related instructional materials *Development Number Concepts* (Richardson, 1998). Richardson developed *AMC Anywhere* and the instructional materials abased on her experience teaching mathematics to children.

The APLUS grant was written in conjunction with faculty at two universities and five school districts around North Carolina. The grant provided funding for three cohorts of teachers who participated in the project for 11 months and each cohort included between 200-250 teachers. At the time of writing this manuscript, the third cohort is in progress. This study focuses on the second cohort of teachers since the professional development activities had been refined after year one, and teachers in the second cohort provide the most current data from the project.

Each cohort began the project with an intensive 5 day, 40-hour summer experience. During this time, teachers learned about the formative assessment system, the underlying mathematics concepts, and related mathematics activities that align to the concepts that are assessed. Teachers also are given time to practice using the assessments and analyzing data from actual students, in order to provide an authentic experience that mirrors actual classroom praxis as much as possible. The intensive summer professional development began on the first day with a teacher practices survey and on the last day ended with the same survey. Teaching practices were measured with 25 items on a 5-point Likert scale with higher scores on teaching practices suggesting more teacher-centered approach. Thirteen items (Items 1, 2, 3, 4, 8, 9, 10, 13, 14, 18, 19, 22, and 23) were indicators of teacher-centered practices whereas 12 (Items 5, 6, 7, 11, 12, 15, 16, 17, 20, 21, 24, and 25) were indicators of student-centered practices.

During the school year, teachers completed a series of classroom-embedded professional development activities that were facilitated through an online learning management system. These activities were organized into three large modules, which are described in Table 1. Each module required that teachers use the formative assessment system, analyze data, and then answer a series of reflection questions based on their experiences teaching mathematics and using the assessment system.

Module 1 focused on reminding teachers about the *AMC Anywhere* assessment system from the summer by watching a video and having them assess their students. Teachers also had to share about how they have organized their classroom to allow for differentiated, small group instruction. Module 2 allowed teachers to work more with the *AMC Anywhere* system with a focus on analyzing the data and making an instructional plan for their students. Module 3 focused on Number Talks as an instructional activity to promote discourse and conversations about number sense. Module 3 also allowed teachers to assess their students and analyze the data with a focus on struggling students in their class.

Participants

Teacher-participants in this study all taught in a large urban school district. In order to contrast the characteristics between high fidelity and low fidelity teachers, we purposefully selected (Patton, 2015) five teachers who had demonstrated a high fidelity of implementation of formative assessment pedagogies

Table 1. Overview of online professional development modules

	Time of Year	Activities
Module 1	First two months of the school year	Teachers assess their students using the *AMC Anywhere* system. Teachers design and share their plan for organizing their mathematics instruction to differentiate activities based on data. Teachers collaborate via online discussion boards sharing ideas about instructional activities to use.
Module 2	Middle of the school year	Teachers assess their students using the *AMC Anywhere* system. Teachers design and share their plan for intensive targeted support for a group of their students who require specific differentiation. Teachers collaborate via online discussion boards their successes, barriers to implementation, questions, and progress of their students.
Module 3	Last two months of the school year	Teachers assess their students using the *AMC Anywhere* system. Teachers provide results and updates about their students' growth, the use of the *AMC Anywhere* system and associated instructional materials. Teachers learn about Number Talks, a process for facilitating conversation about number sense, and implement at least one Number Talk in their classroom.

and five teachers who had demonstrated a low fidelity of implementation. All teachers were classroom teachers and licensed by the state to teach Grades Kindergarten through Grade 6. Lastly, each participant attended and completed all of the summer professional development workshops.

Data Collection

The data used for this study was collected from the academic year 2013-2014 which was year two of the MSP grant. The AMC Anywhere site provides spreadsheets for each of the nine assessments available that show students' performance on those tasks. A student will have several lines in the spreadsheet that show each instance that their teacher assessed them in that particular assessment. Reports for the four most used assessments (Counting, Hiding, Number Arrangements and Combination Trains) were generated, combined, and sorted to show how many assessments were administered for each student. These reports clearly showed the usage pattern for the teacher participants. From these reports a list of teachers that were using the assessments several times with each student was created along with a list of teachers that were assessing their students less than twice.

The online professional development (PD) was set up in three Modules that included activities, discussion boards, videos, and a requirement to respond to other teachers. These modules were examined to connect the teachers that were using AMC assessments regularly and had high participation in the online PD and those teachers that were using AMC assessments minimally and were either not engaged in the required PD or did not complete all modules.

The participants participation in both pre and post survey is also included. The online participation was scaled as 0 –did not participate, 1- participated less than the required amount, 2- exceeded requirements. Fidelity was measured by the use of the formative assessment technology. Again, a scale of as 0 –did not participate, 1- participated less than the required amount, 2- exceeded requirements. This project included 6 districts of teacher participants; the largest district was used for purposeful sampling. The rationale behind using the largest district for purposeful sampling was to have teachers experiencing similar demands and schedules for the mathematics instruction.

Data Analysis

The module data were analyzed using inductive, thematic analysis (Coffey & Atkinson, 1996) and researchers organized the data into categories by themes (Ezzy, 2002). The themes found in each of the modules focused on depth of response, intentionality of teaching practices, evidence of data driven instructional practices, level of interaction with their professional community. The data from the internet-based assessment system was examined to determine the amount of assessments that were administered per student and per teacher. The survey on teacher practices was administered at the beginning of the summer week long professional development and again at the end of the PD that week. The survey included open ended responses that were analyzed along with the pre/post paired sample t-test. The mean scores and significance are reported.

FINDINGS

The teachers were selected based on their participation in the online modules and their activity within the AMC system. The high fidelity group consists of teachers that were active in all three modules of the online professional development and used AMC anywhere assessments with their students regularly. Regularly was defined as students being assessed from 2 to 4 times throughout the year. The low fidelity group of teachers was identified as those that had minimal to no participation in the online modules and had minimally assessed their students with the AMC Anywhere system. The high and low group consisted of 5 teachers. There were several themes that were identified in the comparison of their participation in the online modules.

Learning Environments

Professional development focused on using AMC Anywhere web-based formative assessments and creating a learning environment that promotes hands-on learning and mathematical talk. Module one of the online professional development centered on teachers' classroom learning environment and routines for mathematics instruction.

High fidelity teachers: The teachers identified as high fidelity showed a level of thought and reflection in the module responses that was noticeably than other participants. The responses below are representative of the high fidelity group. The response is taken from Module one where teachers are asked to describe their classroom environment and mathematics routines.

My classroom environment facilitates a safe environment by providing students the opportunity to take ownership of their learning and growth. I have students grouped according to their abilities but each group has students with varying strengths and weaknesses. This is to have helps and support when I can't get to them right away. Each group has a student who is strong in all areas and then the other members of the learning team have different degrees of strength in mathematical ability. My space is set up so that manipulatives are readily available and students can access them on their own. Independence is the word for the year!!

The teacher's response to the question on environment and mathematics instruction reveals a level of intentionality in the construction of her classroom that is more focused on the learners. She purposefully creates groups that have ability differences, but seems to move beyond high and low ability and looks to have students working together that have different strengths to offer. She has an overall goal of creating independent learners and thinkers.

Another participant wrote:

Our math routine changes depending on the need of the students…We also do an estimate of magnetic chips as well as number talks that include "how did you see it?" Students are shown a dot card and then they have to tell me the amount, then I call on several students to tell me how they saw it. The students love this!!!!

Primary Grades Teachers' Fidelity of Teaching Practices during Mathematics Professional Development

This teacher's response conveys a sense of enthusiasm for facilitating an environment that her students can thrive. That same sense of enthusiasm along with flexibility and responsiveness appears in the response about classroom routines. The learners are at the center of the planning and therefore there is constant change in the routine based on those needs.

Low fidelity teachers: The teachers identified as low fidelity responded to the questions on environment and routines in a way that provides the details prompted by the question; however, the responses are limited in the planning and reasoning behind these decisions. One teacher wrote:

We have math from 1:30-3:00 Monday-Wednesday, and 2:15-3:00 on Thursday and Friday. Each math session begins with a math word problem. Then, students share their strategies for solving the problem. Then, we move into a math talk, often using tens frames or place value rods. On some days, the class then divides into groups and I am able teach small group lessons to target specific skills. The independent groups will play a Kathy Richardson or Investigations game, complete independent work, or practice a math skill on the computer. On other days I introduce or review a Kathy Richardson or Investigations game. The math time ends by coming back together to share strategies that we used that day during math.

The same teacher briefly summarized her mathematics instructional time by writing:

We have math from 1:30-3:00 Monday-Wednesday, and 2:15-3:00 on Thursday and Friday. Each math session begins with a math word problem. Then, students share their strategies for solving the problem. Then, we move into a math talk, often using tens frames or place value rods.

The second response provides the answer to the module question in a list-like fashion. The details of why mathematics instruction is structured in that way are not provided and there is little elaboration of the overall objectives and goals. The response fails to show the level of enthusiasm offered in the first response. She includes math problems, math talk, grouping, games, and sharing in the response; however, the intentionality and purpose of using these strategies are not shared. The routine question is met with what appears to be copy and paste from the previous response. This question may have been a place to elaborate on the reasoning behind the environment and agenda choices, but it is merely a reiteration of the first response.

Use of Student Data

The next topic in module one asked about the ways in which the teachers collected and used data. This particular district, as in many school districts, employs many different types of both formative and summative assessments. The example response from high fidelity teachers exhibits more reflection on those assessments.

High fidelity teachers: Participants' use of data was not a completely new idea to teachers. Many teachers, regardless of their fidelity of implementation, commented about the use of data from curriculum-based assessments, quarterly assessments, and end of unit tests. One high fidelity teacher discussed her transition from only using curriculum-based assessments to also using the data from *AMC Anywhere*.

Last year data came from Math Investigation Pre and Post-testing. We also gave students timed tests to determine as well as build fluency with addition and subtraction within a certain number (I did 5, 10,

15, 20, 30). Data in the form of Pre and Post-testing allowed me to know what they could do and what they need to work on. However, it wasn't giving me the skills that my students had difficulty in acquiring. I knew they couldn't subtract, but I didn't know why? If that makes sense. So, if my students did well on the Pre-test for addition, subtraction, word problems, measuring, etc. then we worked on the next "lesson skill" coming up...Data is used to not only plan the next steps for students, but it is also used to have an understanding of where they are and then provide activities that students can do (workshop) that will build upon what they already know. Now, differentiation in workshop and even homework has changed this year in order to meet students where they are mathematically. Data is used for groupings and for informing parents as it has been in the past. The difference now is that we know where they need to go because of what they need to work on in hopes of getting them where they need to be by the years end. Growth is now more evident from the things we have been doing with AMC. High Fidelity Teacher

This response describes the data that the teacher was and still is using, the strengths of that data, the ways in which that data was not providing the full picture, and details on how that data was used in instruction, with parents, and for grouping. She evaluates AMC Anywhere data and notes that while the data provides evidence on students' learning like the curriculum-based assessments did, the AMC Anywhere reports are offering more insight into the specific ways students are struggling and their growth.

Low fidelity teachers: Low fidelity teachers focused their comments primarily on district-mandated and end-of-use data. Further, low-fidelity teachers provided scant information about how the data is used to inform future instruction. The teacher response below provides a list of assessments that have been used in the past and present.

In previous years, our team used common assessments (10 questions every 10 days). We also created assessments based on standards for mid and end of quarter assessments. The data was used at conferences to share student progress. It was also used in intervention team meetings to determine what steps to take with struggling students. Now, we share Kathy Richardson data at grade level meetings. We also look at MAP scores across the grade level. These assessments help us to create small groups for specific skills in math.

The ideas of small groups, intervention, and determining struggling students are listed in the use of certain assessments. The MAP scores are examined by grade level, but it is unclear how they are used for student learning. Similarly, AMC assessments are only mentioned as something discussed at grade level meetings and not directly connected to planning.

Implementation of AMC Anywhere

The professional development workshops in the summer provided video-based examples and allowed teachers to use AMC Anywhere with students in a summer camp. These engaging experiences were strategically part of the professional development to help teacher participants begin the school year ready to implement AMC Anywhere in their classrooms. The online professional development also included videos of teachers administering AMC Anywhere formative assessments and our participants needed to evaluate the student performance and share what level and what type of instruction they may need based

Primary Grades Teachers' Fidelity of Teaching Practices during Mathematics Professional Development

on the video. This allowed participants to share their evaluation with other participants and get ideas for instruction. Both the open-ended questions on the survey that was administered in the summer and the online participation showed a variance perception from the high fidelity and low fidelity teachers regarding ease of implementation.

High Fidelity Teachers: Participating teachers completed a pre/post survey during the summer professional development. The post survey included the question below that asked teachers about their plan for collecting data. The high fidelity teachers' responses to this question suggested they feel *AMC Anywhere* will be an effective and easy to use formative assessment.

How did the PD influence how you plan on collecting and using data this year?

I feel a lot more comfortable going in as a 1st year teacher. I think this data will give me exactly what I need for each student. It will be easier to adapt instruction based on data

This has given me such a better understanding of math concept progression. I feel like I will have assessments that I can use to direct my instruction. So awesome. I am really looking forward to using. Thanks very much

The responses to the survey show a level of enthusiasm and excitement for implementing this program in their classroom. Both responses suggest the teachers will be using the data to direct their instruction. The next responses were included in the online modules from high fidelity teachers and suggest they were using AMC without difficulty and were using the data for instruction.

I think the AMC data is giving us so much more [data]! I found out where my kids were in math quickly. I like how it is easy to work with.

I love how the AMC Anywhere testing results help us determine groups for math.

The responses from the high fidelity teachers continue to exude a positive and enthusiastic outlook for using the AMC Anywhere program. The first response shows the data provided by AMC Anywhere was more comprehensive than other assessments, pinpointed students' understanding, and was easy to use. The second response focuses on the data report created by AMC Anywhere and the ease in using those reports for grouping students. Both responses reveal the teachers are not having difficulty implementing AMC Anywhere. The high fidelity teachers expressed their challenges in a way that suggested they were engaging with the professional development to work toward creating an environment that supported their learners.

Low fidelity teachers: The teachers that were identified as low fidelity teachers in this study have responses that demonstrate a level of struggle that may be limiting their successful implementation of the ideas and AMC assessment program that were part of this grant. The responses of the low fidelity teachers are limited to Module One; they did not participate in Module Two and Three. The lack of participation in these last two modules also displays a lack of implementation fidelity, reflection, and collaboration with regards to this particular project. Their responses to the post survey at the end of the summer professional development also reveal barriers to implementation.

How did the PD influence how you plan on collecting and using data this year?

We may need magnetic 2 color sided counters at our school (WSE). Suggestions: I would like to see a video/s of model classrooms set up/designed for Kathy Richardson. A video library would be helpful.

I will be able to get much more detailed information about my students learning. I will be able to tell how students got their answers rather than just the answer. I have specific activities to address student needs. I would love to go to a model class that uses Kathy Richardson to get an idea of how it will actually look in a classroom. It would be great of we could get magnetic red and yellow chips to use in number talks.

The first response presents ideas for more materials and support that would be helpful to get started, there are no details about how the summer professional development will impact their data collection for the coming school year. It appears that without more materials and video support the collection of data is hindered for this particular participant. The second response exhibits a more positive view toward using AMC Anywhere; however, the plans for the year are non-specific and the request for more materials and modeling indicates the actual implementation of AMC Anywhere may be impeded. The next responses were posted in the online modules.

Being new to this material, I am feeling a bit overwhelmed with trying to familiarize myself with the materials and prepare the materials. I often feel like there just isn't enough time.

This is where I would like to be more familiar with the Kathy Richardson activities so that I could easily access the necessary prerequisite activities for these children. Being new to this material, I am feeling a bit overwhelmed with trying to familiarize myself with the materials and prepare the materials. I am eager to hear how others have designed their math instruction because I am definitely in the market for suggestions. Low Fidelity Teachers

The responses illustrate the teachers' struggle with dedicating time to participating in this project and becoming familiar with the program, strategies, and professional development. These responses, as noted, are coming from Module One and show feelings of being overwhelmed from the beginning of the project. Even though the second response appears to be seeking collaboration with other participants the teachers does not continue with the modules and therefore limits the chance to exchange ideas. The low fidelity teachers shared a sense of being overwhelmed that prevented them from engaging or from continuing to engage in the professional development

Collaboration

The online professional development required participants to thoughtfully respond to the posts of their peers. The requirement was designed to encourage teachers to collaborate with one another and share ideas. The high fidelity teachers actively sought out collaboration and appeared to genuinely want feedback from their peers.

High fidelity teachers: High fidelity teachers participated in the online professional development in a way that supported collaboration among their peers through the discussion board posts. Their posts revealed they valued and wanted the input of the other participating teachers.

I agree with you on what works for one may not work for all. I find that very difficult to work around. Again, differentiation I find that there are times when I need to work with just one student and I can't devote the time that I need as I have about six students who have different needs. I am working to find a solution. Any ideas?

My "to do" list going forward is to keep math talks, number of the day, and the dot cards for "how did you see it?" My students have grown just from seeing how others process the dot cards and what number combinations they are seeing to get a particular number. Any suggestions for a better way to do place value will be greatly appreciated!!

(Responding to a teacher's concern about balancing time constraints and small group instruction) I totally agree with the challenge you are facing. That is where I struggle as well. Any thoughts on how to combat this from the group would be greatly appreciated!! High Fidelity Teachers

The responses above show the teachers have read the responses of other colleagues, they affirm those concerns, share their own challenges, and open the conversation for ideas from their peers. There is also a sense of diligence conveyed in these concerns that suggests the teachers are challenged, but persistent in working through those challenges.

Low fidelity teachers: The low fidelity teachers included limited posts about collaborative experiences that they had with their colleagues during the school year. All teacher-participants are required to collaborate weekly with their grade level teams during mathematics planning. During this planning time, teachers are supported by an administrator or instructional facilitator/coach to guide this process. Despite the fact that collaboration was not mentioned by the low fidelity teachers, they did collaborate weekly with their teachers regarding mathematics instruction.

Reflection about Implementation and Experiences

The questions included in the professional development modules were designed to encourage teachers to reflect on their practice, share their challenges and successes, and to provide new ideas from peers.

High fidelity teachers: High fidelity teachers posted reflective responses that evaluated their practices, highlighted challenges, and shared ideas with others on the discussion board for helping their students.

That is an area I need to work on too. I tend to like things a little too quiet sometimes! I have definitely seen the kids learning a lot for each other this year. For this to really be successful they need to be able to talk to each other.

I agree with this reflection. One of the challenges of having the students work in small groups is that when I look over and see that the work is not going as I had planned, my initial reaction is to run over to the students and "help" them fix it. I need to learn to give them time to work through issues on their own.

When reading this post it really helped me realize that if I conducted number talks on a regular basis, I would reinforce and practice these key skills constantly.

All three responses begin with the acknowledgement of having read another teachers' post, thoughtfully considered the ideas presented, followed by describing their challenges and a plan to adjust instruction. The plans include allowing more discussion between students even if the volume tests the teachers comfort level, allowing more time for students to think through problems, and implementing math talk more consistently. These ideas are reinforced in the professional development and seem to be becoming part of the mathematics routines of high fidelity teachers.

Low fidelity teachers: The low fidelity teachers did not include any posts that included reflective thoughts or ideas regarding the professional development or the use of the *AMC Anywhere* system. While these teachers may have had successes or struggles they did not include them. Discussion posts were simply just a presentation of factual information.

Focus on Student Learning

Teachers varied in their comments about their focus on student learning. The goal of the APLUS project was to improve student learning by supporting teachers' use of formative assessment processes. High fidelity teachers wrote in-depth responses about student learning, while low fidelity teachers did not mention student learning in detail.

High fidelity teachers: High fidelity teachers continued to complete all three online professional development modules and included many posts that emphasize the benefit of using the assessments and noticeable student growth. The observation of student growth may be one of the factors that contributed to the teachers' fidelity to the program.

I completely agree. My students are much more fluent within 10 and 20. AMC really proves to work!

Kathy has changed math workshop for my students as well. I feel more informed and am challenged to meet the needs of my students who still aren't performing at grade level. The tools from Kathy Richardson that I have implemented have strengthened math work time for my students and I can see a difference from the growth they are making. Last year it was hard to see growth. Classroom observations are now spent seeing how students are growing and using the terminology and thinking about math more.

I have seen so much growth already, and I am excited to watch them learn and experience math through differentiated workshop.

My students have achieved so much more! They are fluent within 10. Most of my students are even fluent within 12. They have grown so much since the beginning.

I have found that some of my higher level thinkers sometimes try to out think each other! They hear somebody else's strategy that was the same one they actually used too. Then they try to come up with another strategy that becomes more complicated than the original strategy.

I am seeing improvement all around. My struggling students have been able to master fluency within five and are almost there within ten.

As noted earlier the responses of the high fidelity teachers show a level of enthusiasm for the project and especially the growth they are experiencing with their students. They are reflecting on the way students are developing and how they are interacting with one other. The responses include growth in the area of fluency, using mathematical terminology, and problem solving strategies. The first response indicates this particular teacher found identifying growth and progress with students' number sense to be a challenge the year before and AMC Anywhere has made a positive difference. The teacher continues to note that the data on student growth has allowed her classroom observations to take on a new focus. Their responses indicate they are invested in the professional development and following implementation with reflection

Low fidelity teachers: The low fidelity teachers' mentioned some information about their use of data and students' growth. However, their responses lacked the specificity and enthusiasm presented in high fidelity responses.

The Kathy Richardson assessments allow me to ability group my students based on specific skills and with specific numbers to review. I've always had flexible grouping, but for many skills, the groups would stay the same. Now that I have more data to support my grouping decisions, I truly have had more movement between groups depending on the skill we are working on and those that a child needs more practice or has mastered and is ready for a higher number or greater challenge.

Kathy Richardson has allowed me to change the way that I use data in my classroom as it really organizes student performance based on specific skills.

The focus of both responses is primarily on grouping students. The first response alludes to groups having greater flexibility than prior years due to the data offering more insight into the student learning. It is assumed that movement of students to different groups is a movement of growth due to an increase in their understanding. The response lacks details to better understand how the groups are created, how the data influences the grouping, and how impactful the program has been on student growth. The second response also focuses on organization of students by their performance on specific skills, but does not include a description of student growth.

Examining Teachers' Responses to the Summer Survey

The paired t-test analysis of the pre and post survey indicated both the high and low fidelity teachers had mean scores that moved more towards student centered practices in the classroom; however, the difference in mean scores from pre ($M = 3.26$, $SD = .11$) ($M = 3.05$, $SD = .31$) to post ($M = 2.96$, $SD = .36$) ($M = 2.73$, $SD = .74$) for each group were not statistically significant ($t(4) = 2.10$, $p > .05$)($t(4) = .79$, $p > .05$). The survey included a small section on assessment goals, both the high and low fidelity groups mean scores went up from pre ($M = 3.26$, $SD = .11$) ($M = 3.16$, $SD = .55$) to post ($M = 3.76$, $SD = .79$) ($M = 3.84$, $SD = .74$) indicating they gained self-efficacy in their ability to use assessment with their students. The increase was not statistically significant for either group ($t(4) = -1.77$, $p > .05$) ($t(4) = -1.43$, $p > .05$). Hence, there was no empirical connection between teachers' implementation of the professional development with fidelity and their responses on the survey at the end of the 40-hour summer experience.

Summary of Differences between High Fidelity and Low Fidelity Teachers

The data analysis of discussion board posts indicated that teachers who used the AMC Anywhere system and related instructional activities with a high degree of fidelity resembled specific characteristics. High fidelity teachers organized their classroom in a flexible manner in which the learning environment had structure but could be modified to best meet the academic needs of their students. Further, high fidelity teachers espoused a belief that the data from the *AMC Anywhere* system was beneficial to them, and could be used with other data sources to help them make effective instructional decisions. High fidelity teachers also discussed the growth they were seeing in their students and the benefits of making data-based decisions in their classroom. Lastly, high fidelity teachers wrote more reflective comments about their experiences, and posted comments in which the reaffirmed and supported their peers on the discussion board posts.

DISCUSSION

The findings from this study highlight the differences that exist between a high fidelity teacher and a low fidelity teacher. Ideally, professional development is planned with the goal of creating high fidelity teachers that are effectively implementing the learning tool to address student learning in a meaningful way. The factors pertaining to in the classroom practices, out of the classroom practices, and student progress were where we found differences between high and low fidelity teachers. These findings warrant further discussion.

In Classroom Factors

Several objectives included in the professional development were centered on implementation of the AMC Anywhere web-based formative assessment and creating a learning environment that would allow the data to be used effectively.

Learning environment: The professional development provided participating teachers with instruction for using the AMC Anywhere program and materials were provided to help teachers connect the formative assessment data directly to the learning environment they would create for their students. Linking formative assessment data with instructional practices has been shown to produce gains in student learning (Polly et al., 2014; Black & Wiliam, 1998; Wiliam, 2007b).The first module of the professional development revealed high fidelity teachers had structure and routines that were fluid and adapted based on data. Their responses indicated they implemented the strategies discussed in professional development and were directed by student data.

Implementation: The AMC Anywhere program is designed for students to be regularly assessed. Formative assessment collected and analyzed at the individual level consistency produces significant gains in student learning (Fuchs &Fuchs, 1986). The APLUS teacher participants were required to assess students at least three times during the school year. The high fidelity participants adhered to and exceeded this requirement. Their discussion responses throughout the on-line modules showed they valued the data and it became instrumental in designing their classroom and instructional strategies. Low fidelity teachers struggled to meet the requirement and in most cases assessed their students only once. Formative assessment research affirms that consistent assessment that produces data that directly impacts practice is essential for increasing student growth (Black & Wiliam, 1998; Wiliam, 2007b).

Student growth: The professional development supported the implementation of AMC Anywhere formative assessment, provided teachers with additional learning materials, and illustrated ways to facilitate a learning environment that is flexible to student needs. These objectives were intended to increase students' growth in their mathematical thinking. The high fidelity teachers used the assessment consistently and used the data in their instruction. This was evident in the AMC Anywhere data and their online posts. Their posts indicated they were seeing their students grow in their number sense and with specific skills. Low fidelity teachers responded in less specific terms and in some cases failed to mention student growth. Formative assessment research suggests regular assessment produces growth (Black & Wiliam, 1998); therefore the inconsistency of low fidelity teachers may have impeded their ability to see growth with their students. Future research studies need to examine how professional development can further assist teachers in connecting data to a learning environment that promotes student growth. This may occur through mentorship between high fidelity teachers and low fidelity teachers to create a more specific network of support.

Out of Classroom Practices and Factors

Several out of classroom practices and factors were identified during the data analysis process. They include teachers' use of data, collaboration with colleagues and their reflective practices.

Use of data: The goal of the APLUS project was to support teachers' use of the *AMC Anywhere* formative assessment system to collect data on their students' mathematics understanding and then use the data to make sound instructional decisions. High fidelity teachers used the *AMC Anywhere* consistently and reported specific details in their discussion board posts about how they were using their data to make instructional decisions. Low fidelity teachers did not talk specifically talk about the use of *AMC Anywhere* data. However, in some cases these teachers did mention other data sources, such as district-wide assessments or curriculum-based assessments.

Research indicates that teachers' use of data collected for formative assessment processes directly indicates student learning (Wiliam, 2007b; Black & Wiliam, 1998). Further, teachers who do not effectively use formative data to make instructional decisions are missing a potentially rich opportunity to modify and differentiate instruction based on students' academic performance (Wiliam, 2007b). It is imperative that future studies examine how exactly teachers are using their data sources to make instructional decisions, as well as what factors teachers possess in order to effectively conduct formative assessment processes (Martin & Polly, 2015; Polly et al., under review).

Collaboration: High fidelity teachers used the online discussion forum as a tool to collaborate and interact with their colleagues. The comments made by high fidelity teachers spoke consistently about their thoughts and experiences, and also affirmed or offered suggestions to their peers on the discussion forum. All teacher-participants in this project collaborated on mathematics instruction weekly with their grade level teams, but the high fidelity teachers extended their collaboration using the discussion posts. The low fidelity teachers, however, did not post in depth responses to each other and did not seek out collaboration.

One possibility for the low fidelity teachers' lack of evidence of collaboration was that they may be working in a school that lacks collaborative efforts around the use of the *AMC Anywhere* system. Research studies on programs that embody LCPD found that teachers are more likely to implement new knowledge and skills from professional development if they have school-based support and collaboration from their peers (Polly, 2006; Polly & Hannafin, 2011; Heck et al., 2008; Loucks-Horsley et al., 2010).

Individuals who design online asynchronous professional development programs need to intentionally think about ways to increase teachers' collaboration with others. Further, subsequent research studies should examine the design and influence of online professional development projects that seek to improve the amount of collaboration between teacher-participants.

Reflective practices: Low fidelity teachers simply stated facts and did not post reflective comments about their instruction, their use of the *AMC Anywhere* system, or students' learning. High fidelity teachers, on the other hand, shared reflections about their students' growth, their experiences using the formative assessment system, and their experiences making data-based instructional decisions. Additionally, high fidelity teachers demonstrated reflective practices as they shared how they reflected on their student data to differentiate instruction.

LCPD research supports professional learning activities in which teachers complete classroom-based work and then reflect on their experiences as well as the impact on student learning (Loucks-Horsley et al., 2010). Formative assessment processes require teachers to be reflective about their students' performance, their data sources, and how student learning has been impacted by previous instruction (Wiliam, 2007a, 2007b). Future online LCPD projects should continue to look for ways to support and scaffold teachers' use of reflective practices. This could occur through more structured activities that require teachers to collect data followed by a series of tasks that promote analysis and reflection about the data.

CONCLUSION

This chapter closely examined the teacher participants in a professional development project, Assessment Practices to Support Mathematics Learning and Understanding for Students *(APLUS)*. The teachers participated in the summer professional development and completed a survey related to their teaching practices and goals for assessment. At that point in the project the differences between participants were difficult to discern and there were not statistically significant changes in the pre post means; however, as the project progressed the on-line modules and assessment data revealed teacher participants that were considered high fidelity and those that were low fidelity. The high fidelity teachers exhibited several characteristics that seemed to show they were fully engaged and actively using the AMC Anywhere program and instructional supports to the benefit of their students. Low fidelity teachers exhibited a sense of being overwhelmed and discontinued their engagement in the on-line professional development and limited their use of the AMC Anywhere formative assessment. Some implications of this study are to include more structured activities with tasks that increase analysis and reflection, identify high fidelity teachers and find ways to give them leadership and mentorship roles, and increase support for teachers that begin to show low fidelity characteristics. Future research that examines how teachers use data in their instructional decisions, the factors of teachers that are effectively using formative assessment, and how online professional development should be designed to foster collaboration and teacher support is essential.

This particular study used data produced from an internet based PD and formative assessment usage reports. This provided insight into the effect of PD on participant practices; however, it is difficult to discern between what teachers reported in reflections and their actual behavior. This limitation has been noted by the researchers and the third year of the grant includes observations that will be used as our research continues.

REFERENCES

Abrams, L. M. (2007). Implications of high-stakes testing for the use of formative classroom assessment. In H. McMillan (Ed.), *Formative assessment classroom: Theory into practice* (pp. 70–98). NY: Teachers College Press.

Ball, D. L., Thames, M. H., & Phelps, G. (2008). Content knowledge for teaching: What makes it special? *Journal of Teacher Education, 59*(5), 389–407. doi:10.1177/0022487108324554

Black, P., Harrison, C., Lee, C., Marshall, B., & Wiliam, D. (2004). Working inside the black box: Assessment for learning in the classroom. *Phi Delta Kappan, 86*(1), 8–21. doi:10.1177/003172170408600105

Black, P., & Wiliam, D. (1998). Assessment and classroom learning. *Assessment in Education: Principles, Policy & Practice, 5*(1), 7–71. doi:10.1080/0969595980050102

Borko, H. (2004, November 01). Professional development and teacher learning: Mapping the terrain. *Educational Researcher, 33*(8), 3–15. doi:10.3102/0013189X033008003

Clark, L. M., DePiper, J. N., Frank, T. J., Nishio, M., & Capmbell, P. F. et al. (2014). Teacher. characteristics associated with mathematics teachers' beliefs and awareness of their students' mathematical dispositions. *Journal for Research in Mathematics Education, 45*(2), 246–284. doi:10.5951/jresematheduc.45.2.0246

Ezzy, D. (2002). *Qualitative analysis: Practice and innovation*. London: Routledge.

Fuchs, L. S., & Fuchs, D. (1986). Effects of Systematic Formative Evaluation: A Meta-Analysis. *Exceptional Children, 53*(3), 199–208. PMID:3792417

Hawley, W. D., & Valli, L. (2000). *Learner-centered professional development. Research Bulletin, No. 27*. Phi Delta Kappa Center for Evaluation, Development, and Research.

Heck, D. J., Banilower, E. R., Weiss, I. R., & Rosenberg, S. L. (2008). Studying the effects of professional development: The case of the NSF's local systemic change through teacher enhancement initiative. *Journal for Research in Mathematics Education, 39*(2), 113–152.

Heritage, M. (2007). Formative assessment: What do teachers need to know and do? *Phi Delta Kappan, 89*(2), 140–145. doi:10.1177/003172170708900210

Koellner, K., Colsman, M., & Risley, R. (2011). Multidimensional Assessment. *Teaching Exceptional Children, 44*(2), 48–56.

Loucks-Horsley, S., Stiles, K. E., Mundry, S., Love, N., & Hewson, P. W. (2010). *Designing professional development for teachers of science and mathematics* (3rd ed.). Thousand Oaks, CA: Corwin Press.

Martin, C. S., & Polly, D. (2015). Using the AMC Anywhere web-based assessment system to examine primary students' understanding of number sense. In D. Polly (Ed.), *Cases on Technology Integration in Mathematics Education* (pp. 366–377). Hershey, PA: IGI Global; doi:10.4018/978-1-4666-6497-5.ch018

McGee, J. R., Wang, C., & Polly, D. (2013). Guiding teachers in the use of a standards-based mathematics curriculum: Perceptions and subsequent instructional practices after an intensive professional development program. *School Science and Mathematics, 113*(1), 16–28. doi:10.1111/j.1949-8594.2012.00172.x

National Mathematics Advisory Panel. (2008). *Foundations for Success*. Washington, DC: U.S. Department of Education.

Patton, M. Q. (2015). *Qualitative Research & Evaluation Methods* (4th ed.). Thousand Oaks, CA: Sage.

Polly, D. (2006). Participants' focus in a learner-centered technology-rich mathematics professional development program. *The Mathematics Educator, 16*(1), 14–21.

Polly, D. (2011). Teachers' learning while constructing technology-based instructional resources. *British Journal of Educational Technology, 42*(6), 950–961. doi:10.1111/j.1467-8535.2010.01161.x

Polly, D., & Hannafin, M. J. (2010). Reexamining technology's role in learner-centered professional development. *Educational Technology Research and Development, 58*(5), 557–571. doi:10.1007/s11423-009-9146-5

Polly, D., & Hannafin, M. J. (2011). Examining how learner-centered professional development influences teachers' espoused and enacted practices. *The Journal of Educational Research, 104*(2), 120–130. doi:10.1080/00220671003636737

Polly, D., Martin, C. S., Wang, C., Lambert, R. G., & Pugalee, D. K. (under review). Primary grades teachers' instructional decisions while participating in mathematics formative assessment professional development.

Polly, D., McGee, J. R., & Martin, C. S. (2010). Employing technology-rich mathematical tasks to develop teachers' technological, pedagogical, and content knowledge (TPACK). *Journal of Computers in Mathematics and Science Teaching, 29*(4), 455–472.

Polly, D., Wang, C., Martin, C. S., Lambert, R. G., Pugalee, D. K., Stephan, M., & Ringer, C. (2014, April). Examining the influence of professional development on primary students' mathematical achievement. Paper presented at the 2014 Annual Meeting of the American Educational Research Association. Philadelphia, PA.

Richardson, K. (1998). *Developing Number Concepts: Counting, Comparing, and Pattern*. New York: Dale Seymour.

Richardson, K. (2012). *How Children Learn Number Concepts: A Guide to the Critical Learning Phases*. Bellingham, WA: Math Perspectives.

Sherin, M. G., & Drake, C. (2009). Curriculum strategy framework: Investigating patterns in teachers' use of a reform-based mathematics curriculum. *Journal of Curriculum Studies, 41*(4), 467–500. doi:10.1080/00220270802696115

Stipek, D. J., Givvin, K. B., Salmon, J. M., & MacGyvers, V. L. (2001). Teachers' beliefs and practices related to mathematics instruction. *Teaching and Teacher Education, 17*(2), 213–226. doi:10.1016/S0742-051X(00)00052-4

Wiliam, D. (2007a). Keeping learning on track: Formative assessment and the regulation of learning. In F. K. Lester (Ed.), *Second Handbook of Mathematics Teaching and Learning* (pp. 1053–1098). Greenwich, CT: Information Age Publishing.

Wiliam, D. (2007b). *What does research say the benefits of formative assessment are? National Council of Teachers of Mathematics Research Brief.* Retrieved from http://www.nctm.org/uploadedFiles/Research_News_and_Advocacy/Research/Clips_and_Briefs/Research_brief_05_-_Formative_Assessment.pdf

Wiliam, D., & Thompson, M. (2007). Integrating assessment with instruction: what will it take to make it work? In C. A. Dwyer (Ed.), *The future of assessment: shaping teaching and learning* (pp. 53–82). Mahwah, NJ: Lawrence Erlbaum Associates.

William, D. (2010). An integrative summary of the research literature and implications for a new theory of formative assessment. In H. Andrade & G. Cizek (Eds.), *Handbook of formative assessment* (pp. 18–40). New York, NY: Routledge.

Chapter 4
A Paradigm Shift for Teachers' Professional Development Structure in Turkey:
Moving from Instruction to Learning

Murat Günel
TED University, Turkey

Melike Özer-Keskin
Gazi University, Turkey

Nilay Keskin-Samancı
Gazi University, Turkey

ABSTRACT

This chapter concerns the importance of in-service training programmes for the professional development of science teachers. A description will be given of the general structure of in-service training activities in Turkey and the results will be presented of an in-service training project, which was conducted as part of a three-year longitudinal study. Within the scope of the project, an in-service training programme for science teachers was conducted based on the argument-based inquiry approach and the theoretical premises upon which it is built. The project aimed to direct science teachers towards student-centred teaching. The training activities focused on the scientific thinking underpinning the teachers' professional knowledge and practices, their perceptions on learning, and their pedagogical practices and epistemological beliefs. The extent to which these activities affected classroom applications and learning processes was investigated and the findings suggest that they had a statistically significant impact on the teachers' pedagogical development and on the students' academic performance and thinking skills.

DOI: 10.4018/978-1-4666-9471-2.ch004

INTRODUCTION

The Importance of Professional Development Programmes for Science Teachers

Considering today's competition-based systems and developments on the international stage, one can appreciate the importance of raising individuals possessing the skills that respond to the requirements of our age (Miaoulis, 2009). For this reason, investment in science, technology, engineering, and mathematics (STEM) literacy are very much on the increase. In STEM education, as in all educational systems, this investment and support focus on the *students, teachers,* and *training programmes* and the efficiency and effectiveness of educational systems depend on these three elements moving in harmony towards a specific target. A breakdown, weakness, ineffectiveness, or malfunctioning in any of these elements is bound to lower the efficiency of the whole system. Today, academic performance and a positive change in students in terms of various skills are considered to be the barometers of efficiency and success in education.

The most important factor in ensuring these positive changes in students in terms of various skills and academic performance is, undoubtedly, the teacher (Rivkin, Hanushek, & Kain, 2005), because, as pointed out by researchers who have studied the link between the exercise of the profession and the learning outcomes, a crucial relationship exists between teachers' adequacy and students' performance (Hoy & Miskel, 2008; Junor-Clarke & Fourniller, 2012; Guskey, 2014). Training well-qualified teachers is only possible through an effective implementation of the pre-service and in-service educational activities (Darling-Hammond, 1999; Darling-Hammond & Bransford, 2005). In order for teachers to keep up with the contemporary requirements of the educational sector in their professional lives and to educate individuals possessing the skills demanded of them, they need to constantly refresh their capabilities and take part in the in-service training activities organized for this purpose. The link between in-service training programmes and teachers' professional development directly affects school development and students' learning quality (Kennedy, 1998). When this interaction is taken into account, the need for a proper assessment of the targets and structuring of these in-service training programmes cannot be missed.

Structure and Implementation of Professional Development Programmes

All over the world, traditional in-service training programmes are implemented in the form of seminars and presentations to raise the teacher's teaching abilities and knowledge however, improving teachers' performance in the classroom requires developing their practical skills (McCann, Alan, & Gail, 2012). In-service training programmes should not only present teachers with the opportunity to learn new things but also provide them with a setting where they can put their theoretical knowledge into practice (Avalos, 2011). Only in this way can in-service training programmes achieve their main goal of bringing about a difference in teachers' attitudes and beliefs, their ways of teaching, and their students' performance (Guskey, 2002). From this perspective, traditional in-service training concepts appear to have become *a learning environment for all*. This transition has had an impact on the administrators, teachers, and the schools which are continuous research settings for students (Fullan, 2001; Knight, 2007; Loucks-Horsley, 1995; Loucks-Horsley, Stiles, & Hewson, 1996).

In addition to being a process that needs prioritized planning and implementation that will allow educational reforms to be applied and new approaches to be put into practice, in-service training for teachers has an important role in determining the quality of education and making improvements along the way (Supovitz & Turner, 2000). Educational reforms in many countries seem to fail because teachers' beliefs, values, and practical levels/skills are not taken into account (Al-Daami & Wallace, 2007; McDonald, 2003). This is despite the widely known effects of in-service training on improving the field knowledge and teaching skills of teachers who are in the foreground in the structuring and implementation of teaching programmes (Bybee & Loucks-Horsley, 2000; Garet et al,. 1999).

According to the literature, teachers' beliefs concerning the theory of knowledge and their classroom practices are indispensable components that need to be tackled together within in-service training programmes if significant changes are to be brought about in learning and teaching settings (Kennedy, 1998; Luft, 2001). Research shows that grasping learning theories (and in particular the structural learning theory) and reflecting them in educational settings do not suffice on their own and must be complemented by considerations of teachers' willingness, motivations, and beliefs on learning and teaching (Simon, 1995; Simon & Schifter, 1987; Hand & Treagust, 1995; Luft, 2001; Wellington & Osborne, 2001; Windschitd, 2002). Therefore, it follows that in-service training programmes must be structured to take such components of knowledge theory into account.

Teachers' theoretical ideas on how effective learning takes place directly influence their ways of teaching and the pedagogical decisions that they make (Simon, 1995). In this context, many researchers hold that professional development programmes must include teachers' beliefs about their students' ways of learning and thinking and interact with teachers' actual practices (Millar, Osborne, &Nott, 1998; Millar & Osborne, 1998; Richardson & Placier, 2001). The design of in-service training programmes must also include teachers' beliefs on learning and teaching, elements of classroom management, and components of student assessment (Fishman et al,. 2003).

The success of the in-service training programmes also depends on the content, structure, and format as well as how thoroughly they were initially planned. Besides, when planning in-service training, it is important to ensure that activities are student-centred, have substantial content, consider learner needs, and conform to the legal regulations (Guskey, 2000). There are several international studies that recommend comprehensive theoretical and practical structures to improve teachers' professional adequacies in this context. Determining and improving the perceptions, structures, and practices of in-service training in Turkey are the main areas to be prioritised.

The Current State of Professional Development Programmes in Turkey

In the international arena, the importance of teachers' professional development has been underlined by many studies, and acknowledged with large funds from national budgets. In Turkey, as in all other countries, the importance of in-service training for teachers was recognized in the early years of the Republic, and a number of studies were undertaken by individual researchers or commissioned by various institutions concluding that well-qualified and experienced teachers are an indispensable element of education and multi-faceted training is required for teachers to meet the needs of their classrooms (The Holmes Group, 1996; Thair & Treagust, 2003; Seferoğlu, 2004). The European Commission Report on Improving the Quality of Teacher Education (2007) stated, "teachers should be able to improve their teaching skills with in-service training programmes" and highlighted the importance of these skills being open to development in light of suggestions and feedback (Auhl & Daniel, 2014).

In line with the principles of lifelong learning, in-service training programmes provide a great opportunity for teachers to keep pace with the advances in the field of education and apply them in their classrooms. In Turkey, in-service training programmes for teachers are mostly organized by the Ministry of National Education (MoNE), Directorate-General for Teacher Training, Department of Professional Development and Monitoring. MoNE has organized in-service training activities since 1960 to raise teachers' efficiency in their teaching practices and prepare them for future assignments. The first example of these activities was the two seminars held in 1960 with 85 participants. Since then, a total of 11,081 activities have been organised with the participation of 391,829 staff (Directorate-General for Teacher Training and Development, 2014). The in-service training programmes organized by the MoNE can be grouped, according to their objectives, as *orientation training for newly appointed teachers, candidacy training, preparatory training for higher appointments, training for expert educators, training for personal and professional development,* and *adaptation training for field-switching teachers*. The stages of organization and implementation of these in-service training programmes are summarized in the following section.

Determining Educational Needs

Studies on teacher efficacy in Turkey have risen due to the constant changes in the responsibilities of teachers, and the competencies that are required. In this context, MoNE has, to a certain extent, collaborated with universities and specified 'Teacher Competencies' (MoNE, 2008). Although MoNE aims to take into account these teacher adequacies when planning educational activities in order to respond to teachers' constantly evolving and changing needs, the national report cards and research studies show that the proclaimed alignments are barely reflected in the professional development plans and implementations.

In addition, MoNE plans educational activities in the light of teachers' demands, challenges in the regulations, advances in science and technology, inspection reports by the administration, and similar action plans. In recent years, the MoNE has determined teachers' in-service training needs through surveys on the teaching profession, information technologies, and personal development. For instance, planning for central and provincial in-service training programmes in 2014 was undertaken according to the results of a survey of 37,450 teachers; however, the participants were a fraction of the 800,000 plus teachers and administrators in Turkey.

Since teachers inevitably have different in-service training needs, it is important that programmes are designed and implemented to meet these various needs (Gokdere & Cepni, 2004; Onen *et al.*, 2009; Fok *et al,*. 2005; Rubba, 1985; Klein, 2001). Studies suggest that teachers' needs have not been taken fully into account by MoNE in the planning process of the in-service training activities, and, consequently, the activities fail to meet the needs of the teacher participants (Gultekin, Cubukcu, & Dal, 2010; Budak & Demirel, 2003).

Planning Educational Activities

Every year, the in-service training programmes for teachers are planned and implemented by the Ministry in the capital and by local education authorities in the remainder of the country. Unfortunately, studies have drawn attention to the failure to assign qualified staff to plan and design needs-based content, and also to the lack of implementing a sufficient number of these training events (Gultekin, Cubukcu & Dal, 2010; Onen *et al.,* 2009; Gokdere & Cepni, 2004; Gokdere & Kucuk, 2003).

Implementation of In-service Training Activities

To attend the in-service training activities teachers need to apply on-line through the MoNE portal then the participants are chosen following an evaluation of the applicants. These evaluations are often considered subjective since they are based on the criteria laid down by the region/state the teacher works in and previous trainings they attended. The central training activities are conducted by the Ministry at the seven In-service Training Institutes. Training by Local Education Authorities is offered using the facilities of schools and other educational institutions. Face-to-face as well as distance training activities are offered. The orientation training for newly appointed teachers and the professional development training for pre-school, elementary, middle and high school teachers are centrally planned and carried out as distance training through video-conferencing.

According to various studies there are a number of problems in the implementation process of these in-service training activities such as; short periods allocated to the activities, certificates of participation being issued without any kind of assessment, very few or no long-term activities, unsuitable settings for the content of the activities, abundance of theory-based activities, and very little or no practical training (Onen *et al.* 2009; Kanli & Yagbasan, 2001; Gokdere & Cepni, 2004; Gonen & Kocakaya, 2006).

Monitoring and Assessment

The monitoring and assessment of MoNE's in-service training programmes are carried out through surveys. The assessment of training is based on the participants' response to questions concerning pre-training, planning and programming, training staff, training centre, organization and management, what teachers acquired from the training, and an overall evaluation.

The in-service training programmes designed and implemented by the MoNE are based on short-, mid-, and long-term planning according to teachers' needs, but the majority is of short duration (30 hours on average, between one and 10 days). The monitoring and assessment of these programmes are limited to the evaluation performed only at the end the programmes. There is no long-term post-training monitoring or assessment to determine how the teachers put the results of the training into practice in their classrooms. In other words, how much the teacher acquired from the training is not followed up. It is of paramount importance that the outcomes of the professional development programmes are monitored in the long term in terms of both changes in teachers and their impact on students. In this context, long-term in-service training programmes for science teachers incorporating classroom-monitoring processes are needed, particularly in Turkey.

In order to meet this need, within the last 5 years, in-service training programmes have been organized for science teachers as part of a three-year longitudinal research project supported by TUBITAK in co-operation with four universities. The training activities were designed taking into account the problems reported in the relevant literature. This project aimed to reveal, through teacher training, both the changes in teachers and the reflection of these changes upon their students. This aspect makes the project a first in science education in Turkey and a contributor to the limited literature worldwide on *the impact of in-service training on learning*. It is also considered that the in-service training programme designed as part of the project is an exemplary model in terms of planning, implementation, monitoring, and assessment.

The Theoretical Framework, Aim, and Structure of the Longitudinal Professional Development Programme

The Science Writing Heuristic (SWH) developed by Hand and Keys (1999) is a theoretical framework stressing the importance of language use in learning and forming the basis of scientific debate in the conceptual sense. This approach was later modified with an emphasis on 'argumentation' and named the Argument-Based Inquiry (ABI) (Hand, 2008; Hand, 2009; Norton-Meier et al. 2009). Today, the objective of ABI is to make a difference in teachers' perspectives on learning and teaching to support students' science-learning through the arguments they build on the ideas derived from their research. Many studies in the literature worldwide have attempted to prove the effectiveness of the ABI approach (Hand & Keys, 1999; Keys, Hand, Prain & Collins, 1999; Wallance, Yang, Hand & Hohenshell, 2001; Hohenshell & Hand, 2006; Rudd, Greenbowe, Hand & Legg, 2001; Grimberg, Mohammed & Hand, 2004; Akkus, Gunel & Hand, 2007).

The project aimed to improve teachers' professional knowledge and bring about change in their practices within the scope of the theoretical framework of the ABI approach through the organised in-service training programmes. Since teachers undergo pedagogical changes over a long term, five-day in-service training programmes were organized every six months over the course of three years as part of the project. These programmes aimed to equip the participating teachers with the knowledge, skills, and attitudes in line with the ABI approach. In order to determine whether the expected change occurred in the teaching pedagogy, the changes in the students' field knowledge, critical thinking, and scientific processing skills as well as their attitude to science were also investigated.

The project aimed to detect the pedagogical change in science and technology teachers through in-service training in line with the ABI approach, and the impact of this change in the classroom. A detailed information about the participating teachers, in-service training programmes, and implementation processes are summarized in the following section.

Participating Teachers

The teachers' participation in the project was completely voluntary. At the project proposal stage, approximately 500 science and technology teachers were contacted by e-mail for the selection of the participants. These teachers had previously taken part in the in-service training programmes organized by MoNE and conducted by the project leader. The e-mail contained information about the content and main objectives of the project, and an invitation to participate in the training programmes.

Data obtained from the State Planning Organization (SPO, 2003) was used for the selection of the voluntary teachers. The SPO (2003) divided provinces in Turkey into groups by level of development with reference to their socio-economic parameters. This parameter was considered for the selection of the participants so that provinces with different levels of development could be represented. In this way, 30 voluntary teachers working in 21 different provinces were selected as participants.

In-Service Training Programmes

Through in-service training, the project aimed to direct science teachers towards student-centred teaching. The training activities focused on the scientific thinking underpinning the teachers' professional knowledge and practices. In line with the project goals, longitudinal in-service training programmes were conducted over a period of three years in order for the teachers to efficiently apply the ABI approach to their classroom practices. The participating teachers took part in a total of five in-service training programmes twice every year.

All the in-service training activities were designed considering the teachers' needs and the project goals, and geared to the acquisition of the ABI approach by the participants. Each programme focused on an educational theme that was considered important in the ABI approach. The teachers were helped acquire knowledge, skills, and attitudes in the light of the ABI approach using themes; such as learning, conceptual underpinnings of ABI, importance of questioning, sharing changing experiences in teaching pedagogy and planning.

Research suggests that the success of in-service training programmes rises when they are designed as more than just an ordinary professional development programme with well-defined and clearly laid-out objectives, and when supported by seminars, team work, workshops, conferences, visits, and consultation services as well as on-line and face-to-face educational activities (Guskey, 2014; National Research Council, 1996; Evans, 1986). From this point of view, planning was considered to be one of the most important factors for an effective in-service training programme (Klein, 2001), and all the project activities were planned with due diligence over the course of three years.

All in-service training activities were structured around an assessment of the teachers' practices in the previous programme and a debate on what needed to be done to improve teachers' ABI practices. The teachers were asked to share their experiences relating to their ABI practices in the classroom with the other participants and the project team. Proposals were formulated to overcome the challenges experienced in these practices, which were then taken into consideration in the planning of subsequent in-service training programmes.

One of the primary goals of these in-service training programmes was to allow participating teachers to experience the process as 'learners'. For this purpose, learning environments were set up where the participants would be aware of, and reflect upon, their own learning. Current studies on the basics of professional development highlight the significant role of the knowledge contributed by teachers to in-service training programmes, and underline their existing beliefs on learning and teaching as a highly effective factor in the success of the process (Loucks-Horsley, 1995). In this context, many published studies and reports (Posner, Strike, Hewson & Gertzog, 1982; Driver, Asoko, Leach, Mortimer & Scott, 1994; National Research Council (NRC), 1996, 2000) stress that teachers, just like students, need to "acquire an experience of questioning as learners", and underline the important role of professional development programmes in improving the ways, in which science is taught. For this reason, learner-focused ABI activities on the field knowledge of physics, chemistry, and biology were designed as part of the in-service training activities for the science teachers. In the course of these activities, data on the basic patterns of the ABI approach was obtained, which led to the formulation of claims with corroborating evidence. In this way, the question-claim-evidence triangle, which is an important component of the ABI approach, was established. Furthermore, writing to learn activities were included as one of the language practices in the ABI approach. Sample writing activities that can be used in different levels of education were presented, and the participants took part in these activities.

Throughout the training, in addition to directly experiencing the learning process, the teachers were presented with further opportunities to work in collaboration with their colleagues and the researchers. During the planning and the ABI practices in their own classrooms, the participating teachers took direct responsibility and structured the process in collaboration with their colleagues and the researchers. Many studies on the effectiveness of in-service training programmes underline the importance of participants taking direct responsibility in the planning, application, and assessment processes, and structuring the training in collaboration (Evans, 1986; Hutson, 1981; Klein, 2001).

Over the course of the project, all in-service training programmes were evaluated on a daily basis in addition to an overall evaluation at the end of the project. These assessments sought to elicit the participating teachers' views on the training process, which shed light on the needs, problems, and aspects for improvement. The results helped review the already flexible structure of the process and provided new suggestions for solutions when needed.

As stated above, in the planning and application of all in-service training programmes, the focus was primarily on clear and lucid educational goals. It was also ensured that the programmes were flexible enough to respond to the needs that might arise and included room for manoeuvre, assessment processes, and contingency plans. Amendments were made to the programmes as and when needed in the light of the participants' needs, and all information available on the processes were shared with the teachers.

In order to increase the teachers' self-efficacy and support them in their practices, the researchers shared the results of video analyses and assessments with the participants, and visited the teachers in their schools to provide feedback on their classroom ABI practices (follow-up assistance). The data obtained from the video assessment of the teachers' ABI practices in the classroom were shared with the teachers on an individual basis to demonstrate the periodic changes due to the longitudinal nature of the project. This provided an opportunity for the teachers to be aware of their own progress and to reflect upon the changes in their pedagogical knowledge. In addition, sessions on critical consideration and assessment were organized, where the teachers were presented with opportunities to evaluate their own practices.

In all in-service training activities, a great deal of importance was attached to integrating the existing teaching programmes with the ABI approach. It was frequently stressed that the ABI approach was an instrument in learning the basic concepts laid out in the curriculum, and that the students needed to improve their higher-level thinking skills.

Another primary goal of the project was to explore the changes in students' academic performance following the change in their teachers' pedagogy. To this end, after each in-service training programme, the teachers were asked to engage in ABI practices in their classrooms. In addition, in the final days of the programme, after selecting units for practice the teachers prepared for teaching the units under the supervision of the researchers and in collaboration with their colleagues. Those who selected the same units for practice worked in groups. Each group agreed upon a main idea from their practice units. Later, ABI activities and progress tests were drafted for assessment purposes.

As part of the project, the data analysis results obtained from the teachers' classrooms were also shared with the teachers. The performance evaluations of the participating teachers in terms of their ABI practices were put into reports and shared with them, including recommendations to handle the shortcomings.

Data Collection

Within the scope of the in-service training programmes, the participating teachers engaged in ABI practices in their primary education sixth-, seventh-, and eighth-year science and technology classes. Classes where the teachers practiced the ABI approach were used as the experiment groups. In the control groups, the teachers carried on using the traditional teaching methods.

The researchers visited the teachers in their schools to observe their ABI practices in the classroom settings. With these on-site visits, proper assessments were made and guidance was offered to the teachers. Figure 1 presents a summary of this process.

The data presented in Figure 1 was collected from the participating teachers and their classes forming the experiment / control groups. For data collection, the Scientific Process Skills Test (Smith & Welliver, 2006), Cornell Critical Thinking Skills Test (Ennis, Millman & Thomko, 2005), Science and Technology Attitude Scale (Nuhoglu, 2008), and Unit-Based Achievement Tests designed collectively by the researchers and teachers were used.

Video recordings of the teachers' ABI practices were also used for data collection to help determine their ABI practice levels. These recordings were analysed by the project team using the Revised Teacher Observation Protocol (RTOP). The RTOP observation form to be used for the assessments was designed in light of the recommendations and standards set forth by the US National Council of Teachers of Mathematics (NCTM) and the National Science Education Standards. The observation form contained 17 items this allowed the ABI practices in the classroom to be evaluated according to the student, teacher, reasoning and scientific process skills, and questioning sub-dimensions.

The application stages of the project outlined above were; in-service training activities, ABI practices in the classroom, and data collection and analysis. Unlike the traditional concept of in-service training, the basic dynamics of this project required a longitudinal programme over a period of three years. This was based on the idea that it takes time for teachers to change their teaching practices. Feedback from the participating teachers and the results of the data analysis suggest that long-term in-service training programmes are more satisfactory for teachers.

Furthermore, the participating teachers' pedagogical knowledge as well as their field knowledge was developed and improved as a result of the ABI practices directly experienced by the teachers who wore learner's hats. In this way the learners' (aka the students), needs were taken into consideration in the design of the training programmes. The participating teachers were given feedback based on the analysis of the video recordings of their ABI practices in the classroom and the field notes collected during the visits of the research team. Furthermore, the teachers shared and reflected upon their experiences with their colleagues, and opportunities were created for critical thinking in the training programmes devised by the project team and the forums with the teachers.

Figure 1. Project application and data collection process

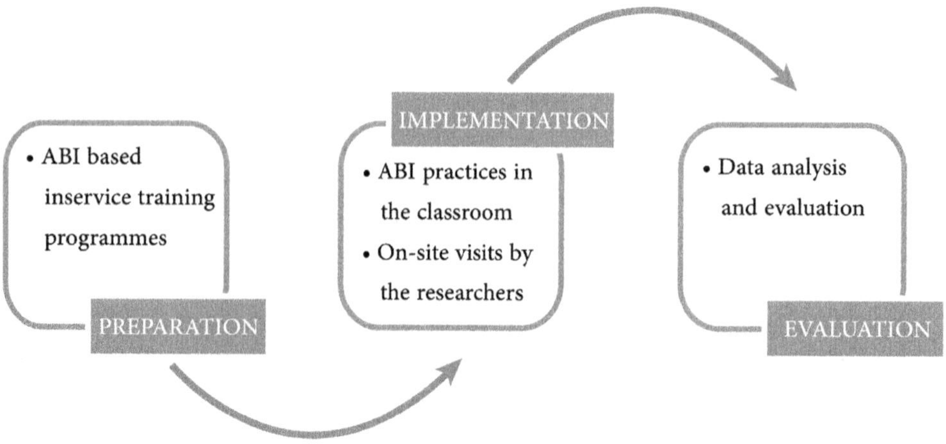

Studies in the literature demonstrate the need for considering five crucial criteria in the assessment of in-service training programmes; the participants' views on the activities, their acquisition of new knowledge and skills, organizational change and support, the participants' ability to use their newly acquired knowledge and skills, and the students' learning outputs (Guskey, 2000; 2002). In this context, it can be suggested that the training programmes within the scope of the project have a strong structure in terms of meeting these criteria.

The Effects of the In-Service Training Programme on the Knowledge, Beliefs and Practices of the Teachers

The concluding section of this chapter is two-folded. The first part of the section presents the impact of the professional development activities and classroom implementations on the teachers' beliefs, pedagogical practices of the argument-based inquiry approach, and in-service trainings. The second part incorporates the findings on students' conceptual understandings of various science topics, critical thinking skills, argumentation competencies, writing proficiencies, and attitudes toward science and science learning.

The Process of Change in Teachers over the Course of the Project

The structure of modern in-service teacher training in Turkey was first established in the 1960s and has been subject to change due to political shifts over the decades. In their comprehensive and comparative review of in-service teacher training literature, Gunel and Tanriverdi (2014) suggested that the current state of in-service teacher training in Turkey is far from the international norms or a state-of-the-art structure. The most significant deviations of the current setting from international tendencies are concerning the purpose and structuring of the trainings. In other words, the in-service trainings in Turkey have shifted, over time, from a learner (teacher) centred to a centralized and content-oriented framework. Thus, the main purpose is now to deliver certain content and curriculum materials to more teachers regardless of the current developments in the literature regarding teacher learning and research findings.

The MoNE, which is the main actor and stakeholder in the Turkish education system, has shifted the majority of in-service teacher trainings to distance learning to meet the short-term legislation needs and cover subjects that are popular among the education community (Directorate-General for Teacher Training and Development, 2014). There are only a limited number of studies or small-scale projects that have adapted the Turkish education setting to international in-service training norms (Gunel & Tanriverdi, 2014). These studies point out the need for and underline the significance of effective learning environments, where teachers' pedagogical and epistemological readiness, as well as their pedagogical competencies, are taken into account and improved through longitudinal and colleague interactions (Loucks-Horsley, 1995; Klein, 2001).

In our study, the implemented professional development programme was based on the blueprints of international norms since it is longitudinal, teacher epistemology and competency based, learning outcome oriented (for both teacher and student), and geared to colleague interaction.

In our study, the implemented professional development programme was based on the blueprints of international norms since it is longitudinal, teacher epistemology and competency based, learning outcome oriented (for both teacher and student), and geared to colleague interaction. Within the scope of the project, Tanriverdi, Gunel, Asci & Ocak (2013) conducted semi-structured interviews with the participating teachers to investigate the impact of professional development programmes and on-site support activities within the project on bringing about change in teachers' pedagogical practices and epistemological beliefs and on students' learning outcomes. The findings point out that the structure of in-service activities was highly effective in terms of promoting pedagogical development and a strong understanding about learning, teaching, and argument-based inquiry approach (Mutlu-Pehlivan, Yesildag-Hasancebi, Tanriverdi & Gunel, 2013). Furthermore, the participating teachers emphasized the value and importance of the on-site support mechanism as well as co-teaching, and reflection-in-action and reflection-on-action framework.

In Tanriverdi *et al.* (2013), one of the significant findings was how the teachers' interacted with their peers. In their study, teachers expressed their appreciation, awareness, and willingness to continue the professional interaction created among the teachers who participated in the training. While the teacher community in the Turkish school settings is generally only framed around the social interaction base, the project provided the teachers with an opportunity to create new dimensions for interaction that led to the formation of a 'community of practitioners'. This type of community provided a safe learning environment for teachers to learn from each other and the project staff based on an ongoing discussion concerning their beliefs, practices, and observations during PD activities and in-class implementations (Gunel, 2013). On the other hand, other research studies conducted within the project framework highlighted the importance of students' learning outcomes and teachers' own learning, which is a salient feature of in-service training programmes (Gunel, Yesildag-Hasancebi, Keskin-Samanci, Demir, Ozgur, Gundogan & Akbay, 2012; Gunel & Tanriverdi, 2012).

The above-mentioned studies are based on teachers' view and perceptions on the structure and impact of the project from their own learning experience and epistemology. The qualitative findings of these case studies emphasize the significance of PD practices in the project that bridge teachers' beliefs, perceptions, and day-to-day routines about teaching and learning, and the basics of student-centred learning and the argument-based inquiry approach. Similarly, in other studies where pedagogical changes in teachers were evaluated through teaching observation protocols over the course of a project, changes were observed over time.

Teachers' pedagogical implementation levels were assessed using the RTOP as outlined in the methodology section. The project staff and independent reviewers evaluated all the video recordings from each school term. A brief explanation of the components in the competency scale is given below:

- **Exploring:** A low level implementation where the learning environment is highly teacher-centred and can mostly be classified as a direct instruction.
- **Developing:** A moderate level implementation where the teacher questions his/her practices as well as beliefs to move toward an inquiry-based and student-centred approach.
- **Transitioning:** A high level implementation where the majority of the basic characteristics of an argument-based inquiry approach is evident.
- **Implementing:** An exemplary level of implementation where the teacher can successfully revise and implement new curriculum topics and materials in line with the argument-based inquiry approach.

Earlier studies that reported on the end of first-year implementation levels of the teachers showed that around 90 percent of the teachers were in the exploring level, and while a third of the participating teachers remained there, approximately two thirds moved onto the developing level (Gunel, Akkus & Ozer-Keskin, 2011; Gunel, Akkus, Ozer-Keskin & Keskin-Samanci, 2012). This means that at the beginning of the project almost all the teachers were fairly low in their pedagogical implementation; however, they moved up to higher levels of implementation over the course of the project. Such pedagogical shifts also continued in the second and third years of the project.

At the end of the second year of the project, around 60 percent of the teachers were in the developing level, 20 percent in the transitioning level and another 20 percent in the implementing level (Gunel, Akkus, Ozer-Keskin &Keskin-Samanci, 2013). Finally, in the final year of the project, the teachers' implementation levels were found to be 20 percent developing, 60 percent transitioning, and 20 percent implementing (Gunel, Akkus, Ozer-Keskin &Keskin-Samanci, 2014). The above-mentioned pedagogical shift originated in very low levels and carried on to the highly anticipated level, and took time, practice, reflection as well as cooperative effort. Contrary to the current PD frameworks, content and beliefs in the Turkish educational settings (short-term and content-oriented), the results of this project show that pedagogical changes in teachers require at least two years of continuous effort. These findings are in line with the international studies as well as the standards and norms regarding in-service teacher training. To reveal how and why such a significant pedagogical shift occurred, the researchers focused on the teachers' evaluation of their own change over the course of the project.

The participating teachers stressed the importance of observing their own change and students' learning outcomes as the project progressed. Since the project staff shared the implementation reports with the teachers every six months, the teachers were able to see and reflect on their own practices, strengths, and areas to improve in the long term (Tanriverdi & Gunel, 2012). Furthermore, Gunel (2013a) and Gunel (2013b) reported that being able to see and align teachers' own progress with their students' academic achievements and improvement in thinking skills was a crucial motivation for the participants to pursue the change and development.

As in the case of in-service training programmes in any sector, generating and scaffolding internal motivation towards a sustainable change is an essential element in professional development activities for teachers. While the current in-service practices in the Turkish educational settings have shifted towards content delivery through distance education, the structure of the programmes also suffers from the lack of assessment, absence of motivation, and inconsistency of the content due to daily practices (Gunel &Tanriverdi, 2014). On the other hand, the current project activities in relation to the professional development of teachers provide an opportunity to adopt effective, data-driven, sustainable, and value-added in-service practices in the Turkish educational settings. Despite being the rudiments of professional development programmes in an international setting, these components are still far from being embedded in the Turkish teacher-training policies and practices.

The Process of Change in Students over the Course of Project

Reaching out to the students is the ultimate goal of any in-service teacher training programme across the globe. Therefore, aligning the purposes, structure, and implementation of PD with expected learning outcomes in students is a key element during the planning and enactment phases of in-service trainings. However, as argued by Gunel and Tanriverdi (2014), up-to-date PD legislation, programmes and practices in the Turkish educational settings do not consider students' learning outcomes. The implemented programmes do not assess the effects of PD on teachers' pedagogy or students' learning enhancements. While one would argue that such shortcomings are a blueprint of most Turkish legislative and operative actions, the inclination for the PD accountability calls for a robust relationship between what is done within the PD and how it is reflected in students' learning.

The project was framed around relevant measurement areas of students' learning outcomes including academic achievement, critical thinking skills, argument competencies and writing comprehensions. While some studies reported on the practice of a single teacher to explore the impact of the implementation of the ABI approach (experiment) as opposed to traditional practices (control) on students' learning outcomes, other studies investigated the differences in students' learning outcomes depending on the group (ABI-experiment or control) as well as the teachers' implementation level (such as exploring and developing, etc.). Furthermore, there are also studies focusing on teachers' ABI group competency developing over a term or a school year. In this section, the above-mentioned assessment areas are discussed in light of the findings of the previously published research.

Researchers have conducted small-scale studies to investigate the impact of PD programmes on students' learning of various science subjects in different learning environments. Arli and Gunel (2012) investigated the impact of the ABI implementation on the academic achievements and argument competencies of students who were also seasonal agricultural workers. They studied a single teacher and her students. The participant teacher worked in the south-eastern part of Turkey and the students attended school only three months in a year due to their seasonal agricultural work, and their academic performance was quite low compared to the national average. The findings suggest that the ABI implementation group, aligning with the PD project, significantly outperformed the control group on academic achievement tests and argument generation scores of students' writing samples (Arli & Gunel, 2012; 2014). Furthermore, in the ABI group, the students' skills for generating questions, claim, evidence, and reflections increased over the school year (Arli, 2014).

Similarly, Yesildag-Hasancebi and Gunel (2013) investigated the impact of the ABI approach on science achievements and writing comprehensions of students from lower socio-economic classes in comparison to the control group students. They also reported that when compared to traditional approaches, the ABI implementation significantly increases students' understanding of scientific concepts as well as their writing skills (Yesildag-Hasancebi, 2014). Furthermore, small-scale investigations focusing on different science concepts; such as electricity, and force and motion all indicate that the content of the PD programmes and the ABI approach create significant learning enhancements, which add to the teachers' existing teaching methods. These findings in an individual teacher's case provide evidence on the measurable effects of the in-service training programme on students' science learning outcomes as well as their argumentation and written comprehension. Thus, it is crucial to investigate the comprehensive impact of the programme on students' learning outcomes when all teachers participating in training programme are considered.

In their annual project impact evaluation studies, Gunel *et al.* (2012), Gunel *et al.* (2013), and Gunel *et al.* (2014) reported that when all participating teachers were considered, ABI instruction groups outperformed the control group on unit-based science achievement regardless of the topic. Moreover, the participating teachers' implementation level of the ABI approach was found to have considerable effects on students' academic achievement. That is, while ABI group students collectively outperformed the control students, the achievement gap was greater when the teacher's implementation level got higher. On the other hand, Cikmaz (2014) analysed the writing samples of the students of three teachers over the course of the project to explore the relationship between the teachers' implementation levels and the development of their students' writing skills. Cikmaz found that as the teachers' implementation level improved, their students' writing skills enhanced. Considering the teachers' pedagogical competency change as argued in the first part of the findings, and its impact on students' academic performance and skill proficiencies considered, one could argue that the PD program demonstrated measurable value-added impact on both teachers' professional growth and students' science learning and competencies.

In their research on the development of thinking skills including project implementation, Gunel (2013) and Gunel *et al.* (2014) reported that students' performance in the Cornell Critical Thinking Test (CCTT) depended on their group (ABI or control), their teachers' implementation level, and the length of their participation in the project. That is, students in the ABI group significantly outperformed those in the control group. This was also due to teachers' implementation level and the time the data was collected. If a teacher's ABI implementation level was higher, their students performed better in the CCTT. Furthermore, since the teachers' implementation levels improved over the course of the project, their students' performance increased; and the results obtained from the second and third years of the project were higher than those obtained from the first year. However, the CCTT performance mainly depended on the group and implementation level.

The findings of Gunel (2013) and Gunel *et al.* (2014) are particularly important since their assessment tool was independent of science content and the skill development was dependent on the PD content (ABI approach) and teacher development. The authors reported that the effectiveness of the PD programme was reflected in the content (independent variable) and time. The effect of the PD programme was observed in not only the understanding of conceptual science but also the development in the thinking skills of the students, which can be considered to be the ultimate goal of any content teaching, even the whole education system. In addition, the arbitrated impact of the approach, implementation level and time give clear indication as to how effective the structure of the in-service training programme was in terms of influencing the students. Findings also demonstrate the necessity of the PD programmes to be comprehensive and longitudinal, two characteristics that lack in the current Turkish educational settings.

When the general structure of the on-going PD programmes are considered, it appears that MoNE heavily concentrates on content delivery with only some emphasis on teachers' needs. Furthermore, those implemented programmes are evaluated not only to bring about a change in teachers' pedagogy but also to improve students' learning. Despite the small sample size in this study, the structure of the PD, implementation procedure, teacher change process and enhancement of student learning outcomes make a contribution to the future direction for in-service training in the Turkish educational setting. By far the most important implication for the future is the need to adopt the international norms of PD and implement state of the art in-service training as discussed by Gunel and Tanriverdi (2014). That is, the PD programmes needs to adopt the perspective of the teacher as learner by doing and interacting, being longitudinal and structured around teacher change trajectory over the time, being related to and evaluated in connection with students learning outcomes and demonstrating the collaborative learning partnership between PD trainers, teachers and students. However, creating such a paradigm and initiating a practical shift in a large system with inveterate perception is a challenge to be faced.

From our perspective evidence-based practices are the first and most important elements that can trigger systematic change in the education world. While a small scale implementations or local success stories framed around data driven frameworks always play important role in this process, there is a strong need for comprehensive scale-up setups. We argue that PD studies such as that described in this chapter can be implemented across larger populations of teachers. The most significant shortcoming for the development of training programmes is the lack of qualified trainers. To improve the situation, it is suggested that teachers who have attended training programmes can receive trainer training and assist in the future scale-up PD programmes. Furthermore, following the PD programme, these teachers can support other teachers in their school or local area, thus continue to reinforce the fundamental tenets of these programmes. Although, there are further efforts needed to determine the dimensions and requirements of the scaled-up PD programmes, first we, as researchers, policy makers, and teachers need to have the commitment and determination to move the idea forward.

CONCLUSION

The multifaceted findings of the PD project show that there is a fine line between the structure of an in-service teacher programme and students' learning outcomes. It appears that in our educational setting that those who should be the ultimate beneficiaries, that is, the students, are ignored or forgotten as we think, talk, and act upon teachers' professional development. It could be argued that reverse engineering processes should be employed in policy making, PD planning and implementation, and the measurement of outcomes if we aim to fulfil the needs of our students. In conclusion, answering the question of why teachers need in-service training can be an excellent starting point for discussion among all stakeholders of education if we dare to place the teachers as learners. Consequently, by accepting that in the first layer of the PD programme the teachers are learners and we, the in-service providers, treat them as learners providing them with proper tools and structures, then these teachers will become more competent in helping their learners – the students.

REFERENCES

Akkus, R., Gunel, M., & Hand, B. (2007). Comparing an inquiry based approach known as the Science Writing Heuristic to traditional science teaching practices: Are there differences? *International Journal of Science Education*, *29*(14), 1745–1765. doi:10.1080/09500690601075629

Al-Daami, K. K., & Wallace, G. (2007). Curriculum reform in a global context: A study of teachers in Jordan. *Journal of Curriculum Studies*, *39*(3), 339–360. doi:10.1080/00220270601057790

Arli, E. E. (2014). *Argumantasyon Tabanli Bilim Ogrenme (ATBO) Yaklasiminin uygulandigi ilkogretim fen ve teknoloji siniflarinda ogrencilerin arguman olusturmadaki degisim ve gelisimlerinin yazili metinler uzerinden incelenmesi*. (Unpublished master thesis). Ataturk University.

Arli, E. E., & Gunel, M. (2012). *Akademik basari duzeyleri dusuk ogrencilerin fen kavramlarini ogrenmelerinin desteklenmesi: Argumantasyon tabanli bilim ogrenme uygulamalari*. Paper presented at the 10th Annual Meeting of National Science and Mathematics Education Conference (UFBMEK), Nigde.

Arli, E. E., & Gunel, M. (2014). *Dezavantajli ogrencilerin egitiminde dusunme becerileri odakli fen egitimi yaklasimi: mevsimlik tarim iscisi ogrenci orneklemi*. Paper presented at the 11th Annual Best Practices in Education Conference (EIOK), Istanbul, Turkey.

Auhl, G. & Daniel, G.R. (2014).Preparing pre-service teachers for the profession: creating spaces for transformative practice. *Journal of Education for Teaching: International Research and Pedagogy*, *40*(4), 377-390.

Avalos, B. (2011). Teacher professional development in teaching and teacher education over ten years. *Teaching and Teacher Education, 27*(1), 10–20. doi:10.1016/j.tate.2010.08.007

Budak, Y., & Demirel, O. (2003). In-service training needs for teachers. *Educational Administration in Theory and Practice, 33*(1), 62–81.

Bybee, R., & Loucks-Horsley, S. (2000). Advancing technology education: The role of professional development. *Technology Teacher, 60*(2), 31–36.

Caglayan, N., Yesildag-Hasancebi, F., Tanriverdi, K., & Gunel, M. (2013). *Implementation of the argumentation based science inquiry approach to the targets of electricity unit.* Paper presented at the 1st International Conference on Immersion Approaches to Argument-based Inquiry (ABI) for Science Classrooms, Busan, Korea.

Cikmaz, A. (2014). *Examining two Turkish Teachers' Questionning Patterns in Secondary School Science Classrooms.* (Unpublished master thesis). University of Iowa, Iowa City, IA.

Darling-Hammond, L. (1999). *Teacher Quality and Student Achievement: A Review of State Policy Evidence.* Seattle, WA: Center for the Study of Teaching and Policy, University of Washington.

Darling-Hammond, L., & Bransford, J. (Eds.). (2005). *Preparing teachers for a changing world: What teachers should learn and be able to do.* San Francisco: Jossey Bass.

Demir, M., Yesildag-Hasancebi, F., & Gunel, M. (2013). *Unit Preparation Process in The Applications of Argumentation Based Inquiry Approach.* Paper presented at the 1st International Conference on Immersion Approaches to Argument-based Inquiry (ABI) for Science Classrooms, Busan, Korea.

Directorate-General for Teacher Training and Development. (2014). 2013 In-Service Training Activity Report. Ankara, Turkey: Author.

Driver, R., Asoko, H., Leach, J., Mortimer, E., & Scott, P. (1994). Constructing scientific knowledge in the classroom. *Educational Researcher, 23*(7), 5–12. doi:10.3102/0013189X023007005

Ennis, R. H., Millman, J., & Thomko, T. N. (2005). *Cornell Critical Thinking Tests Level X & Level Z Manual.* The Critical Thinking Co.

Evans, T. P. (1986). Guidelines for effective science teacher inservice education programs: Perspectives from research. In B. S. Spector (Ed.), *A guide to inservice science teacher education: Research into practice* (pp. 13–56). Columbus, OH: Association for the Education of Teachers in Science and SMEAC Information Reference Center.

Fishman, B., Marx, R., Best, S., & Tal, R. (2003). Linking teacher and student learning to improve professional development in systemic reform. *Teaching and Teacher Education, 19*(6), 643–665. doi:10.1016/S0742-051X(03)00059-3

Fok, S., Chan, K., Sin, K., Ng, A. H., & Yeung, A. S. (2005). *In-Service Teacher Training Needs in Hong Kong.* Paper presented at the Annual Meeting of the Australian Association for Research in Education, Sydney, Australia.

Fullan, M. (2001). The meaning of educational change. In M. Fullan (Ed.), *The New Meaning of Educational Change*. London: Routledge.

Garet, M., Birman, B., Porter, A., Desimone, L., Herman, R., & Suk Yoon, K. (1999). *Designing effective professional development: Lessons from the Eisenhower program*. Washington, DC: U.S. Department of Education.

Gokdere, M., & Cepni, S. (2004). A study on the assessment of the in-service needs of the science teachers of gifted students: A case for science art center. *Gazi University Journal of Gazi Educational Faculty, 24*(2), 1–14.

Gokdere, M., & Kuçuk, M. (2003). Science education of gifted students at intellectual area; a case for science art centers. *Educational Sciences: Theory and Practice, 3*(1), 101–124.

Gonen, S., & Kocakaya, S. (2006). An evaluation of high school physics teachers' oppinions about in-service education. *Pamukkale University Journal of Educational Faculty, 19*(1), 37–44.

Grimberg, I. B., Mohammed, E., & Hand, B. (2004). *A grade six case study of cognitive involvement and attitudes towards scientific inquiry using the SWH*. Paper presented at the International Conference of the Association for Educators of Teachers of Science, Nashville, TN.

Gultekin, M., Cubukcu, Z., & Dal, S. (2010). In-service training needs of the primary school teachers regarding education-teaching. *Selcuk University Journal of Ahmet Kelesoglu Educational Faculty, 29*, 131–152.

Gunel, M. (2013). *The relationship between science teaching and critical thinking skills: Where does the teacher stand for?* Paper presented at the First African Conferences on Research in Chemistry Education, Addis Ababa, Ethiopia.

Gunel, M. (2013a). *Problems faced and strategies developed by teachers implementing inquiry based science teaching approaches*. Paper presented at the 1st International Conference on Immersion Approaches to Argument-based Inquiry (ABI) for Science Classrooms, Busan, Korea.

Gunel, M. (2013b). *Structuring, organizing and implementing longitudinal professional development project focusing on argumentation based science inquiry; a case of Turkish research setting*. Paper presented at the 1st International Conference on Immersion Approaches to Argument-based Inquiry (ABI) for Science Classrooms, Busan, Korea.

Gunel, M., Akkus, R., & Ozer-Keskin, M. (2011). *Implementing the argumentation based science learning approach in middle school setting through professional development programs and investigating the impact of the approach on teachers' pedagogy and students' academic achievements, skills and perceptions toward science*. Paper presented at the annual meeting of the European Science Education Research Association (ESERA), Lyon, France.

Gunel, M., Akkus, R., Ozer-Keskin, M., & Keskin-Samanci, N. (2012). *The effect of the SWH implementation in Turkish school system: results from a scale up research project*. Paper presented at the Annual Meeting of the National Association for Research in Science Teaching (NARST), Indianapolis, IN.

Gunel, M., Akkus, R., Ozer-Keskin, M., & Keskin-Samanci, N. (2013). *Improving students' conceptual understanding of science through argument based science inquiry implementations: a case of nationwide professional development project*. Paper presented at the 1st International Conference on Immersion Approaches to Argument-based Inquiry (ABI) for Science Classrooms, Busan, Korea.

Gunel, M., Akkus, R., Ozer-Keskin, M., & Keskin-Samanci, N. (2014). *Enhancing students' critical thinking skills through argument based inquiry: results from a scale up research project in Turkey*. Paper presented at the Annual Meeting of the National Association for Research in Science Teaching (NARST), Pittsburgh, PA.

Gunel, M., & Tanriverdi, K. (2012). *Boylamsal arastirma projesi: Hizmetici egitim ve sinifici uygulamalarinin, ogretmen pedagojisine, ogrenci akademik basarisina, dusunme becerilerine etkisinin arastirilmasi*. Paper presented at the 10th Annual Meeting of National Science and Mathematics Education Conference (UFBMEK), Nigde.

Gunel, M., & Tanriverdi, K. (2014). In-service teacher training from international and national perspectives: The retention and loss of institutional and academic memories. *Education & Science, 39*(175), 73–94.

Gunel, M., Yesildag-Hasancebi, F., Keskin-Samanci, N., Demir, M., Ozgur, S., Gundogan, F., & Akbay, Y. (2012). *Ogretirken Ogrenen Ogretmenler: Profesyonel Degisim ve Gelisim*. Paper presented at the 10th Annual Meeting of National Science and Mathematics Education Conference (UFBMEK), Nigde.

Guskey, T. R. (2000). *Evaluating Professional Development*. Thousand Oaks, CA: Corvin.

Guskey, T. R. (2002). Professional development and teacher change, *Teachers and teaching. Theory into Practice, 8*(4), 381–391.

Guskey, T. R. (2014). Planning professional learning. *Educational Leadership*, 11–16.

Hand, B. (2008). *Science Inquiry, Argument and Language: A Case for the Science Writing Heuristic*. Rotterdam, The Netherlands: Sense Publishers.

Hand, B. (2009). Negotiating Science: The Critical Role of Argument in Student Inquiry, Grades 5-10. Portsmouth, NH: Heinemann.

Hand, B., & Keys, C. (1999). Inquiry investigation: A new approach to laboratory reports. *Science Teacher (Normal, Ill.), 66*, 27–29.

Hand, B., & Treagust, D. F. (1995). Development of a constructivist model for teacher inservice. *Australian Journal of Teacher Education, 20*(2), 28–38. doi:10.14221/ajte.1995v20n2.4

Hohenshell, L. M., & Hand, B. (2006). Writing-to learn strategies in secondary school cell biology: A mixed method study. *International Journal of Science Education, 28*(2-3), 261–289. doi:10.1080/09500690500336965

Hoy, W. K., & Miskel, C. G. (2008). *Educational administration: Theory, research and practice* (8th ed.). Boston: McGraw-Hill.

Hutson, H. M. (1981). Inservice best practices: The learning of general education. *Journal of Research and Development in Education, 14*(3), 1–10.

Junor-Clarke, P. A., & Fournillier, J. B. (2012). Action research, pedagogy, and activity theory: Tools facilitating two instructors' interpretations of the professional development of four preservice teachers. *Teaching and Teacher Education, 28*(5), 649–660. doi:10.1016/j.tate.2012.01.013

Kanli, U., & Yagbasan, R. (2001). In-service teacher training summer courses for physics teachers. *Gazi University Journal of Gazi Educational Faculty, 21*(3), 39–46.

Kennedy, M. (1998). *The Relevance of Content in Inservice Teacher Education*. San Diego, CA: American Educational Research Association.

Keys, C., Hand, B., Prain, V., & Collins, S. (1999). Using the science writing heuristic as a tool for learning from laboratory investigations in secondary science. *Journal of Research in Science Teaching, 36*(10), 1065–1084. doi:10.1002/(SICI)1098-2736(199912)36:10<1065::AID-TEA2>3.0.CO;2-I

Klein, B. S. (2001). *Guidelines for* effective elementary science teacher inservice education. *Journal of Elementary Science Education, 13*(2), 29–40. doi:10.1007/BF03176218

Knight, P., Tait, J., & Yorke, M. (2007). The professional learning of teachers in higher education. *Studies in Higher Education, 31*(3), 319–339. doi:10.1080/03075070600680786

Loucks-Horsey, S., Stiles, K., & Hewson, P. (1996). *Principles of effective professional development for mathematics and science education: A synthesis of standards*. Madison, WI: University of Wisconsin at Madison, National Institute for Science Education.

Loucks-Horsley, S. (1995). Professional development and the learner centered school. *Theory into Practice, 34*(4), 265–271. doi:10.1080/00405849509543690

Luft, J. A. (2001). Changing inquiry practices and beliefs: The impact of an inquiry-based professional development programme on beginning and experienced secondary science teachers. *International Journal of Science Education, 23*(5), 517–534. doi:10.1080/09500690121307

McCann, T. M., Alan, C. J., & Gail, A. (2012). *Teaching matters Most, A School Leader's Guide to improving classroom instruction*. Thousand Oaks, CA: Corwin Sage.

McDonald, M. (2003). *The integration of social justice: Reshaping teacher education*. (Unpublished doctoral dissertation). Stanford University.

Miaoulis, I. (2009). *Engineering the K-12 curriculum for technological innovation*. USA Today's Engineer Online.

Millar, R., & Osborne, J. (1998). *Beyond 2000: Science education for the future*. London: Nuffield Seminar Series: Interim Report V3.

Millar, R., Osborne, J., & Nott, M. (1998). Science education for the future. *The School Science Review, 80*(291), 19–25.

MoNE. (2008). *Teacher competencies: general and specific areas competencies for the teaching profession*. Ankara, Turkey: The Directorate of State Books.

Mutlu-Pehlivan, N., Yesildag-Hasancebi, F., Tanriverdi, K., & Gunel, M. (2013). *Dusunen, tartisan, uygulayan ogrenciler icin ATBO uygulamasi: Alan bilgisi ve bilim ogrenme sureci ogrenme sureclerinde ogretmen yaklasimlari*. Paper presented at the 10th Annual Best Practices in Education Conference (EIOK), Istanbul, Turkey.

National Research Council. (1996). *National science education standards*. Washington, DC: NRC.

National Research Council. (2000). *Inquiry and the National Science Education Standards: a guide for teaching and learning*. Washington, DC: National Academy Press.

Norton-Meier, L., Hand, B., Günel, M., & Akkuş, R. (2009). *Teaching in the service of learning: A 3-year mixed methods study of embedding authentic language and science practices within elementary science classrooms*. Paper Presented at Annual Meeting of American Educational Research, AERA Annual Conference, San Diego, CA.

Nuhoğlu, H. (2008). The development of an attitude scale for science and technology course. *Elementary Education Online, 7*(3), 627–638.

Onen, F., Mertoğlu, H., Saka, M., & Gürdal, A. (2009). The effects of in-service training on teachers' knowledge about teaching methods and techniques: OPYEP Case. *Ahi Evran University Journal of Educational Faculty, 10*(3), 9–23.

Ozgur, S., Tanriverdi, K., Gunel, M., & Porikli, A. B. (2012). *Cevre ve mufredat entegrasyonu: canlilar ve hayat unitesinde deniz kestaneleri etkinligi*. Paper presented at the 10th Annual Meeting of National Science and Mathematics Education Conference (UFBMEK), Nigde.

Posner, G. J., Strike, K. A., Hewson, P. W., & Gertzog, W. A. (1982). Accommodation of a scientific conception: Toward a theory of conceptual change. *Science Education, 66*(2), 211–227. doi:10.1002/sce.3730660207

Richardson, V., & Placier, P. (2001). Teacher change. In V. Richardson (Ed.), *Handbook of Research on Teaching* (4th ed.; pp. 905–947). Washington, DC: American Educational Research Association.

Rivkin, S. G., Hanushek, E. A., & Kain, J. F. (2005). Teachers, schools, and academic achievement. *Econometrica, 79*(2), 417–458. doi:10.1111/j.1468-0262.2005.00584.x

Rubba, P. A. (1985). Chemistry teachers inservice needs: Are they unique? *Journal of Chemical Education, 58*(5), 430–431. doi:10.1021/ed058p430

Rudd, J., Greenbowe, T., Hand, B., & Legg, M. (2001). *Using the science writing heuristic to promote conceptual understanding of equilibrium*. Paper presented at the 221st National Meeting of the American Chemical Society, San Diego CA.

Seferoğlu, S. S. (2004). Öğretmen yeterlikleri ve mesleki gelişim. [Teacher competencies and professional development]. *Bilim ve Aklın Aydınlığında Eğitim, 58*, 40–45.

Simon, M. (1995). Reconstructing mathematics pedagogy from a constructivist perspective. *Journal for Research in Mathematics Education, 26*(2), 114–145. doi:10.2307/749205

Simon, M. A., & Schifter, D. (1987). *Teacher education from a constructivist perspective: The educational leaders in mathematics project*. Washington, DC: National Science Foundation (TEI-8552391).

Smith, K. A., & Welliver, P. (2006). The development of a science process assessment for fourth-grade students. *Journal of Research in Science Teaching, 27*(8), 727–738. doi:10.1002/tea.3660270803

State Planning Organization. (n.d.). *The study of socio-economic development ranking of the provinces*. Retrieved from http://www.dpt.gov.tr/DPT.portal

Supovitz, J. A., & Turner, H. M. (2000). The effects of professional development on science teaching practices and classroom culture. *Journal of Research in Science Teaching, 37*(9), 963–980. doi:10.1002/1098-2736(200011)37:9<963::AID-TEA6>3.0.CO;2-0

Tanriverdi, K., & Gunel, M. (2012). *Ogretmen pedagojisinde kritik sorun: Degisime karsi direnc*. Paper presented at the 10th Annual Meeting of National Science and Mathematics Education Conference (UFBMEK), Nigde.

Tanriverdi, K., Gunel, M., Asci, O., & Ocak, A. (2013). *365 day in-service training*. Paper presented at the 1st International Conference on Immersion Approaches to Argument-based Inquiry (ABI) for Science Classrooms, Busan, Korea.

Thair, M., & Treagust, D. F. (2003). A brief history of a science teacher professional development initiative in Indonesia and the implications for centralised teacher development. *International Journal of Educational Development, 23*(2), 201–213. doi:10.1016/S0738-0593(02)00014-7

The Holmes Group. (1996). *Tomorrow's teachers: A report of the Holmes Group*. East Lansing, MI: The Holmes Group.

Wallance, C., Yang, E.-M., Hand, B., & Hohenshell, L. (2001). *Using a science writing heuristic to enhance learning from laboratory activities in seventh grade science: Quantitative and qualitative outcomes*. Paper presented at the annual meeting of the National Association for Research in Science Teaching, St. Louis, MO.

Wellington, J., & Osborne, J. (2001). *Language and literacy in science education*. Philadelphia, PA: Open University Press.

Windschitd, M. (2002). Framing constructivism in practice as the negotiation of dilemmas: An analysis of the conceptual, pedagogical, cultural and political challenges facing teachers. *Review of Educational Research, 72*(2), 131–175. doi:10.3102/00346543072002131

Yesildag-Hasancebi, F. (2014). *Argumantasyon Tabanli Bilim Ogrenme Yaklasiminin (ATBO) Ogrencilerin Fen Basarilari, Arguman Olusturma Becerileri ve Grup İci Etkilesimleri Uzerine Etkisi*. (Unpublished PhD thesis). Ataturk University.

Yesildag-Hasancebi, F., & Gunel, M. (2013). Effect of the argumentation based inquiry approach on disadvantaged students' science achievement. *Elementary Education Online, 12*(4), 1056–1073.

Yesildag-Hasancebi, F., & Gunel, M. (2014). Delving into the effect of argumentation based inquiry approach on learning science from multiple perspectives. *Journal of Research in Education and Society, 1*(1), 23–44.

Chapter 5
Systematic Support for STEM Pre-Service Teachers:
An Authentic and Sustainable Four-Pillar Professional Development Model

Reenay R.H. Rogers
University of West Alabama, USA

Jodie Winship
University of West Alabama, USA

Yan Sun
University of West Alabama, USA

ABSTRACT

Developing a strong STEM teacher workforce is essential to improve K-12 (kindergarten to 12th grade) STEM education and to strengthen the STEM talent pipeline in the United States. Based on the successful experience in Project Engage, a grant funded by the U.S. Department of Education, this chapter proposes an authentic and sustainable four-pillar STEM professional development model. Grounded on social constructivist and interactive approaches, this professional development model is intended to cultivate STEM pre-service teachers' ability to provide K-12 students with authentic STEM learning experience as defined in the four types of authenticity (i.e., context authenticity, task authenticity, impact authenticity, and personal/value authenticity) identified by Strobel and his colleagues (Strobel, Wang, Weber, & Dyehouse, 2013).

INTRODUCTION

While no one would deny that the U.S. economic growth and innovative capacity are ever increasingly relying on discoveries and advances made possible by STEM (science, technology, engineering, and mathematics) disciplines, there is no secret that U.S. students are scared of STEM and have been lagging behind their international peers in STEM. The attrition rates for U.S. undergraduate students who major

DOI: 10.4018/978-1-4666-9471-2.ch005

in STEM disciplines are high (Hayes, Whalen, & Cannon 2009; Moakler & Kim, 2014; Tinto, 1993). Data from the 2004/2009 Beginning Postsecondary Education Longitudinal Study indicates that many students who begin college in STEM majors will either change to a non-STEM major or leave college completely. In the U.S. about 28% of students seeking a bachelor's degree or associate degree between 2003 and 2009 entered a program of study in a STEM field. An attrition rate of 48% for bachelor's degree candidates and an attrition rate of 69% for associate degree candidates were obtained for the assessed period (Chen, 2013). As a result, the number of science and engineering graduates produced in the U.S. is among the lowest in the world (National Science Board, 2004).

To boost economy and to maintain its innovative capacity, the United States must deal with the urgent need of improving K-12 STEM education and cultivate its domestic STEM talent pool. The question is, how? Teachers do make a difference in student learning experience and learning outcomes, and this is particularly true in STEM disciplines (CADRE, 2011). Cultivating among K-12 students an interest in STEM and encouraging them to study STEM in college and later pursue STEM as a career requires developing a strong STEM teacher workforce who not only has solid STEM content knowledge but possesses in-depth understanding of STEM careers and how STEM disciplines are used in the workplace. The development of such a STEM teacher workforce should start with STEM pre-service teachers.

While most U.S. students do not get a series of good teachers, STEM teachers are particularly poorly prepared (CADRE, 2011). Teacher related issues, such as a dearth of well-prepared teachers, teachers' lack of STEM content knowledge, and lack of effective STEM teacher professional development (Abel & Lederman, 2007; Fulp, 2002; National Academy of Engineering, 2009; Sun & Strobel, 2013, 2014; van Driel, Beijaard, Verloop, 2001; van Driel, Verloop, de Vos, 1998), render it a daunting task to develop a strong STEM teacher workforce. The present chapter seeks to contribute to the effort of developing a strong STEM teacher workforce in the U. S. by proposing an authentic and sustainable four-pillar professional development model for preparing pre-service STEM teachers. This pre-service STEM teacher professional development model was developed based on *Project Engage*—a three-year grant (2011-2014) funded by the U.S. Department of Education at the University of West Alabama.

Grounded in authentic learning theories and applying social constructivist and interactive approaches, the authentic and sustainable four-pillar professional development model is intended to provide systematic support to STEM pre-service teachers allowing them to enrich their STEM content knowledge and STEM pedagogical content knowledge (PCK), gain insights into STEM careers and real-world STEM applications, and to broaden their horizons of the STEM disciplines..

BACKGROUND

Status Quo of K-12 STEM Education

The importance of strengthening and improving K-12 STEM education to the U.S. economy and competitiveness on global markets has long been acknowledged (NAE, 2004; NAS/NAE, 2007; NSB, 2007; NSB, 2008). Despite the importance and the estimation that STEM related jobs will grow 70 percent faster than other jobs in the next six years (Vann, 2013), low numbers of students pursing STEM disciplines and degree programs have been a big national concern (National Science Board, 2010). Troubling statistics persist: while 25% of high school kids drop out of high school and 57% out of those who do

Systematic Support for STEM Pre-Service Teachers

graduate lack comprehension of even remedial mathematics (ACT, 2011), it is reported that 44% of middle school students would rather take out the trash than do math homework (Research Now, 2012). According to the 2012 National Assessment of Educational Progress (NAEP), only 40% of fourth graders nationwide were proficient in math, and students across grade levels were especially weak in inquiry-based science (Rosen, 2012).

The situation of STEM learning for minority students is even worse. The achievement gap between white and minority students in mathematics and science is well documented in numerous research and statistical reports (e.g., Condition of Education, The Nation's Report Card, Science and Engineering Indicators). According to statistics from the National Center for Educational Statistics and the NSF Division Resources Statistics (National Research Council, 2011), white, Hispanic, and black students respectively have a gain of 116 points, 113 points, and 101 points in average mathematic scores from kindergarten to 8th grade. By 5th grade, the gap between white and black students in average mathematics scores was 24 points, and the average score of black 5th grade students was equivalent to the average 3rd grade score of white students. Similar mathematics achievement gaps persist through high school (Ingels, Pratt, Rogers, Siegel, & Stutts, 2004; Riegle-Crumb & Grodsky, 2010). The educational shortfall is not limited to a specific region, race, or socioeconomic group; it is a national problem (Gottfried & Williams, 2013).

The above alarming trends of low STEM learning outcomes and achievement gap go side by side with K-12 students' disinterest in STEM disciplines. As indicated by previous research, students begin to lose interest in STEM near the middle school years (Finson & Enochs, 1987; Barmby, Kind, & Jones, 2008; Bennett & Hogarth, 2009). K-12 STEM education in the U.S. has to deal with three big challenges: improving student overall STEM learning outcomes, narrowing the STEM achievement gap, and promoting student interest in STEM. Dealing with these three challenges, as the key to strengthening the U.S. STEM workforce pipeline, relies heavily on preparing qualified STEM teachers. Although improving K-12 STEM education is indispensable of organizational elements, such as school leadership and staff collaboration (CADRE, 2011), STEM teacher quality is essential because, working directly with students on a daily basis, STEM teachers are the most active agents who can bring changes to the K-12 STEM education landscape.

Professional development, as a widely accepted conventional and promising intervention to improve teacher quality (Buczynski & Hansen, 2010; Goldschmidt & Phelps, 2009), has assumed an important role in preparing teachers for STEM education in the past decade. Teacher professional development is a key mechanism not only for improving classroom instruction but also for improving student learning outcomes (Ball & Cohen, 1999; Cohen & Hill, 2000; Yoon, Duncan, Lee, Scarloss, & Shapley, 2007). A report on 1,300 studies addressing the effect of teacher professional development (Yoon, Duncan, Lee, Scarloss, & Shapley, 2007) finds that teachers who receive substantial professional development can boost their students' achievement by 21 percentile points. However, although previous research (e.g., Cunningham, Lachapelle, & Keenan, 2010; Diaconu, Radigan, Suskavcevic, & Nichol, 2012; Hsu, Cardella, & Purzer, 2010; McDermott & DeWater, 2000; Supovitz, Mayers, & Kahle, 2000) has yielded findings regarding the positive effects of STEM professional development, STEM professional development was criticized to be "often short, fragmented, ineffective, and not designed to address the specific need of individual teachers" (Wilson, 2011). The overall mixed record of STEM professional development (CADRE, 2011) heightens the need to review the current practice of K-12 STEM professional development and to rethink about its future directions.

Current K-12 STEM Professional Development: What Is Missing?

Focusing on STEM content knowledge and STEM pedagogical content knowledge (PCK) has been the norm of STEM professional development. Research has pointed that it is necessary for STEM professional development to cultivate both content knowledge and PCK in STEM. Leaving suggestions from research aside, there are practical reasons for STEM professional development to focus on STEM content knowledge and STEM PCK: (1) the fast changing nature of STEM disciplines and (2) the fact that K-12 teachers are not well prepared for STEM teaching. An estimated 10–20% of science and math teachers in U.S. middle and high schools are not certified in their subjects—nor did they major in a related field in college (CADRE, 2011). While low course-taking in science and mathematics by elementary and middle school pre-service teachers has been identified by many states as a major factor in poor teacher quality and poor learning outcomes, engineering is not a discipline traditionally taught in K-12 classrooms and K-12 teachers, elementary teachers in particular, are not familiar with Design, Engineering, and Technology (DET) (Hsu, Cardella, Purzer & Diaz 2010; Yasar et al, 2006). Avery and Reed (2013) postulated that professional development was a means to prepare STEM educators to "effectively integrate various instructional approaches" (p. 55).

K-12 STEM teachers are not well prepared in their STEM content knowledge, let alone well prepared pedagogically to teach STEM to their students. Professional development, consequently, becomes a useful means to provide STEM teachers with training to enrich their STEM content knowledge and their PCK in STEM. PCK, first proposed by Shulman (1986), refers to knowledge of how to make the subject comprehensible to learners based on understandings of the learners' characteristics, interests, abilities, as well as their conceptions and content-related difficulties. With growing appreciation of the importance of STEM PCK in improving STEM teaching in the K-12 community, STEM professional programs typically cover specific STEM content integrated with pedagogy seeking to promote a deep understanding of the subject matter along with appropriate pedagogical practices.

Although focusing on STEM content and pedagogy has long become the common practice in STEM professional development, the question remains: Are STEM content knowledge and STEM PCK enough to enable STEM teachers to help their students develop an interest in STEM and motivate them to learn STEM in college and even pursue it as a career? It is true that enhanced STEM content knowledge and PCK in STEM would improve teachers' ability to make STEM content comprehensible to their students. But far more than this needs to be done to reach the ultimate goal of K-12 STEM education of cultivating a STEM-proficient workforce and a STEM-literate citizenry to increase the United States' competitiveness in the global economy. The problem with the current STEM professional development practice of focusing mainly on STEM content and STEM PCK is centering on STEM teachers' teaching and knowledge needs, dismissing students as passive knowledge receptors and inactive agents in the STEM learning process.

The authors of the present chapter call for a new K-12 STEM professional development paradigm that treats students as an active agent that can wield influence on the learning process and affect the learning results. This new paradigm sets on an understanding about the reciprocal relationship between teachers and students in the learning process. Teaching as a practice of human improvement indicates that teaching "practitioners depend on their clients to achieve any results" (Cohen, 1988, p. 57). Labaree (2000) elaborated this idea when discussing the nature of teaching by comparing teachers with surgeons and lawyers: "A surgeon can fix the ailment of a patient who sleeps through the operation, and a lawyer can successfully defend a client who remains mute during the trial, but success for a teacher depends

Systematic Support for STEM Pre-Service Teachers

heavily on the active cooperation of the student" (p.228). Labaree quoted Dewey (1933) that "There is the same exact equation between teaching and learning that there is between selling and buying" (as quoted in Labaree, 2000, p. 228), and pointed out that there is a reciprocal relationship between teachers and students: "you can't be a good salesperson unless someone is buying, and you can't be a good teacher unless someone is learning" (Labaree, 2000, p.228).

This reciprocal relationship reveals the importance of STEM teachers' ability to enable their students to feel motivated and willing to learn STEM in order to make real STEM learning happen. This ability should be directly related to teachers' ability to create authentic STEM learning experiences for their students given the well-documented motivational benefits of authentic learning for students (e.g., Herrington & Oliver, 2000; Huang, 2002; Lombardi, 2007; Newmann & Wehlage, 1993). Adopting the four types of authenticity (i.e., context authenticity, task authenticity, impact authenticity, and personal/value authenticity) identified by Strobel and his colleagues (Strobel et al, 2013) as a theoretical framework, this chapter proposes the authentic and sustainable four-pillar professional development model guiding future STEM professional development efforts to cultivate STEM pre-service teachers' ability to create authentic STEM learning experience for students and to concurrently improve STEM pre-service teachers' STEM content knowledge and PCK in STEM.

New Paradigm of K-12 STEM Professional Development and Authentic K-12 STEM Learning Experience

As proposed by the authors of this chapter, the new paradigm of STEM professional development emphasizes authentic learning experiences for K-12 students and treats cultivating teachers' ability to create authentic STEM learning experience as equally important as enhancing their STEM content knowledge and PCK in STEM. Snape and Fox-Turnbull argued (2011) the necessity of "devising practical, adaptable education programmes" (p. 67) which inspire students to develop understanding of their world through authentic learning. Integrating the above three aspects (i.e., the ability to create authentic STEM learning experiences for K-12 students, STEM content knowledge, and PCK in STEM) into STEM training is the new promising direction for future K-12 STEM professional development.

Although, as pointed out by Petragli (1998), authenticity has become the "desideratum of the American educational system" (p.10), the need still exists to define authenticity in the context of K-12 STEM education. The authors of this chapter defined the meaning of authentic K-12 STEM learning based the four types of authenticity (i.e., context authenticity, task authenticity, impact authenticity, and personal/value authenticity) identified by Strobel and his colleagues (Strobel et al, 2013) (See Table 1).

Approaching K-12 STEM education from the lenses of the four types of authenticity, the K-12 STEM education community would realize that, to allow K-12 students to develop an interest in STEM and to prepare them for studying STEM in college and pursuing STEM as a career, authentic K-12 STEM learning experience should: (1) help K-12 students develop an understanding of real world STEM careers; (2) allow K-12 students to experience real world STEM applications to gain a personal understanding of STEM impact; (3) scaffold K-12 students' development of STEM knowledge and skills; and (4) provide hands-on experience with real world STEM problems. These four aspects define the meaning of authentic K-12 STEM learning.

In addition to applying the Vygotskian concept of the zone of proximal development (Vygotsky, 1978) in scaffolding K-12 students' STEM knowledge and skill development, the authentic K-12 STEM learning experience defined above emphasizes cultivating K-12 students' motivation and interest in

Table 1. Authenticity model (Strobel et al., 2013)

Categories	Description/Key Definition	Curricula Features
Contextual Authenticity	1. Contains a real-world professional environment 2. Provides everyday experience 3. Resemble social challenges or social interactions 4. Align school and professional outcomes	1. Provide input from diverse stakeholders 2. Be a complex problems solving context and interdisciplinary context 3. Provide situations of collaboration, access to tools and resources, and ownership
Task Authenticity	1. Students are engaged in tasks similar to professionals 2. Reflect or develop professional skills for students 3. Challenge students in decision-making in practical contexts	1. Contain ill-structured problems, no pre-specifications 2. Contain open-ended creative activities. 3. Promote disciplined inquiry 4. Ask students to interpret ambiguous data
Impact Authenticity	1. Actions in cultural practices 2. Social events, issues or impact 3. Students' role as effective citizens 4. Students as collaborators of industry	1. Professional community standards in relative area 2. Project results influence people outside of school 3. Minorities' experiences in the role of engineers or scientists
Personal/Value Authenticity	1. Produce knowledge with values in students' lives and studies beyond simply proving their competence 2. Integrate everyday life experience, personal interests, professional target and cultural values 3. Develop a sense of identity and sense of confidence	1. Problematizing the subject matter 2. Perceive relations between the practices and the use of value in them 3. Pursue personal goals and have personal choice 4. Be engaged in personal construction of new knowledge in learning task-environments

STEM by promoting their self-efficacy beliefs about STEM and by allowing them to see the relevance of STEM through personal experience. Underpinning this emphasis are learning theories regarding self-efficacy beliefs and motivational effects of relevance. Bandura (1997) defined self-efficacy beliefs as "beliefs in one's capabilities to organize and execute the courses of action required to produce given attainments" (p. 3).

The terms *mastery experience* (also known as *enactive experience*) and *vicarious experience* (also known as *modeling*) were identified by Bandura (1986, 1988) as two important sources of perceived self-efficacy. While mastery experiences are real and direct experiences that increase one's self-efficacy by allowing the individual to experience performance successes, vicarious experiences are indirect experiences that are able to increase one's self-efficacy beliefs by allowing the individual to observe similar others experiencing performance successes (Bandura, 1988). The authentic STEM learning experience defined in this chapter will give K-12 students both *mastery experience* and *vicarious experience* with STEM respectively through hands-on projects solving real world problems and through personal experience of exploring STEM facilities and interacting with STEM professionals, and consequently increase K-12 students' self-efficacy beliefs about STEM. Informal learning through enriched STEM experiences can create authentic learning experiences for pre-service teachers. Huang, Lee & Lim's research (2012) proposed "when a pedagogy of experimentation exists in schools, learning becomes more authentic because students can anchor learning within rich contexts" (p.1087). In addition, as suggested by Keller's ARCS (Attention, Relevance, Confidence, and Satisfaction) motivational theory and ARCS model of motivational design (Keller, 1988, 2004; Keller & Suzuki, 1988), relevance is a key component to intrinsically motivate student learning. The authentic K-12 STEM learning experience allows students to see the relevance of learning STEM through personal experience of real world STEM applications and their impact and the perceived relevance will serve as a trigger to arouse students' motivation to learn STEM.

Centering on the above four aspects of the authentic K-12 STEM learning experience, the authors of this chapter proposed the authentic and sustainable four-pillar STEM professional development model. As illustrated in Figure 1, the four-pillars of the model are targeting the four aspects of the authentic

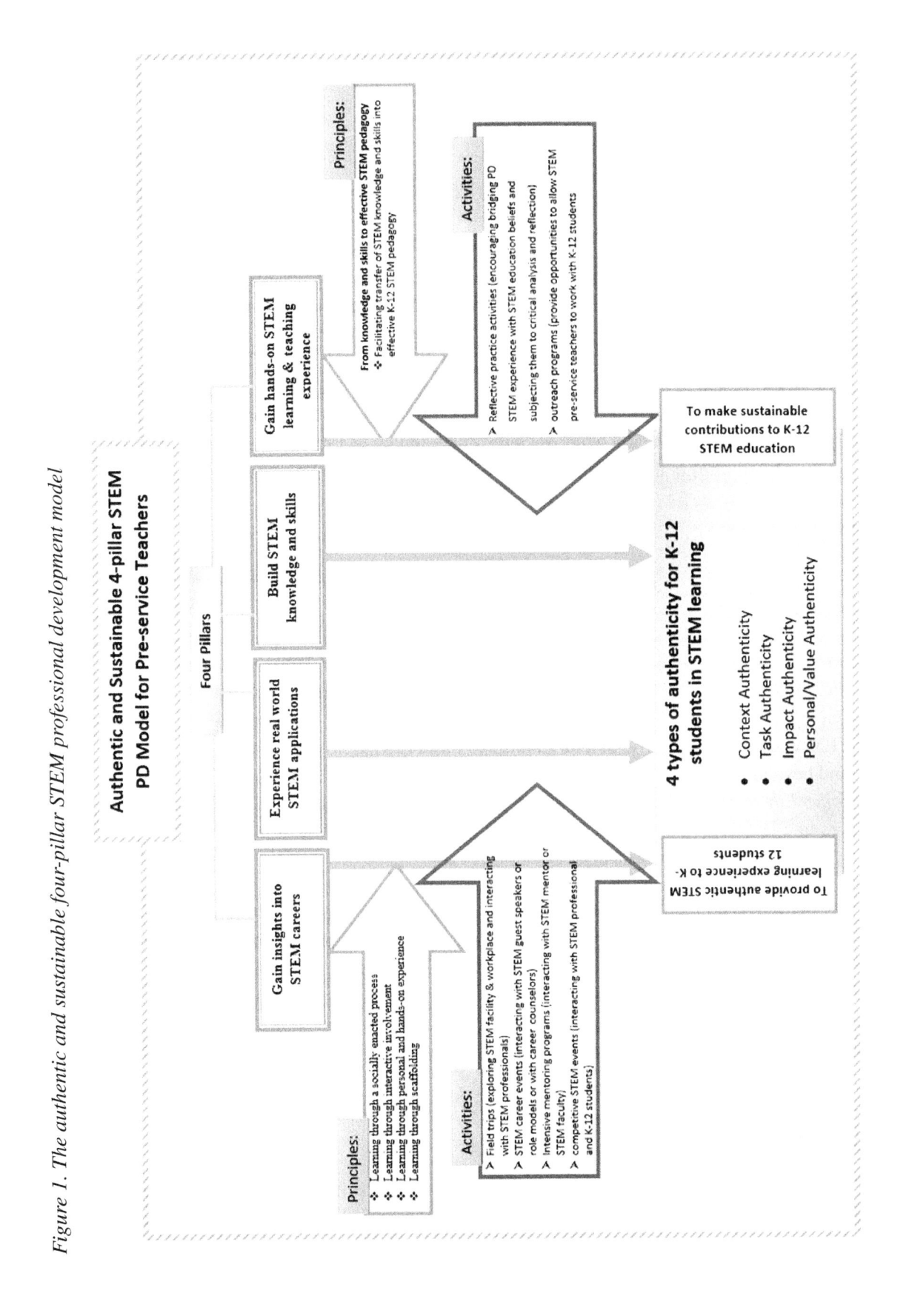

Figure 1. The authentic and sustainable four-pillar STEM professional development model

K-12 STEM learning experience. The rationale of building the professional development model upon the four pillars is to allow pre-service teachers to experience and gain knowledge about authentic STEM learning before providing it to their future students.

THE AUTHENTIC AND SUSTAINABLE FOUR-PILLAR STEM PD MODEL

The four-pillar STEM professional development model proposed in this chapter is authentic and sustainable in the sense that this model intends to provide STEM pre-service teachers with resources, knowledge, and authentic experiences that would enable them, after entering the teaching profession, to give their students authentic STEM learning experience and to make sustainable contributions to K-12 STEM education. This professional development model was developed based on the authors' experience in *Project Engage* funded by the U.S. Department of Education. This section, after giving a brief overview of *Project Engage*, focuses on the authentic and sustainable four-pillar STEM professional development model introducing the theoretical underpinnings of the model and illustrating the professional development learning activities in the model using those learning activities from *Project Engage*.

Project Engage

Project Engage is a three-year grant (2011-2014) funded by the U.S. Department of Education at the University of West Alabama (UWA). UWA enrolls 21% of its student body in STEM degree programs, of which half are minority students. Primarily, *Project Engage* was designed and implemented for the purpose of increasing the retention rates of minority STEM undergraduates between their freshman and sophomore years through intensive academic and personal mentoring, and exposure to opportunities inherent in STEM fields. A second purpose of *Project Engage* is to increase graduation rates of minority STEM undergraduates through their continued participation in project activities during the second year and beyond.

Project Engage participants were all freshmen students pursuing STEM majors including pre-service teachers in STEM education. These STEM pre-service teachers were similar to other participants of *Project Engage*: lacking educational preparation and experiences in STEM, lacking motivation in STEM, and having limited access to STEM professional role-models. In *Project Engage*, the STEM pre-service teachers participated in STEM-enhanced curricula, received strategically-designed mentoring, participated in guided STEM career exploration, engaged in early, ongoing STEM inquiry, interacted with fellow cohort members, STEM faculty, and STEM experts currently employed in various STEM-related disciplines while receiving on-going encouragement and support resulting in graduation from UWA. Based on experience working with the STEM pre-service teachers in *Project Engage*, the authors of this chapter developed the four-pillar STEM professional development model.

Theoretical Underpinnings of the Four-Pillar STEM Professional Development Model

The four-pillars in the STEM professional development model proposed in this chapter reflect the new STEM professional development paradigm of cultivating STEM teachers' ability to create authentic STEM learning experiences along with enhancing their STEM content knowledge and their PCK in

STEM. Learning activities falling under the four pillars were designed and developed using social constructivist and interactive approaches that emphasize knowledge construction through social interaction and through shared rather than individual experience (Vygotsky, 1978). Specifically, these activities are based on the assumptions that learning is a social activity, knowledge is a product of human interaction, and knowledge is socially and culturally constructed that is influenced by the group and its environment. Embracing these assumptions, the model applies two guiding principles in developing the learning activities: (1) individuals create meaning through interaction with others and the environment they live in, and (2) meaningful learning occurs only when individuals are engaged in social activities. Adopting these principles, the learning activities under each of the four-pillars allow pre-service teachers:

- To gain insights into STEM careers by interacting, in STEM career events, with guest speakers or role models from STEM professions or with career counselors;
- To experience real world STEM applications by exploring STEM facilities and workplaces and by interacting with STEM professionals in field trips;
- To build STEM knowledge and skills by interacting with STEM mentors or STEM faculty in intensive mentoring programs;
- To gain hands-on experience both about STEM learning and STEM teaching by interacting with STEM professionals and K-12 students in competitive STEM events.

Running through the learning activities in the four-pillar STEM professional development model are the principles of promoting learning through scaffolding and facilitating learning though hands-on and personal experience. These principles reflect the intention to maximize STEM pre-service teachers' Zone of Proximal Development (ZPD) (Vygotsky, 1978) with the help of more capable or knowledgeable others (e.g., STEM professionals and STEM faculty) and to improve STEM pre-service teachers' self-efficacy beliefs about teaching STEM through enriched *mastery experience* (Bandura 1986, 1988).

Learning Activities from *Project Engage*

Each of the four pillars in the STEM professional development model proposed in this chapter has its corresponding learning activities. To illustrate the possible forms and content of these learning activities, this section introduces and describes some learning activities from *Project Engage*.

Career Counseling

Career development professionals play a key role in aiding the nation in developing a diverse STEM development workforce (Byars-Winston, 2014). Byars-Winston proposed a framework for career intervention with areas focusing on multicultural STEM careers awareness, communication about STEM, and counselor skills and practice. As a result, Career Counseling is a learning activity embedded in *Project Engage* that can be used to serve the purpose of helping pre-service teachers to gain insights into STEM careers. In *Project Engage*, Career Counseling affords opportunities for *Project Engage* participants to foster relationships with professionals working in STEM industries. The career counselor is responsible for individual career counseling sessions with project participants and development of a comprehensive professional exploration program. The project participants meet with the career counselor twice during the first academic semester for comprehensive needs assessment and general guidance. The Career

Counseling activity requires project participants to enroll in a UWA 102 career exploration class during the second academic term where they receive aptitude testing, an interest inventory, interview skills training, and other related career guidance activities. The career counselor is required to meet with project participants once per academic term through graduation to collaborate on the development of an individual career exploration portfolio. The guided career exploration and intensive career counseling provided in the Career Counseling activity are intended to cultivate undergraduate STEM students to ensure preparation for careers in STEM fields including STEM education.

Professional Enrichment Trips and Access to STEM Professionals

The learning activities of professional enrichment trips and access to STEM professionals in *Project Engage* are good activities that can help STEM pre-service teachers to experience real world STEM applications and to gain insights into STEM careers. In *Project Engage*, professional enrichment trips augment the STEM college classroom experience with real world STEM practice by providing exposure to STEM professionals in their work environment. Pre-service teachers in *Project Engage* have interacted with STEM professionals such as NASA scientists and other related NASA careers with trips to the Marshall Spaceflight Center; environmental scientists, engineers, and educators at the Alabama Nature Center; and biologists and biotech engineers at the Hudson Alpha Biotech Center. Interactions with STEM professionals in the work setting provide a deeper understanding of STEM applications that pre-service teachers can take with them into their future classrooms.

Project Engage has also afforded project participants with the opportunity to engage with STEM professional speakers. Project participants have listened to a NASA project director discuss the future of space flight; engaged in an interactive science show; and built boomerangs along with a world champion boomerang thrower. The most significant occasion for Project Engage participants was the lectures by a former U. S. Surgeon General who provided inspiration as well as realistic advice for success in STEM careers. On-going professional development for pre-service teachers in the form of enrichment trips to STEM industries as well as access to real-life practitioners working in STEM-related fields reinforces the significance of STEM education at the K-12 level.

UWA STEM 101 Course

In *Project Engage*, the UWA STEM 101 course was designed and implemented to help project participants build STEM knowledge and skills. *Project Engage* faculty and staff developed a curriculum and syllabus to be used with the UWA STEM 101 course. The specialized curriculum requires STEM UWA 101 students to investigate a STEM topic of their choosing as part of class assignments facilitated by their STEM UWA 101 professor. One example is the investigation of various topics through the "How Does It Work?" exercise. In this activity, which promotes understanding of the scientific method, students engaged in their own research throughout the semester, seeking answers to their questions, conferring with experts in the subject (faculty members, researchers, mechanics, engineers, scientists, etc.), and sharing their discoveries with fellow classmates. Supported by Engage mentors, STEM faculty, and a Career Counselor, in-class activities offer participants opportunities for directed study into personal areas of interest. The UWA STEM 101 course offered a new way to improve STEM pre-service teachers' STEM knowledge and skills.

Invention Convention

The Invention Convention in *Project Engage* is a learning activity that can be used to improve STEM pre-service teachers' STEM knowledge and skills, and gain hands-on experience about STEM learning and STEM teaching. The Invention Convention in *Project Engage* focuses on involving STEM undergraduate students and K-12 students in competitions which foster STEM creativity and discovery. During year one of *Project Engage*, STEM undergraduate students were involved in a robotics competition hosted in-house at the University. The undergraduate STEM students were taught programming in several sessions, divided into teams, and given the challenge of building/programming a robot to complete a task. Survey results indicated students agreed (58%) or strongly agreed (24%) that the robotics competition increased their knowledge in STEM. However, during year two the robotics competition was coupled with an enrichment trip to the Marshall Spaceflight Center where undergraduate STEM students were exposed to programming and robotics under the tutelage of NASA scientists. As a culminating activity, STEM undergraduate students competed in a robotics competition on site at the Marshall Spaceflight Center. Results from the year two survey showed an increase in the percentage of students from 24% to 63% strongly agreeing that the robotics competition increased their STEM knowledge. Working with the NASA scientists at Marshall Spaceflight Center had a positive effect on STEM undergraduate students' perception of their increased STEM knowledge.

The K-12 component of the Invention Convention has taken various forms including 1) creating inventions from recycled materials, 2) building and testing egg drop carriers, and 3) making boomerangs. UWA STEM students received hands-on experience working with K-12 students as the K-12 students competed head-to-head in these various STEM –themed events. The experience of leading and assisting the K-12 students as they competed provided an authentic "teaching" experience as the undergraduate pre-service teachers developed the skills needed for teaching success. First-hand experience working with K-12 students is invaluable preparation for pre-service STEM educators.

STEM Challenge

The STEM Challenge component of *Project Engage* is another activity that can be used to help STEM pre-service teachers gain hands-on experience with K-12 students. The STEM Challenge incorporates all facets of STEM (science, technology, engineering, and mathematics) using a crime scene investigation theme to pose a real world problem for Project Engage and local K-12 students to solve. During year one, both undergraduate STEM students and K-12 students worked on the same crime scene to collect and analyze evidence as well as create and present their solutions to the crime scenario. The setting for the STEM Challenge was complete with a judge, bailiffs, and suspects creating an authentic atmosphere for the crime solving. Feedback from the undergraduate STEM students indicated they preferred more of a teaching/leading role in the STEM Challenge, thus for year two, the STEM undergraduate students were assigned as leaders for the various K-12 student teams rather than as competitors in the event. Fifty-six percent of the K-12 participants in year two indicated that the STEM Challenge increased their interest in STEM. The excitement of working with college-level students to solve a simulated crime promotes a curiosity about STEM fields which can inspire future generations of STEM majors.

Outcomes from *Project Engage*

The overall goals of *Project Engage* centered on recruitment and retention of underrepresented students in STEM majors. The four-pillar model of professional development for pre-service teachers was developed as a by-product through the implementation of this grant program, *Project Engage*. Data is still being collected at this juncture of implementation and further data collection and analysis is needed. At this stage, results during year one of the program indicated retention of freshmen STEM majors, previously significantly less than freshmen non-STEM majors, equalized at 56%. Current retention data for year two indicates the proposed model has increased retention rates of freshmen STEM majors (70%) above that of non-STEM majors (62%). Retention of students in STEM majors is only one aspect of the effectiveness of *Project Engage*. By keeping undergraduate students in STEM majors, including STEM education majors, this program stands to prepare more highly qualified STEM professionals and in the end will result in a more highly skilled workforce.

SOLUTIONS AND RECOMMENDATIONS

This chapter argues that one of the possible solutions to improving K-12 students' STEM learning outcomes, promoting their motivation and interest in STEM, and narrowing the STEM achievement gap, is to cultivate STEM teachers' ability to create authentic STEM learning experience for their students. Avery and Reed (2013) concluded that professional development "is important to STEM education" (p. 55) and affords STEM educators the opportunity to learn methods of integrating new teaching practices. The authentic and sustainable four-pillar STEM professional development model is proposed as being able to prepare pre-service teachers for providing authentic STEM learning experiences to their future students and for making sustainable contributions to K-12 STEM education. But the fact exists that it is often difficult for teachers to translate knowledge gained through professional development into effective teaching practice (Duffy, 2004; Gordon, 2004) and this is especially true for pre-service teachers who normally have no previous teaching experience. This knowledge transfer problem is reflected in the common lore among teachers: teaching as happening in classrooms and "talk about teaching" as happening in universities are incommensurable. Because of the knowledge transfer problem, the "from knowledge and skills to effective STEM pedagogy" component (see Figure 1) has been added into the professional development model. Pre-service teacher professional development providers are recommended to emphasize this component in their professional development programs and employ appropriate professional development activities (e.g., reflective practice activities and outreach programs) to facilitate the transfer of knowledge from STEM professional development into effective K-12 STEM teaching practices.

FUTURE RESEARCH DIRECTIONS

The authentic and sustainable four-pillar STEM professional development model proposed in this chapter is intended to provide STEM pre-service teachers with training that will not only improve their STEM content knowledge and their STEM PCK but also cultivate their ability to create authentic STEM learning experiences for K-12 students. Such training is rather comprehensive in nature. Pragmatically, it might be difficult to add such professional development training into already tightly-packed teacher preparation programs. Future research is needed to provide clues regarding effective and feasible ways or formats that can make the training possible.

This chapter uses learning activities from *Project Engage* as examples that can be used to achieve the purposes specified in the four-pillars of the professional development model. However, there is no empirical evidence regarding the effectiveness of these learning activities. Research needs to be conducted to either determine the effectiveness of these activities or to help decide what kind of learning activities should be designed and developed instead. Possible future research efforts include: (1) investigating the effects of a particular learning activity on STEM pre-service teachers' self-efficacy beliefs about STEM teaching, (2) investigating the effects of a particular learning activity on STEM pre-service teachers' STEM content knowledge and PCK, (3) conducting longitudinal research revealing the effects of a particular learning activity on pre-service teachers' future STEM teaching performance.

CONCLUSION

This chapter argues that (1) STEM teachers' ability to provide their students with authentic STEM learning experience is crucial to cultivating among K-12 students an interest in STEM and encouraging them to study STEM in college and later pursue STEM as a career; (2) it is not enough for STEM professional development to focus mainly on improving teachers' STEM content knowledge and their PCK in STEM; and (3) the task of cultivating STEM teachers' ability to create authentic STEM learning experiences for their students should be put on STEM professional development programs' agenda. The authentic and sustainable four-pillar professional development model is proposed in this chapter reflecting the above opinion regarding K-12 STEM professional development.

This professional development model as illustrated in Figure 1, is intended to guide the development of STEM professional development training for STEM pre-service teachers that will not only aim to improve their STEM content knowledge and their STEM PCK but also to cultivate and enhance their ability to create authentic STEM learning experiences for K-12 students. It is envisioned that future research will be conducted to test the validity of the model and to improve it to better serve STEM pre-service teacher preparation purposes. Also, it is hoped that research efforts will be made in the future to modify this model to be used to provide effective STEM training to in-service teachers as well.

REFERENCES

Abel, S. K., & Lederman, N. G. (2007). *Handbook of research in science education*. New Jersey: Erlbaum.

ACT. (2011). ACT Profile Report: Graduating Class 2011 National. Retrieved from http://www.act.org/newsroom/data/2011/pdf/profile/National2011.pdf

Avery, Z. K., & Reeve, E. M. (2013). Developing effective STEM professional development programs. *Journal of Technology in Education*, 25(1), 55–69.

Ball, D. L., & Cohen, D. K. (1999). Developing practices, developing practitioners: Toward a practice-based theory of professional development. In G. Sykes & L. Darling-Hammonds (Eds.), *Teaching as the learning profession: Handbook of policy and practice* (pp. 30–32). San Francisco, CA: Jossey-Bass.

Bandura, A. (1986). *Social foundations of thought and action: A social cognitive theory*. Englewood Cliffs, NJ: Prentice-Hall.

Bandura, A. (1988). Organizational Application of Social Cognitive Theory. *Australian Journal of Management, 13*(2), 275–302. doi:10.1177/031289628801300210

Bandura, A. (1997). *Self-efficacy: The exercise of control*. New York: W.H. Freeman and Company.

Barmby, P., Kind, P., & Jones, K. (2008). Examining Changing Attitudes in Secondary School Science. *International Journal of Science Education, 30*(8), 1075–1093. doi:10.1080/09500690701344966

Bennett, J., & Hogarth, S. (2009). "Would you want to talk to a scientist at a party?": High school students' attitude to school science and to science. *International Journal of Science Education, 31*(14), 1975–1998. doi:10.1080/09500690802425581

Buczynski, S., & Hansen, C. B. (2010). Impact of professional development on teacher practice: Uncovering connections. *Teaching and Teacher Education, 26*(3), 599–607. doi:10.1016/j.tate.2009.09.006

Byars-Winston, A. (2014). Toward a framework for multicultural STEM-focused career interventions. *The Career Development Quarterly, 62*(4), 340–357. doi:10.1002/j.2161-0045.2014.00087.x PMID:25750480

CADRE. (the Community for Advancing Discovery Research in Education). (2011). Preparing and supporting STEM educators. Retrieved from http://successfulstemeducation.org/sites/successfulstemeducation.org/files/Preparing%20Supporting%20STEM%20Educators_FINAL.pdf

Chen, X. (2013). *STEM Attrition: College Students' Paths Into and Out of STEM Fields (NCES 2014-001)*. Washington, DC: National Center for Education Statistics, Institute of Education Sciences, U.S. Department of Education.

Cohen, D. K. (1988). Teaching practice: Plus a change. In P. W. Jackson (Ed.), *Contributing to educational change: Perspectives on research and practice* (pp. 27–84). Berkeley, CA: McCutchan.

Cohen, D. K., & Hill, H. C. (2000). Instructional policy and classroom performance: The mathematics reform in California. *Teachers College Record, 102*(2), 294–343. doi:10.1111/0161-4681.00057

Cunningham, C. M., Lachapelle, C. P., & Keenan, K. (2010). Elementary teachers' changing ideas about STEM and STEM pedagogy through interaction with a pedagogically supportive STEM curriculum. Paper presented at the P-12 Engineering and Design Education Research Summit, Seaside, OR.

Dewey, J. (1933). *How we think*. Lexington, MA: D.C. Heath.

Diaconu, D., Radigan, J., Suskavcevic, M., & Nichol, C. (2012). A multi-year study of the impact of the Rice model professional development on elementary teachers. *International Journal of Science Education, 34*(6), 855–877. doi:10.1080/09500693.2011.642019

Duffy, F. M. (2004). *Moving upward together: Creating strategic alignment to sustain systemic school improvement*. Lanham, MD: Scarecrow Education.

Finson, K. D., & Enochs, L. G. (1987). Student attitudes toward science-technology-society resulting from visitation to a science-technology museum. *Journal of Research in Science Teaching, 24*(7), 593–609. doi:10.1002/tea.3660240702

Fulp, S. L. (2002). *2000 National Survey of Science and Mathematics Education: Status of elementary school science teaching*. Chapel Hill, NC: Horizon Research.

Goldschmidt, P., & Phelps, G. (2009). Does teacher professional development affect content and pedagogical knowledge: How much and for how long? *Economics of Education Review, 29*(3), 432–439. doi:10.1016/j.econedurev.2009.10.002

Gordon, S. P. (2004). *Professional development for school improvement: Empowering Learning Communities*. New York: Pearson.

Gottfried, M. A., & Williams, D. N. (2013). STEM Club Participation and STEM Schooling Outcomes. *Education Policy Analysis Archives, 21*(79), 1–23.

Hanover Research. (2011). K-12 STEM education overview. Retrieved from http://www.hanoverresearch.com/wp-content/uploads/2011/12/K-12-STEM-Education-Overview-Membership.pdf

Hayes, R. Q., Whalen, S. K., & Cannon, B. (2009). *2008–2009 CSRDE stem retention report*. Norman: Center for Institutional Data Exchange and Analysis, University of Oklahoma.

Herrington, J., & Oliver, R. (2000). An instructional design framework for authentic learning environments. *Educational Technology Research and Development, 48*(3), 23–48. doi:10.1007/BF02319856

Hsu, M., Cardella, M., & Purzer, S. (2010). Assessing elementary teachers' design knowledge before and after introduction of a design process model. Paper presented at American Society for Engineering Education 2010 annual conference.

Huang, D., Lee, S., & Lim, K. Y. T. (2012). Authenticity in learning for the twenty-first century: Bridging the formal and the informal. *Educational Technology Research and Development, 60*(6), 1071–1091. doi:10.1007/s11423-012-9272-3

Huang, H. M. (2002). Towards constructivism for adult learners in online learning environment. *British Journal of Educational Technology, 33*(1), 27–37. doi:10.1111/1467-8535.00236

Ingels, S. J., Pratt, D. J., Rogers, J. E., Siegel, P. H., & Stutts, E. S. (2004). *Education Longitudinal Study of 2002: Base-Year Data File User's Manual (NCES 2004-405)*. Washington, DC: National Center for Education Statistics, Institute of Education Sciences, U.S. Department of Education.

Keller, J. M. (1987). Development and use of the ARCS model of instructional design. *Journal of Instructional Development, 10*(3), 2–10. doi:10.1007/BF02905780

Keller, J. M., & Suzuki, K. (1988). Use of the ARCS motivation model in courseware design. In *D. H. Jonassen (ED.) Instructional designs for microcomputer courseware*. Hillsdale, NJ: Lawrence Erlbaum.

Keller, J. M., & Suzuki, K. (2004). Learner Motivation and E-Learning Design: A Multinationally Validated Process. *Journal of Educational Media, 29*(3), 229–239. doi:10.1080/1358165042000283084

Labaree, D. F. (2000). On the nature of teaching and teacher education: Difficult practices that look easy. *Journal of Teacher Education, 51*(3), 228–233. doi:10.1177/0022487100051003011

Lombardi, M. (2007). Authentic learning for the 21st century: An overview. Retrieved from http://net.educause.edu/ir/library/pdf/ELI3009.pdf

McDermott, L. C., & DeWater, L. S. (2000). The need for special science courses for teachers: two perspectives. In J. Minstrell & E. H. van Zee (Eds.), *Inquiring into inquiry science learning and teaching.* Washington, DC: American Association for the Advancement of Science.

Means, B., Confrey, J., House, A., & Bhanot, R. (2008). STEM high schools: Specialized science technology engineering and mathematics secondary schools in the U.S. (Bill and Melinda Gates Foundation Report). Retrieved from http://www.hsalliance.org/stem/index.asp

Moakler, M. W. Jr, & Kim, M. M. (2014). College Major Choice in STEM: Revisiting Confidence and Demographic Factors. *The Career Development Quarterly, 62*(2), 128–142. doi:10.1002/j.2161-0045.2014.00075.x

NAS/NAE. (2007). *Rising above the gathering storm: Energizing and employing America for a brighter economic future.* Washington, D. C.: National Academies Press.

National Academy of Engineering. (2004). NAE Annual Report 2004. Retrieved from https://www.nae.edu/File.aspx?id=43371

National Academy of Engineering. (2009). *Engineering in K-12 education: Understanding the status and improving the prospects.* Washington, DC: National Academies Press.

National Research Council. (2011). *Expanding Underrepresented Minority Participation: America's Science and Technology Talent at the Crossroads.* Washington, DC: National Academies Press.

National Science Board. (2004). *Science and engineering indicators 2004.* Arlington, VA: National Science Board.

National Science Board. (2007). *National Action Plan for Addressing the Critical Needs of the U.S. Science, Technology, Engineering, and Mathematics Education System.* Arlington, VA: National Science Foundation.

National Science Board. (2008). *Science and engineering indicators 2008.* Arlington, VA: National Science Foundation.

National Science Board. (2010). *Science & Engineering Indicators 2010.* Arlington, VA: National Science Foundation.

Newmann, F. M., & Wehlage, G. G. (1993). Five standards for authentic instruction. *Educational Leadership, 50*(7), 8–12.

Petraglia, J. (1998). *The rhetoric and technology of authenticity in education.* Mahwah, NJ: Lawrence Erlbaum.

Research Now. (2012). Math Relevance to U.S. middle school students: A survey commissioned by Raytheon Company. Retrieved from http://www.raytheon.com/newsroom/rtnwcm/groups/corporate/documents/content/rtn12_studentsmth_results.pdf

Riegle-Crumb, C., & Grodsky, E. (2010). Racial ethnic differences at the intersection of math course-taking and achievement. *Sociology of Education*, *83*(3), 248–270. doi:10.1177/0038040710375689

Rosen, L. (2012). STEM gets a boost from Business: Business leaders are partnering with elementary schools to help increase students' interest and achievement in STEM. Retrieved from https://www.naesp.org/book/export/html/4708

Shulman, L. S. (1986). Those who understand: Knowledge growth in teaching. *Educational Researcher*, *15*(2), 4–14. doi:10.3102/0013189X015002004

Snape, P., & Fox-Turnbull, W. (2013). Perspectives of authenticity: Implementation in technology education. *International Journal of Technology and Design Education*, *23*(1), 51–68. doi:10.1007/s10798-011-9168-2

Strobel, J., Wang, J., Weber, N. R., & Dyehouse, M. (2013). The role of authenticity in design-based learning environments: The case of engineering education. *Computers & Education*, *64*, 143–152. doi:10.1016/j.compedu.2012.11.026

Sun, Y., & Strobel, J. (2013). Elementary engineering education (EEE) adoption and expertise development framework: An inductive and deductive study. *Journal of Pre-College Engineering Education Research*, *3*(1), 32–52.

Sun, Y., & Strobel, J. (2014). From knowing-about to knowing-to: Development of engineering PCK by elementary teachers through perceived learning and implementing difficulties. *American Journal of Engineering Education*, *5*(1), 41–60.

Supovitz, J. A., Mayers, D. P., & Kahle, J. B. (2000). Promoting inquiry-based instructional practice: The longitudinal impact of professional development in the context of systemic reform. *Educational Policy*, *14*(3), 331–356. doi:10.1177/0895904800014003001

Tinto, V. (1993). *Leaving college: rethinking the causes and cures of student attrition* (2nd ed.). Chicago, London: University of Chicago Press.

Van Driel, J. H., Beijaard, D., & Verloop, N. (2001). Professional development and reform in science education: The role of teachers' practical knowledge. *Journal of Research in Science Teaching*, *38*(2), 137–158. doi:10.1002/1098-2736(200102)38:2<137::AID-TEA1001>3.0.CO;2-U

Van Driel, J. H., Verloop, N., & de Vos, W. (1998). Developing science teachers' pedagogical content knowledge. *Journal of Research in Science Teaching*, *35*(6), 673–695. doi:10.1002/(SICI)1098-2736(199808)35:6<673::AID-TEA5>3.0.CO;2-J

Vann, C. B. (2013). Pioneering a new path for STEM education. *Industrial Engineer*, *45*(5), 30–33.

Vygotsky, L. S. (1978). *Mind and society: The development of higher mental processes*. Cambridge, MA: Harvard University Press.

Wilson, S. M. (2011). Effective STEM teacher preparation, induction, and professional development. Paper presented at the National Research Counci's Workshop on Successful STEM Education in K–12 Schools, Washington, DC.

Yasar, S., Baker, D., Robinson-Kurpius, S., Krause, S., & Roberts, C. (2006). Development of a survey to assess K–12 teachers' perception of Engineers and familiarity with teaching design, engineering, and technology. *The Journal of Engineering Education*, *95*(3), 205–216. doi:10.1002/j.2168-9830.2006.tb00893.x

Yoon, K. S., Duncan, T., Lee, S. W. Y., Scarloss, B., & Shapley, K. (2007). Reviewing the evidence on how teacher professional development affects student achievement (Vol. 033). Washington, DC: US Department of Education.

KEY TERMS AND DEFINITIONS

Authentic Learning: A wide variety of educational and instructional techniques focused on connecting what students are taught in school to real-world issues, problems, and applications.
Content Knowledge: knowledge about the actual subject matter that is to be learned or taught.
Professional Development: Form vocational training that allow someone to acquire new knowledge and skills that relate to his/her profession, job responsibilities, or work environment.
Scaffolding: The support given during the learning process to facilitate learning.
Social Constructivist Theory: A theory that suggests that social interaction plays a fundamental role in the development of cognition and the construction of knowledge.

Chapter 6
The Role of Teacher Leadership for Promoting Professional Development Practices

Patricia Dickenson
National University, USA

Judith L. Montgomery
University of California Santa Cruz, USA

ABSTRACT

This chapter examines the status of teacher professional development in mathematics and explores the role of teacher leadership to promote innovative professional development strategies that sustain the growth and development of an organization. Survey data was collected from teacher leader participants of one mathematics professional development organization to understand how participants' growth and development as a teacher leader not only shaped their mathematics instructional practices, but influenced their choices in leadership roles. Further the authors share how the learning environment and pedagogical choices of the project director supported a teacher-driven professional development approach. Recommendations as well as a model for developing a teacher-driven professional development organization are provided for replication.

INTRODUCTION

The authors' of this chapter explore the development and growth of ten mathematics' teachers and one program director in a University-based mathematics professional development organization that has been established for over ten years in Northern California of the United States of America. Teacher leaders' profiles, motivations and beliefs about mathematics practices were examined to determine what elements of belonging to a professional mathematics development organization shaped their classroom practices and role as a teacher leader in a professional development organization. Interviews with the director of the organization were conducted to gain insight to the evolution and progression of the organization through social changes, political policies and reform efforts. The organization capitalizes on the idea of

DOI: 10.4018/978-1-4666-9471-2.ch006

"teachers-teaching-teachers" and the human desire of belonging, to grow and sustain teacher membership. The approach to a teacher-centered professional development is teacher-driven and created and rooted in a constructivist approach of learning whereby participants construct knowledge about how children best learn mathematics through active techniques such as applying approaches to their classroom practice and demonstrating practices and student work for feedback and replication. Further, participants share their ideas with colleagues in informal group meetings and demonstrate their best practices at professional development seminars to share with other teachers for investigation.

Traditional Professional Development Scenario

The last bell of the school day has rung, Ms. Myer scrambles around her fourth grade classroom to gather student workbooks to review while she attends staff development in the school cafeteria. Ms. Myer has been a teacher at Longview Elementary for the past few years, where every Wednesday the teachers listen to a presentation given by the school administration or guest speaker. Fresh baked cookies and coffee are located in the back of the room where the teachers sign in as they enter. Ms. Myer values the time to work with her grade level peers and share what she is doing in her classroom, but professional development at Longview Elementary does not leave much time for teachers to collaborate and share best practices. Before the presentation begins and whenever breaks occurs Ms. Myer shares a few ideas and hears what her colleagues are doing but rarely do they speak during the presentation.

Although this week's presentation is on problem solving in mathematics a topic Ms. Myer class is struggling with, she finds the presenter misses the mark when it comes to what can actually work in her classroom. The strategies that are shared may be appropriate for typical fourth graders but this year her class is struggling with reading and comprehension so she usually skips this section in the student textbook.

Ms. Myer feels a sense of relief as she closes the last of her student's workbooks and records their grades just before the presentation draws to a close, "time well spent" she thinks to herself. She asks her colleague for name of the presenter to place on the top of the form and quickly completes the evaluation consisting of questions where she has to rate the presenters' style and content, rather than reflect on her experience. When asked "What did you enjoy the most?" she writes "problem solving" but thinks silently "this won't work in my classroom". Yes it is not surprising to hear that while 90 percent of teachers reported participating in professional development, most of the teachers also reported it was totally useless (Darling-Hammond et al, 2009).

If student achievement is the desired result than teacher professional development must ensure that teacher participants are actively involved in the process and ideas are transferrable to the classroom. Much like the students who enter the K-12 classroom, teachers also bring their experiences, beliefs and views of learning into professional development. Shaping a teacher's beliefs and pedagogical practices takes time, commitment and support. Teacher professional development however is often presented through a traditional teaching lens where participants are passive receivers of information rather than active participants. This model of instruction is outdated and lacks impact to teachers' daily practice. As such in the case study of Ms. Myer teachers "check out" when the traditional professional development approach does not require participants to be actively involved in the process. It is necessary for professional development models take into account what Confucius has been credited in saying "I hear and I forget. I see and I remember. I do and I understand." Research has found traditional professional development fails to produce substantive or sustained change in teachers' practice (Cohen and HIll, 2001; Parsad et al., 2001; Porter et al., 2000). Traditional professional development usually consists of in-service days

The Role of Teacher Leadership for Promoting Professional Development Practices

through the district in which techniques or ideas are shared (Little, 1993) or university based courses which teachers attend that focus on academic perspectives (Stein, Smith, & Silver, 1999). Other modes of professional development such as one-day workshops often make teacher professional development "intellectually superficial, disconnected from deep issues of curriculum and learning, fragmented, and noncumulative" (Ball & Cohen, 1999, pp.3-4). There are four critical characteristics of professional development that improve instruction (Knapp, 2003) they are:

- Aligned with reform initiatives
- Ongoing
- Grounded in a collaborative and inquiry-based approach to learning
- Embedded in the context-specific need of a particular setting

In mathematics shifting the paradigm of traditional teacher professional development is imperative in a time where problem solving, conceptual understanding and critical thinking are essential skills for students to enter higher-level mathematics course and without access to higher-level mathematic students may not have the prerequisites to enter college or professional careers and this is especially true for disadvantaged and minority students (Achieve, 2008). But such a shift in teacher professional development requires not only changing the model but the decision making process. It requires a growth-driven approach that is ongoing and collaborative from the moment planning begins. Research has found when professional development is driven by the needs of the participants their content knowledge and practice grows and this directly impacts the students in their class (Darling-Hammond and McLaughlin 1995; Little 1998). The purpose of this chapter is to examine one such model of professional development in mathematics. The present study examines an established and successful teacher professional development organization and the teacher participants' motivations and reasons for engaging and becoming part of the organization. Through this lens it is the hope that other organization can develop best practices for designing and supporting teacher-centric professional development practices that fosters leadership skills and promotes collaborative practices within a professional organization. The goals of this chapter are:

1. Discuss present research on Teacher Professional Development in Mathematics and the Role of Teacher Leadership.
2. Identify teacher leaders' motivation for participating in professional development.
3. Explain the process of developing a Teacher Leadership team.
4. Describe how a volunteer leadership team designs and executes a mathematics professional event.

BACKGROUND

Teacher Professional Development

Research suggests what hinges on reducing the achievement gap is not just a students' home address, but the quality of the classroom teacher (Center for Public Education, 2005). While the achievement gap in the United States between minority and non-minority students continues to persist and an even greater international gap appears when students from the United States are compared to their international peers (Timms, 2011). Professional development is a critical means of shaping teachers practices especially in a time when reform initiatives require significant changes to the way teachers teach and students are assessed.

There are numerous models in which teacher professional development is conducted however the end goal is usually the same, to improve teachers' practice for the benefit of student learning. According to Yoon and colleagues (2007) professional development affects student achievement through three steps:

First, professional development enhances teacher knowledge and skills. Second better knowledge and skills improve classroom teaching. Third improved teaching raises student achievement. If one link is weak or missing, better student learning cannot be expected. If a teacher fails to apply new ideas from professional development to classroom instruction, for example, students will not benefit from the teachers' professional development (p.11).

Numerous studies have revealed the positive correlation between teacher effectiveness and student achievement (Haycock, 1998; Hanushek & Rivkin, 2003; Marzano, 2003; Nye, Konstantopoulos, & Jedges, 2004). Further value-added studies by Sanders and Rivers (1996, as cited in Haycock, 1998) found that students who were assigned to three effective teachers in a row scored up to 30 percentile points higher in mathematics assessments than children assigned to three ineffective teachers in a row. Whether a reform initiative is successful in education is largely determined by the qualifications and effectiveness of the teachers who are implementing it. Teacher professional development is a major focus of systemic reform initiatives (Corcoran, 1995; Corcoran, Shields, & Zucker, 1998).

In the United States, the Common Core State Standards (CCSS) was developed to establish consistency in what students should be able to know and do at every grade level across the states for mathematics and English Language Arts. The goals of the initiative is to raise the achievement of students as compared to international peers, reduce remediation in college courses, and ensure all students are college and career ready (Common Core State Standards Initiative, 2015). In mathematics the CCSS require teachers to change what they teach as well as how they teach. There is a greater focus on fewer topics at each grade level and a higher expectation for students to master the concepts. Pedagogical practices form a balanced approach to teaching that includes conceptual understanding, procedural skills and fluency. Adopting a reform approach of teaching will require effective professional development for teachers to learn new approaches to teaching concepts.

Mathematics Professional Development

In a review of the research on mathematics teaching and learning conducted for the National Council of Teachers of Mathematics, James Hiebert (1999) found teacher learning shared several core features:

ongoing (measured in years) collaboration of teachers for purposes of planning with the explicit goal of improving students' achievement of clear learning goals, anchored by attention to students' thinking, the curriculum, and pedagogy, with access to alternative ideas and methods and opportunities to observe these in action and to reflect on the reasons for their effectiveness . . . (p. 15).

Yoon and colleagues (2007) also examined 1,300 studies of professional development research to find which types of programs had the greatest impact on student achievement. Programs that were lengthy and

The Role of Teacher Leadership for Promoting Professional Development Practices

intensive had the greatest impact. In fact several studies have found the duration of professional development is related to the depth of teacher change (Shields, Marsh, & Adelman, 1998; Weiss, Montgomery, Ridgway,& Bond, 1998). Teachers much like students need an opportunity to practice and rehearse new skills prior to implementing them in the classroom. In fact research has found teachers need at least twenty instances of practice to master a new skill (Joyce & Showers, 2002). Further instructors of professional development can identify and address misconceptions as well as answer questions related to teaching strategies when teachers have an opportunity to develop expertise. In his research of teacher transferring new skills Bush (1984) found that about 10 percent of teachers could transfer a skill to practice when the training simply describes a skill to teachers. Darling-Hammond and colleagues (2009) analysis of well designed experimental studies found that professional development that includes over six to twelve months of contact hours with at least 30 to 100 hours in total spread over six to twelve months showed a positive and significant effect. In addition when professional development included at least 49 hours in a year, student achievement was raised by approximately 21 percentile points.

Research also shows that teachers will change their beliefs about how to teach something only after they see success with students (Guskey, 2002). Therefore it is imperative that professional development practices abandon the one-shot approach and develop ongoing dialogues that support a community of practice for all learners. Further giving teachers much like students time to achieve mastery, provides the facilitator with an opportunity to scaffold learning and support participants. Teachers are more likely to abandon a new practice and teach the way they were teaching when they do not see success, regardless of the research.

Additional research is needed to determine the efficacy of various types of professional development activities, such as colloquiums, pre-service and in-service trainings, workshops, and summer institutes. Studies are needed to evaluate professional development activities that are extended over time and across broad teacher learning communities to identify the processes and mechanisms that contribute to the development of teachers' learning communities (Bransford, Brown, &Cocking, 1999, p. 240).

In review much of the research shared with regards to professional development suggests teachers need to be engaged in learning opportunities that are continuous and lengthy and connected to practice. Teachers need multiple instances to practice new skills and see success in using the skills with students. Further teacher professional development should be a collaborative process that provides time for teachers to meet, plan curriculum, use data to design instruction and learn from each other. In high achieving countries about 60 percent of work time is classroom instruction whereas the remaining time is to collaborate with colleagues and develop curriculum and instruction, in the United States teachers spend about 80 percent of their time in classroom instruction (Darling Hammond, et al., 2009). Thus the present study is timely and much needed to understand how to develop and sustain teacher engagement in professional development practices.

THEORETICAL FRAMEWORK

Teacher Professional Development through a Constructivist Lens

The idea that teachers must learn more about the subjects they teach, and how students learn these subjects has been argued for quiet some time (Shulman & Sparks, 1992). Shifting to a mastery approach to teaching mathematics requires teachers to develop a greater understanding of subject matter as well as pedagogical practices that will support their students in applying, transferring, and constructing knowledge in different contexts. In addition teachers need to determine what skills, and knowledge a student has in order to design and scaffold instruction, and support students toward mastery. That being said planning for professional development requires a sophisticated understanding of the participants' level of understanding to bridge the gap between prior knowledge and new knowledge. Beyond the usual icebreaker, professional development models often fail to assess teachers' knowledge before they begin instruction. Working from a constructivist model to design professional development requires data to be used to design instruction, informal and formal assessment to be embedded within the context of the training, training to be ongoing and monitored, and content delivery to be an active learning experience. School and districts can transform into a community of learners when adults are motivated to grow and learn through professional development (Zepeda, 1999).

When it comes to mathematics professional development teaching strategies to promote multiple representations and ways of knowing is essential, especially in a time where reform practices are valued. However in order for strategies to transfer into teachers' classroom practice authentic activities must be embedded to provide an opportunity to experiment and explore new concepts, construct knowledge, engage in dialogue with peers and develop the confidence to master new strategies. Adult learners need to see the results of their efforts as well as get feedback on their progress toward reaching their goal (Zemke and Zemke, 1995). Additionally, there is value when teachers not only hear their colleagues share successful teaching methods but see colleagues demonstrate these practices. Much like students modeling for their classmates, having a relevant peer demonstrate a task or share an experience provides evidence that such a goal is obtainable (Omrod, p. 259). Opinions about our own abilities are often formed by observing the successes and failures of other people, especially those with ability levels similar to our own (Dijkstra et al., 2008; Usher & Pajares, 2008; Zeldin & Pajares, 2000).

Teacher Leadership

According to Angelle & DeHart, (2011) teacher leadership is as varied as the context in which educators work, therefore there is not one singular meaning when it comes to teacher leadership. Educators may take on formal roles such as academic coach or grade level chair that require them to work outside the classroom or informal roles such as teacher advisor or mentor that focus on student development in the classroom. For this study, we will use Angelle and DeHart's (2011) definition of teacher leaders as:

those teachers who maintain focus on student learning, seek lifelong learning for themselves, use facilitation and presentation skills, engage others in shared vision and meaning, develop and maintain relationships, work with a sense of integrity, and plan and organize. (p. 143)

The field of leadership study has increasingly included the importance of teacher as leader in school reform (Crowther, Kaagan, Ferguson, & Hann, 2002; Frost, Durrant, Head, & Holden, 2000; Katzenmeyer & Moller, 2001; Murphy, 2005). Increasing the extent of teacher leadership in a school can bring positive change to schools, transforming the school into a place of adult, as well as student, learning (Ryan, 1999). Expertise is critical to the teacher leader, according to Snell and Swanson (2000), because teacher expertise is what establishes credibility with peers. Along with credibility, Childs-Bowen, Moller, and

The Role of Teacher Leadership for Promoting Professional Development Practices

Scrivner (2000) identified teacher competency as a major component of teacher leadership. Odell (1997) also stressed the importance of teacher competency by stating that "one cannot be an effective teacher leader if one is not first an accomplished teacher" (p. 122). Literature informs us that teacher leaders are those who have the ability to "encourage colleagues to change" (Wasley, 1991, p. 23) and have the willingness to "lead beyond the classroom and contribute to the community of learners" (Katzenmeyer & Moller, 2001, p. 17). In a traditional school structure teacher leaders are elected to serve in a position, are selected for a role or volunteer to take on a leadership position. What makes the teacher leaders in this chapter unique is their participation and willingness to serve is intrinsically driven by their desire to learn and improve their practice. The roles and responsibilities they take on for the organization are outside their school workplace.

Most teachers who take on leadership roles do not see themselves as leaders, as the term leader is often associated with those who take on formal positions such as principals or district supervisors. They perceive that most of their work is done informally through collaboration (Moller et al., 2001). Teacher leadership in an atmosphere of collaboration was found to be an element in successful change throughout the literature (Dimmock, 2002; Harris, 2002; Turk, 2001; Wikeley, Stoll, & Lodge, 2002).

What we know about teacher leaders is they must not operate in a vacuum to be effective. Teacher leaders must share their ideas, and beliefs with their colleagues and peers. Further when teachers learn from one another teacher leadership is significantly enhanced (Little, 1995). Boles and Troen (1994) characterized teacher leadership as a form of collective leadership in which teachers work collaboratively. Having the time, space, and opportunity for collaboration are essential for teacher leaders to reach their potential (Clemson Ingram & Fessler, 1997; Gehrke, 1991; Stone et al., 1997). The importance of sharing leadership to improving schools has been shown through out the literature (Harris, 2002; Moller et al., 2001; Snell & Swanson, 2000; Suranna & Moss, 2002). Similarly the idea of sharing leadership is aligned with the inner workings of the Monterey Bay Area Mathematics Project (MBAMP). Without the sharing of leadership in this volunteer leadership team the organization would not be able to sustain and support year round professional development for over ten years.

Teacher Leadership and Teacher Professional Development

Creating a bridge between teacher leadership and professional development is essential for two reasons: to enhance teacher leadership and to improve teacher practice. Previous research has suggested that teacher leadership can only be successful with the support of the school leadership (Harris, 2002; Moller et al., 2001). Further schools with the greatest extent of teacher leadership are led by principals who are empowering, treat teachers with respect, and value the work of teacher leaders (Acker-Hocever & Touchton, 1999). Unlike the traditional school leadership model which is administrator driven and selected the MBAMP organization is voluntary and teacher-driven as leadership roles and responsibilities take place outside of the traditional school day. This approach to developing a leadership team does not limit an organization in valuing the specific skills and styles of a selected group of teachers rather participation is teacher initiated allowing teachers to share their unique skills, knowledge and experiences.

Research has suggested that teacher leadership in a school is dependent on whether the top-level administrators in a school are able to relinquish power to teacher leaders (Little, 2002). MBAMP's model is based on the idea that teacher leadership can happen outside of the school district. Leadership should not be limited to a administrator directed process, as all teachers should be given the opportunity to lead. MBAMP is based on the teachers' desire to receive the benefits that come from being an MBAMP teacher leader. As a result of the teacher leadership opportunity MBAMP participants gain districts and schools are utilizing the leadership of these participants to support and train other teachers at their respective school site. Districts are funding teacher participants to attend MBAMP summer institutes so they can reap the benefit of having their teachers engage in year long professional development that impacts not only the participants classroom but their colleagues as well.

CONTEXT, RESEARCH DESIGN, AND MODES OF INQUIRY

Context

This research project took place over the course of one year examining the profile of participants who are involved with a university based mathematics professional development program in Northern California of the United States. The University based professional development program is one of 19 sites supported by the state of California and residing in a public university to support K-12 mathematics initiatives. The program offers year round professional development and support to teachers of students in grades K-12 through a variety of events including summer institutes, consulting services with local school districts, independent study programs and weekend seminars.

Research Design and Modes of Inquiry

Participants Survey: A total of ten participants responded to this survey. Survey questions were created based on the existing literature of professional development practices and teacher leadership and included both closed-ended and open-ended questions that allowed participants to share their beliefs, knowledge and experiences. A sample of an open-ended question is "How did your participation in the Teacher Leader team shape your classroom instruction?" Survey Monkey, an online web survey tool was used and a link was emailed to all participants of the University project. The survey had five parts: demographic information, reasons and motivations for working with MBAMP, qualities of the director, type of participation, and benefits of participation.

In-depth Interview: The director of the program was interviewed four times throughout the school year to understand how she develops and grows her professional development community. Multiple interviews were conducted to examine how her practices might change throughout the school year. Questions were asked to understand the processes to organize and structure mathematics professional development events, as well as establishing a professional development community that is teacher-driven and focused on the collective strengths of teacher leaders.

Analyzing Documents: In order to understand the history and context of the professional development organization as well as the growth and development over the last ten years meeting notes and documents from event planning as well as research grants were analyzed. Content analysis was conducted to interpret the various types of communication within the organization as well as the structure and process for developing professional development.

RESULTS

Demographics of Teacher Leaders: Table 1 displays the overall teacher leader participants' demographic data. The study focuses on ten participants who have been involved with the University of California Santa Cruz mathematics project for an average of more than five years.

70% of the participants in this survey identified as a K-12 teacher. In addition most of the participants held at least a Masters degree (80%) and a multiple subject teaching credential, which permits them to work at the K-6 grade level in a self-contained classroom.

Hours of Reported Work with MBAMP

Participants were asked to report the number of hours they have contributed as part of the MBAMP organization. This includes planning, presenting and attending MBAMP events. Results appear in Figure 1.

Overall the majority of participants reported more than 100 hours of work with MBAMP. 40% of participants shared they have contributed at least 30 to 50 hours and 10% contributed 50-70 hours of professional development.

Identified Roles as MBAMP Teacher Leader

Participants were asked to identify the roles they have engaged in while actively involved in the MBAMP professional development organization (see Table 2).

Table 1. Overall teacher participation

	N	P
Professional Position		
Teacher (K-5)	4	40%
Teacher (6-12)	3	30%
Administrator	1	10%
Retired Teacher (K-12)	1	10%
College Professor	1	10%
Years as Teacher Leader		
1-5	1	10%
5-10	4	40%
10-15	6	60%
Education Level		
Bachelors Only	1	10%
Masters	8	80%
Doctorate	1	10%
Credential		
Multiple Subject	7	70%
Single Subject	3	30%

Figure 1. Hours of work with MBAMP

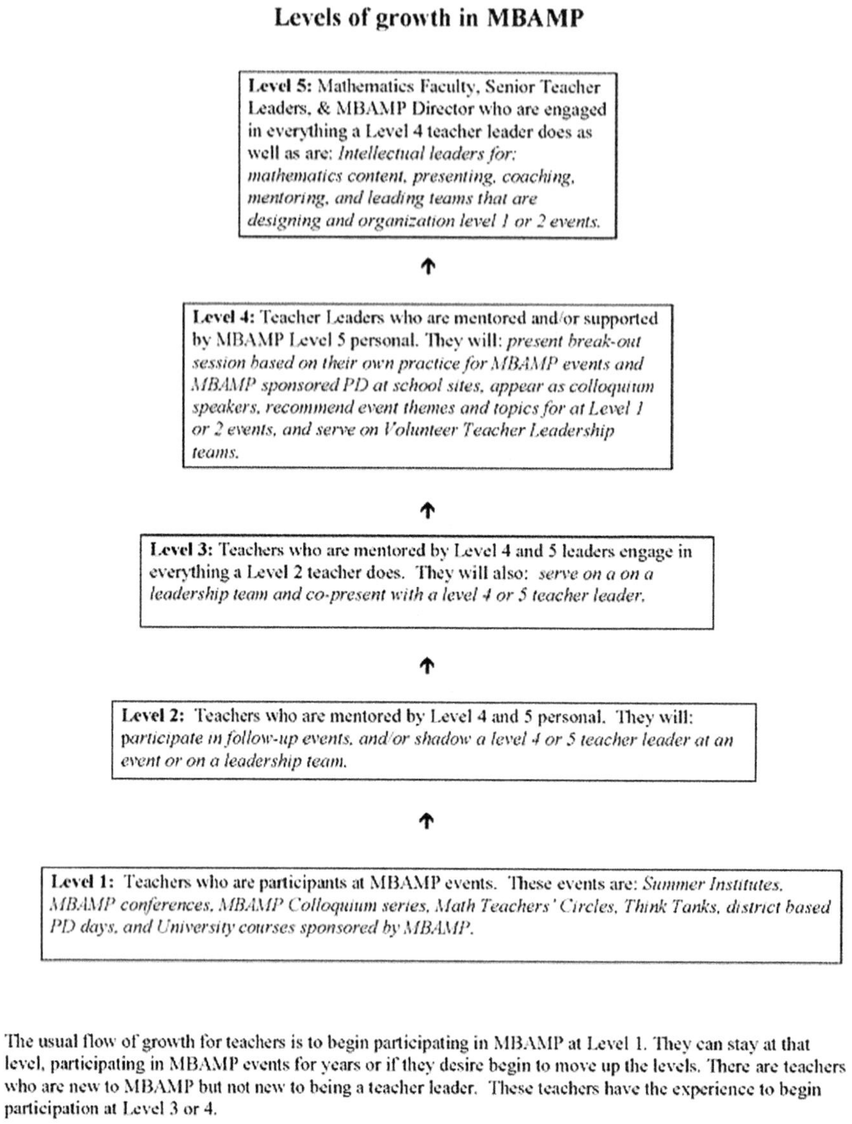

Levels of growth in MBAMP

> **Level 5:** Mathematics Faculty, Senior Teacher Leaders, & MBAMP Director who are engaged in everything a Level 4 teacher leader does as well as are: *Intellectual leaders for: mathematics content, presenting, coaching, mentoring, and leading teams that are designing and organization level 1 or 2 events.*

↑

> **Level 4:** Teacher Leaders who are mentored and/or supported by MBAMP Level 5 personal. They will: *present break-out session based on their own practice for MBAMP events and MBAMP sponsored PD at school sites, appear as colloquium speakers, recommend event themes and topics for at Level 1 or 2 events, and serve on Volunteer Teacher Leadership teams.*

↑

> **Level 3:** Teachers who are mentored by Level 4 and 5 leaders engage in everything a Level 2 teacher does. They will also: *serve on a on a leadership team and co-present with a level 4 or 5 teacher leader.*

↑

> **Level 2:** Teachers who are mentored by Level 4 and 5 personal. They will: *participate in follow-up events, and/or shadow a level 4 or 5 teacher leader at an event or on a leadership team.*

↑

> **Level 1:** Teachers who are participants at MBAMP events. These events are: *Summer Institutes, MBAMP conferences, MBAMP Colloquium series, Math Teachers' Circles, Think Tanks, district based PD days, and University courses sponsored by MBAMP.*

The usual flow of growth for teachers is to begin participating in MBAMP at Level 1. They can stay at that level, participating in MBAMP events for years or if they desire begin to move up the levels. There are teachers who are new to MBAMP but not new to being a teacher leader. These teachers have the experience to begin participation at Level 3 or 4.

The tasks were organized by type to identify the most common kinds of tasks that participants selected in their role of teacher leader. For administrative tasks, 90% of participants reported attending face-to-face meetings and 80% selected communicating via email for schedules, surveys, and flyers. For mentoring tasks, teacher leaders were most likely to report allowing visitors to come into their classroom for observation (60%) and least likely to report supporting a new teacher leader (20%). For advising tasks, 70% of teacher leaders reported they were most likely to engage in activities that include determining the direction of the 1-day conference, determining the direction of an institute (60%) and serving as a liaison between MBAMP and school districts (50%). Presenting and planning tasks that were commonly reported include planning and presenting an entire content session without support (80%) and breakout

Table 2. Identified roles as MBAMP teacher leader

	N	P
Administrative Tasks		
Promoting MBAMP events	10	10%
Attending face-to face planning meetings	9	90%
Writing grants or funding	4	40%
Giving email feedback		
For flyers, surveys or schedules	8	80%
For participants survey	5	50%
Daily schedule of an event	7	70%
Networking for MBAMP	7	70%
Mentoring Tasks		
Working with UCSC Pre-service Teachers	3	30%
Supporting a new Teacher Leader	2	20%
Attending Teacher Leader session to support	3	30%
Opening your classroom for visitor observation	6	60%
Advising Tasks		
Determining the direction of 1 day conference	7	70%
Determining the direction of an institute	6	60%
Assisting to start a new leadership team	4	40%
Finding other Teacher Leaders	3	30%
Serving as a liaison between MBAMP and school districts	5	50%
Presenting/Planning Tasks		
Breakout sessions with another teacher leader	6	60%
Entire content for session without support	8	80%
Solo Producing an entire event without director	2	20%
Producing an entire event with another teacher	3	30%
3 day institute	1	10%

session with another teacher leader (60%). Solo producing an entire event without director support was not commonly reported (20%). Teacher leaders were also less likely to report producing an entire event with another teacher (30%).

Perceived Benefit of Mathematics Professional Development Organization

Participants were asked to report the benefits they received from working with MBAMP. Teacher responses were organized into three categories: teaching skills, sense of belonging, and professional development skills (see Table 3).

90% of participants reported their experience with MBAMP deepened their pedagogical understanding. 80% of participants also reported their mathematical understanding deepened and they learned new teaching practices. Tasks that were identified as developing a teachers' sense of belonging were highly

Table 3. Perceived benefit of MBAMP

	N	P
Teaching Skills		
Deepening my mathematics understanding	8	80
Deepening my pedagogical understanding	9	90
Learning new teaching practices	8	80
Sense of Belonging		
Part of a professional community of educators	10	100
Feeling connected an less isolated	7	70
Sharing my teaching experience with teachers	10	100
Being a professional outside of the class	8	80
Sharing about your work with MBAMP	8	80
Professional Development Skills		
Developing a session to present	6	60
Developing the skills to present to other teachers	7	70
Spreading the word on effective practices	10	100
Planning an institute	8	80
Planning a 1-day conference	7	70

rated and include 100% of the participants reported a benefit of being "part of a professional community of educators". Participants also reported sharing their teaching practices (100%), being a professional outside of the classroom (80%) and sharing what they are doing at MBAMP (80%) to be a benefit as well. The most common professional development skill reported was 100% of participants identified spreading the word on effective practices to be a benefit of their work at MBAMP. They also reported planning an institute (80%) and 1-day conference (70%) to be a benefit as well.

Shaping Classroom Instruction

Participants were asked to share how their participation in the MBAMP organization shaped their classroom instruction. Similar to the results from the survey above the participants' responses were generally related to three specific areas: teaching skills, sense of belonging, and presentation skills. With regards to teaching skills one participant shared "I have learned specifically how to implement number talks and use different engagement strategies which encourage my students to communicate and be part of our discussions about math." Participant responses also indicate the value of belonging to a professional development organization with regards to their own motivation and teaching style "being involved in leadership helps me to stay motivated to teach the way we preach" and "MBAMP helps inspire me to keep stretching for the next best practice". Sense of belonging to a professional development organization was also evident in teacher responses as one teacher shared "It has sustained me through difficult times" and "I bring more of a spirit of curiosity into my classroom now than I did previously". With regards to presentation skills teachers reported "I became more confident in my presentation skills" and "I use my classroom as a lab to try new lessons or ideas that I consider sharing with other teachers."

Participants were also asked to provide a specific example of how MBAMP supported their work in the school or classroom. Participant responses reflect not only how specific professional development shaped their practice but also how the opportunity to partake in a leadership role influenced their professional growth and school community, one participant shared:

MBAMP provided needed support and structure for organizing professional development at our school site throughout the year, from the Winter Colloquium to the Summer Institute. Those opportunities allowed us to not only develop our leadership as math training facilitators, but also as offered a regular forum for deeper and informed professional collegial conversations about math practice. From there we have been able to carry the message to others and share resources at our individual schools.

Several other participants also shared how their involvement in the organization continued to further their professional growth as an educator. One participant shared "MBAMP has supported me by offering resources such as model lessons from other teachers and the opportunity to borrow materials and books to try in my class" and "As a science lecturer and student teacher supervisor, I am constantly using MBAMP material with my students."

Leading Teacher Leaders

Participants were asked "what qualities do you find important in working with the director of the MBAMP organization" and "share what the director does well and can improve". Several themes emerged in the participant responses as valuable qualities of a director. Flexibility emerged as a strong theme in participants' responses. Participants stated the director was flexible and would provide time for the leaders to develop and grow into teacher leaders. "Judith's flexibility, creativity and enthusiastic response to meeting teacher training needs provides a needed contrast to more traditionally structured professional development. That flexibility encourages others to take leadership." Figure 2 shows the most reported comments regarding qualities of a director. The qualities were organized into four categories: management style, personal qualities, vision and technical knowledge.

For Technical knowledge and personal qualities one participant shared:

The director of MBAMP does a really good job of bringing people together. Everyone loves the leadership dinner we have at the beginning of the school year where we discuss plans for the year and share a good meal. I also think she stays on top of current information in the field of mathematics education, and shares these resources with all of the leaders. She also makes it clear how much she appreciates the team and our input.

DISCUSSION

The results of this study found all of the participants reported at least 30 hours of work with MBAMP. This finding is significant as Hammond and colleagues found at least 30 hours of professional development a year leads to significant impact in student achievement (2009). More than 60% of participants indicated they spent more than 50 hours a year engaged in professional development. Hammond and colleagues found participants who engage in at least 49 hours in one-year student achievement by approximately

Figure 2. Qualities of director

```
              Management Style:          Personal Qualities:
                 Efficient                Sense of Humor
                 Productive                   Passion
                Encouraging                 Enthusiasm

                   Vision:              Technical Knowledge:
                    Open                 Content Knowledge
                  Flexible               Current Research
                  Creative               Teaching knowledge
```

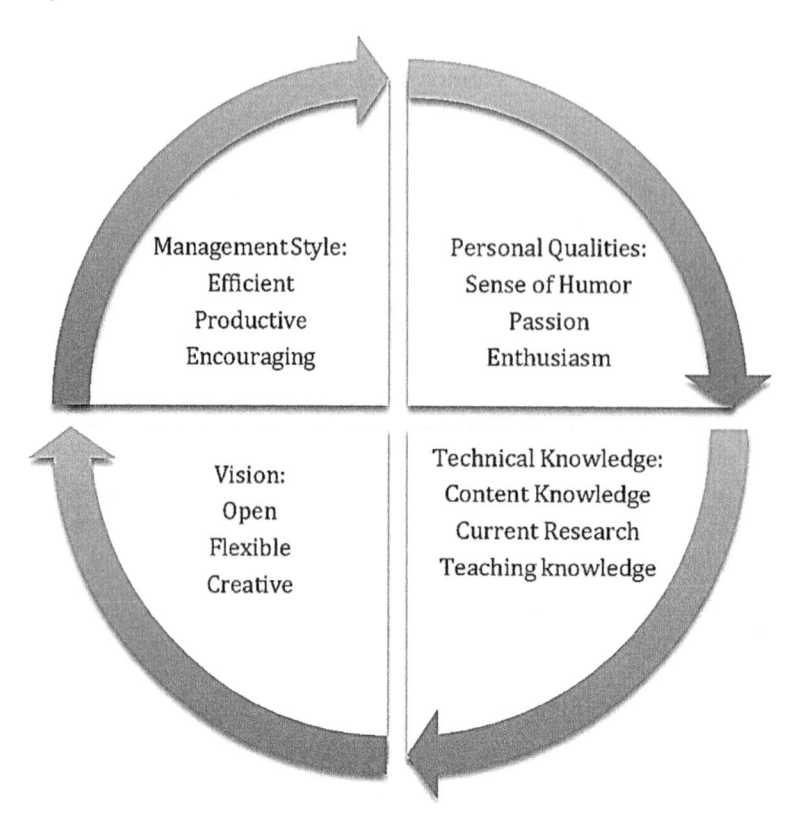

21 percentile points. Although the purpose of this study was not to identify if student achievement was gained as a result of professional development, it is worthy to note that the participants in this study are engaged in activities that have been found to have significant impact on student achievement. Future research should examine if the impact from professional development does lead to an increase in achievement from a classroom and school level.

The types of roles teacher leader participants engage in extend beyond the typical task of planning and presenting material. Results from this study show in order for an organization to be successful and thrive participants need to contribute to the growth and direction of the organization. Networking and sharing information beyond just the day of the event is essential to build capacity and to create a sense of community and belonging in an organization that extends beyond the traditional school day. Although digital tools are available and accessible, the research from this study suggests it is still of value for team members to meet face-to-face in order to establish a bond and commitment among colleagues. A sense of belonging emerged in both the quantitative and qualitative data from teacher participants as a valuable benefit of their work with MBAMP.

The most common administrative task included attending face-to-face meetings this finding suggests participants see the value in making personal connections with colleagues to support the work they are doing together. Communicating via email regarding administrative tasks such as schedules, flyers and surveys were also commonly reported by participants (80%) suggesting that teacher leaders are able to distinguish between the types of tasks that can be completed without personal communication and the types of tasks that can be delegated among peers. Moreover participant responses also indicate the feeling that their time face-to-face was well spent, highly structured and organized. Higher-order tasks that require participants to think critically and negotiate meaning are more valuable during face-to-face meetings whereas lower-level demand tasks can be managed and completed via electronic communication.

Mentoring tasks that were highly reported include allowing a visitor to observe (80%) but least likely to include supporting a new teacher leader (20%) this finding suggests the teacher leaders in this study were less likely to take on a coaching and supportive role. This could be an area for growth for this organization. The program director and/or experience teacher leaders may consider ways to promote teacher mentoring. Teacher leaders were more likely to report engaging in activities such as allowing someone to observe them in their class, but less likely to engage in activities that new teacher leaders often need to develop their competence and confidence as a teacher leader. Since teacher leaders were also less likely to report finding other teacher leaders (30%) this may be an area for growth within the organization. Training and advisement may be necessary to support teacher leaders in this task.

Common advising tasks include determining the direction of a conference (70%) and institute (60%). This is aligned with the types presenting and planning tasks that were commonly reported by teacher leaders such as planning and presenting a breakout session and doing this without the support of a teacher leader. These findings suggest teacher leaders appreciate the autonomy and choice that the director provides in designing and delivering professional development. Only two of the participants shared they were able to produce an entire event without the director. More training may be necessary by the director or Level 5 teacher leaders to give teacher leaders the support to produce an entire event independently.

Establishing a University-School Model of Teacher Professional Development

The Monterey Bay Area Math Project (MBAMP) is a site of the California Math Project (CMP) and part of the California Subject Matter Project (CSMP). CMP was founded in the early 1980s through a grant from the University of California Office of the President (UCOP) in order to provide Professional Development (PD) to K–12 math teachers. The original seed money funded a 21-day summer retreat for 15 to 30 teachers and teacher-leaders and UC faculty to support the participants in pedagogy, mathematics content and leadership skills. At first, there was no need for MBAMP to write grants or partner with school districts because the UCOP funding covered all program expenses. At this point, all of MBAMP staff was able to spend all their time in service of summer institutes and developing teacher-leaders. In 2001, however, UCOP reduced their funding by 70 percent. As a result, the originally promised "seed" funding became conditional. In order to receive the money, each site needed to develop a plan outlining how they would find additional funds for developing teacher leadership; staffing the site; offering the summer institute; continuing to work with Mathematics faculty and Mathematics Education faculty; serving a minimum of 200 teachers from low-performing school districts; working with regional Mathematics PD providers; building relationships and partnerships with local school districts; building relationships and partnerships with other university programs involved with PD. The requirement to "develop teacher-leadership" forms the cornerstone of all CMP work. It is the presence of teacher-leaders that enables the program's unique "teachers-teaching-teachers" approach to professional development. In the face of little to no funding for this foundational requirement, MBAMP director developed the Volunteer Teacher Leadership method. This helped MBAMP change so it could thrive despite lack of funding and continue developing teacher-leaders.

Volunteer Leadership Team

The Volunteer Leadership Team (VLT) is the backbone of every MBAMP event. Whether conducting a one-day conference; Teacher Learning Community (TLC); or a monthly colloquium series; the VLT plays a vital support role. Each team collectively operates to advise the MBAMP director, helping with and consulting about every aspect of the event.

In today's financial climate, it is a challenge to reward the leadership team for their keystone role. MBAMP cannot pay teacher-leaders the compensation that their invaluable work merits. Furthermore, MBAMP asks teachers to do high quality work outside of their regular working day—work that their district is not particularly interested in. However after teachers become MBAMP teacher leaders districts typically want to use them at a district level.

In Figure 3 MBAMP Teacher Leader Growth and Governance there are five levels of teacher-leaders. As noted in the model each level denotes a certain level of content knowledge and professional development (PD) responsibilities. The model consists of five levels of participation for teachers in MBAMP events. These are the ways a teacher can grow with MBAMP. Teachers can enter at any level they are qualified to.

- Level 1 is where a teacher might be introduced to MBAMP for the first time. This might be the first time a teacher has done any professional development outside of their district.
- Level 2 is for teachers who are interested in going a bit deeper with MBAMP. They make a commitment to attend a monthly colloquium session, work on an independent study or be mentored (usually by email) by the director or a senior teacher-leader.
- Level 3 is for teachers who want to become teacher leaders they take a co-leadership role on a leadership team or assist a senior teacher leader in a presentation.
- Level 4 is for teachers who are ready to present a PD session independently. They want the support provided by the director or a senior teacher leader to have the session as part of an event. Many teacher leaders stay at this level, because they do not have the desire or possibly the time to take on more responsibility.
- Level 5 is for teachers who are ready to head up a leadership team or produce an event on their own. They determine when the director needs to give them support. These teacher leaders are often paid an honorarium for the work they do.

Teacher Leader Developing A Mathematics Professional Development Event

At level 5 teacher leaders can construct a MBAMP event independent of the support from a senior teacher leader and director. They determine when the director will need to support them as she is available to meet or via email. The teacher leaders can develop their own leadership team and schedule meetings to determine the planning and outcomes of an MBAMP event. The teachers determine how much time they have to spend on their MBAMP work. The below excerpt is a detailed outline of what transpired for the MBAMP 2015 Winter conference in terms of work and time spent.

The Role of Teacher Leadership for Promoting Professional Development Practices

Figure 3. Teacher leader growth and governance

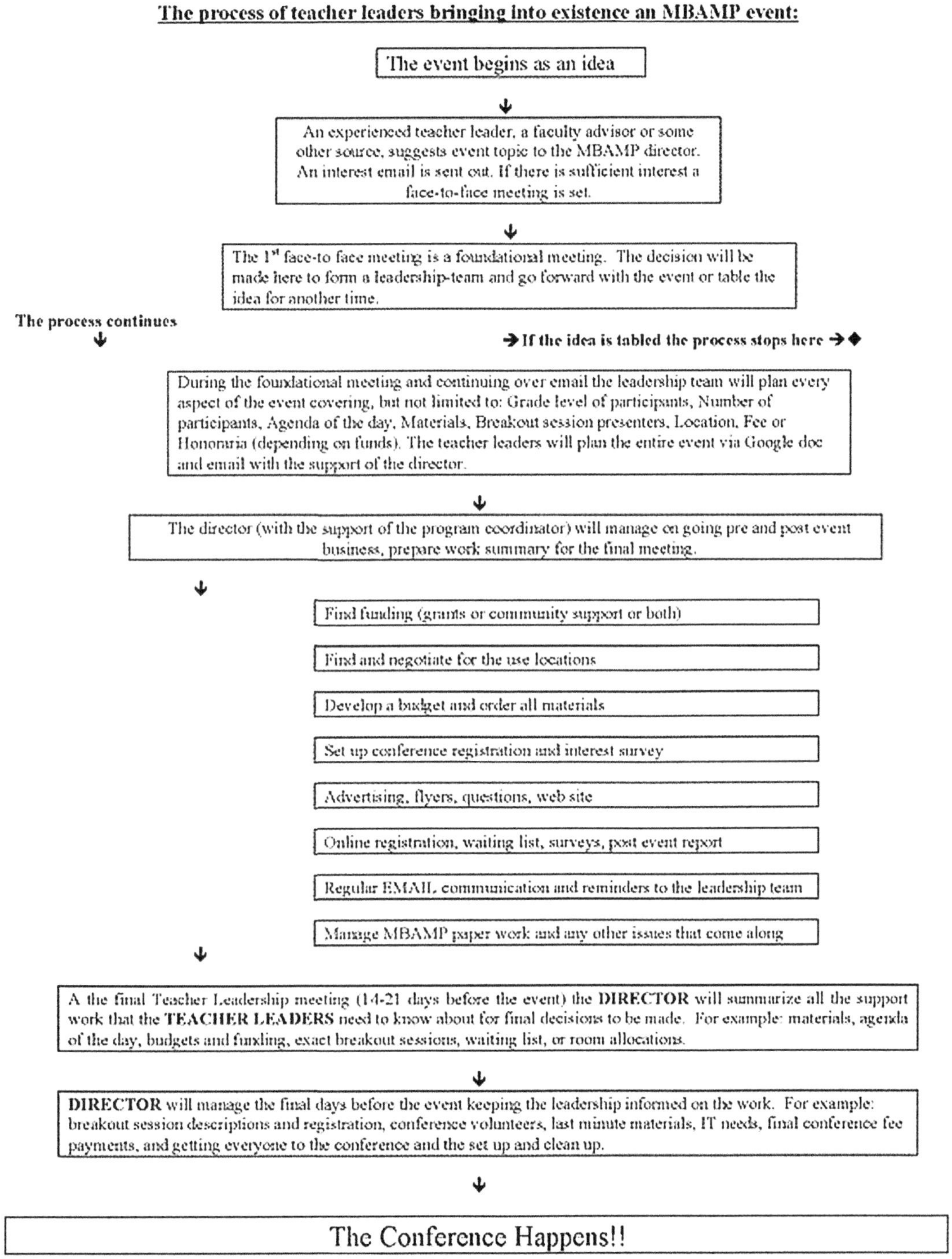

The process of teacher leaders bringing into existence an MBAMP event:

The event begins as an idea
⬇
An experienced teacher leader, a faculty advisor or some other source, suggests event topic to the MBAMP director. An interest email is sent out. If there is sufficient interest a face-to-face meeting is set.
⬇
The 1st face-to face meeting is a foundational meeting. The decision will be made here to form a leadership-team and go forward with the event or table the idea for another time.

The process continues
⬇   ➔ **If the idea is tabled the process stops here** ➔ ◆

During the foundational meeting and continuing over email the leadership team will plan every aspect of the event covering, but not limited to: Grade level of participants, Number of participants, Agenda of the day, Materials, Breakout session presenters, Location, Fee or Honoraria (depending on funds). The teacher leaders will plan the entire event via Google doc and email with the support of the director.
⬇
The director (with the support of the program coordinator) will manage on going pre and post event business, prepare work summary for the final meeting.
⬇

- Find funding (grants or community support or both)
- Find and negotiate for the use locations
- Develop a budget and order all materials
- Set up conference registration and interest survey
- Advertising, flyers, questions, web site
- Online registration, waiting list, surveys, post event report
- Regular EMAIL communication and reminders to the leadership team
- Manage MBAMP paper work and any other issues that come along

⬇
A the final Teacher Leadership meeting (14-21 days before the event) the **DIRECTOR** will summarize all the support work that the **TEACHER LEADERS** need to know about for final decisions to be made. For example: materials, agenda of the day, budgets and funding, exact breakout sessions, waiting list, or room allocations.
⬇
DIRECTOR will manage the final days before the event keeping the leadership informed on the work. For example: breakout session descriptions and registration, conference volunteers, last minute materials, IT needs, final conference fee payments, and getting everyone to the conference and the set up and clean up.
⬇

The Conference Happens!!

- February 2014:Teachers read an initial email, sent by the MBAMP director inviting them to a meeting about the start of a possible teacher leadership team around the subject of Mathematics PD and the arts. (Teachers 5-min, Director 25-min)
- March 2014: A venue (often a coffee shop) is chosen for a face-to-face meeting to discuss with all interested teachers and an electronic poll is sent out to determine the day and time. (Teachers 5-min, Director 25-min).
- March 2014: The face-to face meeting happens, the director makes the pitch for math and art and describes a bit of the history around the idea and explains why each person was invited. Each person has a chance to share their thoughts, their interest in math and art and ask each other questions. At the end of the meeting 5 teachers volunteered to be part of the leadership team. A follow up meeting for planning is set for August (90 minutes).
- March 2014: The meeting notes are sent out to all the participants with the date of the next meeting. (Director 25-min)
- August 2014: At this 2nd face-to-face meeting the teacher leaders commit to participation. They decide the date for the MBAMP Winter conference on Jan 24, 2015. Four people on the team will present and they will look for outside presenters. They decide the possible topics for the Math and Art day are: literature, music, dance, visual art, graphic art and math walks. They decide the event will be held at a school site as they would like an auditorium for the dance and music. (90 minutes)
- Between August 2014 and December 2014 Teacher-leaders are connected by email and the director does the work to get location and participants. The following tasks are completed via electronic communication:
    - Sending out flyers electronically to past participants, and contacts from districts and county offices.
    - Setting up online registration (The registration is also a survey that will be used to inform the leadership team when they do their final planning for the breakout sessions)
    - Keeping leadership team informed as the event fills.
    - Monitoring the registration and setting up the waiting list when the event is full.
    - Contacting districts about POs for conference fees
    - Emailing participants with conference information
    - Finalizing the details for the school site (a teacher liaison from the school for the event, insurance, required rooms, school rules, etc…)
    - Setting up the final face-to-face meeting
- Jan 2015 the last face-to-face meeting happens. This time the team meets at the school site where the event will be with the teacher liaison. The team tours the site, reviews the registration survey, determines the agenda and the breakout sessions of the day and decides which rooms they want to use for the event. Four members of the team are also presenters. There will be only one outside presenter. (90 minutes)
- Jan 24, 2015 the day of the event. For leadership team members who are not presenting they will be at the event setting up and monitoring the event. For leadership members who are presenting they will prep their session and also help when they are not presenting. (8 hours, + prepping time for presenters)
- February 2015 All teacher leaders and participants will be sent an event post survey. For the leadership it will focus on their experience as a leadership team member and their impressions of the

The Role of Teacher Leadership for Promoting Professional Development Practices

event. For participants it will be a post survey about experience at the conference and what it will lead to. (Director: 1 hour to make the survey, Teacher-leaders and Participants: 30 min to take the survey)
- February 2015: Using the survey results the director composes a Math/Art conference report. It will be sent to all districts who paid for teachers to attend and to the leadership team.

The hours of work time for teacher leaders will range from 15 - 20 hours to 40 hours. The hours of work time for the director will be about 80 hours. The work will take place over a period of 1 year. The remote work is done at everyone's convenience using computers, phone or tablets. The flexible remote aspect makes the time spent very efficient. Teacher leaders are involved in email streams about parts of the conference they care about. The teachers determine how much or how little they work.

Planning a Professional Development Event

The planning of a Monterey Bay Area professional development event begins with an idea (see Figure 4).

The critical INPUT is an idea for a topic and interested teacher leaders. The OUTPUT for the teachers is the work of directing and producing the event, for the director it is using the infrastructure of MBAMP in service of supporting the vision of the teacher leaders, being the person with the institutional knowledge, helping the leadership team to make sure they do not overlook any details. The teacher participants who

Figure 4. Planning an MBAMP event

INPUT +	OUTPUT =	OUTCOMES	
		Teacher Leaders	**MBAMP's region**
• MBAMP Infrastructure • Teacher Leaders who self identify as Leadership Team Members • Potential Teacher Leaders who self identify or are discovered by Level[1] 4 or 5 MBAMP personal.	• Teacher Leaders nominate themes for events • Teacher Leaders design, organize and present at MBAMP events • Teachers take event content back to their classroom • Teacher do Independent studies with Teacher Leaders • Teachers and Teacher Leaders communicate via the online forum • Teachers borrow MBAMP materials and books. • Teacher Leaders mentor each other • At appropriate times, Teacher Leaders network for MBAMP in their district meetings	• Teacher-to-teacher mentoring occurs through out MBAMP's region • Online forum helps teachers feel connected and encourages them to develop their practice • Teachers visit other teacher in their classroom • Teachers in any given school collaborate across grades, providing year to year consistency for students • Teacher Leaders pedagogical and content knowledge flourish • Teachers move from Level to Level in MBAMP participation	• Teachers parents and administrators are talking about MBAMP and MBAMP's profile raises • Students respond with increased: 　○ Mathematical intuition and understanding 　○ Higher achievement on assessments 　○ Positive feelings associated with mathematics
Continually Developing Resources: Curriculum, Funding, Teacher Leaders, and Professional Relationships (University, Districts, County, Community)			

Teacher Leadership Promotes Teacher growth: A LOGIC MODEL

---
[1] See MBAMP Levels of participation chart.

attend the event will hopefully benefit from the experience, but is there an impact beyond the individual teachers who participate? That is what the Logic Model addresses. Teacher leadership teams are planning MBAMP events throughout the year. The OUTCOME is the impact beyond the experience of the participants. The Logic Model in Figure 4 details INPUTS and OUTPUTS of planning an event and also shows desired outcomes:

1. All Teachers' pedagogical and content knowledge increase.
2. MBAMP's profile raises.
3. Students' respond with increased mathematical intuition and understanding.
4. Districts Administrators are motivated to support MBAMP events, because these events are training some of their district teachers to be leaders (see Figure 5).

These outcomes are larger than a single event. They are the impact seen over time on the districts and the counties that the teacher leaders come from. The results from exit surveys of MBAMP events overwhelmingly suggest teachers are reporting they have increased pedagogical and content knowledge. Further the MBAMP Director is being contacted frequently in district and county outreach. When asked why this model of teachers-training-teachers works the project director stated:

Figure 5. Logic model of MBAMP

INPUT +	OUTPUT		= OUTCOMES
Key Elements	Volunteer Teacher Leadership Team Tasks	MBAMP Director or program coordinator tasks	For Teacher Leaders and the MBAMP's region
• Topic for the event • Teachers who self identify as Leadership Team members with an interest or experience in the topic and willing to serve. • MBAMP Director and/or program coordinator and/or Level[1] 5 MBAMP personal • MBAMP infrastructure	Determine: • Audience • Date and time • Breakout sessions (as determined by the pre survey) • # Of participants • Budget • Format of the day • Location • Materials • Session speakers from the Leadership team and outside the leadership team	• Funding, locations and advertising • Online registration, waiting list pre and post survey and breakout sessions • Guiding the Leadership team to see and complete tasks, stimulate team via email • Manage all paper work, write final event report	• All Teachers' pedagogical and content knowledge increases • MBAMP's profile raises • Students' respond with increased Mathematical intuition and understanding • Districts Administrators are motivated to support MBAMP events, because these events are training some of their district teachers to be leaders.
On going pre and post event: Curriculum Development, Funding, Partnerships & Dissemination			

Volunteer Teacher Leadership Teams Creating MBAMP Events Promotes Change in the Teachers and the Region

---

[1] See MBAMP Level of Participation Chart

The Role of Teacher Leadership for Promoting Professional Development Practices

I think what works well is the teachers who are attending the conference see the value and relevancy from the teachers who are presenting ideas. The teacher leader who is presenting might say this is what I did last week and these are teachers that are actually teaching kids with the material they are working with. (J. Montgomery, personal communication, November 12, 2014).

Teachers are reporting by applying the strategies they are learning their students are explaining their mathematical thinking. The director has reported "school district administrators continue to fund MBAMP events and reap the rewards of their teachers participating by asking their MBAMP trained teachers to do in house PD" (J. Montgomery, personal communication, September 14, 2014).

FRAMEWORK FOR TEACHER-DIRECTED PROFESSIONAL DEVELOPMENT

The flowchart in Figure 6 outlines the steps to follow and the components to include for a Teacher Leadership Team to direct and produce an MBAMP event. This general flowchart can be applied to any event whether it is a 1-day conference or a multiple day summer institute. It begins with an informal discussion of thought and ends with teacher participants at an event.

SOLUTIONS AND RECOMMENDATIONS:

Supporting Teacher-Directed Professional Development

It is the belief of the program director that a Volunteer Leadership Team (VLT) functions best when it is composed of teachers who believe in the team's mission. This earnest commitment not only provides a common language between MBAMP and the team, but also creates a nourishing reciprocal relationship

Figure 6. Framework for PD

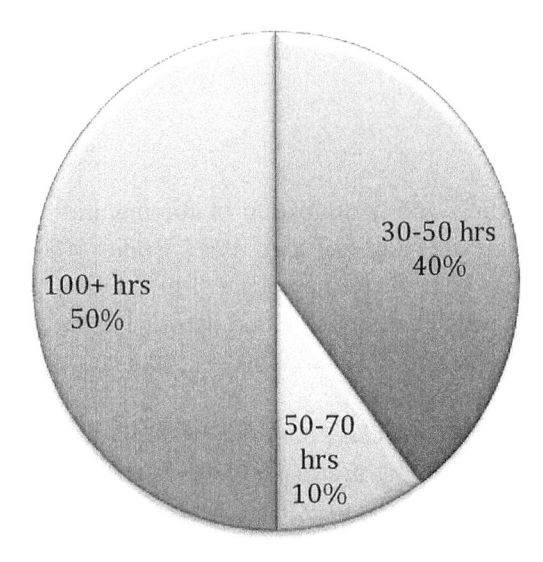

between the two parties. Teachers feel like MBAMP works for them by facilitating service opportunities; MBAMP benefits from teacher-leaders assistance at events. For the teacher's sake and for the benefit of the event itself, the leadership team requires support and nurturing. A motivated, well-supported VLT means participants who deeply understand the content of the event, affects the desired change in the teaching practice of the participants and ultimately benefits students of the participants. The MBAMP director works to nurture the leadership team members in a variety of ways including but not limited to: maintaining regular email contact, visiting classrooms, facilitating team-wide meetings, taking the team to conferences, and helping teachers present at conferences. It is important to note that—beyond the event itself—the teacher-leaders act as ambassadors to their district and their county. In the end, each team member is promoting an ideal that they believe in by doing service to their community. The VLT is truly a body that affects positive change.

Volunteer leadership teams that are a grassroots movement are a successful way to produce professional development and train teacher leaders. This model is geared toward an apprenticeship approach, whereby people interested in teacher leadership move through the five different stages to become teacher leaders who are self-sustaining and growth oriented. Applying a growth model approach to a professional development organization sustains the membership of teachers as they become intrinsically motivated to improve their practice and develop leadership skills.

One of MBAMP's core values is to support teachers in developing a trajectory toward leadership growth. In Figure 5 we make a case that teacher leadership in a team is an opportunity for teachers to organically grow into powerful leadership roles. Teachers might start being little more than an observer on a team, but 4 years later they can be leading their own team and explaining mathematics content and pedagogy that used to elude them. This approach to teacher leadership promotes:

- Teacher-to-teacher mentoring
- Teachers visit other teacher in their classroom
- Collaboration across grades
- Sharing and developing pedagogical and content knowledge.

One place that illustrates this outcome is the movement of the teachers from level to level in MBAMP participation, the outcomes are difficult to document, but they are being observed by the MBAMP director.

CONCLUSION

Collaboration, community building, and participation in communities of learners are key features to high quality professional development (Ball & Cohen, 1999; Borko, 2004; Loucks-Horsley, et al, 2003; Wilson & Berne, 1999). We also believe one key element in learning to participate in a professional community is valuing the unique skills, experience and knowledge that each teacher brings with them as a teacher leader. MBAMP professional development is centered on what teachers are doing in the classroom and the expertise they have to share.

As one teacher leader stated "I use my classroom as a lab to try new lessons or ideas that I consider sharing with other teachers". Approaching professional development from a constructivist stance is a powerful method as it allows group members to explore an area of interest and develop expertise at their own pace. When teacher leaders view their classroom as a learning lab they are demonstrating what is referred to as a "stance of inquiry (Ball & Cohen, 1999). From this perspective teacher leaders are using their teaching practice as a source of inquiry and continued professional learning. When they have developed expertise using a particular strategy then they are able to demonstrate mastery by presenting this approach to their colleagues at a professional development session. As stated by the MBAMP director, "Professional development becomes so embedded in what they do that they are creating a mindset of consistently reflecting and thinking about their practice with a goal of improving their practice" (personal communication, November 13, 2014).

REFERENCES

Achieve, (May, 2008). The Building Blocks for Success: Higher level math for all students. National Research Council Retrieved from: http://www.achieve.org/files/BuildingBlocksofSuccess.pdf

Angelle, P. S., & DeHart, C. A. (2011). Teacher Perceptions of Teacher Leadership: Examining Differences by Experience, Degree, and Position. *NASSP Bulletin, 95*(2), 141–160. doi:10.1177/0192636511415397

Ball, D. L., & Cohen, D. K. (1999). Developing practices, developing practitioners: Toward a practice-based theory of professional development. In G. Skyes & L. Darling-Hammonds (Eds.), *Teaching as the learning profession: Handbook of policy and practice* (pp. 30–32). San Francisco, CA: Jossey-Bass.

Bush, R. N. (1984). Effective staff development in making schools more effective: *Proceedings of three state conferences*. San Francisco, CA: Far West Laboratory.

Center for Public Education. (2005). Teacher Quality and Student Achievement: Research Review. Retrieved from www.centerforpubliceducation.org/Main-Menu/Staffingstudents/Teacher-quality-and-student-achievement-Research-review.html

Cohen, D. K., & Hill, H. (2001). *Learning policy: When state education reform works*. New Haven, CT: Yale University Press. doi:10.12987/yale/9780300089479.001.0001

Darling-Hammond, L., Chung Wei, R., Andree, A., & Richardson, N. (2009). *Professional learning in the learning profession: A status report on teacher development in the United States and abroad*. Oxford, OH: National Staff Development Council.

Darling-Hammond, L., & McLaughlin, M. (1995). Policies That Support Professional Development in an Era of Reform. *Phi Delta Kappan, 76*(8), 597–604.

Dijkstra, P., Kuyper, H., van der Werf, G., Buunk, A. P., & van der Zee, Y. G. (2008). Social comparison in the classroom: A review. *Review of Educational Research, 78*(4), 828–879. doi:10.3102/0034654308321210

Hanushek, E. A., & Rivkin, S. G. (2004). *How to improve the supply of high-quality teachers* (pp. 7–25). Brookings Papers on Education Policy doi:10.1353/pep.2004.0001

Haycock, K. (1998). Good teaching matters…a lot. *Thinking K-16, 3*(2), 1-14.

Knapp, M. S., McCaffrey, T., & Swanson, J. (2003, April). District Support for Professional Learning: What Research Says and Has Yet to Establish. Paper presented at the Annual Meeting of the American Education Research Association, Chicago, April 21-25.

Little, J. W. (1998). Seductive Images and Organizational Realities in Professional Development. In A. Lieberman (Ed.), *Rethinking School Improvement*. New York: Teachers College Press.

Marzano, R. J. (2003). *What works in schools: Translating research into action*. Alexandria, VA: Association for Supervision and Curriculum Development.

Nye, B., Konstantopoulos, S., & Hedges, L. V. (2004). How large are teacher effects? *Educational Evaluation and Policy Analysis, 26*(3), 237–257. doi:10.3102/01623737026003237

Parsad, B., Lewis, L., & Farris, E. (2001). *Teacher preparation and professional development. 2000 (NCES Publication No. 2001-088)*. Washington: D.C. National Center for Educational Statistics.

Porter, A., Garet, M., Deimone, L., Yoon, K., & Birman, B. (2000). *Does professional development change teaching practice? Results from a three year study*. Washington, D.C.: US Department of Education.

Stein, M. K., Smith, M. S., & Silver, E. A. (1999). The development of professional developers: Learning to assist teachers in new settings in new ways. *Harvard Educational Review, 69*(3), 237–269. doi:10.17763/haer.69.3.h2267130727v6878

Usher, E. L., & Pajares, F.Timms Study Usher. (2008). Sources of self-efficacy in school: Critical review of the literatures and future directions. *Review of Educational Research, 78*(4), 751–796. doi:10.3102/0034654308321456

Youngs, P. (2013). *Using teacher evaluation reform and professional development to support Common Core assessments*. Washington, D.C.: Center for American Progress.

Zeldin, A. L., & Pajares, F. (2000). Against the odds: Self-efficacy beliefs of women in mathematical, scientific and technological careers. *American Educational Research Journal, 37*(1), 215–246. doi:10.3102/00028312037001215

Zemke, R., & Zemke, S. (1995). Adult Learning: What Do We Know For Sure? *Training (New York, N.Y.), 32*(6), 31–40.

Zepeda, S. J. (1999). *Staff Development Practices That Promote Leadership in Learning Communities*. Larchmont, NY: Eye on Education.

Chapter 7
Teachers' Professional Development in the Digitized World:
A Sample Blended Learning Environment for Educational Technology Training

Emsal Ates Ozdemir
Istanbul Sehir University, Turkey

Kenan Dikilitaş
Hasan Kalyoncu University, Turkey

ABSTRACT

Professional development for in-service English language teachers has increasingly become a need in higher education not only in Turkey but across the world. Due to the limited time teachers have and the distance between the source of service and the potential participants, using digitized activities and materials have naturally become a necessity. The purpose of this research is to report the potential impact of the course described below and discuss the role of blended learning experience of professional development on the participating teachers. The theoretical background of the study is experiential learning initiated by Kolb and socio-constructivist learning theory by Vygotsky in that both theories highlight the role of experiencing the change and focus on personal meanings and learning with and from others in real and online environments.

INTRODUCTION

Professional development for in-service teachers has increasingly become a need in the education field not only in Turkey, but across the world. Due to the limited time teachers have and the distance between the source of service and the potential participants, using digitized activities and materials have naturally become a necessity. In the digitized world, teachers are expected to develop their technological pedagogical knowledge so as to keep up with the developing pedagogical innovations.

DOI: 10.4018/978-1-4666-9471-2.ch007

With the growth of digital facilities, professional development activities for teachers have become more visual and comprehensible. However, in developing countries, teachers who grew up with non-technological environment experience challenges in the digitized world, which makes it really difficult to deal with the changing nature of the training materials for their professional development. Turkey is one of the examples of such educational settings with several contextual constraints for the integration of digitized teacher development activities. Moreover, teachers do not have enough opportunities offered by their institutions. However, they attempt to develop professionally by searching materials on the Internet and attending relevant conferences or short courses.

It has also been observed that professional development activities which are more regular, organized and focused on the integration of technology into teaching rather than learning about how to use technological tools are needed. The training program offered in this study is planned according to this need. The purpose of this research is to report the potential impact of 'The Certificate Program for Educational Technology' (ETUSP) course described in this study and discuss the role of blended professional development program on the participating teachers. The theoretical background of the study is experiential learning initiated by Kolb and socio-constructivist learning theory by Vygotsky in that both theories highlight the role of experiencing the change and focus on personal meanings and learning with and from others in real environments.

Literature Review

It is widely believed that teachers are key to putting information technologies in the hands of students by integrating it into the teaching and learning process. By using technology as a natural and necessary part of classroom practice, teachers can give students the knowledge and experiences they need. Therefore, for students to be better prepared to 'learn with technology, teachers need to be better prepared to 'teach with' technology (Luke, Moore, Sawyer, 1998 as cited in Fossum, 2010).

There are also pedagogical theories to guide technology integration in classrooms. Technological Pedagogical Content Knowledge (TPACK) is a framework for teacher knowledge for technology integration prepared by Koehler and Mishra (2006). They argue that developing good content requires a skillful interweaving of three sources of knowledge: technology, pedagogy and content. They also assert that there is no single technological solution that addresses every teacher, every course or every view of teaching. For a productive technology integration teachers should consider all three issues within complex relationships rather than in isolation.

The Substitution Augmentation Modification Redifinition (SAMR) is another model for technology integration. This model was prepared by Puentedura (see Figure 1). It displays a new way to look at the different levels of integrating technology into the classroom.

As Dexter, Anderson and Becker (1999, p.223) explained, 'For teachers to implement any new instructional strategy, they must require new knowledge about it and then weave this together with the demands of the curriculum, classroom management and existing instructional skills'. Teachers need information about how, as well as why, to use technology in meaningful ways. Lack of knowledge regarding either element can significantly decrease the potential impact that these powerful resources might have on student learning. Lock (2006) explains in his study that described shortcomings in traditional professional development models have started a shift toward community based models to provide the continuous support teachers need to promote for teaching better, thus enhancing student learning. With advances in Information Communication Technologies (ICT) and ICT infrastructures in schools, online

Figure 1. SAMR Model by Dr. Ruben Puentedura, http://hippasus.com/rrpweblog

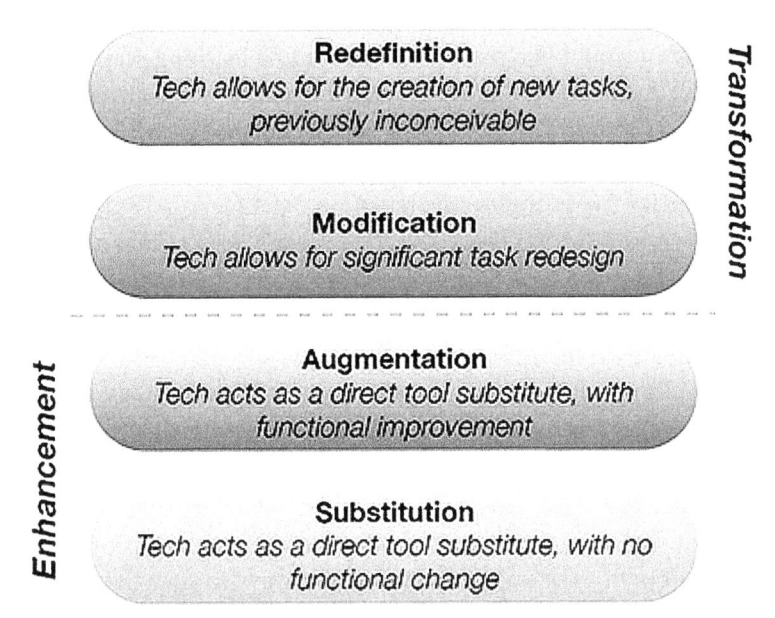

environments can be designed, implemented and developed in a meaningful way to support teachers' professional practice and continuous development. The community of participating teachers in the current course exemplifies such a group who wanted to promote their skills for integrating technology into their lives, classrooms, and schools.

Potter and Rockinson-Szapkiw (2012) state that researchers are aware of the fact that adult learners do not respond favorably to conventional, behavioral pedagogy and methods of instruction; they respond more favorably to social constructivist pedagogy and methods. Similarly Vygotsky's (1978) social constructivism also underlines the fact that learning is a social collaborative activity He adds that an instructional guide is necessary and should use the Zone of Proximal Development (ZPD) to improve instruction. The learning activities should extend into real world activities, so they should be applicable. Knowles (1980) also states in his theory of andragogy that adult learners have prior knowledge and experience to build upon and prefer experiential learning; they are more motivated to learn what is relevant.

Various trainings have been held and are still being held by many institutions. The impact these trainings create on the teachers' practices and future plans are not reported or investigated extensively. Therefore, one of the aims of this paper is to inform about a teacher training that has been recently held and how it has affected its participants in time (after 8 months) the training.

ETUSP 2 (Digitized Course)

This blended professional development course was designed and delivered by a group of professionals whose common feature is their experience in integrating technology into teaching; they are four technology specialists. These trainers specialized themselves in the integration of technology through their academic studies or joining some training activities abroad and in Turkey. They are also working at 1:1 schools where they lead the technology integration into teaching.

The course is a five-week program through which the participants meet face to face once a week with the trainers in a computer lab and follow activities such as doing homework, participating in forums during the week at any time they would like throughout the online learning platform. Moodle was chosen as the learning platform as it gave the trainers the chance to share feedback, lesson materials, samples, homework and to discuss via a forum. The trainers had worked on the curriculum for two years before they came up with the final version. It took a while to decide on what to include in the training and to create the written content for Moodle. They employed simulations, sample lesson plans, videos to enhance the education program for teachers. They got feedback from the teachers in their schools as they wanted to include the most needed technological tools and their integration into teaching. The name of the course was derived from the initials of the phrase 'Egitim Teknolojileri Uzmanlığı Sertifika Programı' which meant 'Educational Technology Expert Certificate Program'.

8 intern students from Computer Education and Instructional Technology Department at the school where 3 of the trainers work at and 3 other teachers of different subjects working at different private schools (Maths, Turkish and Computer) volunteered to work in the program by helping the creation of the digital content and assisting the trainees during the face to face sessions.

They finalized the digital content as a large group (trainees, trainers, three teachers who volunteered to work with the trainers). Finally, the trainers searched for ways to start this training. They wanted to equip the course participants with a certificate through a continuous learning center of a university. They communicated with the administrative people from a university and they were accepted to use the computer laboratory and the certificate would be given by the university. ETUSP 2 was delivered at a private university as a professional development activity for teachers (teaching at all levels and subjects) who were working in İstanbul and two teachers from other cities. The participants who were able to fulfill the requirements of the course (passing the online quizzes, participating in the forums and doing the homework) would be given a certificate by the university. Any teacher who would like to learn more about technology would apply to the program regardless of their background.

The course consists of six modules which are:

- Social Media in Education
- Digital Citizenship
- Tablets and Web 2.0 Apps
- Pedagogical Models for ICT integration
- Google Apps for Education
- Learning Management Systems

However, the training was limited to 21 teachers thinking that it would be the best number of people to be dealt during face to face training. The educational technology training program was announced on the following website http://www.egitimtek.com, which was prepared by teacher trainers. 60 teachers applied for the program, and 21 of them were selected for the training. Teachers of different subjects and levels were selected to create a heterogeneous group which could share experiences and be inspired by one another. The group was intrinsically motivated to professionally develop as they volunteered to take the training. Moreover, the number of teachers working at the same school was low thinking that they would form technology support groups within their schools and share their knowledge with their colleagues.

Teachers' Professional Development in the Digitized World

The face to face sessions and the digitized section of the course went smoothly. The teachers seemed engaged in the activities they were doing and doing their tasks on time. They were also working in groups and sharing their projects in the classroom with the other teachers. However, the researchers thought an investigation about the teachers' perspectives on the integration of technology throughout a blended learning program was necessary. They wanted to find out how the teachers felt after the process of training. The researchers also aimed to find out the transfer of learning into their professional contexts and changing practices in using educational technology and its effect on their teaching. This experiential and hands-on training course would provide critical insights into the dimensions of development and teacher change. The study will also focus on the reflections, feelings and experiences of teachers after the course.

METHODOLOGY

Research Questions

1. What are the expectations of the teachers from the digitized technology training course?
2. How did the participating teachers feel after the digitized training course (ETUSP)?
3. What was the impact of the digitized technology training course on the participating teachers?

Participants

Participant demographic information presented in Table 1.

Data Collection Tools

Data to evidence impact of the training n the teachers were collected three times in the following order to triangulate the data sources.

1. Pre-course data
   - Background information survey to reveal about the context
   - Written report from the participating teachers in order to reveal the impact of the course on their development

Table 1. Demographic information about the participants

Area of Teaching	N	Experience	Gender
History	1	4-7	Male
Homeroom Teacher	4	3 - 17	4 Female
Mathematics	6	4-22	1 Female 5 Male
English	2	8-17	2 Female
Science and Technology	3	0-12	2 Female 1 Male
Turkish	1	8-12	Male
German	4	8-17	4 Female

2. While-course data
   ○ Interview for immediate impact
   ○ Analysis of completed tasks and documents
3. Post-course Data
   ○ Written report from the participating teachers in order to reveal the impact of the course on their development
   ○ Written report to reveal the impact on the institution

Data Analysis

The data collected from the participants through written reports and the participants' posts on the social media. An open, axial, and selective coding (Strauss & Corbin, 1998) was followed in the analysis. In open coding, transcribed data was sorted out as sentences or larger groups sentences that contain single ideas. A code was given to the emerging concept. The items from the open coding analysis were reduced to concepts through axial coding. During selective coding, these concepts were then gathered as two central categories (expectations and impact on professional development. The two central categories were further divided into sub-categories, presented in Table 2 and 3 respectively.

Table 2. Central themes regarding participants' expectations from the course

Learning to Integrate ICT	• As it will relate to how I can use technology in my classroom • To experience how technology can be integrated into classrooms • In order to learn how to use it more effectively in my classroom • To find an answer to how I can use technology better in my classroom • By developing professionally, I want to learn how I can adapt technology into my classrooms • To learn about new technological applications and reflect over how I can integrate them into my classroom • To find technology-integrated applications from lessons
Self-Development	• To improve myself and learn new things • To update myself about technology and develop myself • Promote my skills in the use of technology in education • It will be informative for me • To enhance my professional knowledge and competency • To learn more about how students are learning in the 21st century and developing a perspective in order to teach more • To learn about alternative technology-based methods of teaching as it is needed in this century • To share to learn and to self-develop
Curiosity	• I am curious about technology and keen on generating through technology • I love technology. • I am always interested in trainings on the use of technology for educational purposes • I have developed tremendous curiosity about using technology in lessons recently
Training	• I want to run workshops in my school and share with them what is new about the use of technology • To share what I have learnt about technology with my colleagues
Fun	• To make my lessons more interesting and fun • To teach in a way that is enjoyable and appealing to students
Awareness	To raise my awareness towards educational technology
Motivation	To increase students' motivation to learn

Table 3. The prospective impact of the training on teachers' professional development

Major Impact	Specific Impact	Excerpts
Professional	Classroom Practice	I will generate ideas for how to use it better.
		I already start to think about specific ways of using web 2.0 tools, Google documents and LMS.
		I have already started to integrate. I put technology into the lesson plans.
		I am sharing what I have learnt with my students and then we implement the technological tools.
		I am implementing several new applications in the classroom now.
		I will use it in the assignment checking.
		I am using technology for consolidation activities and students' evaluations.
		I am implementing technology for creative writing and collaborative writing
	Student learning	I am planning to use technology inside and outside the classroom where ever possible to increase student motivation and learning.
		The students reported that they feel more motivated and learn better and more.
		Students are learning better with individual and groups work and have greater motivation now.
	Planning	It has already integrated. What I used to do on the basis of trial and error became more planned and with more awareness.
		I have become more professional when I am planning to integrate technology in my classes.
		I have been thinking about ways of integrating technology into my lesson plans considering the target topics.
		I have started to organize technology-enhanced implementation especially for classroom management.
	Development	The training taught me how to catch fish rather than gave me fish to eat whenever I need.
Institutional	Change	I will reconsider the content of my lessons as a leader of change in my institution.
		I have been given an opportunity to become technology leaders in my school so that I can enrich instructional varieties.
		I have already set up a Google Drive to share with 21 colleagues the syllabuses, meetings sheets, and etc.,.
		I plan to become technology leader in the institutions I work for especially in the area of integration of ICT in the classrooms.
		I am preparing applications and implementations in line with the curriculum.
		I want to become an agent of change in my school and environment.
	Expertise	I am sorting out problem arising at school through the use of technology.

FINDINGS

Analysis of the pre-course written report: *The expectations of the participants before the course*

21 participants responded to the first question of the online course evaluation survey. Table 2 presents the central themes participants mentioned regarding the specific and personal reasons for attending the course, ETUSP.

From the 26 responses of the 21 participants, 7 central themes were grounded. The responses are very positive and all have connotations with intrinsic motivation to develop their digital and technological literacy as teachers. There seems to be a tendency to grasp the importance of technology use in classroom because 8 responses were directly related to classroom implications. This also shows the changing nature of classroom instruction and teachers' growing awareness towards the need to integrate ICT in their instruction. Another most mentioned theme was self-development. The participants were well aware of the need to self-develop in the area of the use of ICT in the classroom. The initial positive stance towards technology integration and self-reported needs for integration positively influence the commitment they have put into learning from the training. In addition to these, some mentioned that they would like to lead their colleagues in terms of using technology and guide them towards the correct usage. This brings another perspective to teachers' practices in the teachers' room. Learning from a peer is something natural for these participants, which makes the sharing of best practices useful for all teachers.

The Impact of the Training on Teachers' Professional Development

The scope of the impact of the training on teachers turned out to have layers such as personal, and institutional. On the personal layer, they want to be more skillful, to be able to cater the needs of the 21st century learners. As they are aware of the different profile of students who are born in a technological world, they think they need to improve themselves professionally. The teachers participating in the digitized course volunteered to learn more about the integration of technology. They state that they would like to keep up with the needs of their learners. One of the participants was unemployed and she participated the course to be more skillful in the use of technology and look for a job then. She thought she would find a job more easily with the skills she acquired at the digitized course.

When it comes to the institutional layer, it is noted that some participants were working at schools where there were 1:1 computing projects, however where techno centric view dominates. They were just given the devices and could not use these devices effectively in the classroom. Therefore, the teachers participated in the course especially to contribute to their school's success through their own personal development. They were aware of the critical role played by teachers in contributing to a school's development through direct impact on their and other teachers' classroom practices. Table 3 shows the various areas of the prospective impact on teachers.

The major impact of the training on teachers seems to be the one on their classroom practices. The ultimate aim of any training is to impact the teaching and learning in the classroom. As can be seen in Table 3, the impact reported by the participants can be categorized into two general themes: professional and institutional.

The participants were asked to comment on the initial immediate impact of the course after the training, which could also indicate the commitment to the long-term impact. The immediate responses can be categorized under three themes such as pedagogical technological knowledge, change, and technological network.

Immediate Impact After the Training

The teachers were based to fill out an online written survey where they reflected on the immediate impact of the participation in the training. The responses were categorized as presented in Table 4.

OECD report entitled 'Education and New technologies: Teacher Training and Research' states that the potential of the new information technologies for improving learning and teaching will not be realized unless teachers are well trained and retrained in the pedagogical use of technology in the classroom (OECD, 1992, as cited in Orhun, 2002).

Table 4. The experienced impact areas immediately after the training

Pedagogical technological knowledge	I am feeling more competent in technology now.
	My knowledge increased about different technological tools.
	I learnt a low and feel competent to make interdisciplinary connections. I also developed ideas about what I can do in the lessons.
	I feel that I am more equipped with educational technologies
	I have overcome the fear of using technology after the training.
	I feel that I have developed new ways of using technologies.
	I feel that I want to learn more of educational technologies.
	I feel that I can actively use these tools autonomously
	I realized that there is still more to learn about educational technologies.
	I think the training made me feel that I am promoting my pedagogical technological further skills.
Change	I have started to change my perspective of teaching via technology.
	I feel that I am changing in terms of personal development and views about teaching.
	I feel impressed and satisfied with new skills I have learnt.
	I have more alternative ideas about new applications when I make lesson plans.
	I feel that I am learning and developing skills that I lacked before.
	I feel synergetic and happy to equipped new ideas about technology use in the classroom.
Technology network	I have been part of a network where I can find support and share my ideas
	I now know that teachers can make difference in the way they use technologies when they are connected to others.

DISCUSSION

ETUSP 2 was designed as a digitized in-service teacher training program to enhance the integration of technology into teaching such various subjects like Maths, Science, English,Turkish. Teachers were given the online content and guided feedback on their lessons to have better outcomes in teaching and learning. The participants had the chance to work in groups and could visit other groups to see how they integrate various tools into their subjects. This worked well and teacher had to share their group work with some other teachers during the training. It created a positive atmosphere to exchange ideas for the same goal. Similarly, Overbauch and Lu (2008 in Potter & Rockinson-Szapkiw, 2012) came up with the idea that an increased emphasis on technology integration was positively correlated to collaborative efforts. Moreover, Potter & Rockinson-Szapkiw (2012) state that as teachers' technological competence and confidence increased, so did their self-efficacy. Overbaugh and Lu (2008) state that the increase in self-efficacy resulted in more experimentation with technology in the classroom and in the teachers' immediate environment i.e. their colleagues and the school. This was also observed in the answers teachers provided about the short-term impacts of the course. The teachers who participated the online course expressed that they felt themselves more knowledgeable after seeing and practicing various technological tools into their teaching during the training. This encouraged them to continue learning and disseminate their knowledge to other teachers through conferences and social platforms (writing posts on Twitter, on technology blogs, Facebook).

Another positive impact of the digitized course ETUSP 2 was teachers spending more time on planning before integrating any kind of technology in their lessons. One of the modules in the training was on the 'Pedagogical Models for Tech Integration' and teachers were introduced with TPACK Framework (Technological Pedagogical Content Knowledge) by Mishra & Koehler (2006), the SAMR model (Puentedura, 2012). Having investigated these models teachers were trying to be more careful and focus on the teaching goals more than the technological tools to be used. One of the main goals of this digitized course was to make teachers aware of these models and to be more meticulous. That's why they started to question more, think more before using any kind of technological tool in their lessons. In line with this, Weinbaum, A., Allen, D., Blythe, T., Simon, K., Seidel, S., & Rubin, C., (2004 as cited in Lock, J, 2006) mention that when teachers develop and work from an inquiry stance and in collaborative inquiry groups, it opens them to questioning, exploring issues as they believe as important, making their work public, gaining new ideas on their work and students' work and providing avenues for intellectual growth and renewal as the teacher. This study supports this view as most of the teachers reported greater growth as a professional teacher who is able to share experience and knowledge particularly in an experiential way within their own context. The professional and social growth gained during the training led to greater awareness and further needs for creating opportunities to benefit from their developing experience. The while- and post-training sharing in the specific context made the outputs of the training program pedagogically more valuable especially because the participants became agents of change and development through their personal attempts to disseminate the new ideas and innovative practices. A further study in which the participants of the course are planned to be surveyed after a longer time to see if the impacts of the training have undergone any change.

REFERENCES

Dexter, S. L., Anderson, R. E., & Becker, H. J. (1999). Teachers' views of computers as catalysts for changes in their teaching practice. *Journal of research on computing in education, 31*(3), 221-239.

Duran, M., Fossum R. (2010). Technology Integration into Teacher Preparation: Part 1—Current Practice and Theoretical Grounding for Pedagogical Renewal. *Ahi Evran Üniversitesi Egitim Fakültesi Dergisi, Cilt 11, Sayı 2, Agustos, Sayfa 209-228*

Herreid, C. F., & Schiller, N. A. (2013). Case studies and the flipped classroom. *Journal of College Science Teaching, 42*(5), 62–66.

Knowles, M. (1980). The modern practice of adult education: From pedagogy to andragogy (2nd ed.). Englewood Cliffs, NJ: Prentice Hall/Cambridge.

Lock, J. V. (2006). A new image: Online Communities to Facilitate Teacher Professional Development. *Journal of Technology and Teacher Education, 14*(4), 663–678.

Mishra, P., & Koehler, M. (2006). Technological pedagogical content knowledge: A framework for teacher knowledge. *Teachers College Record, 108*(6), 1017–1054.

Orhun, E. (2002). Information and Communication Technologies in Education. In E.P.A. Orhun M., & Kommers (Ed.), Ege Üniversitesi: İzmir.

Overbaugh, R., & Lu, R. (2008). The impact of a NCLB-EETT funded professional development program on teacher self- efficacy and resultant implementation. *Journal of Research on Technology in Education*, *41*(1), 43–62. doi:10.1080/15391523.2008.10782522

Potter, S. L., & Rockinson-Szapkiw, A. J. (2012). Technology integration for instructional improvement: The impact of professional development. *Performance Improvement*, *51*(2), 22–27. doi:10.1002/pfi.21246

Puentedura, R. (2012). SAMR Model (Image). Retrieved from http://hippasus.com/rrpweblog

Puentedura, R. R. (2012). The SAMR model: Background and exemplars.

Strauss, A., & Corbin, J. (1998). Basics of qualitative research: Procedures and techniques for developing grounded theory. Thousand Oaks, CA: Sage.

uentedura, R. (2012). SAMR Model (Image). Retrieved from http://hippasus.com/rrpweblog

Vygotsky, L. S. (1978). *Mind in society: The development of higher psychological processes* (M. Cole, V. John-Steiner, S. Scribner, & E. Souberman, Trans. & Eds.). Cambridge, MA: Harvard University Press.

Chapter 8
Introducing Educational Technology into the Higher Education Environment:
A Professional Development Framework

Linda Van Ryneveld
University of Pretoria, South Africa

ABSTRACT

Over the past decade or two advancements in educational technology have taken place so swiftly that it threatens to revolutionize the education system. This phenomena seem to drive higher education institutions to respond with costly roll out plans that bring state of the art computing hard- and software, together with other highly specialized educational technologies, to their campuses. The dilemma is that these investments in educational technology are often made in isolation, without consideration for imperative aspects such as professional development. To progress, educators need to acquire the skills, knowledge and attitudes necessary to make optimal use of the technology. This can be achieved, among other, by means of well-structured professional development programmes. In this chapter the author explores the role of educational technology in higher education and establishes the need for capacity building by means of carefully designed professional development programmes. It furthermore suggests an alternative professional development framework.

INTRODUCTION

Over the past decade or two advancements in educational technology have taken place so swiftly that it threatens to revolutionize the education system (Quinn, 2003). This phenomena seem to drive higher education institutions to respond with costly roll out plans that bring state of the art computing hard- and software, together with other highly specialized educational technologies, to their campuses. The dilemma is that these investments in educational technology are often made in isolation, without consideration for imperative aspects such as professional development (Tlhoaele & Van Ryneveld, 2007).

DOI: 10.4018/978-1-4666-9471-2.ch008

Cuban (2001) makes a strong case when he argues that the mere fact that educational technologies are available, does not, by itself, change the educational practices inherent in an institution. In fact, there is little conclusive evidence that investments in hard- and software alone, make any significant difference in the teaching and learning practices of Universities. To progress, educators need to acquire the skills, knowledge and attitudes necessary to make optimal use of the technology. This can be achieved, among other, by means of well-structured professional development programmes.

In order to teach effectively in the current networked educational environment, educators require applied knowledge, coupled with a functional awareness of the potential of the various technologies. They need a sound educational foundation, as well as practical skills to meaningfully integrate the technology into their learning programmes. Ignoring the need for professional development may therefore come at a high cost for institutions that expect a return on their initial investment in educational technologies. The anticipated results are unlikely to materialise without the proper empowerment of staff.

As a result of this threat, some institutions do, in fact, launch impressive training programmes which normally take the form of a series of workshops and seminars scheduled throughout the academic year. The effectiveness and value of such a decontextualised approach is questionable with practitioners labelling them as '*hit-and-run*' (Darling-Hammond and Ball, 1997), or '*learning-where-to-click*' workshops (Greyling, 2007) and '*button pushing clinics*' (Carlson, 2002).

This chapter first explores the role of educational technology in higher education and establishes the need for capacity building by means of carefully designed professional development programmes. It highlights the outdated elements of the workshop approach and suggests an alternative professional development framework. The chapter concludes with a summary of lessons learnt and recommendations for professional development practice aimed at integrating technology into higher education.

TEACHING AND LEARNING WITH TECHNOLOGY AT A UNIVERSITY OF TECHNOLOGY

At one of the prominent Universities of Technology (UoT) in South Africa, a variety of educational technologies was introduced over time, with the aim to improve student success rates and to address challenges that surfaced due to abnormally lage classes. In some cases, educational technology was brought in to address quality assurance issues, for example, standardising the teaching of similar courses across geographically dispersed campuses. Online tutorials, simulations and drills were introduced to provide additional support to underprepared learners, whilst online assessment opportunities were utilised by lecturers for continuous and formative assessment purposes.

Rethinking Traditional Professional Development Activities

In an attempt to get lecturing staff on board, workshops and training programmes were developed and offered each time when a new technology or a new functionality became available. Frustrations with the workshop format of professional development, however, included the fact that these sessions often only focussed on the 'Click here, click there' activities and as such lacked the educational/pedagogical grounding that was required to make the outcome of the workshop optimal. Furthermore, lecturers had difficulty to attend workshops that spread over anything from 3 hours to 3 days due to their own heavy workloads and teaching schedules.

Due to these time constraints, lecturers also struggled to find the time needed to develop their teaching and learning materials, using the skills they mastered at the workshop. As such, months sometimes passed before a lecturer would have the time to sit down and develop learning materials or opportunities, by which time they had long since forgotten what they have learnt in the workshop.

Sometimes, training sessions would focus on new technologies/software packages that were not yet available for use in a particular department. Workshops then added to the levels of frustrations experienced by teaching staff as they now knew what was possible, but due to financial or other constraints were not able to utilise the new funcitonalities.

Another constraint is the everpresent emphasis on research and research outputs, as is prominent in all higher education institutions world-wide. Acknowledging that learning to use and implement new educational technologies takes an initial time investment, it is obvious that time spent in this manner competes with that of other academic key performance areas, specifically time to do research.

As a result of the abovementioned realities, the Partners@Work project was thus conceptualised and implemented.

Research Methodology

The Partners@Work programme was introduced when it became clear that the traditional workshop-based approach to professional staff development was not going to be effective in empowering educators to adequately address the problems experienced in higher education. With this sense of dissonance in mind, the professional development framework was designed as described below. The Partners@Work framework for the empowerment of educators who are interested in using technology in their teaching, was firmly grounded on the theories of adult learning (Decker, 2002; Rogers, 1993; Cross, 1981; Knowles, 1959) and further informed by the motivation theories of Lieb (1991), O.Houle (1988), Malone and Lepper (1987), Csikszentmihalyi (1975), Herzberg (1959) and Maslow (1954).

The case study has been hailed as a major methodological tool in social science inquiry and as a distinctive means for providing valid social knowledge (Sjoberg et al. 1991). The term case study, however, has multiple meanings. It can be used to describe a unit of analysis or to describe a research method. Stake, in Denzin and Lincoln 2000, argues that a 'case study is not a methodological choice but a choice of what is to be studied. By whatever methods, we choose to study the case.' In this study, the Partners@Work professional development programme as it was presented at the University of Technology in question, was selected as the unit of analysis.

According to Patton (1987) the 'evaluation of any research data should take into consideration a multiplicity of evidence gathered through numerous data collection methods and incorporate both quantitative ad qualitative methods.' Data was therefore collected by a variety of means including questionnaires, surveys, focus groups, personal interviews, research diaries, electronic communication (email and bulletin board messages), reflective journals (webblog entries), video reflections, group and informal individual discussions, course statistics and exploratory visits to other higher education institutions. Literature concerning professional development, capacity building and academic development were also scrutinized. These data sources acted as powerful instruments to investigate the extent to which a professional development programme can address the challenges faced by a higher education institution.

Introducing Educational Technology into the Higher Education Environment

PARTNERS@WORK: EMPOWERING EDUCATORS TO USE TECHNOLOGY IN EDUCATION

In essence the Partners@Work programme is a professional development programme, extended over the course of a year, aimed at empowering educators to meaningfully use technology as part of their teaching and learning practices. The programme focuses on the development and consequent implementation of well-rounded technology-enhanced courses that address specific challenges such as low pass rates, geographically dispersed learners and large classes. One of the strengths of the programme is its underlying focus on action research relating to the use of educational technology.

The Partners@Work programme consists of 4 components. The first component is a capacity-building empowerment phase that equips lecturers with the skills, knowledge and attitudes needed to successfully introduce technology into their teaching practices. The next component is a design and development phase, during which lecturers create technology-enhanced teaching and learning materials. Once the materials are developed, the third component follows in the form of an implementation phase. In this phase, lecturers pilot the materials that they developed previously. The final component focuses on research and in this phase lecturers study and report on the impact of their interventions. As a result this component produces tangible research outputs in the form of journal articles, conference papers and research posters. The 4 components are shown in Figure 1.

In the section below, each of these components will be unpacked with detail from the Partners@Work programme, as it was presented at the University of Technology in question.

Preliminaries

A number of activities had to take place before the official launch of each year's new Partners@Work programme. A call for nominations typically went out 6 months prior to the launch of a new group. Interested lecturers then had the opportunity to discuss their wish to participate in the programme with their Deans and Heads of Departments (HODs), who in turn, had to scan their environments for courses that could benefit from the introduction of educational technology.

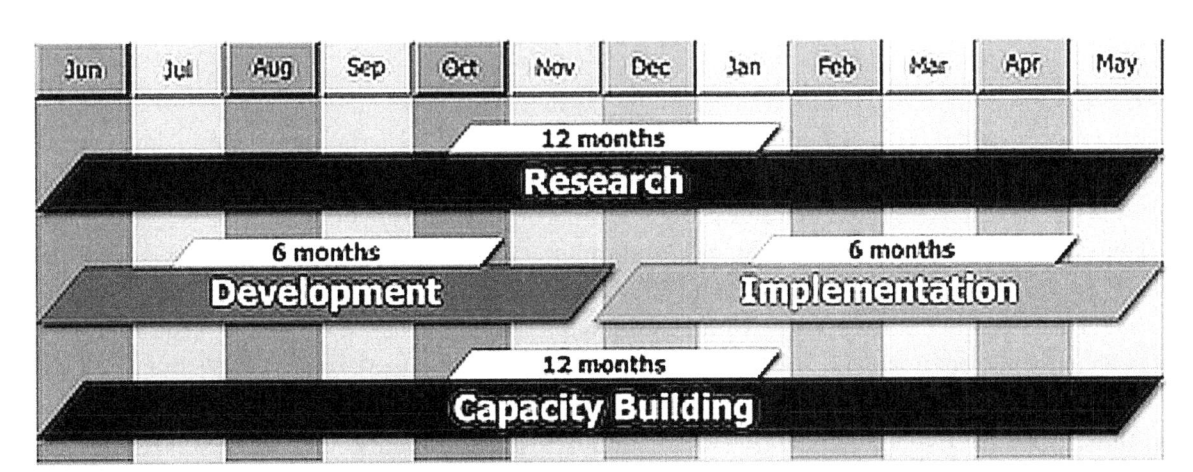

Figure 1. The 4 phases of the Partners@Work programme

The various Deans subsequently nominated the lecturers representing their Faculties. Once the nominations were received, the *Directorate for Teaching and Learning with Technology* (TLT) arranged an introductory lunch to which the Dean, the relevant HODs and the new nominees (also known as Partners) were invited. At this occasion, approximately 3 months prior to the commencement of the programme, the Partners@Work concept was explained in detail, and all parties were informed of their distinct roles and responsibilities. Contracts were signed, and after the HODs had the opportunity to introduce their 'candidate' to the audience, a celebratory lunch was offered.

After the lunch, the selected lecturers had to undergo a 2 hour long computer skills assessment that tested their computer fundamentals, essential word processing skills, typing speed and accuracy, and basic Internet browsing and searching skills. Afterwards, each lecturer received a report indicating possible areas for further training. Training opportunities (presented in-house) were also highlighted. This activity managed to raise the lecturer's awareness of the skills that they needed and most of them made a concerted effort to improve these before their official Partners@Work programme started.

Lecturers (the new Partners) were also given the outline of a typical project plan, and were requested to draw up a draft plan for the project they intended to work on. The plan profiled the subject area that the Partner were to develop and provided background information with regards to the profile of their students, the number of lecturers involved in teaching the programme involved, mention of the campuses where the subject was offered, previous pass rates, and other illuminating facts about the programme. Unique challenges and problems experienced in the programme were also highlighted. During the first week of the Partners@Work programme, these documents then served as a starting point for a thorough needs analysis.

In the mean time, the HOD and the Dean had to find and appoint a replacement for the seconded lecturer from their faculty. Financial support for the replacement was made available to replace the lecturers in the form of seed funding. These funds were provided by Top Management in support of the University's strategic vision to lead through innovative teaching practices that include the use of technology.

It was agreed that the Partner would be replaced in totality for the first six months on the programme. During this time they would be seconded to the *Directorate for Teaching and Learning with Technology (TLT)*. Since they were substituted in their Faculties, and as a result 'lost' access to their offices, alternative arrangements had to be made to accommodate the lecturers on the programme. They were, therefore, provided with a laptop, pre-loaded with all the necessary software and drivers, and Internet connectivity. During the initial offerings of the Partners@Work programme, fixed line broadband Internet connections were provided at lecturer's homes, however in later programmes, these were replaced with wireless connections.

The abovementioned provisions enhanced mobility and made it possible for lecturers to work wherever they wished. The TLT classroom was often used as a social gathering space, and some Partners preferred working there rather than at their own homes. They benefited from the close proximity of the instructional designers who were close by to assist if needed. Others preferred to work in the comforts of their own homes and kept in touch by means of online instant messaging, email and the telephone.

For the last six months on the programme, Partners returned to their departments on a part-time basis. Partners had to be in a position where they could implement their technology-enhanced materials in an authentic environment, and still have enough time left to rework or expand sections based on student feedback. Partners also spent time on their research projects during this time and as such Deans and HODs were advised to limit the Partners' lecturing load to the subject they were working on only.

The Capacity-Building Component

During the first six months of the Partners@Work programme, lecturers were empowered to function independently by means of an extensive capacity-building programme. This programme involved a two-month initial face-to-face block session, followed by weekly one-day contact sessions thereafter, and a variety of online training courses throughout their time on the programme. Active participation in the online courses, earned Partners certificates that stated the specific levels of their achievements. At the initial block session, and thereafter during the weekly contact sessions, time was spent networking with other partners, sharing progress, taking part in workshops and hands-on training sessions facilitated by experts, and by asking and answering questions related to their own development activities.

Skills development activities, focused on applications such as the learning management system, assessment software, website development and video editing programs. Knowledge development activities included among other: Writing a scientific article, Preparing and presenting a conference paper, Designing an outcomes-based curriculum, Instructional design for elearning purposes, Facilitating and managing online learning, Encouraging online collaboration and interaction, Implementing high quality electronic learning activities, Implementing interactive multimedia products, Creating and administering quality electronic assessments, and Managing a technology-enhanced course. Constructive attitudes were fostered through heated class debates and journaling by means of reflective weblogs.

During this phase lecturers also attended a series of workshops on the basic principles of conducting a research project. Apart from simply absorbing the facts, Partners were encouraged to start thinking about a possible problem or hypothesis that could be examined during the research phase. Having done this, lecturers could plan specific design and development outcomes with the aim to support the research data required later.

The Design and Develop Component

This component ran parallel with the capacity-building phase. Lecturers spent the majority of their time during their first six months on the Partners@Work Programme actively designing and developing technology-enhanced teaching and learning materials and learning activities for their courses with the help of an expert team consisting of specialists such as programmers, instructional designers, curriculum designers, student development officers, quality experts, graphic artists, and video editors. During this phase, time was spent designing and developing materials for a particular subject using the technologies, applications, tools and services available at the institution. These included the Internet, animations, graphics, interactive multimedia, electronic testing, video- and audio conferencing, mobile learning and video productions.

For example, in a management course, a case study on leadership styles included a video clip of the current president of South Africa, Mr Jacob Zuma, making a speech. The video clip paused at particular points and was then interspersed with thought provoking questions with regards to leadership issues. The aim was for students to reflect on the various characteristics of this particular leadership style, and to provide a stimulus for group discussions, either online using a bulletin board or a wiki, or in group discussions face-to-face.

The lecturers on the programme met their instructional designers weekly for individual sessions to plan and discuss areas of concern. This ensured that the lecturer got personalised advice and support in the areas that they still lacked experience. They also stayed in contact with each other during the time between contact sessions by means web-based technologies. They interacted using the e-mail and bulletin facilities available in Blackboard (the learning management system), as well as instant messaging facilities such as Yahoo Messenger and Skype, and as such become part of an online support community. The instant messaging feature in particular was extremely popular due to the immediacy of the interpersonal contact that it managed to facilitate. The lecturers reported that they experienced these interactions as their lifeline when they sat struggling, for example, with a particular piece of software in the late hours of the night. Moral and technical support was easily available from others who were synchronously online.

The lecturers on the programme were required to schedule stakeholder meetings to which they invited all people with a direct interest in what they were doing. Stakeholders such as the Dean, HOD, fellow lecturers, a student representative, the subject librarian, and the computer laboratory technician all joint the lecturer in these meetings. The Partners@Work lecturers presented their progress and defended their instructional design decisions at these meeting. They also got the opportunity to discuss and plan for the logistics of the implementation phase. For example, if their design included regular continuous electronic assessments, they had to schedule weekly contact sessions in a computer laboratory. This aspect had to be booked into the laboratory schedule for which the IT technician had to prepare specific settings (for example, loading Java-enabled scripts). These contact sessions also had to be incorporated into the students' time table for which the Faculty's scheduling officer had taken responsibility. Fellow educators had the opportunity to question learning programme-specific issues, whilst the librarian had to take note of the sections where specific library resources would be required (for example, if an assignment required students to watch a copy of a particular video clip, the library's multimedia section had to be informed and consulted).

The research activities that took place in this phase culminated in a mini-conference as described below. At this event, the lecturers showcased the technology-enhanced materials that they designed. For example, they demonstrated their interactive multimedia and specialised animations and graphics, shown their video clips, explained their electronic assessment strategies, explained their learning activities, and talked the audience through examples of other resources and facilities available in their online classrooms. The audience typically included their peers and other interested educators, but all stakeholders were invited.

The Implementation Component

Following the last 6 months on the programme, lecturers piloted their new technology-enhanced learning programmes, with actual students in an authentic learning environment. This phase provided formative feedback for refinement purposes. Lecturers monitored students' reactions and analysed what was happening as they implemented their technology-enhanced teaching and learning materials. In the light of this analysis and the associated reflection, they subsequently refined their thinking and made changes where needed. Some lecturers shared their newly created materials with colleagues presenting the same subjects, and in doing so they started the required mentorship relationships in their departments.

This phase turned out to be the most difficult one, from the perspective of the Directorate for Teaching and Learning with Technology. Since many influencing factors were out of the management control of the instructional designers, contingency plans often had to be made on the fly, for example when technical problems hampered progress in the computer laboratories.

During this phase lecturers had to collect the data needed to answer their research questions or to validate the hypothesis of their research projects. Some of these projects focused on a single intervention, whilst others used data mined throughout the entire course.

The Research Component

One of the most significant components of the Partners@Work programme is the fact that lecturers were guided through a structured research process. This phase demonstrated the ease with which research and teaching responsibilities can be integrated meaningfully. Even though research is one of the three key performance indicators (teaching, research and community service) for educators employed at a higher education institution, many of the Partners on board have had preciously little previous research experience. Therefore the mandatory research project in itself significantly contributed to the lecturer's professional development as it aimed to strengthen these important skills. This component culminated in 4 research outputs, namely a research poster, two conference papers, and a scientific journal article.

As part of their exposure to research activities during the first 6 months of the programme the lecturers had to design a research poster. This assignment required the lecturers to reflect on, and then defend their instructional design decisions during the design and development phase. They may have set out to design a particular piece of interactive multimedia, and in this poster, the lecturers had to explain what the learning problem was that they hoped to address and why they had chosen this particular medium to support both their teaching and the learning of their students.

As a surprising number of the lecturers had never presented papers at research (or practitioner) conferences, the Partners@Work programme included two in-house conferences to serve as a learning and preparatory experience. In both cases, an open invitation to attend went out to all staff members of the University, but stakeholders in particular were personally invited to attend. The first in-house conference, at the end of the design and development phase, was dubbed a 'mini-conference'. At this occasion, Partners presented their design decisions that were made based on the original challenges that they experienced during their courses. They also showcased the technology-enhanced teaching and learning materials that they designed. The mini-conference mirrored a typical 'practitioner'-style conference and created a safe in-house environment in which they could hone their presentation skills and gain experience at presenting in front of an audience of peers. Many of the Partners reported this as an extremely worthwhile experience, especially since they had to be prepared to respond to unexpected questions from the audience, simulating the exposure they were bound to get at national and international conferences.

The second in-house conference was held at the end of the Partners@Work year and was dubbed the *Annual Teaching and Learning with Technology Research Indaba*. According to the Free Dictionary (http://www.thefreedictionary.com/indaba) an 'Indaba' is seen as "a council or meeting of indigenous peoples of southern Africa to discuss an important matter". The TLT Research Indaba emulated a typical national conference in order to give Partners exposure to all the processes involved. These ranged from a call for papers, deadlines, abstracts and full paper submissions, peer reviews, short CVs for the session chairs, test runs with the equipment in the auditorium, presentation timekeepers, and question and answer sessions. At this conference, the lecturers had to present their research findings, and as such a typical national research conference were simulated. The conference was typically held over a period of two days and lecturers had the opportunity to present their research findings to the broader academic community of the University and other interested parties. In most cases, the focus of the papers was on how the technology-enhanced learning materials that they developed during the course of their Partners@ Work year influenced the challenges (such as low pass and retention rates) that the University faces.

Finally, the research activities of this phase culminated in a proper scientific journal article that had to be of such quality that it could be submitted to a respected accredited journal in their discipline, or alternatively, in relevant fields such as higher education or elearning. These articles were written as part of a structured writing programme throughout the final six months of the programme. The article started out as a research proposal and was developed, as data was collected and analysed into a fully fledged article in the end. Weekly peer reviews gave much needed feedback as each lecturer was a member of a research syndicate, as part of which they were required to critically read each others' work and provide constructive feedback. This important aspect of the programme, contributed to a higher level of critical academic attitude. Research professors from their own disciplines were appointed to act as mentors throughout the period of six months, and together with the inputs from the instructional designers and a language editor, the articles were finalised for submission.

The purpose of the research phase of the programme was, among other, to build and nurture a scholarly community that focus on the use of technology in teaching and learning within the institution. The research phase also provided lecturers with the opportunity to improve their qualifications to a Masters, Doctorate or Post Doctorate level. This became possible as a result of the extended nature of some of the research projects.

The Closing Component

To conclude the lecturer's year on the programme, a 'graduation' ceremony was held where awards were made for exceptional quality, and certificates of achievement and competence were handed out. At this ceremony, the next year's group of Partners@Work lecturers were also inaugurated. All stakeholders were invited and a celebratory cocktail party usually followed.

After the graduation, seasoned lecturers returned to their departments in a full time capacity, but still remained active as part of the Partners@Work community and played an important role as mentors for the new lecturers who were embarking on their own educational technology journeys. Deans and HODs were encouraged to use the new abilities of the lecturer in question to the benefit of the entire Faculty.

Many lecturers continued their design and development work in the years following their participation in the programme. Having gained the necessary skills, knowledge and attitudes to survive using technology to enhance their teaching practices, these lecturers tackled the next subject and developed it in a similar manner. Others spent their time following the programme, improving the existing materials, developing more technology-enhanced materials, and focusing on the empowerment of their peers.

A FRAMEWORK FOR PROFESSIONAL DEVELOPMENT IN THE FIELD OF EDUCATIONAL TECHNOLOGY

The Partners@Work programme, as it was presented at this University of Technology, underwent a number of iterations before most of the challenges were ironed out. It is believed that the current format of the programme can add value to other higher education institutions who grapple with staff development challenges when introducing new educational technologies. The professional development framework described in this chapter, relies on a number of critical components to ensure success.

At first, the buy in and support of the university's top and middle management structures is essential. Whilst the programme is unlikely to be successful without the support of the Dean and Deputy Deans of a Faculty, it is essential to also ensure that the Heads of Departments and Section Heads are on board.

Secondly the identification of the right Partners is of the utmost importance. Not only should Partners be foreward-thinking, passionate about teaching, and enthusiastic about participating in the programme, but the modules that they develop should also be selected based on their strategic importance in the Faculty. Selection of the modules should explicitly consider existing challenges, for example large classes or low success rates.

Thirdly, the programme should make provision for the full range of supporting resources, fulfilling hardware, software and connectivity needs. During the development phase, Partners must have access to high end computing equipment, preferably in the form of mobile technology, to ensure that they can work any time and anywhere. All the required software programs that may benefit the development of the module, should be licenced and available on such a mobile device. Furthermore, 24/7 access to a stable and fast Internet connection is a minimum requirement.

During the implementation phase, lecture halls and other spaces where staff have face-to-face contact with their students should be equiped to handle the modality in which the module is presented. For example, data projectors, sound systems and computer laboratories should be available when required, and should be well supported by trained technical staff. Students should also have access to all the required technologies, albeit in or outside of class, in residences, in computer laboratories, and/or in the library.

Fourthly, since academics are typically torn between their teaching, research and community service as competing key performance areas, time constraints for development work are often a concern. The successful introduction of any new educational technology however, relies heavily on staff having the time to develop their teaching and learning materials thoroughly. As such, the framework discussed above, allows for 'teaching sabbaticals' where a staff member gets dedicated time off for the purpose of developing their technology-enhanced module.

The fifth important component of the framework is empowerment. In order for staff to fully embrace the enhancements that adding educational technologies bring to a module, they need to be empowered. This component of the programme could include workshops and seminars, but also encourages peer teaching. Each of the Partners comes with a unique set of expertise and effort should be put into getting these Partners to share their knowledge and skills, and to teach the others in the group. Empowerment should also overtly focus on educational theory, sound instructional design principles and teaching with technology.

Without support a programme such as the Partners@Work would not be successful. As mentioned above, management backing is essential, however, provision should also be made for significant IT and logistical support as well as instructional design support. If the research component is included, additional reseach support is also required, especially in the case of novice researchers.

CONCLUSION

As higher education invest in technologies that support teaching and learning, it has become a priority to ensure that lecturing staff are adequately trained. The traditional workshop approach did not succeed in empowering lecturing staff to the point where they are able to use educational technology independently.

This chapter proposed a comprehensive professional development framework that stretches over a period of a year, and consists of four distinct components. The framework makes provision for building the necessary capacity, providing time, resources and support in the development and implementation of technology-enhanced learning materials, and provided lecturers with the opportunity to conduct research based on their improved teaching activities.

The Partners@Work framework is heralded as a highly successful professional development programme to build capacity and elearning leadership in the University of Technology where it was implemented. As a result of the success stories that were generated by the lecturers involved with the programme, the number of academic staff interested in enhancing their teaching with technology multiplied manyfold. Another significant consequence that two other higher education institutions has adopted this approach, opening the scope for inter-institutional collaboration and further refinement of the framework.

REFERENCES

Carlson, S. 2002. Wired to the Hilt: Saint Joseph's University stakes its future on a $ 30 million bet. *The Chronicle of Higher Education: Information Technology.* Retrieved from http://chronicle.com/free/v48/i29/29a03301.htm

Cuban, L. (2001). *Oversold & Underused: Computers in the Classroom. Harvard.* University Press.

Darling-Hammond, L., & Ball, D. L. 1997. Teaching for high standards: What policymakers need to know and be able to do. *National Educational Goals Panel.* Retrieved from http://www.negp.gov/Reports/highstds.htm

Greyling, F. C. 2007. *The why and how of technology-assisted learning: Authentic professional development for higher education practitioners* [Unpublished doctoral thesis]. University of Johannesburg, Johannesburg.

Quinn, D. M. (2003). Legal Issues in Educational Technology: Implications for School Leaders. *Educational Administration Quarterly, 39*(2), 187–207. doi:10.1177/0013161X03251152

Tlhoaele, M. J., & Van Ryneveld, L. (2008). What's in it for me? An analysis of the need for credit-bearing professional development modules on the topic of elearning. *SAJHE, 22*(6), 1279–1291.

Chapter 9
Supporting the Enactment of Standards-based Mathematics Pedagogies:
The Cases of the CoDE-I and APLUS Projects

Drew Polly
University of North Carolina at Charlotte, USA

Chuang Wang
University of North Carolina at Charlotte, USA

Christie Martin
University of South Carolina at Columbia, USA

Richard Lambert
University of North Carolina at Charlotte, USA

David Pugalee
University of North Carolina at Charlotte, USA

ABSTRACT

In order for professional development in the STEM fields to be effective, teachers need worthwhile experiences to simultaneously develop their knowledge of content, pedagogy, and understanding of how students' learn the content. In this chapter we provide an overarching framework of learner-centered professional development and describe the implementation of two mathematics professional development projects designed to support elementary school teachers' mathematics teaching. We follow our description by highlighting some of the findings from our line of professional development research and provide implications for the design of learner-centered professional development programs in mathematics.

OVERVIEW

The Need for Mathematics Professional Development

Professional development continues to be held up on a pedestal as a potentially powerful vehicle for supporting practicing teachers' adoption of new pedagogies and knowledge (Borko, 2004; Darling-Hammond, Wei, Andree, Richardson, & Orphanos, 2009; Desimone, 2009; Polly & Hannafin, 2011). In the field of mathematics education, administrators and district leaders must provide effective profes-

DOI: 10.4018/978-1-4666-9471-2.ch009

sional development so that teachers have a robust understanding of mathematics content and are also prepared to enact the most effective strategies in their classrooms (Loucks-Horsley, Love, Stiles, Mundry, & Hewson, 2010; United States Department of Education, 2008).

In the United States, this has been especially true in the last few years with the large-scale adoption of the both standards-based (reform-based) mathematics curriculum as well as the Common Core State Standards in Mathematics ([CCSSM]; Common Core State Standards Initiative, 2010). More school districts than ever before have adopted standards-based mathematics curriculum; these sets of instructional resources are described by having alignment with the National Council for Teachers of Mathematics ([NCTM], 2014) *Principles to Action*, in that students learn mathematics by exploring cognitively-demanding mathematical tasks and mathematics games, engaging in discussions about mathematical tasks and concepts, and reasoning and justifying their paths to solving tasks and problems.

Learner-Centered Professional Development

Large-scale syntheses of research studies on professional development have yielded components of highly effective learning experiences for teachers (Garet et al., 2001; Darling-Hammond, et al., 2010). The construct learner-centered professional development (LCPD) (Polly, 2006; Polly & Hannafin, 2011; Hawley & Valli, 2000) has been used to describe professional development programs that focus on meeting the specific professional needs of teachers and align with the American Psychological Association's *Learner-centered Principles* (hereafter *Principles*) (APA Work Group, 1997). The *Principles* were grounded on empirical findings related to teaching and learning and reflect both cognitivist and constructivist views of how people learn (Alexander & Murphy, 1998). Hawley and Valli (2000) identified nine primary design recommendations associated with LCPD:

1. LCPD should focus on content that students need to learn and problems that students face learning that content;
2. LCPD should be driven by addressing the difference between goals and standards for student learning and actual performance;
3. LCPD should involve allowing teachers to identify their own learning needs, and when possible, involve them in the design of professional learning activities;
4. LCPD should be primarily school based and integral to school operations;
5. LCPD should relate to individual learning needs but should include collaborative problem solving;
6. LCPD should be continuous and ongoing involving follow-up and support for further learning;
7. LCPD should include an evaluation that includes multiple sources of information including classroom implementation;
8. LCPD should allow teachers to develop a deep theoretical understanding of the content and pedagogy;
9. LCPD should be part of a comprehend change process that addresses impediments to and facilitators of student learning.

Many of these nine design recommendations have been verified by an extensive synthesis of the *Principles,* Hawley and Valli's (2000) recommendations and research on professional development (Polly & Hannafin, 2010). To that end, LCPD provides a robust framework for the design of professional development programs.

Mathematics LCPD Programs

Mathematics professional development research studies have examined the influence of programs that align with LCPD. In one line of work, researchers examined how the InterMath professional development program influenced teachers' knowledge of mathematics content, pedagogical content knowledge, and their use of technology (Polly, 2006; Polly & Orrill, 2012). In one study, teacher-participants reported focusing on varying aspects of the professional development including learning about technology, mathematics content, or the intersection of how to use technology to better teach mathematics (Polly, 2006). The learner-centered framework allowed teachers to hone in and focus their learning on their greatest perceived need.

In a subsequent study (Polly & Orrill, 2012), the participants reported gains in both knowledge of technology and knowledge of mathematics, but did not report gains in more frequent uses of integrating technology into their mathematics study. One possible conclusion is that the LCPD framework allows teachers to focus their learning, but in some cases boundaries are needed to ensure that the goals of the professional development are met.

An example of LCDP that had boundaries or more structure would be the nation-wide Australia Numeracy Project (Higgins & Parsons, 2009). This nationwide professional development program included numerous aspects of LCPD activities, but limited teachers' choice and ownership of activities until it was time to implement the emphasized pedagogies in their classroom. The professional learning activities were pre-determined, and included active, ongoing learning, collaborative tasks, a balance of knowledge about pedagogy and content, as well as a focus on addressing problem areas regarding students' learning (Higgins & Parsons, 2009).

Based on the theoretical underpinnings of LCPD and the research regarding professional development that embodies the LCPD principles, there is definite potential for these types of teacher learning experiences. However, there is a need to closely examine the specific activities in an LCPD program and look at how these activities specifically influence teachers' practice and student learning outcomes. In the next section we describe two multi-year LCPD programs designed to support elementary school teachers' mathematics teaching and their students' learning.

EXAMPLES OF LEARNER-CENTERED PROFESSIONAL DEVELOPMENT IN ELEMENTARY SCHOOL MATHEMATICS

Content Development to Teach Investigations (CoDe-I)

Content Development to Teach Investigations (CoDe-I) was a project funded by the (state) Mathematics and Science Partnership (MSP) grant program for teachers from Grades Kindergarten through Grade 5. The goal of the project was to support teachers' adoption of standards-based mathematics practices through the use of the mathematics curriculum *Investigations in Number, Data, and Space* (TERC, 2008). During the project the (state) Department of Education adopted the Common Core Mathematics Standards, so the Common Core was also a focal point of the professional development.

The *Investigations* curriculum is a standards-based curriculum that includes components designed to support the development of students' mathematical thinking. The lessons include cognitively-demanding mathematical tasks (NCTM, 2014) that include all students to use concrete mathematical manipulatives, pictorial representations, and transitional mathematical procedures to support students' computation and mathematical understanding. The curriculum also includes mathematics games to build students mathematical fluency (Russell fluency article).

The project included teachers from two school districts in <state> from the United States. Each district had similar professional development experiences but they were implemented separately. District 1 was a large urban school system that had 98 elementary school teachers during the project. Approximately 180 District 1 teachers participated for each of the three years of the project. District 2 was a small, suburban school system that had 5 elementary schools. Approximately 30 District 2 teachers participated for each of the three years of the project.

Goals

The goals of the CoDe-I project were to:

1. Develop teachers' knowledge of mathematics content related to the mathematics in the Kindergarten through Grade 5 mathematics standards.
2. Develop teachers' knowledge of connections between mathematics topics related to the mathematics in the Kindergarten through Grade 5 mathematics standards.
3. Support teachers' shifts to more favorably teaching in a standards-based manner.
4. Develop teachers' skills related to selecting, modifying, and creating cognitively-demanding mathematical tasks.
5. Develop teachers' skills related to analyzing how the *Investigations* curriculum can support students' mathematics understanding.
6. Increase teachers' enactment of standards-based mathematics pedagogies.
7. Positively influence student achievement in mathematics.

Description of Activities

The Mathematics Science Partnership projects require teacher-participants to engage in an intensive summer institute and follow up activities during the year. As a result there was an 8 day summer institute and various experiences during the school year. The summer institute focused on three main concepts: 1) solving and exploring cognitively-demanding mathematical tasks in order to explore the mathematics concepts heavily emphasized in elementary school classrooms; 2) analyzing the activities and lessons in the *Investigations* curriculum and considering alignment to standards; and 3) examining how to differentiate *Investigations* and other activities for both struggling and high-achieving students.

The exploration of tasks occurred in multi-grade breakout sessions which allowed teachers from various backgrounds to collaborate to explore and discuss the mathematics embedded in each task. The other activities were carried out in grade-level specific sessions, which enabled teachers to work with others at their grade level to intensively focus on the analysis of grade-level specific resources, standards, and how to meet the needs of learners.

During the school year, both districts supported teacher-participants through half-day workshops and classroom-embedded projects. The half-day workshops mirrored the work of the summer institute with more of a focus on mathematics concepts that teachers were about to teach in their classrooms. These projects included conducting a video analysis of a mathematics discussion in their classroom, conducting a thorough data analysis of student work on a cognitively-demanding mathematical task, and facilitating a professional development session for their colleagues.

Supporting the Enactment of Standards-based Mathematics Pedagogies

Summary of Findings

During each year of the three-year project numerous data sources were collected. They included a Teacher Beliefs Questionnaire (TBQ; Swan, 2006), Teacher Practice Questionnaire (TPQ; Swan, 2006), and pre- and post-test data for three units for each grade level. In some instances the evaluation team also collected classroom observation data in order to examine teachers' instruction as a function of the CoDe-I project.

In the first year of the CoDe-I project teachers reported a shift from teacher-centered to student-centered practices, while others who were student-centered before the project reported enacting similar pedagogies (Wang. Polly, LeHew, Lambert, & Pugalee, 2013). Teachers also demonstrated significant growth in their mathematics content knowledge. Further, some teachers reported a shift towards more traditional beliefs about teaching mathematics, which was contradictory to the goals of the professional development. The study also indicated a statistically significant relationship between teachers' shift from teacher-centered to student-centered practices and increases on curriculum-based assessments. In another study about teachers who participated in the first year of the CoDe-I project, teachers were observed and interviewed and found to be implementing *Investigations* with a high level of fidelity, which included increases in their enactment of cognitively-demanding mathematical tasks and higher-level questions about mathematical reasoning (McGee, Wang, & Polly, 2013). Further, many teachers reported embracing this student-centered way of teaching; however, teachers also expressed apprehension using the curriculum and student-centered pedagogies in upper elementary school grades due to the pressure on statewide high-stakes tests (McGee, et al., 2013).

Research from the second and third years of the project continued to find statistically significant findings between teachers' content knowledge and their students' achievement (Polly, Wang, McGee, Lambert, Martin, & Pugalee, 2014; Polly, McGee, Wang, Martin, Lambert, & Pugalee, in press). Teachers also reported shifts from teacher-centered to student-centered practices each year (Polly et al., 2014; Polly et al., in press). The only inconsistency was once again teachers' beliefs, as some teachers reported shifts from traditional to more student-centered beliefs, but others reported shifting from student-centered to traditional beliefs (Polly et al., 2014).

Assessment Practices to Support Mathematics Learning and Understanding for Students (APLUS)

Assessment Practices to Support Mathematics Learning and Understanding for Students *(APLUS)* is a project funded by the (state) Mathematics and Science Partnership (MSP) grant program that involves assisting kindergarten through second grade teachers in learning to effectively use the *Assessing Mathematics Concepts* (*AMC Anywhere*) tool for formative assessment which is then analyzed for instructional purposes. This project includes six school districts throughout a large state in the southeastern United States.

AMC Anywhere is a web-based formative assessment system designed based on children's number sense (Richardson, 2012). There are nine assessments in *AMC Anywhere*: Counting Objects, Changing Numbers, More/Less Trains, Number Arrangements, Combination Trains, Hiding Assessments, Ten Frames, Grouping Tens, and Two-Digit Addition and Subtraction. These assessments include different parts and varying number of activities. The assessments are administered one-on-one with the teachers using an iPad or computer. *AMC Anywhere* assessments produce reports for individual students with the letters A, P+, P, P-, I, and N. The letters stand for apply, practice, instruction, and needs prior skill. The assessment includes + or – with these letters that indicate the degree to which the student is performing in this area. *AMC Anywhere* can provide data on students' learning and recommended instructional activities from *Developing Number Concepts*, a set of mathematics activities focused on number sense. Teachers can take the report and match it up with ways to support their students. The professional development provided with this grant intended to instruct teachers how to use the assessment and provide support to develop number sense.

Goals

The grant lists the overarching goals that guided the implementation of APLUS and served as a tool for evaluation:

1. Strengthen teachers' understanding of number concept development.
2. Build teachers knowledge base for key mathematical ideas underlying number concepts and how children think with numbers and use numbers to solve problems.
3. Develop teachers' abilities to differentiate instruction to support learning for all students.
4. Increase teachers' use of formative assessment data to plan instruction.
5. Extend teachers' own mathematical understanding as they develop new ideas about how students learn mathematics.

The professional development (PD) provided to teachers in the summer for five days (8 hours per day). After the summer PD, follow-up PD (40 hours) was in the form of three on-line modules. The PD focused on instructing teachers on how to use the assessments, how to analyze the data, and how to effectively pair the data with instruction. Facilitators, during the summer sessions, provided background on the development of *AMC Anywhere*, the importance of developing number sense that leads to greater conceptual understanding, and how this one-on-one formative assessment can provide data on individual learners. The PD included video illustrations of students and teachers working with *AMC Anywhere* and toward the end of the week actual students were brought in for teachers to work with directly. Each experience with students on video and in person was paired with an opportunity to work with the Kathy Richardson support texts. Teachers worked in groups to identify next steps from the data they acquired. The support for this work continued through three online modules that included similar activities and asked for teachers to post plans, questions, and challenges.

The goals of this grant were to introduce a web-based formative assessment tool and give teachers the PD needed to become active and effective users. Teachers becoming active and effective users would have a greater understanding of number sense, value formative assessment for instruction, and plan with the individual student in mind, and through this increase student achievement.

Description of Activities

The summer session began with teachers getting introduced to *AMC Anywhere*, this included information on the development and developer of the program, the theoretical foundation of the assessments, and meeting the developer, Kathy Richardson. Richardson spent many years teaching kindergarten and was able to share how she created and used the *AMC Anywhere* assessments in her instruction. She discussed personal experiences in her classroom and instances of assisting other teachers. The facilitators showed the teachers the website and navigated through the assessments, the reports, and used test mode to illustrate the actual questions found in the assessment. As previously mentioned, teachers evaluated videos of students engaged in an assessment, worked with real students, and used actual data with the instructional supports.

The summer session ended and PD continued through online modules. The first module required teacher participants to discuss their classroom environment, describe their mathematics routine, and explain how they use data as an instructional tool. Module two included video assessments of students for teachers to evaluate, a place to propose an instructional plan, and an opportunity to post the implementation follow-up. The last module focused on introducing number talks, developing strategies for number talks, and designing purposeful talks.

Summary of Findings

APLUS is a three year MSP grant that includes an evaluation team that provides a full report yearly. The summer sessions included a pre and post survey that examined teacher versus student centered instruction and included a gauge of the teachers' data collection goals. In addition there were open ended responses. The teachers' responses in the online modules were also collected and evaluated. The assessment data for each student, which identifies who their teacher was that year, how many times they were assessed, the assessments they took, and the level they reached for the assessment.

There were several findings from the quantitative and qualitative data analysis. The summer pre/post survey showed a statistically significant change from teacher-centered to student-centered practices (Martin & Polly, 2015; Polly et al., 2014). In addition, there was a statistically significant increase in teachers' reported scores for being able to collect and analyze data (Wang, Polly, Lambert, Pugalee, Evans, & 2014). Further, teachers in year one of the project who used the *AMC Anywhere* system at least three times saw more significant gains in student learning than teachers who only used the system once or twice (Polly et al., 2014).

The examples below are the open ended responses included on the post survey from teachers. These highlight participants' reactions to the professional development project:

This was such an excellent training workshop that opened my mind up to a more hands on center based classroom. I want my students to leave my room feeling confident about numbers and number sense.

Another teacher-participant commented about her learning about the importance of data-based planning. This "totally changed my thinking. I plan to collect my data first and then plan lessons/activities based on the need of my children"

The responses show support for the quantitative findings from the survey and illustrate the teachers' enthusiasm for using the *AMC Anywhere* that school year. The module findings indicated a divide between high fidelity teachers and low fidelity teachers. Those that were in the high fidelity used *AMC Anywhere*, participated in the PD, offered thoughtful responses, and had the AMC student data that supported their implementation. The low fidelity teachers may have been enthusiastic when the summer session ended; however, their participation waned. It appeared they may have needed more support to continue effective use of the assessments. The actual student data indicated that the teachers that used the assessments often with their students saw the most student growth. The evaluation of the grant is continuing to evolve to better understand how teachers can be supported and the effect of using *AMC Anywhere* formative assessments on student achievement.

IMPLICATIONS AND FUTURE DIRECTIONS

Meeting the Needs of Teachers and Participating school Districts

Learner-centered professional development (LCPD) must be designed to meet the individual and collective needs of teacher-participants and the school districts that they work for (Polly & Hannafin, 2010; Hawley & Valli, 2000). In the two projects described in this chapter there were specific needs related to mathematics instruction and student achievement. Through collaborative partnerships between the university faculty and school district leaders, both projects were designed to address student learning deficiencies and also address teachers' and school districts' needs related to mathematics instruction.

Future professional development projects must include an ongoing collaborative partnership between the professional development facilitators and district or school-based leaders (Polly, 2012). Professional development activities are such a large investment of both time and resources that it is critical that proper planning has been done to ensure that the learning activities meet the needs of teachers (Polly & Hannafin, 2011). As seen in these two projects the benefit of having professional development co-designed by university faculty and district-leaders was that the learning activities were relevant to teachers' needs and aligned to major comprehensive mathematics support efforts in each district.

Teacher Ownership

Teacher ownership is a key principle of learner-centered professional development (Polly, 2011; Hawley & Valli, 2000). In these two projects, the professional development activities were divergent in that specific activities were included in the summer institute workshops, but teachers were given ownership of how they chose to implement and apply the knowledge and skills that they learned in the professional development. In the CoDe-I project, teachers reported shifts from enacting teacher-centered to more instances of learner-centered mathematics pedagogies (Polly et al., 2013; in press). In the APLUS project teachers' online discussion board posts indicated that teachers were applying the content of the professional development differently as they created instructional plans based on their formative instructional data (Polly, Martin, Wang, Lambert, & Pugalee, under review).

Designing Professional Development Activities During the School Year

Participants took part in the program for a year, which included an intensive summer institute as well as school-based learning activities during the school year. The goal of school-based or job-embedded professional development is to develop teachers' knowledge and skills through activities that are closely related or embedded to the daily work of teachers (Hawley & Valli, 2000).

In the CoDe-I project teachers completed job-embedded activities such as assessing and reflecting on student performance through the analysis of curriculum-based assessments, video recorded classroom discussions and spent time reflecting and watching their videos and their colleagues' videos, and facilitating professional development and planning meetings with their colleagues. CoDE-I participants reported that these job-embedded activities provided learning opportunities without adding too much undue burden to the already challenging workload of teachers.

In the APLUS project teachers completed a series of online modules, which included a refresher of how to use the *AMC Anywhere* system, support in setting up data-based instructional activities, as well as learning more content. The job-embedded professional development activities in the APLUS project were focused on the use of the *AMC Anywhere* system, which meant that it was closely connected to the work of teachers who frequently used the tool, but not connected to those teachers who were not consistent in their use of the system.

Future professional development projects need to closely examine the goals of their program and look for ways to capitalize on opportunities to situate teacher learning in classroom-based or job-embedded activities (Polly & Mims, 2009; Polly et al., 2014). While summer or outside of classroom workshops provide an opportunity to intensively engage with content and new pedagogies, the most relevant and related professional learning activities are those embedded in teachers' classroom and daily work.

Evaluation of Professional Development

The evaluation of the impact of professional development on both teachers and their students is quite problematic to assess (Yoon et al., 2007). Part of the potential issue is linking professional development activities to teacher learning and then linking evidence of teacher learning to student learning outcomes.

The evaluation of APLUS includes several challenges that continue to be considered and rethought. The teachers can use any of the nine assessments at any time and usually make their assessment decisions based on evidence they see in their classrooms. This means a student may be assessed with the counting numbers assessment and a few weeks later, based on work in the classroom, the teachers may decide to assess the student using the hiding assessment. If the student is not assessed more than once with the same assessment it is difficult to accurately chart growth. Teachers may also make decisions to assess students at a level that is too high and end up having to make readjustments that also distort the data's picture of student growth. Another challenge for evaluating growth is the ceiling effect. Teachers may have students performing beyond an assessment, this may be a reason for either moving on to a new assessment or a reason the teacher decides to use other resources. Accounting for these decisions and understanding the full picture of student progress is difficult; however, this formative assessment was meant to be adaptable and used at the teachers' discretion and not necessarily be used in a linear fashion.

Another challenge for evaluation of PD is identifying the various causes for lack of participation in the online modules and to understand the responses that were somewhat disconnected from the goals of the PD. The survey at the end of summer session indicated the teachers were excited and felt empowered to use formative assessment to inform their instruction and increase student mathematical performance. The online modules, which lasted throughout the academic year, had a large drop in participation. Researchers are considering the support systems that are in place or lack thereof as a possible cause of the decreased participation. The online module that focused on implementation of instructional plans based on AMC Anywhere data was also analyzed. The prompt specifically asked teachers to reference their AMC Anywhere data and offer a rationale for instructional activities based on their data; however only 67.4% included their data and 43.5% provided a rationale in their response (Polly et al.,, under review). The PD also intended for teachers to be able to use the Developing Number Concepts (DNC) resources provided to support instruction based on AMC data. The instructional plans posted in the module that referenced instructional activities from Developing Number Concepts (DNC) resources were 55.1% and these types of responses closely matched the expectations from the professional development (Polly et al., under review). These areas are being analyzed to provide greater support and to enhance the future PD.

In the CoDe-I project, evaluators used curriculum-based assessments from the *Investigations* curriculum to examine student progress. Students completed identical assessments before and after three different units during the year in order to look at growth. Data analysis indicated that there were empirical links between teachers' instructional practices and content knowledge to gains in student achievement (Polly et al., 2013, 2014). However, the empirical links were inconsistent in various grade levels and across units.

One of the issues with the *Investigations* curriculum-based assessments was that the assessments included few items and some were multi-part. The evaluation team developed rubrics for each item and scored them on a percentage basis in order to provide consistency across grades and units. Future professional development projects should examine empirical links between teacher learning and student learning by examining student assessment data. The use of curriculum-based assessments provided measures that were aligned to the goals of the professional development as well the content that teachers were focusing on in their instruction.

CONCLUSION

Learner-centered professional development has potential to transform how teachers learn as well as how teacher learning impacts both teachers' instruction and student achievement. In this chapter both the CoDe-I and APLUS projects were designed using LCPD principles to support elementary school teachers' mathematics instruction. The findings from the evaluation and research of these LCPD efforts included gains in student learning outcomes, teachers' adoption of student-centered practices, and shifts towards more student-centered instruction. Further, in the APLUS project, teachers documented their successful use of formative data to design developmentally-appropriate instruction for their students. Implications for the design of future LCPD programs includes continuing mutual partnerships between professional development facilitators with district and school-based leaders, the careful design of classroom-based or job-embedded learning activities, and the methods used to evaluate LCPD programs.

REFERENCES

Alexander, P. A., & Murphy, P. K. (1998). The research base for APA's learner-centered psychological principles. In N. M. Lambert & B. L. McCombs (Eds.), *Issues in school reform: A sampler of psychological perspectives on learner-centered schools* (pp. 33–60). Washington, DC: American Psychological Association; doi:10.1037/10258-001

Borko, H. (2004). Professional development and teacher learning: Mapping the terrain. *Educational Researcher*, *33*(8), 3–15. doi:10.3102/0013189X033008003

Borko, H. (2004). Professional development and teacher learning: Mapping the terrain. *Educational Researcher*, *33*(8), 3–15. doi:10.3102/0013189X033008003

Common Core state Standards Initiative (2010). Common Core State Standards for Mathematics. Retrieved from: http://corestandards.org

Darling-Hammond, L., Wei, R. C., Andree, A., Richardson, N., & Orphanos, S. (2009). *Professional learning in the learning profession: A status report on teacher professional development in the United States and abroad*. Washington, D.C.: National Staff Development Council.

Desimone, L. (2009). How can we best measure teachers' professional development and its effects on teachers and students? *Educational Researcher, 38*(3), 181–199. doi:10.3102/0013189X08331140

Garet, M., Porter, A., Desimone, L., Briman, B., & Yoon, K. (2001). What makes professional development effective? Analysis of a national sample of teachers. *American Educational Research Journal, 38*(4), 915–945. doi:10.3102/00028312038004915

Hawley, W., & Valli, L. (2000). Learner-centered professional development. *Phi Delta Kappan Research Bulletin*. Retrieved from http://tlcliteracy.org/images/downloads/Professional_Development/learner_centered_pro.pdf

Higgins, J., & Parsons, R. (2009). A successful professional development model in mathematics: A system-wide New Zealand case. *Journal of Teacher Education, 60*(3), 231–242. doi:10.1177/0022487109336894

Loucks-Horsley, S., Love, N., Stiles, K. E., Mundry, S., & Hewson, P. W. (2010). *Designing professional development for teachers of science and mathematics* (3rd ed.). Thousand Oaks, CA: Corwin Press.

Martin, C. S., & Polly, D. (2015). Using the AMC Anywhere web-based assessment system to examine primary students' understanding of number sense. In D. Polly (Ed.), *Cases on Technology Integration in Mathematics Education* (pp. 366–377). Hershey, PA: IGI Global; doi:10.4018/978-1-4666-6497-5.ch018

McGee, J. R., Wang, C., & Polly, D. (2013). Guiding teachers in the use of a standards-based mathematics curriculum: Perceptions and subsequent instructional practices after an intensive professional development program. *School Science and Mathematics, 113*(1), 16–28. doi:10.1111/j.1949-8594.2012.00172.x

National Council for Teachers of Mathematics. (2014). *Principles to Action*. Reston, VA: Author.

Polly, D. (2006). Participants' focus in a learner-centered technology-rich mathematics professional development program. *The Mathematics Educator, 16*(1), 14–21.

Polly, D. (2011). Examining teachers' enactment of technological pedagogical and content knowledge (TPACK) in their mathematics teaching after technology integration professional development. *Journal of Computers in Mathematics and Science Teaching, 30*(1), 37–59.

Polly, D., & Hannafin, M. J. (2010). Reexamining technology's role in learner-centered professional development. *Educational Technology Research and Development, 58*(5), 557–571. doi:10.1007/s11423-009-9146-5

Polly, D., & Hannafin, M. J. (2011). Examining how learner-centered professional development influences teachers' espoused and enacted practices. *The Journal of Educational Research, 104*(2), 120–130. doi:10.1080/00220671003636737

Polly, D., Martin, C. S., Wang, C., Lambert, R. G., & Pugalee, D. K. (under review). Primary grades teachers' instructional decisions while participating in mathematics formative assessment professional development.

Polly, D., McGee, J. R., Wang, C., Martin, C. S., Lambert, R. G., & Pugalee, D. K. (in press). Linking professional development, teacher outcomes, and student achievement: The case of a learner-centered mathematics program for elementary school teachers. *International Journal of Educational Research*.

Polly, D., & Mims, C. (2009). Designing professional development to support teachers' TPACK and integration of Web 2.0 technologies. In T. T. Kidd & I. Chen (Eds.), *Wired for Learning: Web 2.0 Guide for Educators* (pp. 301–316).

Polly, D., & Orrill, C. H. (2012). Developing technological pedagogical and content knowledge (TPACK) through professional development focused on technology-rich mathematics tasks. *Meridian, 15*. Retrieved from http://ced.ncsu.edu/meridian/index.php/meridian/article/view/44/43

Polly, D., Wang, C., Martin, C. S., Lambert, R. G., Pugalee, D. K., Stephan, M., & Ringer, C. (2014, April). Examining the influence of professional development on primary students' mathematical achievement. Paper presented at the 2014 Annual Meeting of the American Educational Research Association. Philadelphia, PA.

Polly, D., Wang, C., McGee, J. R., Lambert, R. G., Martin, C. S., & Pugalee, D. K. (2014). Examining the influence of a curriculum-based elementary mathematics professional development program. *Journal of Research in Childhood Education, 28*(3), 327–343. doi:10.1080/02568543.2014.913276

Richardson, K. (2012). *How Children Learn Number Concepts: A Guide to the Critical Learning Phases*. Bellingham, WA: Math Perspectives.

Swan, M. (2006). Designing and using research instruments to describe the beliefs and practices of mathematics teachers. *Research in Education, 75*(-1), 58–70. doi:10.7227/RIE.75.5

TERC. (2008). *Investigations in Number, Data, and Space* (2nd ed.). Saddle River, NJ: Pearson.

United States Department of Education. (2008). Foundations for Success: The Final Report of the National Mathematics Advisory Panel. Retrieved from http://www2.ed.gov/about/bdscomm/list/mathpanel/report/final-report.pdf

Wang, C., Polly, D., Lambert, R. G., Pugalee, D. K., & Evans, A. (2014, February). Examining the influence of elementary mathematics professional development on formative assessment of teachers. Presentation given at the Annual Meeting of the North Carolina Association for Research in Education: Greensboro, NC.

Wang, C., Polly, D., Lehew, A., Pugalee, D., Lambert, R., & Martin, C. S. (2013). Supporting teachers' enactment of elementary school student-centered mathematics pedagogies: The evaluation of a curriculum-focused professional development program. *New Waves - Educational.* [PubMed]. *Research for Development, 16*(1), 76–91. Retrieved from http://www.caerda.org/journal/index.php/newwaves/article/view/97/46 PMID:23154410

Work, A. P. A. Group of the Board of Educational Affairs (1997). Learner-centered psychological principles: A framework for school reform and redesign. Washington, DC.

Yoon, K. S., Duncan, T., Lee, S. W.-Y., Scarloss, B., & Shapley, K. (2007). Reviewing the evidence on how teacher professional development affects student achievement (Issues & Answers Report, REL 2007–No. 033). Washington, DC: U.S. Department of Education; Retrieved from http://ies.ed.gov/ncee/edlabs

Chapter 10
Identifying the Target Needs of Non-Native Subject Teachers Related to the Use of English in Their Professional Settings:
A Case from Northern Iraq

Ece Zehir Topkaya
Çanakkale Onsekiz Mart University, Turkey

İbrahim Nişancı
Ishik University, Iraq

ABSTRACT

This study primarily explores the target needs of subject teachers from various disciplines who are all non-native speakers of English and enrolled in a training program preparing them to teach their subjects in English. Secondarily, it looks into the key stakeholders' evaluation of the program to understand its effectiveness to meet the needs of the teachers. For the first question, key stakeholders were interviewed to identify the needs, wants, and lacks of the teachers based on Hutchinson and Water's (1987) needs analysis framework. Then, the pooled items were converted into a questionnaire which was administered to the teachers in the program. To investigate the second question, open-ended questions and semi-structured interviews were used. Findings revealed that participants were in need of developing productive language skills while they reported satisfaction over the program. It is concluded that a more specifically tailored course both in terms of content and practice is needed.

INTRODUCTION

As English has become the language of international commerce, sciences, business, communication, and technology everywhere in the world, it is now considered as a basic skill that every individual needs to be competent at a certain level. Therefore, governments and educational institutions all around the world are now seeking ways to teach English to the younger generations more effectively in order to provide them

DOI: 10.4018/978-1-4666-9471-2.ch010

with "some kind of competitive advantage... in the job market" or global economic market (Graddol, 2006, p. 107). Some are doing it through integrating content and language education and thus adopting an English-across-the-curriculum approach while some are launching bilingual education where the medium of instruction (MoI) is English. Following this trend, "many countries in Asia, Europe and Latin America have already experimented with teaching one or more subjects through [English] programmes and national initiatives" (Hodijah, 2012, p.82).

Like all rapidly developing countries, there has also been a great development in every field of life in Iraq, especially in Northern Iraq, including education since 2003. Although Iraqi universities and higher educational institutions have been cut off from progress in educational curricula, resources, teaching methods, modern technology and research for two decades, there is a great demand for integration with the global academic world as well as the economic market. In such a context, the need for learning English has become one of the major concerns of the country giving rise to a rapid growth in the number of institutions conducting most of the instruction in English. This situation, on the other hand, has brought about the problem of finding subject teachers who can teach in English since it is hard to reach them in Iraq or bring them to Iraq.

Feeling this pressure for qualified teachers who can teach in English, one of the biggest educational institutions offering multilingual education in Kurdish, Turkish, Arabic, and English at different levels in Northern Iraq has initiated a year-long teacher training program for non-native teachers from various subjects such as science, mathematics, and primary school education which comprises a language course segment as well. While pedagogy, intercultural issues, general instructional knowledge and skills form the teacher education segment, the language course segment aims at preparing non-native subject teachers to function in school settings using English as the MoI. It includes a general English language course and English for Specific Purposes (ESP) course run in two separate academic terms.

This unique program has never been investigated in terms of its critical components such as administrative staff, program staff, course attendees, course materials, assessment procedures, or the syllabus since its start three years ago. Yet, based on the knowledge that needs analysis is the starting point for designing and revising programs of any kind, this particular study aims to identify the language needs of the subject teachers attending the language course segment of the program and understanding whether the current program is able to meet these needs. This study is thus guided by the following two research questions:

1. What are the target needs of the non-native subject teachers attending the language course segment of the program?
2. What is the overall evaluation of the key stakeholders -the subject teachers and course manager- regarding the language course segment of the program?

Before moving on the details of the study, however, a brief literature review on the two core issues of it, English as the MoI and needs analysis, are presented below.

English as the Medium of Instruction

As Graddol (2006, p. 82) states, "learners, their families, teachers, governments, employers, textbook publishers, examination providers" are the major stake holders of education who have different opinions and beliefs about how English language should be taught and learnt. For decades, there have been two

Identifying the Target Needs of Non-Native Subject Teachers

major approaches to English language teaching: either as a foreign or as a second language. However, now more governments are interested in making their countries bilingual such as Singapore, Columbia, Mongolia, Chile, South Korea, Taiwan, Malaysia, and Indonesia. In this context, one of the ways of adopting this kind of approach is to start teaching a number of subjects such as science, mathematics, biology, chemistry in English.

Therefore, now an increasing number of teachers in different corners of the world need to use English effectively in order to deliver subject specific content knowledge and skills to their learners (Low, Chong & Ellis, 2014; Othman & Mohd Saat, 2009). While doing so, they need to have certain linguistic competencies and fulfill tasks when using English as the MoI. As listed by Richards (2010 cited in Low, Chong & Ellis, 2014, p. 66),

- To comprehend texts accurately,
- To be good language models,
- To maintain constant and fluent use of the target language in the classroom,
- To give explanations and instructions in the target language,
- To provide examples of words and grammatical structures and give accurate explanations (e.g. of vocabulary and language points),
- To use language appropriate for classroom usage,
- To select appropriate target-language resources,
- To be able to effectively monitor one's own speech and writing accurately,
- To give correct feedback on learner language,
- To provide input at an appropriate level of difficulty, and
- To provide language enrichment experiences for learners

are but some of these competencies and tasks. Moreover, in multilingual settings, the use of English is not just limited to classrooms. Teachers also need to use it as the means of communication with parents, colleagues, school personnel and other stakeholders for various purposes. Therefore, several other linguistic competencies and tasks can be added to the list offered by Richards above.

In this context, educating specialist teachers who can focus on their subjects using English as the MoI is becoming a major concern in several countries around the world. There are certain initiatives that are already underway in several countries both at pre-service and in-service levels. For example, in Malaysia pre-service English language teachers are also trained to teach science at primary schools (Hudson, 2009). In Singapore, where English has been the MoI since 1987, teacher candidates have to take the Entrance Proficiency Test which "provides a threshold proficiency in English for teacher candidates applying to teach English medium subjects" (Low, Chong & Ellis, 2014, p. 65). In Vietnam, where some high schools have started teaching subjects in English recently, there are no official training programs to prepare subject teachers to teach their subject in English but the Ministry of Education and Training is planning to offer such programs for both pre and in-service teachers (Nguyen, 2013). On the other hand, in Finland the University of Helsinki, Department of Teacher Education offers a program in English geared for both Finnish and international pre-service teachers giving official qualifications for teaching in basic and secondary education.

As can be detected from these examples, there are three major policies addressing the training of subject teachers using English as the MoI. One is that teacher candidates take courses on language and teaching skills in order to teach their subject through English, the other one is that teacher candidates receive all of their training in English and the third one is that in-service training is offered to practicing teachers. Each country depending on their own contextual constraints and opportunities seems to adopt the best option available to them.

Together with this accelerated interest in and implementations of teaching other subject through English movement, a parallel increase in studies investigating pre and in-service teachers' perceptions on the challenges of teaching other subject through English with a focus on language needs can be observed. For example, in a small scale study conducted in Malaysia with the participation of 26 science and mathematics teachers using English 92.3% of the respondents reported problems using new terms or words correctly while 88.5% of them had difficulty in expressing themselves correctly in English (Yahaya, Noor, Mokhtar, Rawian, Othman, & Jusoff, 2009). Similarly, another study done in the Malaysian context in 2012 reported that subject teachers of science and mathematics needed "general English language skills, certain specific language aspects such as instructional vocabulary and phrases" (Masuum, Maarof, Zakaria, & Yamat, 2012, p. 1004). In Singapore, Low, Chong and Ellis (2014) found that although the pre-service subject teachers in their cohort fell into the categories of 'very good' and 'good' users of English according to their IELTS scores, they had relatively lower scores in productive skills of speaking and writing, especially in terms of pronunciation features and formal writing styles. In another study in the Malaysian context by Hudson (2009), 50 pre-service teachers at the end of their first year of a Bachelor of Education Studies (Primary Science) degree stated that having not enough time to learn English with the associated science terminology was the biggest barrier for them to learn how to teach science using English as the MoI. They also reported understanding and memorizing science terminology as challenges for them.

As these studies show, general English language skills, field-related terminology and phrases are the major areas that can be regarded as language needs of pre and in-service subject teachers. It is obvious that as school systems, learning and teaching change in this new global context of education, teacher preparation programs and in-service training courses should be designed to support subject teachers using English as the MoI so that they could attain the required highest level of English proficiency needed to teach their subjects effectively.

Needs Analysis

Investigating learner needs is a prerequisite in effective course design and revision. Since the specificity of tasks, genres and discourse in various situations that language learners have to operate change, a "one-size-fits all" approach has proven to be ineffective. Therefore, every language course ought to be considered unique and be designed through needs analysis (NA) (Long, 2005).

It can be better to understand what is meant by needs before discussing NA in detail. Simply put, needs refers to wants, desires, demands, expectations, lacks, deficiencies, goals, aims, purposes and objectives (Jordan, 1997, p. 22). NA, on the other hand, is "the process of establishing the what and how of a course" (Dudley-Evans & St John, 1998, p. 121). Especially in ESP course design NA is "a stage in which the course developers identify what specific language and skills the group of language learners will need" (Bashturkmen, 2010, p. 17). Main directions of needs analysis are goals and content of a course. What students are in need of learning and what they know already are questioned in this process. By doing NA, it is assured that the course will involve germane and beneficial things for learners (Nation & Macalister, 2010, p. 24).

NA can be considered as an umbrella term since it "has become increasingly sophisticated" over the years (Bashturkmen, 2010, p. 17) and several other approaches have been included to it such as target-situation analysis, present-situation analysis, situation analysis, means analysis, strategy analysis and etc. (Jordan, 1997), all of which offer clear descriptions and systematic procedures to conduct a needs analysis (see Basturkmen, 2010; Dudley-Evans & St John, 1998; Hutchinson & Waters, 1987; Munby 1978). Since this study has taken up Hutchinson and Waters' framework of NA as the basic departure point to investigate the research questions posed at the beginning of the study, some more information will be given on their approach here.

Hutchinson and Waters (1987) believe that learners should take active participation in the process of NA since learning is a "process of negotiation between individuals and society" (Jordan, 1997, p. 25). Therefore, NA should not just focus on what is to be learnt, i.e. the content (knowledge, skills, and understanding) but also on the activity through which it is to be learnt (Hutchinson & Waters, 1987, p. 92). With this underlying philosophy, thus, Hutchinson and Waters group needs into two categories as target needs and learning needs. The former refers to the expected abilities; tasks and activities learners will carry out in the target situation while the latter deals with the efforts necessary to learn them. They further divide target needs into three sub categories: necessities, lacks, and wants. By necessities they mean what learners should know to meet the target situation requirements. Lacks is the gap between the present state of the learners and what they need to know, do in the target situation while wants represent learners' individual desires, expectations from the language learning process. Despite the fact that not all of these wants are likely to be addressed in the course design and development, the wants of majority can be negotiated and responded. As can be seen, NA provides the initial data upon which the design and development of any kind of ESP course/program becomes possible and by means of on-going NA, objectives, teaching techniques, materials, assessment procedures can be revised and modified.

Although there is a fast growing body of research on NA, the scarcity of studies on the needs of subject teachers using English as the MoI is noteworthy given the increasing number of countries experimenting with this new educational model. Thus, there is a need for studies to understand what pre and in-service teachers around the world feel they need to know, understand and do in order to teach their subjects effectively. Therefore, this study may have the potential of making a modest contribution to the existing literature on NA and the training of subject teachers to use English as the MoI.

The Present Study: Program Specifics and the Significance of the Study

This program started three years ago with 20 subject teachers as course attendees when an educational institution that offers education to students from pre-school to undergraduate level needed subject teachers from various fields to teach their related subjects in primary, secondary and high schools in English. The vice general director of the educational institution explained how and why they started this specific program in the initial interview. He stated:

Every establishment looks for people whom they can work with well. In previous years, we witnessed that some of the teachers we hired could not keep up with our educational system. Even experienced ones had some difficulties for a number of reasons. Therefore, we looked into those likely reasons and we came up with the idea of organizing a course involving teacher development (general pedagogy and field-related support), language development and cultural orientation concerning the realities of our schools and the country. We put an advertisement on the internet and interviewed with the applicants. Those who were accepted were taken into the course.

As could be understood, the educational institution faced several challenges implementing their desired system in their schools and thus took an action by designing a teacher training and language course program for those selected subject teachers. The vice general director summarized their broad aim as follows: "We plan to overcome many obstacles that our teachers may encounter before they start teaching".

Every year around 40 teachers attend the program. As stated above, it is a multifaceted program with courses covering several issues related to learning English for general purposes, teaching subject matter in English, and general teacher education. Seminars are also given on intercultural perspectives and the vision and mission of the educational institution. The medium of instruction in this teacher-training program is English. The program consists of two terms. In the first term, a general English course is given to the attendees including grammar, main course and four language skills, in total 30 hours a week, which lasts 20 weeks. In the second term, an 8-week ESP program follows, which was designed by the coordinator of the course, who holds an M.A. in TESOL and is an experienced teacher and the head of the English department in the educational institution. The ESP course includes five fields: Primary School Education, Science, Mathematics, Physics, and Biology. The heads of each department simulate sample lessons on one of the topics they teach at school in English. Through these simulations, they highlight possible instructional techniques, classroom management skills, and the use of classroom language. Then, the course attendees micro teach to their colleagues, where they get the opportunity to put the knowledge and skills they learn into practice. In Table 1 the language course segment of the program and its details are given.

The program staff includes one native and three non-native English language teachers who are assigned to deliver general English courses in the first term. The English language teachers also work as the coordinators of the course in general. That is, they develop the curriculum, decide on the procedures, choose the content, and develop/select the materials. In the second term, on the other hand, there are four experienced subject teachers who are the heads of science, mathematics, biology, and primary school education departments.

In the initial unstructured interview, the course manager explained how they decided the methodology and content of the program. For needs analysis, they focused on the in-service teachers' needs and lacks mostly as the aim of the program was to prepare competent teachers for the sector. He stated:

Table 1. Teacher-Training Program: Language Courses

	Courses	Hour/week	Materials	Carried out by
First Term	Grammar	12/20	Reference books	English language teachers
	Main course	8/20	Various course books	English language teachers
	Skills	10/20	Various skill books	English language teachers
Second Term	ESP sample lessons	8/8	PowerPoint slides, handouts	Heads of departments
	Microteachings	12/8	PowerPoint slides, handouts	Course attendees (Subject teachers)
	School observations	4/8		Course attendees (Subject teachers)

We observed about 45 different teachers from different subjects for a year. We worked as a team with the heads of the departments. At the end of the year, we wrote a report concerning the pedagogical and linguistic lacks of in-service teachers. Then, we also had discussions with the administrator about the findings.

It is obvious that the educational uniqueness of this ESP course requires a thorough investigation to identify the needs of all stakeholders in a scientific way. Although the program has been running for three years, the actual needs of the participants, their lacks and wants have not been openly questioned before. Therefore, this study is the first attempt taken to understand subject teachers' needs, lacks, and wants, which will inform the stakeholders about the effectiveness of the program in meeting the needs of the participants and, thus, could certainly give way to a sound program revision and development.

METHODOLOGY

Descriptive research design was chosen to investigate the research questions of this study. While doing so, a mixed methodology approach was taken up in order to create a more complete view on the needs of the participants. Huhta, Vogt, and Tulkki (2013) explain that "[t]his is an approach to needs analysis, which may also be referred to as a triangulation of data, in which the researcher has used a combination of qualitative and quantitative methods to identify the learning needs of stakeholders" (p. 16). Therefore, all parties of stakeholders, the vice general director of the institution, program staff, in-service subject teachers, some of whom already participated in the course and teach at different schools of the educational institution, and the course attendees, i.e. the subject teachers participating in the program, were included in different phases of the study using qualitative and quantitative data collection techniques. The steps of data collection, techniques utilized, and stakeholders involved in each step for each research question (RQ) of this study are shown in Table 2.

As can be seen in the table, unstructured and semi-structured interviews were used to find out about different stakeholders' experiences of the training program and the needs felt by these parties. These interviews also helped to develop the main source of data collection instrument, which was a questionnaire. As known well, self-report questionnaires are the most frequently used data collection technique

Table 2. Details for data collection

	Steps	Data Collection Techniques	Stakeholders	Aims
RQ 1	1	Unstructured interview	Vice general director of educational institution	To identify the needs of the institution
	2	Unstructured interviews	• Subject teachers (in-service teachers) • Program staff	To identify the necessities and lacks of the subject teachers
	3	Questionnaire	Subject teachers attending the program	To identify their perceived necessities, lacks and wants
RQ2	1	Questionnaire (open-ended questions)	Subject teachers attending the program	To identify their opinions and evaluations of the language course
	2	Semi-structured interview	Course manager	To identify his opinions and evaluations of the language course

in descriptive research design. They are administered to large groups efficiently in a short time with minimum effort where financial resources are also used wisely (Dörnyei, 2010, p. 9-10). Lastly, the triangulation of these methodological approaches and data sources provided a basis to enhance confidence in the data and its interpretation.

The quantitative data obtained were analyzed using frequencies and percentages while the qualitative data were analyzed through thematic analysis inductively without referring to a theoretically informed coding frame.

Setting and Participants

The study took place in a special teacher-training program in Erbil, Northern Iraq in 2013-2014 teaching year. The data were collected in May, when the program was about to finish. There were 40 subject teachers from Turkey and Iraq enrolled in the program and 36 of them participated in the study voluntarily. The demographic information about the participants is given in Table 3.

As it can be seen in the table, all participants were young teachers with very minimum teaching experience. Although teaching is generally considered as a feminized profession, the equal distribution of teachers among the participants in terms of gender suggests that male teachers favored this program as much as their female counterparts. A majority of the teachers were Turkish, while only 4 of them were Kurdish, as there was a small number of Kurdish applicants. Lastly, the participants' English language backgrounds differed from one another. As the table reveals, 47.2% of the participants reported to have studied English only for a year and within this particular program. It should be noted that although 44.5% of them had more than 4 years of English instruction before they attended the language course, the proficiency level of the participants did not vary since all learners were elementary level learners.

The other stakeholders included in the needs analysis to have an in-depth understanding were the vice general director of the educational institution (GD) and the course manager (CM) and 3 program staff (PS) and five subject teachers who were the heads of departments (HD). They were coded for anonymity and some details for this group of participants are presented in Table 4.

Table 3. Demographic information about the subject teachers attending the course

Label	Categories	f	%
Age	*20-25*	26	72.2
	26-30	10	27.8
Gender	*Male*	18	50
	Female	18	50
Country/ Ethnicity	*Kurdish*	4	11.1
	Turkish	32	88.9
Work experience	*0-2 year*	36	100
Years of English studied	*0-1 year*	17	47.2
Subject specialization	*2-3 years*	3	8.3
	4-5 years	2	5.6
	6 or more years	14	38.9
	Science	15	41.7
	Mathematics	12	33.3
	Primary school	4	11.1
	Biology	5	13.9

Identifying the Target Needs of Non-Native Subject Teachers

Table 4. Codes and details about different stake holders

Participant Code	Gender	Age	Years of Experience	Subject Specialization
GD	M	49	27	Mathematics
CM	M	47	25	English
PS1	M	36	14	English
PS2	F	32	8	English
PS3	F	30	5	English
HD1	M	39	16	Mathematics
HD2	M	33	11	Science
HD3	M	38	15	Biology
HD4	M	39	16	Primary School Education
HD5	M	34	12	English

Data Collection Instrument and Its Development

In order to find answers to the first RQ posed at the onset of the study, in other words to elicit the target needs, lacks and wants of the participants, a four-part needs analysis questionnaire was designed by the researchers (see Appendix 1). It included both closed and open-ended items. The participants were asked to respond to the closed-ended items by using 3-point Likert scale. For different parts, different anchors were used. The first part of the questionnaire aimed at identifying the lacks of the participants concerning communicative target tasks, i.e. occupational tasks, requiring speaking, writing, reading and listening skills. The second part asked the participants to evaluate their general English skills in order to have a deeper understanding of their lacks. At the right side of each item in these first and second parts, the participants were provided spaces where they were invited to give more in depth information about their target needs. In the third part, they were asked to select those language skills and communicative target tasks given in the first two parts that they would like to develop more in the course. They were also given space to write more about their individual expectations from the course. By this way, their wants were identified. In the last part of the questionnaire, demographic information about the participants was collected.

While developing the needs analysis questionnaire, firstly, three parties of stakeholders, i.e., GD, CM, 3 PSs and 5 HDs were interviewed about the priorities of the course and target needs of the subject teachers related to the knowledge and skills in English. These initial unstructured interviews provided exploratory data in return (Long, 2005). All interviews were tape-recorded. This data were not only used to understand the phenomenon under investigation but also formed the basis of the needs analysis questionnaire in that the interview data were transcribed and analyzed to determine those needs that were emphasized and the ideas were turned into items and pooled according to Hutchinson and Waters' 'target needs' focus. Then, the pooled items were first presented to the interview participants for 'member checking'. As known, member checking is a technique for establishing the validity of an account where participants correct errors, confirm and/or revise the interpretations, and add any new points to the data (Guba & Lincoln, 1989). After this first step, some minor changes in wording took place and the first version of the questionnaire was designed. Secondly, this earlier version was sent to two experts from the ESP field to get their ideas about the face and content validity of the questionnaire. In the light of the feedback taken from them, extra blank columns were added to the first and second part so that the respondents could reflect on the information provided in the questionnaire and write their personal ideas more freely. These parts provided detailed qualitative data about their choices and shed light on their deeper attitudes and feelings related to their necessities, lacks and wants. After these steps taken, the final version of the questionnaire was formed.

In order to assess the degree of consistency of results across items within the survey, the Cronbach's Alpha was calculated for Part 1 and 2 of the questionnaire. The analysis revealed satisfactory levels of internal consistency for both parts; first part's Alpha value was found to be .89 while the second part occurred as .68.

The second RQ of the study sought to investigate the extent to which the current language course meets those occupational needs as specified by the subject teachers. To this aim, firstly, an open-ended item was added to the third part of the questionnaire asking the current participants of the ESP course to reflect upon their expectations from the course and how much these expectations were fulfilled. Secondly, the course manager was interviewed about the feedback the program receives from the sector and his overall evaluation of the language program (see Appendix 2 for the questions used in the interview with the course manager). In the analysis of the data collected for this research question, the steps outlined by Stemler (2001) were followed. Firstly, the two researchers of this study reviewed the transcripts and categorized the themes and topics independently. Next, they compared their notes and agreed on the emergent themes and topics. Then, they went through the data independently again using the consolidated themes and topics. Lastly, they checked the reliability of the coding and found that they maintained a significant degree of similarity between the coding (92%).

FINDINGS

Research Question 1: What Are the Target Needs of the Non-Native Subject Teachers Attending the Language Course Segment of the Program?

As stated before the conceptual framework of this study was constructed upon Hutchinson and Waters' 'target needs' notion. Therefore, to answer the first research question, the findings are discussed in three parts: necessities, lacks, and wants.

Necessities

Necessities of a course simply mean the demands of the target tasks in learners' future professions (Nation & Macalister, 2010). Therefore, in this particular study the first goal was to find out those target situation tasks which are carried out by the subject teachers in English in their working places. To do this, three different parties were involved in the data collection: the GD, the CM, three PSs and five HDs.

The interview data with the GD revealed that the institutions did not have a clearly specified set of target situation tasks to be done in English, but an overall understanding to the competencies that these subject teachers should have when they start teaching through English. He stated:

Identifying the Target Needs of Non-Native Subject Teachers

... [W]e expect our teachers to be very proficient in classroom language, to have a good command of field terminology, and to able to explain their subjects clearly.(GD)

He did not clearly mention what this classroom language or field terminology might include or what the subject teachers should do to clearly explain their subjects. However, it could be assumed that the educational institution puts emphasis on those competencies related to learning and teaching process and knowledge of content. Therefore, the data he provided might indicate those necessities regarding various skills and knowledge related to these competencies such as beginning and ending the lesson, language of classroom management and spontaneous situations, giving feedback, exemplifying a topic, summarizing the main points and etc.

At this stage, the data derived from the other key stakeholders (CM, PSs, HDs) supported the interpretation made above about the necessities, which were just briefly mentioned by the GD. Being the designer and implementers of the course, they stated what these subject teachers should be able to do in English in their work places, which could be linked to six categories of general teacher competencies as described by the Turkish National Ministry of Education (MEB, 2006) including personal and professional values-professional development, knowing the student, learning and teaching process, monitoring and evaluation of learning and development, school-family and society relationships, and knowledge of curriculum and content. Table 5 shows the target situation tasks identified by these participants and the general teacher competencies they may be classified into.

These findings show that subject teachers need to possess pedagogical, professional, personal and social competencies, all carried out in English. The interviewees touched upon a wide range of tasks related to target situation. They cited some tasks similar to the ones listed by Richards (2010 cited in Low, Chong, & Ellis, 2014). However, as Table 5 clearly shows, they reported more detailed and individual occupational tasks unique to their working place as well and they are those necessities related to the competency areas of learning/teaching process, personal and professional values-professional development, and school-family relationship.

Table 5. Target situation tasks as identified by language course coordinators and staff members

General categories	Target situation tasks	Participant Codes
Learning/ Teaching Process	• Presenting a subject (a lesson) in class • Writing questions for my subject (for exams etc.) • Preparing posters and notices • Writing the roll book • Reading the materials of the lesson to prepare a lesson • Reading web sites on my field (blog, wiki, forum etc.) • Listening to videos and audios related to my field to prepare a lesson	CM,HD1, 2, 3, 4, 5, PS 2 HD 1, 2, 3, 4, 5, S 1, 3 CM, HD 1, 5, PS 1, 3 CM, HD 5, PS 2, PS 3 CM, HD 1, 2, 3, 4, 5, S 1 CM, HD 5, PS 3 CM, HD 5, PS 1
Personal and professional values-professional development	• Presenting a subject in department meetings • Reading books, articles on my field • Conversing with supervisors • Reading web sites on my field (blog, wiki, forum etc.) • Writing a CV • Understanding the teacher's book and its audio files • Listening to complementary files of books (video and audio files) • Listening to videos and audios related to my field for professional development • Commenting on colleagues' presentations	CM, HD 1, 2, 3, 4, 5 CM, HD 1, 2, 3, 4, 5 CM, HD 3, 5 CM, HD 5 CM, HD 5 CM, HD 5 CM, HD 5 CM, HD 1, 2, 3, 4, 5, PS 1, HD 5, PS 2

When the number of the participants indicating the necessities is taken into account, the most essential ones seem to be those requiring academic competence and productive skills such as reading the material of the lesson, reading books and articles, reading web sites, and presenting a subject (lesson) or presenting a subject in departmental meetings. The findings of these interviews show that subject teachers around the world lack similar competencies and have some common necessities (see Low, Chong, and Ellis, 2014; Masuum et al., 2012).

Lacks

Lacks means looking at where learners are at present. Although the identification of lacks could be investigated by looking at learners' assignments or test scores and asking lecturers who evaluate these assignments about the weaknesses and strengths of them, the learners are useful source of information about their lacks. We can have them to do self-evaluation by providing a specific checklist (Nation & Macalister, 2010). As already explained in the methodology part, the target situation tasks identified by the HDs, CM and PSs were rephrased and turned into questionnaire items to understand how they were perceived by the subject teachers attending the course and, thus, to determine the lacks as reported by the subject teachers. While doing so, to ease the analysis, the target situation tasks were grouped under two categories: communicative target tasks including speaking and writing skills and comprehension-based target tasks including reading and listening ones. These two categories and the perceived lacks of the participants will be presented under separate subheadings below.

Communicative Target Tasks

Table 6 shows those lacks related to speaking as perceived by the subject teachers attending the ESP course.

The participants of the study reported that they needed practice on most of the speaking tasks on the list except the skill regarding starting the lesson, where almost half of them felt they could cope with this

Table 6. Perceived lacks related to the communicative target tasks: speaking

Communicative Target Tasks	I need a lot of practice on this f	I need a lot of practice on this %	I need some practice on this f	I need some practice on this %	I do not need any practice on this f	I do not need any practice on this %
1- Greeting and checking attendance	-	-	19	52.8	17	47.2
2- Small talk	9	25	23	63.9	4	11.1
3- Communicating with students	15	41.7	17	47.2	4	11.1
4- Speaking on the phone.	12	33.4	21	58.3	3	8.3
5- Presenting a subject (a lesson) in class	8	22.2	26	72.2	2	5.6
6- Presenting a subject in department meetings	17	47.3	16	44.4	3	8.3
7- Commenting on colleagues presentations	6	16.6	24	66.7	6	16.7
8- Conversing with supervisors	20	55.6	12	33.3	4	11.1
9- Giving feedback to parents	17	47.3	16	44.4	3	8.3
10- Welcoming guests and informing them about the school	18	50	14	38.9	4	11.1

target situation task ($n = 17$, 47.2%). Yet, more than half of them still felt they needed some practice ($n = 19$, 52.8%). Presenting a subject (a lesson) in class was identified as one of the top necessities by the participants ($n = 34$, 94.4%) along with presenting a subject in English in department meetings ($n = 33$, 91.6%). However, when the ratings were inspected closely, it is seen that while 17 participants (47.2%) reported a strong need for practicing on the latter task, only 8 of them (22.2%) stated they needed a lot of practice on presenting a subject in class. This finding suggests that these subject teachers felt more concerned about speaking English in front of their colleagues. There can be several reasons for this: the possibility of presenting in front of more able teachers in terms of English language skills might be the likely cause of this perceived lack. Similarly, the prospect of spontaneity in language use in these interactive contexts may be another source of this feeling.

Similarly, the participants rated the task, i.e. communicating with students, as a strong necessity (32, 88.9%). However, surprisingly, 15 participants felt they needed a lot of practice on this. This finding seems somewhat contradictory to the rating given to presenting a subject in class and, therefore, requires interpretation. One interpretation could be that these teachers found teacher-to-student interaction pattern easy to handle while face-to-face, spontaneous interaction much more challenging, which may suggest that these subject teachers attending the language courses need to be given more oral production activities where creativity in language is supported and more unpredictable language could be used and practiced. Definitely, this finding may also indicate that the language proficiency level of these participants was not up to this sort of interaction pattern yet, thus, they might still be in need of more general English language instruction.

In the same line with this argument, the target situation tasks of welcoming guests and informing them about the school, giving feedback to parents, conversing with supervisors, speaking on the phone that require more spontaneous social interaction were equally rated as high-priority necessities, a finding which also supports the interpretations made above regarding the use of English in interactive contexts.

When it comes to the communicative target tasks requiring writing, the participants regarded all the tasks identified as skills they needed more or less practice on (see Table 7). They reported a lower need about writing emails, writing CVs, writing roll book, and writing reports. Although fewer participants indicated these target writing tasks to be their top rated necessities, however, it should be noted that more than half of them still viewed them as tasks they needed to practice. Conversely, a great majority of the subject teachers identified writing meeting minutes ($n =34$, 94.4%), writing a defense ($n =34$, 94.4%), writing information notes to parents ($n =33$, 91.6%), writing reports ($n =30$, 83.3%) and writing questions related to their subject matter ($n = 29$, 80.5%) as the top necessities they felt they needed either a lot of practice or some practice on. These data indicate that, as might be expected, the subject teachers found themselves to be more capable of fulfilling those every day and less demanding communicative writing tasks such as email and CV writing while they considered those writing tasks that require more creative language use, a more formal style and register where cohesion and coherence are more important as challenging. These findings also support the findings already reported above regarding communicative speaking tasks where the subject teachers were found to be more concerned about (Low, Chong, & Ellis, 2014; Masuum et al. 2012; Yahaya et al., 2009). Thus, it could be concluded that these subject teachers were still worried about their general language proficiency while they were found to be more confident about those tasks where more formulaic language can be used.

Table 7. Perceived lacks related to the communicative target tasks: writing

Communicative Target Tasks	I need a lot of practice on this f	I need a lot of practice on this %	I need some practice on this f	I need some practice on this %	I do not need any practice on this f	I do not need any practice on this %
1- Writing e-mails	5	13.9	24	66.7	7	19.4
2- Writing report cards	10	28	19	52.6	7	19.4
3- Writing register book	7	19.4	20	55.6	9	25
4- Preparing posters and notices	10	27.7	20	55.6	6	16.7
5- Writing petitions	13	36.1	20	55.6	3	8.3
6- Writing invitations	10	27.7	24	66.7	2	5.6
7- Writing a CV	6	16.7	25	69.4	5	13.9
8- Writing questions (for quiz, exam etc.)	12	33.3	17	47.3	7	19.4
9- Writing reports	8	22.2	22	61.1	6	16.7
10- Writing information notes to parents	12	33.3	21	58.4	3	8.3
11- Writing a defense	18	50	16	44.4	2	5.6
12- Writing meeting minutes	21	58.3	13	36.1	2	5.6

Comprehension-Based Target Tasks

As identified by the GD, CM and HDs working at schools, some comprehension-based target language tasks, i.e. reading and listening, are also needed while teaching subject matter in English. Therefore, the participants in the study were asked to evaluate themselves with regard to these tasks. The following table shows their responses (Table 8).

As the data in Table 7 show, unlike the target situation tasks based on production, the receptive tasks were not regarded as very strong lacks by the majority of the participants where only some of the participants reported to be in need of a lot of practice. Additionally, when reading and listening tasks are compared, the subject teachers appeared to be a bit more confident in target listening tasks. Field-related

Table 8. Perceived lacks related to the comprehension-based target tasks: reading and listening

Comprehension-based Target Tasks	I need a lot of practice on this f	I need a lot of practice on this %	I need some practice on this f	I need some practice on this %	I do not need any practice on this f	I do not need any practice on this %
1- Reading books, articles on my field	6	16.7	25	69.4	5	13.9
2- Reading the materials of the lesson	1	2.7	29	80.6	6	16.7
3- Reading web sites on my field (blog, wiki, forum etc.)	3	8.3	28	77.8	5	13.9
4- Understanding teacher's book.	1	2.7	29	80.6	6	16.7
5- Listening to videos and audios related to my field.	4	11.1	24	66.7	8	22.2
6- Listening to complementary files of books (video and audio files).	3	8.3	24	66.7	9	25

Identifying the Target Needs of Non-Native Subject Teachers

reading was found to be demanding by these subject teachers as majority of them stated they needed a lot of or some practice on them (for example, reading books, articles and reading the materials related to their fields on the websites ($n = 31$, 86.1%), reading lesson materials and teacher's book ($n = 30$, 83.4%). These findings may indicate a lack in terms of vocabulary knowledge related to their own subject fields. Similarly, these teachers might also be unfamiliar with the genres used in these reading materials. However, to determine the exact reasons for this perceived lack, more in depth research needs to be done.

Lastly, the subject teachers were also invited to evaluate their overall language skills and knowledge (see Table 9). The results revealed that productive skills are the ones the participants did not feel themselves very competent (speaking and fluency). This finding is consistent with the points already identified in communicative target tasks where the participants rated most target speaking and writing tasks as considerably more demanding (see Tables 7 and 8). As could be expected, pronunciation was another skill the subject teachers reported to be weak ($n = 32$, 88.9%). Thus, it could be concluded that speaking was the major skill the participants had problems with. Apart from these, one third of the participants stated that they felt weak regarding the terminology of their subject matters ($n = 12$, 33.3%), which can also be linked to the reported lacks in reading skills as was interpreted for the likely reason of problems with reading above (see the interpretations for Table 8).

Wants

Learning the wants or the subjective needs of learners is of paramount importance since learner motivation largely depends on these perceived wants. To elicit the data regarding the subjective needs of the subject teachers attending the course, they were invited to write their opinions about their expectations/wants from the language course segment of the program while they were filling out the questionnaire. All of them responded this part and their responses were analyzed and grouped under three categories (see Table 10). For anonymity, the code ST is used to refer to the subject teachers.

Table 9. Perceived lacks related to basic language skills and knowledge

Basic Language Skills and Knowledge	I feel myself weak on this		I think I am OK		I think I am strong on this	
	f	%	f	%	f	%
1- Reading	3	8.3	23	63.9	10	27.8
2- Listening	5	13.9	20	55.6	11	30.5
3- Writing	5	13.9	25	69.4	6	16.7
4- Spelling	4	11.1	22	61.1	10	27.8
5- Punctuation	9	25	19	52.8	8	22.2
6- Speaking	13	36.1	21	58.3	2	5.6
7- Fluency	16	44.4	19	52.8	1	2.8
8- Accuracy	5	13.9	24	66.7	7	19.4
9- Pronunciation	8	22.2	24	66.7	4	11.1
10- Classroom language (vocabulary)	4	11.1	30	83.3	2	5.6
11- Everyday English (speaking phrases)	9	25	23	63.9	4	11.1
12- Terminology of my field	12	33.3	20	55.6	4	11.1

Table 10. Wants (subjective needs) of the subject teachers related to the language courses

Categories	Wants (Subjective Needs)	Participants
Speaking practice & Fluency	More practice for speaking and fluency	ST 1, 2, 4, 5, 6, 7, 8, 10, 13, 14, 16, 17, 19, 20, 21, 22, 23, 24, 25, 26, 28, 29, 30, 31, 32, 35
	Course to be in an English-speaking country or visiting one	ST 11, 14, 18, 21, 23, 24, 25, 28, 29, 30, 31, 32, 35, 36
	Always practicing English during and after the lessons	ST 1, 5, 16, 22, 24, 34, 35, 36
	Learning and using daily phrases	ST 1, 3, 7, 26, 27, 30
Reading	Understanding field-related scientific articles	ST 4, 6, 10, 12, 15, 27
Writing	Writing in formal genres	ST 7, 27, 31

As the Table 10 shows, the first major category of wants is related to the speaking skill, where the reported wants are classified under four sub-headings. Firstly, the respondents expressed that they needed more practice for speaking and fluency. As ST 8 stated "here has to be more focus on speaking practice and fluency". Secondly, a lot of participants reported a strong want for the courses to be in an English speaking country or to be financially supported to visit one for some time (ST 11, ST 14, ST 18, ST 21, ST 23, ST 24, ST 25, ST 28, ST 29, ST 30, ST 31, ST 32, ST 35, ST 36). For example, ST 23 stated "Had we had the course in a country where English is the official language, we would have had more chances to use what we had studied and we would not have fluency and pronunciation difficulties now". Another want identified by the subject teachers was having more opportunities to practice speaking as ST 1 stated "… we must be provided with more speaking opportunities". They also offered some suggestion as to how this could be achieved. ST 24 and ST 34 stated that speaking in English in and out of the classroom should be compulsory and that they should not be allowed to use any other languages during the course while ST 5 said that an increase in class hours for speaking skill would be better. ST 24 even wanted the course teachers to force everyone to speak in the target language by saying "The teachers should be insistent that everybody speak in English language all the time". Lastly, the teachers expressed their wants related to the content of what needs to be practiced, i.e. daily phrases and expressions. For example, according to ST 7 "it can be more beneficial for students if there are chances for practicing daily spoken expressions and communication skills".

The next category of wants was related to the reading skill, for which understanding field related articles was reported as a major want. This finding also supports the findings related to reading skills presented in Table 8 and 10 above, where the participants indicated greater competency in general reading skill (Table 9) while they reported understanding field related books and articles as a lack (Table 8). Regarding this point, ST 6 stated 'I would like to have the capacity to understand scientific articles in my field'.

Lastly, three subject teachers (ST 7, ST 27, ST 31) stated that they wanted to learn more about formal writing genres although they reported to have had sufficient writing practice.

In conclusion, the findings presented in this part indicate that the participants mostly referred to those wants that could be classified under general English language competencies rather than professional needs, which might be due to the fact that these teachers did not start teaching at the time of data collection for this study and therefore they developed limited insights into their individual needs as professionals getting prepared to teach their subject through English.

RQ2: What Is the Overall Evaluation of the Key Stakeholders- the Subject Teachers and Course Manager- Regarding the Language Course Segment of the Program?

To find answers to this research question, qualitative data were collected from the subject teachers and the course manager. The data from these two sources were reported under separate subheadings below.

Views of the Subject Teachers Attending the Course

The qualitative data obtained from the subject teachers were categorized under three broad themes of positive and negative opinions regarding the language course segment of the program.

As for the positive opinions, almost all the respondents reported to have benefitted from the program to a great extent. They appeared to appreciate not only the language course but also the professional development segment of the program. For example, ST 13 indicated that "I feel that the course is way more than I had imagined. I have learned many things and developed myself both in terms of language and professional knowledge and skills". Similarly, ST 10 stated that "I had expected to learn English well and to develop my skills as a teacher. When I reflect on the year, I see I have achieved most of it".

Yet, it should be noted that some of the subject teachers also reported to have had some concerns and doubts about the language course at the beginning. ST 27 stated that "At the beginning, I had huge concerns, as I had not studied English before". As could be understood, this doubt seems to stem from the participants' lack of English instruction. Having no or very little prior foreign language experience was an issue for these participants as another respondent, ST 26, also said "When I joined the course… I knew nothing at all except very little English grammar. So I was not sure if I would be able to improve the language or not". The length of the program also seems to have given way to these concerns as ST 29 pointed out that "At first, I thought that in 8 months, I would not be able to learn a language'. However, these initial worries seem to have been replaced by more positive ideas later on. Especially being able to communicate to a certain extent appears to have given the course attendees a sense of accomplishment as ST 27 asserted that "… now as we approach the end of the course, I feel that I can communicate in English better".

Grammar and writing components of the language course segment were identified as more successful. For example, ST 29 stated that "… I have made a great progress especially for writing and grammar". Likewise, ST 32 wrote that "… my writing has developed more than I had expected". This finding also supports those views of the participants about grammar (accuracy) and writing as reported in Table 9, where a majority of them stated they found themselves rather strong on these language areas. Yet, it is worth reminding that the participants felt they needed more practice regarding communicative target tasks requiring writing (see Table 7). In other words, occupational and formal writing was a challenge for these subject teachers. Therefore, this finding should be read as an indication of the participants' present state in language learning as also stated by one of the respondents: "this course has helped us to establish baseline knowledge and skills in English", who also made a comparison between the past and present concluding that "When we consider the fact that we were just beginner-level learners of English when the course started, I believe this course has been successful" (ST 21).

With regard to negative opinions, majority of the respondents stated their dissatisfaction with the speaking component of the course. Some of them expressed their disappointment in their development of oral skills saying that "At the beginning of the year I thought that I would be able to speak accurately and fluently, now I feel that I have not mastered enough" (ST 32). Having the same expectation, ST 10 also reported to "have difficulty in speaking English fluently". Two of the respondents called speaking their "biggest worry" (ST 8, ST 21) since in the near future they would start teaching which requires more face to face oral interaction than anything else.

As for the reasons for this perceived underdevelopment, fear of making mistakes was found to be the major emotional barrier as ST 27 pointed out "... we need to build self-confidence. We do not want to talk in front of people for fear that we would make mistakes". ST 28 also stated that "I avoided the Canadian teacher every time I saw her, because I was scared to make mistakes. I want to communicate with her without feeling any stress". The second identified reason was a lack of opportunities to practice speaking (ST 28, ST 29, ST 9, ST 5, and ST 7). Also, time allocated to speaking in the course was not enough as 12 subject teachers stated that speaking skill was not as much emphasized as writing in the language course schedule (ST 2, ST 4, ST 6, ST 7, ST 8, ST 9, ST 11, ST 17, ST 28, ST 29, ST 34, and ST 36). Apart from these reasons, the insufficient number of native speaker teachers available was another point raised by the respondents as ST 28 clearly stated that "I believe that there must be other native speakers or native-like people to practice English. Only one Canadian teacher is not enough for all the students". However, some subject teachers also assumed the responsibility for not developing their speaking skills as much as they expected. For example, ST 28 stated that "It is partly our fault for we do not try to speak with teachers" while ST 24 indicated that developing fluency in speaking is basically her own "responsibility".

Course Manager's Views

The semi-structured interview with the course manager provided data that were categorized under two major themes: needs and lacks of subject teachers attending the language course and strengths and weaknesses of the language course.

Under the first theme, the course manager firstly stated that subject teachers had similar necessities and lacks regarding certain language skills and sub-skills. Similar to the views of the subject teachers above, he also identified speaking as the major skill they needed although he stated that "all skills ought to be developed". According to him, subject teachers "mostly worry about their accuracy and avoid speaking with the teachers or in the classroom" and this prevents them from developing their oral skills. Listening and writing are the next two main skills the course manager pointed out as lacks to be developed. He pointed out that especially at the beginning of the course, subject teachers lack effective listening skills because they are beginners or elementary learners. He said "they usually cannot answer any questions... since they do not comprehend what is asked or said". In terms of writing, the course manager also mentioned the subject teachers' needs to develop and practice a range of sub-skills from the simplest ones like spelling to more complicated ones like academic essay writing, which also shows the tremendous job that the course tries to achieve in a limited period of time i.e. 8 months. The similarities between the course manager's and the subject teachers' opinions and perceptions as reported in the quantitative and qualitative data analyses prove that the course manager is aware of the needs and lacks of the course attendees.

Under the second theme, on the other hand, the course manager's comments on the strengths and weaknesses of the program were identified. Firstly, he stated that all course attendees are intrinsically motivated and open to new ideas, two traits that are most needed in an intensive program such as this one. He pointed out that the program staff includes experienced teachers from different subject fields "who are good models for the language and methodology in their subjects" mentioning the sample lessons these teachers present. As for micro teaching sessions, the course manager stated that they are good opportunities for these teachers where "they learn from each other" adding that "They usually take note of every new vocabulary because they know that they will need them next year while teaching".

Apart from these general comments on the strengths of the language course, the manager also mentioned specific implementations and learning strategies they employ throughout the course. For example, he stated that "… we have them read at least 100 graded books during the course" and for each skill "we ask them to keep separate notebooks". He also believed that "There are plenty of listening and writing exercises". Finally, he emphasized that "there is constant assessment and evaluation to ensure that the aims and goals of this training program are met".

As for the weaknesses of the course, the manager identified two major ones: lack of enough speaking practice and the intensity of the program. Like the subject teachers, he believed that not having several native speaker teachers is a problem as he pointed out that "We have only one native speaker for them to practice their English in a natural way". Although it was not mentioned by the subject teachers themselves, the course manager also stated that "the intensity of the program was very challenging for some of the teachers especially for those who had just completed their undergraduate studies as they wanted to relax after four years of study".

Consequently, in the light of the findings presented under RQ2 it can be claimed that the program is successful in helping the subject teachers develop especially their basic receptive English language skills. Given the entry proficiency level of the course attendees and the more emphasis put on reading and grammar as stated by the stakeholders, this result may be an expected one. Overall, the similarities between the views of the stakeholders regarding the strengths and weaknesses of the language course have some implications for program revision and development.

CONCLUSION AND IMPLICATIONS

This study primarily investigated the target needs of non-native subject teachers who were attending a specifically designed training program preparing them to teach their subjects in English. Secondarily, the study looked into the key stakeholders' overall evaluation on the language course segment of the program to understand whether the present course is able to meet the needs of the subject teachers.

There are three main conclusions that could be drawn out from the findings of this study. They are presented below and possible implications are discussed:

Firstly, the subject teachers reported to have developed basic English language skills and knowledge related to comprehension-based tasks. The course structure can be a reason for this particular result. As the subject teachers reported not to have enough practice in speaking and some of them indicated that they needed to develop their writing skills, it can be assumed that there is an imbalance in the distribution of skills courses in the language course program. Therefore, the lesson hours allocated to different skills in the weekly program could be revised. Apart from this reason, the teaching methodology used in the language course might be another cause for this perceived underdevelopment of productive skills. Thus, it might be necessary to question whether the program staff utilizes integrated or segregated approach to skills teaching in the language course.

Secondly, the subject teachers reported to need more input and practice regarding those general skills and tasks in learning English since they were observed to rarely identify professional skills and tasks they will have to perform in English as their needs. This might be due to the fact that almost all of these teachers were beginners when they started the program. Therefore, they might not have attained the proficiency level where they would be more concerned about the professional use of English. This can have three implications for this teacher training program. First, the goals of the course (learning outcomes) could be narrowed down to be more manageable and reachable. This might reduce the negative perceptions of the course attendees regarding their lacks. Second, subject teachers could be taken to school observations as early as the first term of the course, which may help them realize the long-term goals of the language course. Third, an in-service teacher training component can be added to the program, where the graduates of the course continue their training as they teach their subjects in English.

Lastly, the subject teachers reported satisfaction over the general English language course components but did not make any comments on the ESP course component. The existence of criticisms and suggestions from both stakeholders (course manager/designer and subject teachers) imply that a more specifically tailored language course in terms of both content and practice should be launched.

The conclusions and implications stated above have direct practical relevance and serve mutually for course designers, program staff and subject teachers taking the course. Any attempt to revise and restructure the existing program will definitely call for future needs analyses.

Further research may also explore the learning needs of course attendees as proposed by Hutchinson and Waters (1987) since this study solely focused on target needs. Yet, what learners bring into the learning context should also be investigated to better understand what language learning strategies work best, which study skills prove to be effective in an intensive course such as this one.

Since this study concluded that the subject teachers were in need of developing professional skills and knowledge regarding teaching their subjects in English, follow-up studies of former course attendees may surely provide more information about the course design not only for this program but also for in-service training programs.

Limitations of the Study

This present study has some limitations. To start with, it should be noted that this study was a case study where a specific program with specific goals and program structure was investigated. Therefore, the study does not claim that the findings of this study are generalizable across different contexts. Secondly, semi-structured and unstructured interviews were used to identify the necessities of the subject teachers. It is possible that only a partial picture of the target situation tasks was elicited through these interviews. Therefore, in future studies the inclusion of observations of subject teachers using English as the MoI in real school settings could help to triangulate the data to have a more complete description of target situation tasks. Thirdly, a self-report questionnaire was used to collect data from the course attendees to determine their lacks and wants based on the data of the initial interviews with different stakeholders. The closed-ended items in the questionnaire might have limited the possible range of responses although the questionnaire included open-ended questions. Therefore, any other future study may include face to face interviews with the participants in order to get more in-depth information about their lacks, wants and overall evaluation of the course.

REFERENCES

Bashturkmen, H. (2010). *Developing courses in ESP*. New York: Palgrave Macmillan.

Brown, J. D. (1995). *The elements of language curriculum: A systematic approach to program development*. Boston: Heinle & Heinle Publishers.

Dörnyei, Z. (2010). *Questionnaires in second language research: Construction, administration, and processing*. London: Routledge.

Dudley-Evans, T., & St John, M. J. (1998). *Developments in English for specific purposes: A multidisciplinary approach*. Cambridge: Cambridge University Press.

Guba, E. G., & Lincoln, Y. S. (1989). Epistemological and methodological bases for naturalistic inquiry. *Educational Communication and Technology*, *30*(4), 233–252.

Graddol, D. (2006). English next. London: British Council; Retrieved from http://englishagenda.britishcouncil.org/publications/english-next

Hodijah, I. S. (2012). Towards the understanding of bilingual education: The views of teaching other subjects through English (TOSTE) at international Standard schools (ISS). *Asia-Pacific Collaborative Education Journal*, *8*(1), 79–88.

Hudson, P. (2009). Learning to teach science using English as the medium of instruction. *Eurasian Journal of Mathematics, Science and Technology Education*, *5*(2), 165-170. Retrieved from http://www.ejmste.com/v5n2/eurasia_v5n2_hudson.pdf

Huhta, M., Vogt, K., & Tulkki, H. (2013). *Needs analysis for language course design: A holistic approach to ESP*. Cambridge: Cambridge University Press.

Hutchinson, T. (1987). *English for specific purposes*. Cambridge: Cambridge University Press. doi:10.1017/CBO9780511733031

Jordan, R. R. (1997). *English for academic purposes: A guide and resource book for teachers*. Cambridge: Cambridge University Press. doi:10.1017/CBO9780511733062

Long, M. H. (Ed.). (2005). *Second language needs analysis*. Cambridge: Cambridge University Press. doi:10.1017/CBO9780511667299

Low, E., Chong, S., & Ellis, M. (2014). Teachers' English communication skills: Using IELTS to measure competence of graduates from a Singaporean teacher education program. *Australian Journal of Teacher Education*, *39*(10).

Masuum, T. N. R. T. M., Maarof, N., Zakaria, E., & Yamat, H. (2012). Content-based instruction needs and challenges in diversified literacy context. *US-China Foreign Language*, *10*(3), 999–1004.

MEB. (2008). *Öğretmen yeterlikleri: Öğretmenlik mesleği genel ve özel alan yeterlikleri* [Teacher Competencies: General and specific field competencies of teaching profession]. Ankara: Devlet Kitapları Müdürlüğü.

Munby, J. (1978). *Communicative syllabus design: A sociolinguistic model for defining the content of purpose-specific language programmers*. Cambridge: Cambridge University Press.

Nation, I. S. P., & Macalister, J. (2009). *Language curriculum design*. New York, London: Routledge.

Nguyen, D. H. (2013, March 25). *Bilingual education in Vietnam: Success and challenges*. Cambridge Educational Leadership Seminar; Ho Chi Mihn City. Retrieved from http://www.cambridgeassessment.org.uk/Images/137032-dr-dong-hai-nguyen-presentation-slides-.pdf

Othman, J., & Mohd Saat, R. (2009). Challenges of using English as a medium of instruction: Pre-service science teachers' perspective. *The Asia-Pacific Education Researcher*, *18*(2), 307–316.

Patel, M., & Powell-Davies, P. (Eds.). (2009). Access English: English Bilingual Education Symposium. Jakarta: British Council; Retrieved from http://www.teachingenglish.org.uk/sites/teacheng/files/download-accessenglish-publications-ebe-proceedings.pdf

Stemler, S. (2001). An overview of content analysis. *Practical Assessment, Research & Evaluation*, *7*(17). Retrieved from http://PAREonline. net/getvn.asp? v=7 &n=17

Yahaya, M. F., Noor, M. A., Mokhtar, A. A., Rawian, R. B., Othman, M. B., & Jusoff, K. (2009). Teaching of mathematics and science in English: The teachers' voices. *English Language Teaching*, *2*(2), 141–147. doi:10.5539/elt.v2n2p141

KEY TERMS AND DEFINITIONS

Hutchinson and Waters: Two key people on ESP who advocate a learner centered approach to ESP. They inspired a lot of researchers and practitioners by coining the term 'target needs' and categorized them as 'necessities', 'lacks', and 'wants'.

Needs Analysis: As Brown (1995) explains, needs analysis refers to "the systematic collection and analysis of all subjective and objective information necessary to define and validate defensible curriculum purposes that satisfy the language learning requirements of students within the context of particular institutions that influence the learning and teaching situation".

Non-Native: If someone is not born or raised in a particular country he/she is considered to be non-native. As for non-native speaker of English, it refers to a person who was not born in an English spoken country or family, and learned it later.

Productive Language Skills: They refer to skills that require production of target language (mainly speaking and writing).

Receptive Language Skills: They refer to skills that require comprehension of target language (mainly listening and reading).

Stakeholders: This term refers to person(s) with an interest or concern in something, especially a business. In this context, it refers to an independent party who has connection with the teacher training program especially in two groups: staff (policy makers and supervisors of the program) and attendees (subject teachers).

Subject Teachers: Teachers who have teaching qualification in the specialist subject such as physics, chemistry, mathematics etc. They are usually graduates of different first degree titles available in universities around the world that require qualifications for entry.

Target Needs: Hutchinson and Waters (1987) group needs into two categories as target needs and learning needs. The former refers to the expected abilities; tasks and activities learners will carry out in the target situation while the latter deals with the efforts necessary to learn them. They further divide target needs into three sub categories: necessities, lacks, and wants. By necessities they mean what learners should know to meet the target situation requirements. Lacks is the gap between the present state of the learners and what they need to know, do in the target situation while wants represent learners' individual desires, expectations from the language learning process.

Teacher Training: It is a process of professional preparation of teachers, usually through course instruction and practice of teaching. This term involves teacher education programs in tertiary educational intuitions, graduate programs, and special courses (certificate programs etc.).

APPENDIX 1

Table 11. Vocational English needs analysis survey for subject teachers

	Part 1. Communicative Target Tasks	I need a lot of practice on this	I need some practice on this	I do not need any practice on this	Your detailed opinion
Communicative (speaking) tasks	Greeting and checking attendance				
	Small talk				
	Communicating with students				
	Speaking on the phone.				
	Presenting a subject (a lesson) in class				
	Presenting a subject in department meeting				
	Commenting on colleagues presentations				
	Conversing with supervisors				
	Giving feedback to parents				
	Welcoming the guests, informing them about the school.				
Communicative (writing) tasks	Writing e-mails				
	Writing report cards				
	Writing a register book				
	Preparing posters and notices				
	Writing petitions				
	Writing invitations				
	Writing a CV				
	Writing questions to my subject				
	Writing reports				
	Writing information notes to parents				
	Writing a defense				
	Writing meeting minutes				
Comprehension-based tasks	Reading books, articles on my field				
	Reading the materials of the lesson				
	Reading web sites on my field (blog, wiki, forum etc.)				
	Understanding teacher's book.				
	Listening to videos and audios related to my field.				
	Listening to complementary files of books (video and audio files).				
	Other (Write yourself)				
	Other (Write yourself)				
	Other (Write yourself)				

continued on following page

Table 11. Continued

Part 2. Basic Language Skills and Knowledge	I believe that my...			
	insufficient	OK	sufficient	Your opinion
Reading				
Listening				
Writing				
Spelling				
Punctuation				
Speaking				
Fluency				
Accuracy				
Pronunciation				
Classroom language (vocabulary)				
Everyday English (speaking phrases)				
Terminology of my field				
Other				
Other				
Other				

Part 3

1. Please put these items in Part 1 & 2 in order of importance for you. (Please prioritize your needs.)
    1. ....
    2. ....
    3. ....
    4. ....
    5. ....
    6. ....
    7. ....
    8. ....
    9. ....
    10. ....

2. What is your overall evaluation of the language course (Term 1 and 2)? Explain the reasons for your evaluation of the program in as much detail as possible, please.

    ....
    ....
    ....
    ....
    ....
    ....

....
....

3. Please use the space below to indicate your suggestions for the development and revision of the language courses in the first and second term of the training program.

....
....
....
....
....
....
....

Part 4

Demographic Information

Gender:
Country/Ethnicity:
Age:
Work Experience: ……………………………………………… (Duration month or year)
If you would like to give more information about your work experience, use the space below, please.
I have been learning English for……………………………… (Duration month or year)
If you would like to give more information about your language learning experience, use the space below, please.
Thank you for your participation and cooperation ☺

APPENDIX 2

Course Manager's Interview Questions

a. Demographics:
   1. How do you describe your job?
   2. What is your field of expertise?
   3. How old are you?
   4. How long have you been working as a teacher trainer?
   5. Can you tell us about your teaching experiences?
   6. How long have you been the manager of the course in this program?
   7. Have you ever had a similar job?
   8. Have you ever taught in a course similar to this before?

b. About the Language Course:
1. How long has this course been running?
2. What is your role in the program?
3. How was English language related part of the program shaped? Who are the other decision makers in the design of the language program? How do you plan the program?
4. Have you ever revised the program? If yes, how many times? How did you decide on the revisions? What parts were revised?
5. Do you have any connections with the sector which look for candidates who can teach in English?
6. What do you think about the needs of the sector which employs subject teachers who can teach in English? What is expected from these subject teachers?
7. What are the needs of the teachers who attend this course?
8. Do you run any needs analysis to find out their needs? If yes, what do you do?
9. Do you think that education provided in the course can meet the needs of both the sector and the course attendees?
    - If yes, to what extend?
    - How do you understand this? In other words, do you have an evaluation process? (For example; do you have any inspectors or do you collect feedback from the schools where your graduates work? Or do you get any feedback from the subject teachers about their experiences?)
10. What are the strengths of the program?
11. What are the weaknesses of the program?
12. Are there any points you would like to add?

Chapter 11
Impact of a Professional Development Programme on Trainee Teachers' Beliefs and Teaching Practices

Yasemin Kırkgöz
Cukurova University, Turkey

ABSTRACT

This study emerged from the concerns experienced by the last-year English language trainee teachers during their school practicum. An increasing number of trainees complained that their existing beliefs conflicted, in many ways, with the school-based mentor's teaching practice. A collaborative action research (CAR) professional development programme (PDP) was established to help prospective teachers resolve many of the dilemmas and improve their classroom practices in a 10-week practicum course. It was found that CAR has a powerful impact upon teacher candidates as it solves many of the dilemmas and concerns. Belief changes of one trainee teacher are presented as an exemplary case. While such findings can improve our understandings of pre-service teachers' cognitive learning and problem solving skills at the practicum site, they also generate useful insights into designing a PDP to promote trainee teachers' school-based professional development in STEM (science, technology, engineering, and mathematic) education.

INTRODUCTION

In the initial teacher education, teaching practice has been recognized as one of the most important aspects of the L2 teacher education programme (Farrell, 2003; Gebhard, 2009; Tang, 2004). Research investigating student teacher practicum reveals that the practicum component constitutes a very important aspect of language teacher learning (Johnson, 1999; Borg, 2006; Farell, 2008). It provides opportunities to apply theoretical knowledge and skills, previously gained through instruction to authentic educational settings (Williams, 2009). During the practicum, trainees can apply their beliefs based on language

DOI: 10.4018/978-1-4666-9471-2.ch011

learning theories they acquired in the course of their university studies. Much evidence points to the value of pre-service student teaching due to the realistic nature of the experience (Slick, 1998). Hascher, Cocard and Moser (2004) state 'it is the best way to acquire professional knowledge and competences as a teacher' (p. 626). As noted by Leshem and Bar-Hama (2008), the practicum is the trainee teachers' first hands-on experience with their chosen career; as such, it has an important impact on trainees' future careers (Myles, Cheng & Wang, 2006; Rozelle & Wilson, 2012). The practicum also serves as a 'protected field for experimentation' and 'socialization within the profession' (Hascher et al., 2004). Thus, a trainee's future in education may be determined by what happens during their training period (Leshem & Bar-Hama, 2008). Zeichner (1990) points out that trainees consider the practicum experience as the most significant element in their teacher training; they benefit more from spending time in the field watching others teach than from attending classes at the university or colleges. Tsui (2003) supports this assertion in her discussion on teachers' personal values and beliefs by claiming that trainee teachers consider classroom experience as the most important source of knowledge about teaching.

Among the important aspects of the practicum, school-based mentor teacher plays a crucial role in shaping trainee teachers' beliefs and teaching skills, contributing to their knowledge base and professional development. By teaching under the supervision of mentoring teachers and engaging in various classroom tasks, trainee teachers can enhance their teaching knowledge and skills and reflect upon their deeply held values and beliefs, which can contribute to their cognitive learning and development (Cheng, Cheng & Tang, 2010; Gebhard, 2009). Additionally, mentors, through their own teaching, "can model appropriate teaching practice, and have a positive impact on mentees' self-confidence, and effectiveness" (Noe, 1988:459).

Ragins and Kram (2007) highlight the crucial effect of mentoring as follows:

At its best, mentoring can be a life-altering relationship that inspires mutual growth, learning and development. Its effects can be remarkable, profound and enduring; mentoring relationships have the capacity to transform individuals, groups, organizations and communities (p. 3).

The literature on mentoring in L2 teacher education has tended to focus on mutual effects of the mentor-mentee relationship, models of mentoring and mentor-mentee roles (Eliahoo, 2011). Yet, the impact of the mentoring on trainee teachers' cognitive change, particularly on the process of trainees' belief change and teaching practice, has remained relatively unexplored (Borg 2006; 2009).

To fill this gap, this study investigates

a) the impact of mentoring on the process of belief change among the trainee teachers, and
b) the impact of an innovative professional development programme (PDP) that highlights cognitive, constructive and interactive aspects of development on trainee teachers' beliefs.

The following chapter aims to present the implementation of an innovative PDP for the last-year trainee teachers of English as part of a 10-week practicum course. First, the collaborative action research is provided as the theoretical grounding for the development of the PDP. The ensuing section gives the rationale for initiating this study and details the methodology that is used to answer the research questions of this study. The process of the collaborative action research (CAR) applied in this study is described, followed by a presentation of a case study of a pre-service trainee teacher's belief changes and teaching experiences to illustrate the impact of the CAR in facilitating the trainee teacher to resolve many of her dilemmas and concerns during the PDP. The article concludes with solutions and recommendations based on our findings and directions that future studies might take.

ACTION RESEARCH

Action research is a methodology through which practitioners study their own practice in order to solve problems in their day-to-day practice (Corey, 1953, cited in Mitchell, Reilly & Logue, 2009), and to improve the quality of action (Elliot, 1991) through systematic inquiry (Bullough & Gitlin, 1995). Of the multiple models of action research, CAR, as a form of inquiry, requires practitioners to engage in a cycle of problem identification, action planning, implementation, evaluation and reflection. The insights gained from the initial cycle are integrated into planning of the second cycle, for which the action plan is altered and the research process is repeated (McKernan, 1991). It also aims to create collaboration with different stakeholders functioning as co-researchers (Mitchell, Reilly & Logue, 2009).

Studies on the impact of CAR in teacher education show that both pre-service and in-service teachers become more reflective, critical, and analytical about their teaching practices as they engage in collaborative research (Carr & Kemmis, 1986; Mitchell, Reilly & Logue, 2009; Kırkgöz, 2014). Case studies involving pre-service teachers and their cooperating teachers have further revealed strong evidence to support collaborative research as a professional development tool (Catelli, 1995; Levin & Rock, 2003; Atay, 2006).

In the present study, CAR was established between a university researcher/teacher educator, the author of this chapter, and eight trainee teachers, to provide the mentorship and support for trainee teachers' professional development. In addition, it was aimed to create an ongoing climate of collaboration among trainees and the supervising teacher in helping trainees resolve their teaching concerns and dilemmas within a supportive framework; it would help trainees develop strategies and meaningful solutions that are trainee-based and process-oriented, so that they were going to improve their classroom practice by adopting a problem based inquiry to learning and teaching. In addition, the process of cognitive change was investigated in trainees' situated classroom context in order to identify potential impacts of involvement in the CAR experience on the professional development of trainee teachers.

MAIN FOCUS OF THE STUDY

This study describes the author's engagement, who is the teacher educator, in implementing a school-based professional development programme (PDP), informed by the principles of collaborative action research (CAR). The study was conducted with Turkish pre-service English language trainee teachers as part of their practicum course (School Experience II) and lasted 10 weeks. An increasing number of last-year trainee teachers complained that their existing beliefs, based on their university course work, conflicted, in many ways, with the school-based mentor's teaching practices they observed in school classrooms. Consequently, trainees experienced discrepancies as their beliefs about teaching English did not match the observed teaching practice of their mentors. They encountered a dilemma as they were left to choose between the teaching methodology recommended by their university tutors and their mentors' teaching practice.

The present study was initiated to identify concerns of trainee teachers on a large-scale, and to conduct a PDP as part of their professional practice that would reconcile those conflicting views by helping trainees develop appropriate strategies, and support them in weighing alternatives for action, and deciding upon the one which best meets specific needs.

Participants and the Research Setting

Participants of the study were final-year trainee teachers of English attending a four-year English Language Teacher Education Programme in a Turkish university, the first three years of which include EFL courses. In Turkey, the Initial Teacher Education for primary and secondary school teachers takes place through a four-year university programme leading to a Bachelor of Education degree. The curriculum of the Teaching Practice at the university where this study took place is typical of other universities in Turkey where the Teacher Education programme is offered. In the first term of their final-year of the teacher education programme, as part of the 'School Experience I' course, trainee teachers are placed in various schools to observe mentor teachers to develop awareness of English language teaching and learning experiences.

In the second term, trainee teachers visit the placement schools, generally twice a week, as part of the 'School Experience II' course, to take responsibility for teaching. A serving teacher from the school is appointed as the mentor, responsible for guiding, supporting and evaluating the trainee teachers' learning. Additionally, each trainee is supervised by a cooperating teacher from the university. All the trainee teachers' teaching performance during the practicum is assessed by their university supervisors.

Data Collection

This multiple-source qualitative study (Denzin & Lincoln, 2000) explored a phenomenon in its natural school setting. A collective case study design was adopted "to examine, in-depth, a case within its 'real-life' context" (Yin, 2003: 111), in order to provide both description about how each trainee teachers engaged in CAR and explanation regarding the Turkish pre-service English language trainee teachers' beliefs and problem solving skills in teaching practicum during the 10-week School experience II course.

Data were collected from multiple sources in two stages as described below:

School Experience I: 150 trainee teachers of English in their fourth-year of teacher education programme were the participants of this part of the study. Assigned to classes in primary and secondary schools, they observed 25 mentors. Before their observation of the mentors, I asked the participants to write what their expectations were from the school-based mentors to investigate the participants' pre-established beliefs about language teaching and learning. At the end of the ten-week mentoring observation period, participants were asked to reflect upon the extent to which their expectations were met by the mentors whose lessons they observed.

Furthermore, the participants wrote two different reports each week: 1) field notes, in which they mostly included their observations of the mentors; 2) a reflective report or a commentary, in which they critically reflected on the experiences they gained from their observation of their mentor; that is, a more personal account of the course of the inquiry. By doing so, they produced a written summary of their evaluations/reactions to their mentor's lesson delivery in terms of how the mentor's teaching influenced (if any) their existing beliefs. Their summative evaluations varied in length from 500 to 600 words. Many respondents wrote extensive reports about their thinking expressing dilemmas resulting from the mismatch between their existing beliefs and what they observed in the mentor's teaching practice. Producing a reflective commentary served an important element of the trainees' professional learning, and gave insights for the design of the PDP to be conducted in the second term of the practicum.

School Experience II: Eight trainee teachers, three male and five female, each supervised by a different school-based mentor, participated in this part of the study. They were from the same cohort of pre-service language teachers (150 in total). They were placed in two schools, which allowed me convenience in data collection and explore the subject in depth.

The Process of CAR Research Teacher Development Programme

The process started with each trainee's identified dilemma or a concern. Then, the trainees started to investigate issues related to the concern and implemented a plan designed to address that concern. Reflection is an important part of an action research. Trainee teachers were actively engaged in the process of critically exploring their own classroom contexts and working toward resolving that concern.

Prior to initiating CAR, a meeting was held with the participants by the author of this study to familiarize them with the basic knowledge on action research and the PDP. I made it clear to the participants that my role was to act as a supporter, organizer, facilitator and resource person (Goodnough, 2003). The active role assumed by the trainees as researchers of their own teaching context was highlighted.

Drawing upon the action relationship principle of CAR (Kemmis, 1998; Mitchell, Reilly & Logue, 2009), each trainee teacher employed a recurring spiral of cycles, focusing on planning, acting, observing, reflecting, re-planning, and re-acting for the attainment of goals which involved investigating dilemmas and/or an authentic problem. They started examining their problem from various aspects, setting up an inquiry in light of the literature as part of the planning process. The action research process involved each trainee teacher conducting research within the school context. First, each trainee prepared action plans to solve their problems or overcome their concerns in the areas in which they felt the need for further improvement. In the following weeks, they read relevant literature, conducted research in their specific school context, and reflected upon the action taken. Each trainee was guided through the entire process lasting 10 weeks covering the whole practicum period. The author visited each trainee class every two weeks. In addition, she had access to mentors through e-mail.

Data Sources during the CAR

Throughout the process of CAR, data were collected from multiple sources; interviews, classroom observations, reflective journals and collaborative meetings about the participants' belief changes and learning experiences in the CAR professional development programme.

Semi-Structured Interviews

During the teaching practicum, trainee teachers' beliefs were investigated with three rounds of semi-structured interviews. These interviews were scheduled before, during and after the teaching practicum to explore potential changes in trainees' beliefs derived from their participation in different professional activities. The participants were guided to reflect on the whole field experience, their belief changes, and the factors influencing their beliefs. All the interviews were conducted in English and audio-taped.

Classroom Observation and Stimulated Recall Interview

The trainee teachers taught 20 lessons (45 min each) during the practicum, and I, as the university supervisor, observed and videotaped the 1st, 7th, 14th, and 20th lesson of each participant with observation notes taken. Each trainee also watched their video recorded lessons and wrote a reflection about their teaching. At the end of each observation, I held a stimulated recall interview with each participant to identify belief changes in their teaching practice. I also identified some teaching episodes based on my observation notes, which might reflect or contradict the beliefs stated by the participants in their interviews.

Participants' Reflective Journals

Each participant maintained a reflective journal to express their beliefs, to record insights they gained during this programme, and how these contributed to their professional development. Each participant's weekly journals (in English) were collected at the end of each week. These writings provided the author with insights into the personal and implicit processes that the trainees experienced in their research process.

Collaborative Meetings

A schedule of three *collaborative meetings* was held during the 10-week practicum. The purposes of the meetings were to share trainees' learning of ideas, practical strategies and solutions they were applying to achieve proposed principles in their teaching, and to collaboratively reflect on the process. All discussions from the meetings were audio-recorded and later transcribed for analyses.

Data Analysis

Given the large number of participants who provided written reflections of school mentors during the first semester of the practicum, a corpus tool was used for analysis. First, the responses were collated. Through repeatedly reading the data, frequently used key words and phrases were identified, i.e., *discipline*, *use of L1* and *classroom management*. Wordsmith was used to search for these key words and create the preliminary categories. Further categories were created through searching the remaining data, and identifying further key words. As for the recorded interviews, I transcribed them all. Afterward, the interview transcripts of each participant were first reviewed to identify the specific beliefs the participant held about language teaching and learning. The emerging beliefs were then categorized and compared across different interviews, paying special attention to the relationships between the identified belief change processes to account for the evolutionary nature of belief development. The videotaped classroom observations were reviewed together with the transcribed stimulated recall interviews and the observation notes. Relevant data from the participants' written reflections were revisited to triangulate with the other data sources (Merriem, 2009).

The research findings are presented according to a case, which provides both a descriptive and analytic account of what the participant's beliefs were like before the teaching practicum, how her beliefs changed as she was involved in teaching and the collaborative research, and what the newly emerged beliefs were.

Illustration of a Case

This section illustrates Özge, as one of the case study participants in the study. The choice of this participant was decided during the study as this particular case produced a rich source of data. In order to shed light on the complex and dynamic processes of the trainee teachers' belief transformation in her situated classroom context, I asked Özge (pseudonym), like other trainees, to express what her expectations were from the school-based mentors to investigate her pre-established beliefs about language teaching and learning.

In terms of her belief, before the practicum, Özge believed that

A language teacher should manage the class very effectively using different techniques and materials. Classroom atmosphere is very important so a teacher should make a good classroom atmosphere. A teacher should arouse the students' interests using different materials, activities and real tasks. I think that during lessons, students should often be given opportunities to work in small groups and with a partner, which might help students feel more comfortable and relaxed and possibly reduce the anxiety related to attempting the target language. Young learners need to speak out! Teachers should struggle to increase the quantity and the quality of English spoken by the students in classrooms. So, it is essential to create a more interactive and communicative classroom, particularly for young learners of English. By also doing this, I believe in creating a S-SS ad S-T interaction in the classroom. Students must be exposed to the target language; therefore, he or she should mostly use L2.

At the end of the ten-week mentoring observation period, her prior expectations from the mentor(s) whose lessons she observed contradicted her beliefs in many ways, as stated below:

In my observation, I saw that the teacher always used the course book, he didn't benefit from any other interesting materials like I expected before. I know that one way to capture students' attention and keep them engaged in activities is to supplement the textbook activities with brightly coloured visuals puppets, or objects. These can also be used for follow-up activities and make the language input comprehensible. Unfortunately students in my class didn't have a chance to study in small groups or in pairs, as I expected before. During my observation period, I clearly understood that one of the most challenging parts of teaching is classroom management. My mentor teacher was not effective in managing the class and involving students in the learning process. We know young learners are very energetic and they have limited attention span, it's not an easy job for teachers. I also have doubts about controlling the class before starting to teach and I'm very scared of not being able to convey what I would.

She explains the impact of the mentor on her beliefs resulting in a real dilemma as follows:

I think I got three contradicting views in my head. On the one hand, I like to follow my university lecturer's advice to use L2 because the students should be exposed to English as early as possible. They should get used to the sound, the structure, the vocabulary... so that they can learn the language unconsciously. And from the approaches course that I received at the university, I thought it would be more logical to use L2 all the time and expect students to respond in English. On the contrary, during the observation, I witnessed that the teacher didn't use the target language as the medium of instruction. He was using a lot of mother tongue.

The next contradiction was related to the methodology used:

I have also learned from my mentor what I should not do. He was using very traditional ways of teaching English like translation or 'repeat after me' technique. Students got bored and they forgot if they did not write and study what they learned. I could see the drawbacks of this implementation. I don't want to teach in a traditional way as my mentor (Interview).

Before the teaching practicum, Özge held a set of conflicting beliefs about language teaching by perceiving a dichotomy between the traditional approach (focusing on translation and drills) and a communicative classroom. Influenced by the university coursework, she believed that "language learning needs to be meaningful and interactive and teachers develop students' communicative abilities, use L2 mostly and manage the class effectively" (Interview).

She further stated the class she dreamed about as:

...full of communication opportunities, materials, audios etc. And when I saw that classroom, I thought it would be impossible to manage young learners and take their attention even with interesting activities and in a friendly way because I couldn't imagine that a teacher chose such a traditional way without trying the others. Briefly, I was hopeless for that (Interview).

However, these beliefs were at odds with her mentor's teaching instruction, dominated by grammar drills and memorization. Thus, she was not certain whether communicative activities could be successfully applied to the real language classroom.

The next interview with the participant was carried out before she started teaching in the practicum, which aimed to investigate her beliefs about language teaching and learning and about herself as a language teacher:

Since I had so many opportunities to observe my mentor in the first term, I made some decisions about my own teaching process. For example, I decided that I would use L2 in class frequently and I would be more a facilitator towards the students. Teaching young learners is like creating a new picture. Those children are looking at your eyes, watching what you will teach them. They are open to new things.

In the following section, changes in Özge's belief system in three areas are presented: (1) the use of L2; (2) classroom management; (3) activities to attract students' attention

Belief Changes in Relation to L2 Use

As noted by Stuart & Thurlow (2000), trainee teachers can engage in dialogic reflection with their mentors in their teaching practice where different ideas and understanding can be shared and developed, which can exert great influence on their belief transformation. First of all, through designing lesson plans and her dialogic interaction with the mentor, her prior perception of language teaching in relation to the use of L1 versus L2 was challenged (Mattheoudakis, 2007), as she reflects in her journal, following her first teaching experience:

In my very first lesson, I had difficulty in using the target language in the classroom not because of myself but because of my mentors. I wanted to use my knowledge that I gained from my university Young Learners Classes but my mentors didn't let me use the target language because they didn't trust the students in understanding the language (Reflective journal).

This incident overturned Özge's prior belief that "teachers should mostly use L2 in the classroom" (Reflective journal). To resolve her dilemma concerning the use of L1-L2 dichotomy, she initiates her action research project. She was offered guidance and was provided a set of articles to read. During this process, she shared her own understanding by relating it to what she had learned in the teacher education courses. Through the dialogic mediation (Vygotsky, 1978) with the author of this study, the supervising teacher, she saw the importance of "forming a situational understanding of the subject matter, the school curriculum, and the students" in teaching (Reflective journal). Such understanding, according to Özge, is "the key to integrating the theoretical knowledge into a coherent and practical framework to guide her teaching" (Reflective journal).

Özge seemed to be going through a slow and gradual process of developing and modifying her beliefs concerning the use of L1 versus L2. She expresses this process in her journal:

I was left alone in the classroom because of my mentor's illness; I did everything as I wanted. My thoughts changed when I was the only authority in the class because in the presence of a mentor, I believed I would not be able to put my plan into practice. So, I planned my lesson, prepared my materials, organized the activities. All of my negative feelings started to vanish. When students started to learn the songs that I taught them and tried to express themselves in English, this motivated me more. Every class listened to songs related to the topics. I tried to find a suitable song for them sometimes spending a whole night. I tried to make them speak in English because the mentor didn't use L2 in the classroom. I struggle with this a lot but when I heard a word of English from them, I was motivated more.

She continues her experience as follows:

I tried to use L2 all the time because the students hadn't been exposed to it till then. They were somehow shocked and puzzled whenever they heard me speak English. All the same, they tried to listen to me and understand what I was saying but they couldn't wholly concentrate on it. I didn't think of using L1, even if I got some problems I thought I could find some other ways not to use L1. I used my body language and put stress on the instruction they had problem with. I realized again that they just began to face with English and I tried to keep on using English without ignoring Turkish because I could summarize the important points in each class through Turkish.

This seemed to be a great opportunity for her as she further stated:

I can't fully motivate the class when there is a mentor because, while I am using L2 in the classroom, the mentor can interrupt to warn me about what the students can and can not understand. This distracts me too much. But when I am alone I don't have any anxiety so I can feel that this class is fully mine (Reflective journal).

As noted by Borg (1999) classroom teaching can play a mediating role in trainee teachers' belief development. Particularly, by critically examining their values and beliefs in classroom actions, trainee teachers could become more aware of the possible convergence and disparity between their beliefs and practices so that their belief systems could be constructed and transformed to guide their teaching (Farrell, 2007).

Özge's belief about the use of L2 was further challenged and reconstructed in her own teaching practice. Her ongoing reflection made her realize that instead of dichotomizing L1 and L2, she could resort to L1 when needed:

When I started to teach, I mostly used L2 in class. After a while, I realized that some students did not understand me. Since I did not want to lose them in teaching process, I tried to speak in a more understandable manner. If they still did not understand me, then I used gestures and theatrical expressions. So the problem was solved. I realized that using L1 is inevitable for young learners only when it is more efficient to use L1 for a difficult expression or a word, we can use it. For instance; for words that students can figure out, we can rely on visuals, realia, and gestures. We should spend class time focusing on those target language objectives rather than spending time trying to make a difficult word or expression comprehensible in English.

Thus, in terms of Özge's beliefs about language teaching, due to the continuous interaction between her field experiences and personal reflections (Stuart & Thurlow, 2000), she modified her original polarized view about the use of L1 and L2 to language teaching, and began to embrace a new belief that "I can use L2 mostly but L1 when needed" (Interview).

Belief Changes in Relation to Classroom Management

The second concern running through the trainees' thoughts was related to classroom management, which involves dealing with misbehaviour, as well as establishing rules and routines, among a host of other teacher activities. The challenge in maintaining control in class throughout the practicum was somewhat further compounded by her not having a good model as stated in the interview:

Unfortunately, I didn't see a good model of classroom management. Children are full of positive feelings and they are very willing to share these feelings with another person. No matter how disrespectful or energetic a child is, you can find a way to effect him/her and maybe with just a couple of words can solve all problems in the classroom. I know that students are very good imitators and they reflect whatever they observe, on their own behaviours. I start to think all of them as I am controlling the classroom.

Through the teaching practicum, Özge expanded and deepened her beliefs of the classroom management. Her concerns related to classroom management began to change as she engaged students with activities as expressed below:

In my first teaching, I wasn't able to manage the classroom because I was inexperienced. When I prepared some materials such as visuals, pictures and games students became more willing to learn English. They did not want to just sit and listen to the teacher. I saw while students were playing a game like 'which one is missing' they were practicing the language actively and they were also learning from each other.

To manage lessons effectively, she tried to establish classroom rules through a reward system:

I realized that managing misbehaviours of students was not a big deal. Because I saw that they were willing to learn English when they had fun during the lessons. For example, in one of my classes I asked students to draw an object. I told them that if they could draw the object and write the name correctly, I would reward those students by putting a star in their notebooks. This may sound very ordinary but I was very surprised when I saw how it made students alert and this activity became more important for me later because the students who were not interested in learning English and were not very attentive to any word of mine suddenly became very enthusiastic about my lessons. Students like rewards and competitions.

Another belief she developed concerning classroom management was that of authoritative stand, as reflected in her journal:

While teachers should be friendly with students, they should also be authoritative in the classroom. During the course of my practicum I also realized that I had to be the authority in the class in order to manage students' misbehaviour. For instance, in 4/H classroom, students knew that I was a trainee teacher in their school so they treated me as if they did not trust my knowledge. When I tried to teach something they made a lot of noise and did not listen to me. I could not implement the management of that classroom. I mean I could not manage them because they did not accept me as their teacher. So, in my opinion students should not know whether the teacher in their classroom is an official teacher or a student-teacher.

Therefore, through her dialogic interaction with the students during the teaching practicum (Johnson, 2006; Tang, 2004), the participant realized the complexities of classroom management, which entails a comprehensive and situational understanding of the subject matter, the curriculum and the students. Contrary to her previous simple belief that teachers should be friendly now she realized that teachers should also be authoritative.

Activities to Attract Students' Attention

Although Özge firmly believed in the value of using a variety of activities, games and songs in the young learner classes, she had a real dilemma as she stated earlier "I am idealist and want to use them in my teaching. However, I don't know whether these can really work in the classroom" (Reflective journal). Her uncertainty could be attributed to her mentor's traditional way of teaching. However, the participant's belief to create a communicative classroom using songs, games and activities were sustained throughout the programme, and she integrated them in her teaching.

To illustrate, the interview, conducted during the 4th week of the practicum, explored the possible change in her beliefs and teaching behaviour derived from her participation in CAR and different professional activities including lesson planning and practical teaching, in the field school. In planning the weekly lesson, she expressed confirmation of her original beliefs to use a variety of activities:

I believe that I have to use games, songs, visuals and physical activities because I have learned to do so in one of my methodology classes, Teaching English to Young Learners. I am aware of the advantageous and disadvantageous of teaching young learners.

Using such activities also contributed greatly to promoting students' motivation and managing the lesson effectively, as she reflects in an interview:

I managed to capture their attention with different activities, colourful pictures, songs, etc... As I stated earlier, taking their characteristics into account helped me to involve them. Of course there were slight distractions during the classes, but they weren't really problematic; I could maintain it by moving from activity to activity. Students were active and took part in games and activities that I'm very proud of them.

In the following section, changes in Özge's belief system in three areas discussed in the preceding section are illustrated by means of a lesson observation.

Lesson Observation

The lesson observation with following stimulated recall interviews documented changes in Özge's belief system. During the stimulated recall, the trainee was asked to stop the videotape every time she recalled what she had been thinking and she was encouraged to share everything she could recall at that point (Meijer, Zanting & Verloop, 2002). As a further data collection tool, the observation notes of the researcher revealed reflection on or modification of beliefs that Özge had mentioned in the previous interviews.

In the first example, Özge prepared a lesson plan to teach foods and drinks for students in grade 2 (age six). The following extract comes from the author's observation notes:

First, she posted pictures of items of foods and drinks, vegetables and fruits on the board. She pointed to each of the pictures and pronounced their names and asked the students to pronounce all together. The next activity involved "Match the names with the pictures". For this, she mixed the names of the items on the pictures and posted them on the board randomly and wanted students to stick the right name under the right item. The next activity "Putting pictures under the right super ordinate", the trainee posted the pictures without their names and wanted students to put appropriate names under the right super ordinate by saying its name and the super ordinate. (i.e., this is an apple. It is a fruit).

Özge commented on this teaching episode in the following stimulated recall interview as follows:

First of all, I knew that I had to be prepared before the lesson. I believed that I had some extra techniques in my mind in order to use when I could not attract students' attention or when they made a lot of noise.

The teaching episode below illustrates how Özge implemented extra techniques to attract students' attention:

The activity is named "What is there in the refrigerator?". She puts up a model refrigerator and hides items of food and drinks. She asks the students to close their eyes and guess what is hidden by giving clues. The students try to guess what is hidden. The students are highly motivated and use the target language effectively (Observation notes)

She commented on the above activity as follows:

I hoped to create S-S and S-T interactions. The students were successful in constructing such interactions, especially S-S interaction; they were active and motivated (Stimulated recall interview).

Stimulated recall interview concerning this lesson further revealed that her aim was to encourage students to communicate:

My aim was to teach the students correct pronunciation and recognition of the super ordinates of the items. I gave importance to fluency instead of accuracy because my first concern is their ability to communicate in the target language. In my first activity, I intentionally separated the names of the items and posted them on the board by letting them see what I was doing because it was the first activity of the topic and I didn't want to raise anxiety. I took care of all students and tried to include all of them in the lesson.

Through classroom teaching, Özge's beliefs about language teaching and learning were further refined and developed. To begin with, she had concerns about the traditional approach to language teaching and she was more inclined towards communicative, activity based language teaching. Özge reflected on how she could turn a lesson into an opportunity for students' learning. In the next lesson, she introduced not only a variety of activities, but she also tried to get the students engaged in the activities. This teaching incident made a strong resonance with her classroom observation as mentioned above, which consolidated her belief that teachers can effectively manage misbehaviour. More importantly, by reflecting on her teaching and seeking improvement (Farrell, 1999; 2007), she enriched her belief and came to realize the teacher' role as a facilitator of the students' learning in the classroom:

Actually my beliefs changed thanks to my own experiences. I saw that the more I practiced on teaching in classroom the more I could deal with difficulties easily because practicing provided me the chance of getting to know students' behaviours and I could comment on them so I could use different techniques accordingly. For example; while I was teaching 'foods and drinks' I used 'smiling face stickers' when they joined to the activities and beyond any doubt every student was willingly interested in the activities (Reflective journal).

Johnson (1994) posits that

if the aim of teacher education programmes is to provide trainee teachers with opportunities to experience real teaching, then teacher educators (in this case the practicum mentors) should make sure that trainee teachers are granted a reasonable amount of control over what and how they will teach, so that they can test their emerging conceptions of teaching (p.47).

Impact of a Professional Development Programme

The last interview took place during the last week in the practicum summarises nicely how Özge perceived her belief changes. Through participation in the CAR, she experienced how the initial ideas of teaching and student learning were brought into reality and her ability to come to terms with many of the dilemmas and concerns improved. This was expressed as follows:

Since I had so many opportunities to observe my mentor in the first term, I made some decisions about my own teaching process. For example, I decided that I would use L2 in class frequently and I would be more facilitator towards the students. Teaching young learners is like creating a new picture. I have been very determined because I tried my way and didn't choose the traditional way though it was really hard, at times. During the lessons, I used L2 as much as possible. And my students were always busy doing the activities. Sometimes these were stir-up activities, sometimes settle-down. I always had two activities about a topic. I gave them the chance to choose which activity they wanted. So they didn't have time to get bored in my classes.

While I was teaching, every class has taught me something. I used realia, songs, games, reinforcements, etc. during the lesson to support my teaching. I gave clear instruction, did a lot of practice, and tried to monitor classroom activities, gave feedback and reinforcement regarding their behaviour. While doing these all, I made use of humour, when suitable, to stimulate student interest or reduce classroom tensions. Thanks to these, I could involve students in lessons and didn't have problems related to classroom management.

SOLUTIONS AND RECOMMENDATIONS

Situated in an L2 teacher education context, the present study reveals that collaborative action research is a valuable tool to promote trainee teachers' problem solving skills in resolving dilemmas and concerns; and, contributing to their professional development during their school practicum, when facilitated in the field school with expert support. Involvement in action research helps teacher trainees reflect upon the concerns originating from observation of mentors and their specific classroom contexts and promotes deeper reflection and the ability to deal with genuine problems. As revealed from reflective journals, interviews and other data sources, all the participants, as well as Özge perceived the implementation of CAR positive despite the fact that action research is an additional workload. In the present study, the CAR was part of formal assessment of school practicum.

Despite the short duration of the teaching practicum, the participants' prior beliefs interacted with the new input and experiences through participation, practice, and reflection. As a result, their beliefs about language teaching and their self-understanding as a language teacher were transformed and developed (Freeman & Johnson, 1998; Kelly, 2006). The study also reveals that trainee teachers' beliefs about language teaching and learning are not stable, but open to change and development, which corroborates Borg's (2006, 2009) claim that significant changes do take place in pre-service teachers' beliefs through the teaching practicum. Given their past learning experience as a language learner and student teacher, trainee teachers could form a set of beliefs about language teaching and learning. As they come to the field school, their encounters with the realities of language teaching could trigger a chain of changes in their beliefs. In the present study, the participant consolidated, confirmed or modified many of her original beliefs, and as a result, her prior beliefs became more established, as in the use of L1-L2 dichotomy, as well as adding some new constructs to her existing beliefs. She elaborated her existing beliefs by adding new input, in her beliefs regarding classroom management during the practicum.

The practicum generally provides trainee teachers with atypical teaching experience that could differ from that of regular teachers. In this study, the trainee teachers taught only 20 lessons in a 10-week practicum. It is uncertain whether and how their beliefs might change when they become real language teachers in the classroom upon starting teaching profession. It is also uncertain whether their changed beliefs in the teaching practicum can be sustained in their future practice where more contextual challenges might emerge. Moreover, in terms of school contexts, while the learning environment in the field school was considered highly favourable, particularly in the case of this participant, it remains unclear whether the trainee teachers' beliefs would have undergone similar changes had they been placed in a school with less support.

The study was conducted with teacher candidates in the context of an (English language) teacher education department in Turkey; as such, it might be considered context-specific. However, this research leads to a deeper understanding of how teacher educators can support and challenge future teachers in their ability to think critically and thoughtfully in coming to terms with dilemmas and concerns in their teaching practicum. It is expected that this study provides insights into designing an innovative programme to promote trainee teachers' school-based professional development in STEM education.

FUTURE RESEARCH DIRECTIONS

The study demonstrates the complex processes of a trainee teacher's belief change in coming to terms with her dilemmas. Such findings can improve our understanding of pre-service teachers' cognitive learning at the practicum site and generate useful implications about how such learning can be facilitated and supported through CAR in teacher education programmes in similar EFL contexts.

The presents study focuses on one participant in a particular school; its findings cannot be generalized to other contexts. Despite this, some insights can be gained from the findings for the design and improvement of the practicum component of the pre-service language teacher education. First of all, it can be pointed out that maximum opportunities should be provided for trainee teachers to take part in various professional activities in the teaching practicum, such as reflective journal writing (Lee, 2008), post-lesson interviews (Watson & Williams, 2004), and collaborative action research (Johnston, 2009; Mitchell, et al.,2009). Through exposure to various forms of professional learning activities, trainees can engage in critical reflection on their perceptions about language teaching and learning (Gao & Benson, 2012), develop an appreciation of the complexities and challenges that comprise teachers' professional practice, and construct a strong self-belief as a language teacher (Borg, 2006; Turnbull, 2005). Further research can investigate in greater depth the long-term belief development of pre-service language teachers, particularly the possible change in their beliefs in their first few years of teaching.

In addition, the data derived from the participants in the present study suggest that school mentors with their obviously grammar-based teaching styles developed a favourable perception about the trainees' more communicative teaching after a rather deprecating initial reaction to the trainees' teaching practices. Noticing that students' attention was enhanced, they greatly appreciated and welcomed such communicative activities. Hence, further research can investigate this area.

A short version of this chapter has been presented at the symposium "Looking Forward and Back: Bridging Pre-Service and In-Service Teacher Education Programs in English Teaching" organized by the British Council / Hacettepe University SFL on 2-3 February 2015, Ankara, Turkey.

REFERENCES

Atay, D. (2006). Teachers' professional development: Partnerships in research. *TESL-EJ, 10*(2), 1–14.

Borg, S. (1999). Studying teacher cognition in second language grammar teaching. *System, 27*(1), 19–31. doi:10.1016/S0346-251X(98)00047-5

Borg, S. (2006). *Teacher cognition and language Education: Research and practice*. London: Continuum.

Borg, S. (2009). Language teacher cognition. In A. Burns & J. C. Richards (Eds.), *The Cambridge guide to second language teacher education* (pp. 163–171). New York: Cambridge University Press.

Bullough, R. V., & Gitlin, A. (1995). *Becoming a student of teaching: Methodologies for exploring self and school context*. New York: Garland.

Carr, W., & Kemmis, S. (1986). *Becoming critical: Education, knowledge and action research*. Basingstoke: Falmer Press.

Catelli, L. A. (1995). Action research and collaborative inquiry in a school-university partnership. *Action in Teacher Education, 265*(4), 25–38. doi:10.1080/01626620.1995.10463216

Cheng, M., Cheng, A., & Tang, S. (2010). Closing the gap between the theory and practice of teaching: Implications for teacher education programmes in Hong Kong. *Journal of Education for Teaching: International Research and Pedagogies, 36*(1), 91–104. doi:10.1080/02607470903462222

Denzin, N. K., & Lincoln, Y. S. (Eds.). (2000). Collecting and interpreting qualitative materials. 2nd Edition. Place: SAGE Publications.

Eliahoo, R. (2011). Dilemmas in measuring the impact of subject-specific mentoring on mentees' learners in the lifelong learning sector. *Practitioner Research in Higher Education, 5*(1), 39–47.

Elliot, J. (1991). *Action research for educational change*. Buckingham, UK: Open University Press.

Farell, T. S. C. (2008). Here is the book, go and teach: ELT practicum support. *RELC Journal, 39*(2), 226–241. doi:10.1177/0033688208092186

Farrell, T. S. C. (1999). The reflective assignment: Unlocking pre-service teachers' beliefs on grammar teaching. *RELC Journal, 30*(2), 1–17. doi:10.1177/003368829903000201

Farrell, T. S. C. (2003). Learning to teach English language during the first year: Personal influences and challenges. *Teaching and Teacher Education, 19*(1), 95–111. doi:10.1016/S0742-051X(02)00088-4

Farrell, T. S. C. (2007). *Reflective language teaching: From research to practice*. London: Continuum Press.

Freeman, D., & Johnson, K. E. (1998). Reconceptualizing the knowledge-base of language teacher education. *TESOL Quarterly, 32*(3), 397–417. doi:10.2307/3588114

Gebhard, J. (2009). The practicum. In A. Burns & J. C. Richards (Eds.), *The Cambridge guide to second language teacher education* (pp. 250–258). New York: Cambridge University Press.

Goodnough, K. (2003). Facilitating action research in the context of science education: Reflections of a university researcher. *Educational Action Research, 11*(1), 41–64. doi:10.1080/09650790300200203

Hascher, T., Cocard, Y., & Moser, P. (2004). Forget about theory - practice is all? Student teachers' learning in practicum. *Teachers and Teaching: Theory and Practice, 10*(6), 623–637. doi:10.1080/1354060042000304800

Johnson, K. E. (1994). The emerging beliefs and instructional practices of pre-service ESL teachers. *Teaching and Teacher Education, 10*, 439–452. doi:10.1016/0742-051X(94)90024-8

Johnson, K. E. (1999). *Understanding language teaching: Reasoning in action*. Boston: Heinle and Heinle.

Johnson, K. E. (2006). The sociocultural turn and its challenges for second language teacher education. *TESOL Quarterly, 40*(1), 235–257. doi:10.2307/40264518

Kelly, P. (2006). What is teacher learning? A socio-cultural perspective. *Oxford Review of Education, 32*(4), 505–519. doi:10.1080/03054980600884227

Kemmis, S. (1998). Action research. In J. Keeves (Ed.), *Educational Research, Methodology, and Measurement: An International Handbook* (pp. 42–49). New York: Pergamon.

Kırkgöz, Y. (2014). A school-university collaborative action research teacher development programme: A case of six Turkish novice teachers of English. *The Asian EFL Journal Professional Teaching Articles, 71*, 31–56.

Leshem, S., & Bar-Hama, R. (2008, July). Evaluating teaching practice. *ELT Journal, 62*(3), 257–265. doi:10.1093/elt/ccm020

Levin, B. B., & Rock, T. C. (2003). The effects of collaborative action research on preservice and experienced teacher partners in professional development schools. *Journal of Teacher Education, 54*(2), 135–149. doi:10.1177/0022487102250287

Mattheoudakis, M. (2007). Tracking changes in pre-service EFL teacher beliefs in Greece: A longitudinal study. *Teaching and Teacher Education, 23*(8), 1272–1288. doi:10.1016/j.tate.2006.06.001

McKernan, J. (1991). *Curriculum action research. A handbook of methods and resources for the reflective practitioner*. London: Kogan Page.

Meijer, P., Zanting, A., & Verloop, N. (2002). How can student teachers elicit experienced teachers' practical knowledge? Tools, suggestions, and significance. *Journal of Teacher Education, 53*(5), 406–419. doi:10.1177/002248702237395

Merriam, S. B. (2009). *Qualitative research: A guide to design and implementation*. San Francisco: John Wiley and Sons.

Mitchell, S. N., Reilly, R. C., & Logue, M. E. (2009). Benefits of collaborative action research for the beginning teacher. *Teaching and Teacher Education, 25*(2), 344–349. doi:10.1016/j.tate.2008.06.008

Myles, J., Cheng, L., & Wang, H. (2006). Teaching in elementary school: Perceptions of foreign-trained teacher candidates on their teaching practicum. *Teaching and Teacher Education, 22*(2), 233–245. doi:10.1016/j.tate.2005.09.001

Noe, R. A. (1988). An investigation of the determinants of successful assigned mentoring relationship. *Personnel Psychology, 41*(1), 457–479. doi:10.1111/j.1744-6570.1988.tb00638.x

Ragins, B. R., & Kram, K. E. (2007). The roots and meaning of mentoring. In B. R. Ragins & K. E. Kram (Eds.), *The handbook of mentoring at work*. London: Sage Publications Ltd.

Rozelle, J., & Wilson, S. (2012). Opening the black box of field experiences: How cooperating teachers' beliefs and practices shape student teachers' beliefs and practices. *Teaching and Teacher Education, 28*(8), 1196–1205. doi:10.1016/j.tate.2012.07.008

Slick, S. (1998). The university supervisor: A disenfranchised outsider. *Teaching and Teacher Education, 14*(8), 821–834. doi:10.1016/S0742-051X(98)00028-6

Stuart, C., & Thurlow, D. (2000). Making it their own: Preservice teachers' experiences, beliefs, and classroom practice. *Journal of Teacher Education, 51*(2), 113–121. doi:10.1177/002248710005100205

Tang, S. Y. F. (2004). The dynamics of school-based learning in initial teacher education. *Research Papers in Education, 19*(2), 185–204. doi:10.1080/02671520410001695425

Tsui, B. M. (2003). *Understanding expertise in teaching: Case studies of second language teachers*. Cambridge: Cambridge University Press. doi:10.1017/CBO9781139524698

Vygotsky, L. S. (1978). *Mind in society: The development of higher psychological processes*. Cambridge, MA: Harvard University Press.

Williams, J. (2009). Beyond the practicum experience. *ELT Journal, 63*(1), 68–77. doi:10.1093/elt/ccn012

Yin, R. K. (2003). *Case study research: Design and method*. Thousand Oaks, CA: Sage.

Yuan, R., & Lee, I. (2014). Pre-service teachers' changing beliefs in the teaching practicum: Three cases in an EFL context. *System, 44*, 1–12. doi:10.1016/j.system.2014.02.002

Zeichner, K. M. (1990). Changing directions in the practicum: Looking ahead to the 1990's. *Journal of Education for Teaching, 16*(2), 105–132. doi:10.1080/0260747900160201

KEY TERMS AND DEFINITIONS

Belief: Implicit assumptions about various aspects of teaching and learning such as the subject matter to be taught, the teacher, students and classroom and they generally have a powerful impact on teachers' or trainee teachers' reasoning and practice.

Collaborative Action Research: A model of action research, in which a university teacher educator or a researcher collaborates with practicing teachers or pre-service trainee teachers to provide support for teachers or teacher candidates' professional development.

Dilemma: It is a situation in which a decision has to be made between two alternatives, as in the case of whether to use L1 or L2 as the medium of instruction. Both alternatives in a dilemma typically contain aspects that are not acceptable.

Mentor: An individual who creates a working relationship with students to improve the quality of student learning.

Practicum: A course that offers trainee teachers the opportunity to apply academic theory and acquired skills from their teacher education programmes in a real school setting. It is supervised by a school-based mentor.

Reflection: A process in which a teacher or a trainee expresses, in writing or in oral, beliefs and ideas about an experience, and think about what s/he would ideally do in a similar situation. Reflection can be recorded through journals, diaries, and be elicited through interviews.

Trainee Teacher: A prospective teacher or a teacher candidate who is undergoing training at schools for the teaching profession. A trainee teacher is supervised by a school-based mentor and a supervising teacher, in this particular case, one from the university.

Chapter 12
Prospective EFL Teachers' Perceptions of Using CALL in the Classroom

Anıl Rakicioglu-Soylemez
Abant Izzet Baysal University, Turkey

Sedat Akayoglu
Abant Izzet Baysal University, Turkey

ABSTRACT

The study focuses on prospective English as a foreign language (EFL) teachers' perspectives on the use of Computer Assisted Language Learning (CALL) resources in teaching English as a foreign language context. In addition to examining prospective teachers' perceptions, the similarities and differences in their perceptions and factors affecting their beliefs about using CALL resources will be addressed. The study aimed to identify the prospective EFL teachers' perceptions of their existing skills to integrate CALL into their future professional practices. The perceived factors that will facilitate and inhibit their future teaching practices by using CALL resources and their expectations from the teacher education program in terms of providing the necessary training to use CALL resources in their teaching practices were examined. The perceived benefits and challenges of using CALL in EFL teaching contexts will be addressed from the participants' perspectives. Finally, the study provides implications for further research in addition to recommendations for EFL teacher education programs.

INTRODUCTION

In the field of English as a foreign language (hereafter, EFL), computer assisted language learning (hereafter, CALL) has received a lot of attention and the uses and effectiveness of integrating CALL practices have been addressed in the current literature (i.e. Brown, 1997; Garcia & Arias, 2000; Kilickaya & Krajka, 2010; Kilickaya & Krajka, 2012; Stokes, 1997). Within the current context of EFL classrooms, CALL has been addressed from three perspectives; one is the theoretical foundations and proposed applications of CALL (Chapelle, 2001; Levy & Stockwell, 2006), the second is the use and effectiveness of CALL

DOI: 10.4018/978-1-4666-9471-2.ch012

practices in the language classrooms as well as using CALL as a language teaching tool (Blake, 2005; Hubbard, 2004); and finally the perceptions of the stakeholders (i.e. Teachers, students and developers) (Jamieson, Chapelle, & Preiss, 2005; Wiebe & Kabata, 2010).

A number of technological learning theories have been used in the literature to define the intentions and perceptions of the subjects' ways of using technology in a teaching context. One of the comprehensive studies on the theoretical frameworks of using technology in teaching, Lee (2010) examined four main theoretical frameworks; the expectation–confirmation model (ECM), the technology acceptance model (TAM), the theory of planned behavior (TPB), and flow theory (Koufaris, 2002) to propose a theoretical model to predict the participants' intentions to continue using computer assisted learning tools in the teaching practices after graduating from the teacher education programs. On the other hand, Decomposed Theory of Planned Behavior (DTPB) developed by Taylor and Todd (1995) drawing on the Theory of Planned behavior (Ajzen, 1991) offers a focus on the attitudes, subjective norms and behavior control to examine the perception of the proposed behavior and in return predict one's actions or future plans to implement. The proposed attitudes, subjective norms and perceived behavior control are explored through decomposing the frameworks of existing beliefs into belief-based indirect measures (Sadaf, Newby & Ertmer, 2012).

Although current studies in the literature address the issues of using CALL in the language classrooms from tripartite perspectives, the perceptions of the prospective EFL teachers (hereafter, PTs) and the processes they are going through during their professional learning experiences within the teacher education programs have not been addressed in an EFL teacher education setting.

Moreover, governments usually ignore the training of pre-service teachers while trying to implement some programs to provide the educational institutions with technological devices. As an example to these projects, one of the high-cost projects started to be put into practice in 2012 in Turkey and it is still in progress. The aim of this project is to provide ICT equipment to classes in order to achieve the ICT supported teaching until the end of 2013 in related to the goals that take place in the Strategy Document of the Information Society, the Development Report, the Strategy Plan of our Ministry and The Policy Report of ICT that have described all activities of our country in the process of being an information society and have been formed within the scope of the e-transformation of Turkey (http://fatihprojesi.meb.gov.tr).

Although the project seems ground-breaking, the training of the pre-service teachers was ignored. In-service training was included in the project, but the curriculum of the pre-service teachers of English remained the same.

Hence, the study in hand is designed to examine PTs' perceptions of using CALL in language teaching, their skills and priorities as well as their reflections of integrating CALL resources in their teaching practices. In addition, a basis for a needs assessment of integrating CALL courses in the curriculum of EFL teacher education programs will be addressed.

Thus, in order to examine the aforementioned aspects of PTs' attitudes toward using CALL resources in their teaching practices, the following research questions will be addressed;

1. What are the prospective EFL teachers' perceptions of using CALL resources in EFL teaching practices?
2. How do prospective EFL teachers currently perceive their skills to use and integrate CALL technologies in their own future teaching practices?

3. What are the factors that will facilitate and/or inhibit prospective EFL teachers' use of CALL in their future teaching practices?
4. What are their expectations from the teacher education department in terms of introducing CALL resources in the teacher education curriculum?

BACKGROUND OF THE STUDY

The literature in CALL field has concentrated on the theoretical foundations of CALL, the effectiveness of the CALL tools mainly, however, some researchers (Volman, 2005; Chapelle, 2006; Kessler, 2006; Robb, 2006; Drent & Meelissen, 2008; Stockwell, 2009; Kılıçkaya & Seferoğlu, 2013) mentioned the need for CALL training in the language teacher education programs as the prospective teachers are expected to use CALL tools effectively in and after their classes. According to them, the teacher education programs should prepare these prospective teachers for the technologically equipped classrooms and for the classrooms of the digital age.

Volman's (2005) carried out a study with 13 interviewees and asked to discuss upon some predetermined themes varying from the expected competencies of the teachers to the new roles of the teachers in teaching profession. At the end of the study, the discussions were transcribed and analyzed. As the result of the study, the changing role of the teacher was also mentioned and summarized as the role of teachers, however, will become more complex rather than simpler. Teachers must know what programs are available that are suitable for their students' individual needs and keep abreast of this. They are the 'arrangers' of students' learning processes: they bring together the educational tools and set them up in a particular way. In addition, they fulfill the role of instructor, trainer, coach, advisor, consultant and assessor.

As mentioned here, the teacher is expected to know what programs are available for their students. In other words, they should competent enough to evaluate the tools on the Internet and bring them into their classrooms and this is only possible with a training in teacher education programs.

The same point was also expressed by Chapelle (2006) as "second-language teachers today need to be able to choose, use, and in some cases, refuse technology for their students" (p. vii). In order to refuse a technology, a teacher should be aware of the potential tools that could be used in teaching a foreign language. In case of a disadvantageous position, they should provide an alternative tool or an alternative activity as well.

Kessler (2006) studied with 240 graduates of master's program. He collected data through a survey, interviews and focus groups. At the end of the study, he went beyond just selecting or refusing the tool and mentioned the appropriate methodology and practices. According to him, teachers should be aware of the CALL methodology and even its history and stated that "CALL use is becoming more prevalent within language programs, particularly as programs gravitate toward the web. Teachers need to become more proficient in their understanding of CALL methodology, practices, history and possibilities." (p. 35). While using the CALL tools in language classrooms, teachers should know which tool is appropriate for the context of the classroom and which tool serve the objectives of the course.

Robb (2006) also cited the importance of teacher training; however, he specifically mentioned the pre-service teachers rather than in-service training. He claimed that teachers should autonomously improve themselves and teacher preparation programs should provide some opportunities with these pre-service teachers for this purpose. He pointed out that "teacher preparation programs must thus look beyond the mere teaching of today's software and skills to ensure that teachers can act autonomously to upgrade their knowledge and be able to apply new technologies to their teaching in a timely manner" (p. 335).

Stockwell (2009) believed that CALL is not something to learn in a course or training, but instead, it is a process in which the teachers should develop themselves continuously. Although he provided a professional development workshop for the part-time teachers working at a private university in Tokyo, he found out that there was a need for autonomous teachers who could choose their tools for their classes, educate themselves continuously. Moreover, he claimed that the success in CALL was mostly dependent on the age of the participant and the available resources for the teachers. If the teacher could not find enough resources, he could easily give up CALL. The institutions and teacher training programs should guide these teachers in the field of CALL.

Finally, the importance of CALL integration was touched upon by Kılıçkaya and Seferoğlu (2013) and some teacher education programs started to offer some courses related to CALL tools for the future teachers. They stated that "recognition of the importance of ICT curriculum integration has already occurred, and most teacher education programs have introduced courses in ICT for future teachers" (p.22-23).

Within this framework, this study was designed to find out the attitudes of prospective teachers of English towards the use of CALL tools and their intentions to use technology in their future classes. The results of the study will give insight into the future use of technology by the pre-service teachers and provide data for the curriculum designers of teacher preparation programs.

METHODOLOGY

This study follows a mixed-method approach as it includes both qualitative and quantitative nature of data collection and analysis procedures (Creswell, 2003). The participants were given an adapted survey and a representative group of participants were interviewed during the data collection process. The collected data were analyzed by means of content analysis and the results of the survey were reported in terms by means of descriptive statistics. Drawing on the proposed framework, the study addressed PTs' perceptions of using CALL and the possibility of adapting CALL resources into their future EFL teaching practices.

Participants

This study was carried out at the Department of Foreign Language Education, Abant İzzet Baysal University in Bolu, Turkey. The study group was composed of junior and senior prospective teachers of the department and the approximate number of enrolled prospective teachers is 150. An online survey was employed through Google Forms. The return rate of the survey is 70%.

The prospective teachers enrolled in the EFL teacher education program have not taken a course related to the use of technology in their curriculum. The reason for excluding freshman and sophomore is that with the beginning of the 2014-2015 academic year, the junior prospective teachers began to take practice related course where they find the chance to explore their teaching practices through macro-teachings. The senior group of the participants is enrolled in practice teaching and has the chance to actualize their teaching practices. The senior group of prospective teachers also has the chance to practice their teaching skills at state-run schools from all levels of proficiency. PTs with an age range of 19 to 24 enrolled in the study. The participants formed a homogeneous group in terms of attending the same program and taking the same courses with the same pre-service instructional experience in their initial teacher education program.

Data Collection Tools

The survey adapted from Sadaf, Newby & Ertmer (2012) was used in the first phase of data collection. The survey had have three sections: (a) demographics of the participants, (b) PTs' attitudes towards using CALL and perceptions of using CALL resources in their teaching practices, and (c) the adapted version of the DTPB (Sadaf, Newby & Ertmer, 2012) survey. Due to the fact that the participants of the study are PTs who do not have any actual teaching experience in real school setting, the wording of the survey was modified and adapted to reflect on the practices of the PTs and to avoid any possible misunderstanding due to technical wording. For instance, the following statement "I feel that using Web 2.0 will help my students learn more about the subject" was rewritten as "I feel that using technology will help my students learn more about English".

The DTPB (Sadaf, Newby & Ertmer, 2012) survey was composed of three subscales in the original version; attitude, subjective norm, and perceived behavior. In the attitude subscale, PTs' perceptions of usefulness, ease of use, and compatibility were addressed. In the perceived behavior subscale, self-efficacy, facilitative conditions in terms of technology and resources were addressed. Due to the fact that the study in hand focused on addressing PTs' perceptions using CALL in their classrooms, the second subscale, Subjective norm, was eliminated. The subjective norm subscale was designed by Sadaf, Newby and Ertmer (2012) to address the influences of student, peer and Superior. However, in the context of the current study, PTs are not offered a course on CALL resources; thus it is assumed that their perceptions should be considered on a personal basis. Therefore, the items of the subscale were eliminated in the analysis. As the researchers eliminated the subjective norm subscale, due to the lack of courses offering CALL applications in the department, 10 items (i1, i15, i17, i18, i19, i22, i23, i24, i25, i26, i27) were eliminated from the analysis.

In addition to the scale items, PTs were asked to reflect on the level of confidence in using computers. PTs were asked three additional open-ended questions to reflect on their description of technology, ways of using technology in English language classrooms, and their readiness to use technology in their future teaching practices. The open-ended questions asked to the PTs were

- What does "technology" mean to you?
- How would you use technology in an English language classroom?
- Are you ready to use technology in your future classes?

The interview protocol of the study was mainly based on the attitudes and perceptions of the PTs' use of CALL and gaining further insights to address their needs and intentions of using CALL in their future classrooms. The semi-structured interviews were conducted with 11 PTs. The interview participants were randomly selected from the group of participants who attended the survey part of the data collection. The duration of the interview was approximately 15-20 minutes. The participants who were selected to participate in the interviews were asked for their consent to participate.

The interview protocol of the study was as follows;

- What do you think about technology resources? Can you name any resources/tools to be used in ELT classrooms?
- Have you ever observed a teacher/an instructor using CALL resources in their classroom?
- Have you ever used any of the resources in your teaching practices [refer to your macro teachings at the department or at the schools?
- What do you think of using technology resources within an English language classroom environment?
- Do you think your existing skills in technology will be enough to integrate into your future language teaching practices?
- Would you use technological tools in your future English language classrooms? Why or why not?

Data Collection and Analysis Procedures

The validation of the both data collection tools were reviewed by three experts in the field. For the comprehensiveness, clarity of the wording and organization of the data collection tools. The three experts who had solid background in the field of foreign language teacher education, were invited to conduct a think aloud procedure (Dillman, Smyth & Christian, 2014) to discuss the content and applicability of data collection tools.

During the implementation of the survey, the participant group was sent a link of the Google forms and asked to fill in the form within a week time.

Data analysis procedures composed of reliability and frequency analysis of the quantitative data in addition to content analysis of the qualitative data. The descriptive statistics of the survey results were also examined in the content analysis of the interviews. Thus, content analysis of the interviews provided the necessary insights to examine the perceptions of the prospective EFL teachers' use of CALL resources in their future teaching practices.

RESULTS

The first section of the survey was the demographics of the participants. In Table 1, the demographics of the participants who participated in the study were presented. As seen in Table 1, the PTs (N=106) participated in the study were at the junior year (N= 51), at the senior year (N=47) and irregular PTs (N=8) who has spent more than four years in the program. The female participants (N=69) of the study constitute the 65% whereas the male participants (N=37) were the 35% of the study participants. The range of the group was 18 to 24+. The majority of the participants were at the range of 20-21 (N=73) which was the 69% of the participants.

The second section of the survey focused on the attitudes and perceptions of PTs' use of CALL in EFL classes. In order to analyze the descriptive statistics of the survey, first a reliability analysis was conducted. Rather than investigating the factor affecting the use of technologies in the classroom, the study in hand focused on addressing the needs of the department where the study was conducted and

Table 1. The demographics of the participants

Variables		*n*	%
Gender	Male	37	34.9
	Female	69	65.1
Age	18-19	1	.9
	20-21	73	68.9
	22-23	21	19.8
	24+	11	10.4
Year at the department	3	51	48.1
	4	47	44.3
	4+	8	7.5

address the perceptions and attitudes of the PTs with regards to the use of CALL resources. Therefore, descriptive statistics were calculated and reported. The reliability of the scale was found high in the analysis (23 items, α=. 952). After conducting the reliability analysis for the required items, descriptive statistics focusing on the mean and standard deviation of the items were analyzed. The items were listed according to descending values of the analysis (see Table 2).

According to the descriptive analysis of the scale, PTs agreed on the statement that using technology is a good idea (M=6.67), and they referred to their future plans as they plan to use technology in their future classrooms (M=4.65) because they believed that technology will be useful in their English language teaching practices (M=4.55). According to the descriptive statistics, PTs believed that they feel comfortable using technology in an English language classroom (M=4.22) and reflected on their intentions to use technology as soon as they start teaching English (M=4.31).

In terms of PTs confidence of using technology in their future classrooms, PTs believed that they could easily use technology on their own in the classes (M=4.24) and they feel that technological tools will be easy to use in an English language classroom (M=4.22). Similarly, PTs highly believed that incorporating technology in their future English language classroom will be easy (M=4.10). By looking at the overall results, PTs beliefs about the usefulness of the technology tools in the classroom were higher than their confidence in figuring out the ways of using technology in their classes. For instance, PTs referred to their knowledge of using technology in an English language classroom (M=3.87) was lower than their belief that technology is a good idea (M=4.67).

PTs not only asked to refer to their confidence and opinions in using technology in the classrooms, they also referred to the extent to which they think that their students will benefit from incorporating technology into the classrooms. According to the descriptive of the scale, PTs have high expectations from using technology in their classrooms in terms of its potential to help students to learn more about the topic of the lesson (M=4.17), improve the students' satisfaction with the course (M=4.37), improve students' evaluation of the topic of the lesson (M=4.17), improve students' grades (M=4. 12) and learn better (M=4.36).

Table 2. Descriptive statistics of the scale

	N	M	SD
7. Using technology is a good idea.	106	4.67	0.70
3. I plan to use technology in my future English language classroom.	106	4.65	0.71
5. Technology will be useful in my English language teaching practices.	106	4.55	0.79
10. I feel that using technology will help my students learn more about the topic of the lesson.	106	4.44	0.81
11. I feel that using technology will improve my students' satisfaction with the course.	106	4.37	0.86
14. To help my students better learn the material, I will incorporate technology in my future English language classroom.	106	4.36	0.83
32. I would feel comfortable using technology in an English language classroom.	106	4.33	0.78
4. I intend to use technology as soon as I start teaching English.	106	4.31	0.84
33. I could easily use technology on my own in my classes.	106	4.24	0.84
29. Using the technology fits well with the way I will teach English.	106	4.23	0.83
8. I feel that technological tools will be easy to use in an English language classroom.	106	4.22	0.87
28. Using technology in the classroom is compatible with the way I will teach English.	106	4.18	0.78
13. I feel that using technology will improve students' evaluation of the topic of the lesson.	106	4.17	0.87
6. The advantages of technology in the English language classroom outweigh the disadvantages of not using it.	106	4.17	0.87
12. I feel that using technology will improve my students' English language grades.	106	4.12	0.92
9. I feel that incorporating technology in my future English language classroom will be easy.	106	4.10	0.85
2. I would have no difficulty explaining why technology may or may not be beneficial in an English language classroom.	106	4.04	0.99
21. I have the knowledge and ability to use technology in an English language classroom.	106	4.03	0.81
30. The technology will be compatible with the computer I will use in the classroom.	106	4.01	0.83
31. I will be able to use technology using any computer connected to the Internet.	106	3.99	0.99
34. I know enough to use technology in an English language classroom.	106	3.87	0.98
20. Using technology in an English language classroom is entirely within my control.	106	3.81	0.98
16. My instructors at the department confirm my ability and knowledge to use technology in my future classroom.	106	3.76	0.98

Although item 16 belonged to the subjective norm subscale, considering the significant others in using technology resources at the department was one of the topics that draw the attention of the researchers. Thus, it was added into the analysis. Moreover, it received the lowest mean value of the whole scale items (M=3.76).

PTs were also asked to reflect on the level of confidence in using computers. The responses to their confidence level of using computers was moderate (M=3.18). PTs were asked three additional open-ended questions to reflect on their description of technology, ways of using technology in English language classrooms, and their readiness to use technology in their future teaching practices.

As for the qualitative data, two questions were asked to the participants. The first one was about how they perceived the technology and how they defined it; and the responses were categorized as shown in Table 3.

Table 3. PTs' proposed features of technology

Feature	f	%
Easiness	54	50.9
Inevitability	35	33.0
Accessibility	30	28.3
Facilitation	19	17.9
Communication	15	14.2

When the qualitative data was analyzed, it could be seen that 50.9% of the participants perceived technology as easiness. The participants believed that life was much easier with the help of the technology, especially by means of the Internet. They could easily communicate, share their ideas and communicate with other users of the Internet. The second category was about its inevitability. Of the participants, 33% believed that technology is inevitable. They could not imagine a world without technology and, as a prospective teacher; they mentioned that it was impossible for them to be a teacher without technology. Another point mentioned very frequently was the accessibility. In today's world, they could easily access whatever they want regardless of their physical conditions. They could find information very easily and this was only possible with the advancements in technology. Fourthly, the participants mentioned that technology was very helpful in all tasks they were responsible for. Not only in educational settings but also in their daily tasks, technology was very helpful. The final feature of technology is communication, which should have been at the top in this list. As it is the age of communication, it should have been mentioned more frequently; however, it the least mentioned category in this list. To sum up, the participants of this study defined technology with the aforementioned features.

The second question was about how they could use technology in their future language classes. The responses were analyzed and grouped under seven headings. The responses were presented in Table 4.

When the responses were analyzed and categorized, it was seen that the most frequently mentioned use of technology was about the materials. However, in these responses, the participants did not utter any word about designing or preparing the material, but they were planning to find and download materials from the Internet. They could download pictures illustrating the target culture; or they could find some worksheets shared on different websites. The participants preferred using the ready materials rather than producing their own materials.

Table 4. Ways of using technology in foreign language classes

The Use Technology	f	%
Material (Pictures, audial materials, worksheets, listening materials)	60	56.6
Video	45	42.5
Hardware (Computer, Interactive White Board, Printer, Speakers, Overhead Projector)	36	34.0
Presentation	21	19.8
Source of Information	21	19.8
Web 2.0. (Blogs, Edmodo)	12	11.3
Communication	7	6.6

The second most commonly mentioned way of using technology in language classes was to show some videos related to the topic from different websites. They found it very authentic to use some videos related to the target culture. Since the percentage of this category was distinguishably high, it was given under a different title.

The third category was about the use of hardware in language classes. The participants expect to find some equipment in their future classes and they stated that they could only use technology in their classes if the required equipment is available.

The use of presentations and slideshows was also mentioned very frequently; 19,8% of the participants perceive technology as slide shows and PowerPoint presentations. The same amount of participants claimed that they could use the Internet as the source of information. They could find some information, or they could search for materials on the Internet.

The final two categories were appropriate for the rationale computer assisted language learning. Web 2.0 tools and communication were among the most important keywords in the field of CALL; however, they were not mentioned in the data. The participants who responded as Web 2.0 tools were the ones who used blogs or an online classroom for their courses at the department. This was also a good indicator of the fact that the students were affected by their instructors at the university.

DISCUSSION

When PTs' confidence levels were asked the mean value of the overall confidence level was moderate (M=3.18). The discrepancy between the overall confidence level and their opinions about the using the technology in the classroom (M=4.67) was obvious. Although they did not feel confident enough to use the computer, the results of the scale suggest that they are aware of the importance of incorporating technology into their future classes.

At the end of the data analysis of the qualitative data, the most commonly observed category in the definition of technology is easiness. However, the participants were not aware of the potential uses of technology in language classes. The use of online platforms requires a teacher to spend many hours on the Internet while designing an activity and evaluating their students.

Moreover, the most frequently observed response about the future use of technology in language classes is about finding out ready materials on the Internet. However, in a CALL course, pre-service teachers could be trained how to create their own materials using podcasts, wikis, blogs, online classes and discussion boards. Since they did not have any idea about designing new materials, they preferred to download ready materials on the internet.

In addition to these, although Warschauer (1996) defined the last phase of CALL as integrative CALL and he mentioned the importance of communication, the percentage of the participants who were planning to use technology for communication was very low.

Since the participants of this study were not familiar with Web 2.0 tools, they had never uttered a word related to Web 2.0 tools. They were cited in some responses; however, the reason for this is the fact that some of their instructors used blogs or online classes for their courses. This can a good indicator of the fact that the students took their instructors as the role model for their future practices.

SOLUTIONS AND RECOMMENDATIONS

Prospective EFL teachers' perceptions about the use of technology in EFL classrooms should be examined and acknowledged in the initial teacher training programs. Prospective EFL teachers and the administration of the program needs to be aware of the possible preconceptions about technology and its integration into the teacher education programs to enable its applications in real classrooms. Therefore, addressing the needs of the 21st Century skills for using technology will be achieved.

The primary aim of the foreign language teacher education departments is to provide the necessary context of professional learning for the prospective teachers. However, the context of professional learning not only requires teacher educators to convey the necessary theoretical knowledge for EFL teaching but also to provide the necessary opportunities for prospective teachers' to practice their possible classroom applications. Thus, the curriculum of the initial teacher education programs should address the possible demands of national education. Although there are specific courses (e.g. Teaching English to Young Learners, Foreign Language Assessment) offered by the Council of Higher Education (1998), there are not any courses offered in the foreign language teacher education programs addressing the use of technology in EFL classrooms which is thought-provoking. The present study, therefore, creates the opportunity for an immediate call for the policy-makers to create opportunities for foreign language teacher education departments to offer necessary courses focusing on the integration of technology in EFL classrooms.

FUTURE RESEARCH DIRECTIONS

The study was not designed as a psychometric analysis to examine the underlying factors of PTs' using CALL in their future classes. Rather, it was designed to reflect on the effectiveness of the practices of the department that the current study was implemented. Therefore, the results of the study provide a reflection on the effectiveness of the instruction provided in the applications of the department to train foreign language teachers.

The study was carried out in one of the EFL teacher education programs with a limited number of participants. Therefore, having more participants will provide a coherent understanding of the beliefs of the PTs to use technology in their classes and their readiness to incorporate technology in their teaching practices. It may also be worthwhile to investigate the opinions of the academic staff working at the initial teacher education program to examine the extent to which they believe that they prepare EFL teachers working at the schools and actively using technological resources in their classrooms.

The study investigates PTs' definitions of technology and ways of using technology in their classes. Thus, the study is design solely on PTs' personal opinions. As a suggestion for the future studies, observations can be conducted during practice teaching and at PTs' first year of teaching. Therefore, future studies focusing on the on-site observations of using technology will display a coherent understanding of PTs' teaching practices.

CONCLUSION

The study presented the results of a case study with a mixed-method design addressing EFL PTs' perceptions of using technology in their future practices to teach English in a foreign language setting. Using technology has received tremendous amount of attention in the recent years (Chapelle, 2001; Chapelle, 2006; Levy & Stockwell, 2006). Although teachers are expected to use technology as an assistant tool to the education, there is not a specific course offered to equip prospective teachers with the necessary skills to use technology at the initial teacher education programs in Turkey. In addition to the lack of a course in the curriculum of foreign language teacher education programs in Turkey, the extent to which the instructors are using technology and incorporating technological resources to their instruction has been addressed in the current foreign language teacher education context in Turkey.

Considering the limited number of cases presented in the study, the findings may not be generalized to all foreign language teacher education programs. Despite this fact, the findings of the study add to the foreign language teacher education literature by providing insights of the prospective EFL teachers' attitudes and perceptions of using technology and CALL resources in their future practices.

REFERENCES

Ajzen, I. (1991). The theory of planned behavior. *Organizational Behavior and Human Decision Processes*, *50*(2), 179–211. doi:10.1016/0749-5978(91)90020-T

Blake, R. (2005). Bimodal CMC: The glue of language learning at a distance. *CALICO Journal*, *22*, 497–511.

Brown, J. D. (1997). Computers in language testing: Present research and some future directions. *Language Learning & Technology*, *1*(1), 44–59.

Chapelle, C. (2001). *Computer applications in second language acquisition: Foundations for teaching, testing, and research*. Cambridge: Cambridge University Press. doi:10.1017/CBO9781139524681

Chapelle, C. (2006). Foreword. In P. Hubbard & M. Levy (Eds.), *Teacher education in CALL*. Amsterdam: John Benjamins. doi:10.1075/lllt.14.01cha

Council of Higher Education (Turkey)) & World Bank. (1998). School-Faculty Partnership, Ankara: YÖK.

Dillman, D. A., Smyth, J. D., & Christian, L. M. (2014). *Internet, Phone, Mail, and Mixed-Mode Surveys: The Tailored Design Method* (4th ed.). Wiley.

Garcia, M. R., & Arias, F. V. (2000). A comparative study in motivation and learning through print-oriented and computer-oriented tests. *Computer Assisted Language Learning*, *13*(4-5), 457–465. doi:10.1076/0958-8221(200012)13:4-5;1-E;FT457

Hubbard, P. (2004). Learner training for effective use of CALL. In S. Fotos & C. Browne (Eds.), *New perspectives on CALL for second language classrooms* (pp. 45–68). Mahwah, NJ: Lawrence Erlbaum.

Jamieson, J., Chapelle, C. A., & Preiss, S. (2005). CALL Evaluation by developers, a teacher, and students. *CALICO Journal*, *23*(1), 93–138.

Kessler, G. (2006). Assessing CALL teacher training: What are we doing and what could we do better? In P. Hubbard & M. Levy (Eds.), *Teacher education in CALL*. Amsterdam: John Benjamins. doi:10.1075/lllt.14.05kes

Kılıçkaya, F., & Krajka, J. (2010). Comparative usefulness of online and traditional vocabulary learning. *Turkish Online Journal of Educational Technology, 9*(2), 55–63.

Kılıçkaya, F., & Krajka, J. (2012). Can the use of web-based comic strip creation tool facilitate EFL learners' grammar and sentence writing? *British Journal of Educational Technology, 43*(6), E161–E165. doi:10.1111/j.1467-8535.2012.01298.x

Kılıçkaya, F., & Seferoğlu, G. (2013). The impact of CALL instruction on English language teachers' use of technology in language teaching. *Journal of Second and Multiple Language Acquisition, 1*(1), 20–38.

Koufaris, M. (2002). Applying the Technology Acceptance Model and Flow Theory to Online Consumer Behavior. *Information Systems Research, 13*(2), 205–223. doi:10.1287/isre.13.2.205.83

Lee, M.-C. (2010). Explaining and Predicting Users' Continuance Intention toward E-Learning: An Extension of the Expectation–Confirmation Model. *Computers & Education, 54*(2), 506–516. doi:10.1016/j.compedu.2009.09.002

Levy, M., & Stockwell, G. (2006). *CALL dimensions: Options and issues in computer assisted language learning*. Mahwah, NJ: Lawrence Erlbaum.

Robb, T. (2006). Helping teachers to help themselves. In P. Hubbard & M. Levy (Eds.), *Teacher education in CALL*. Amsterdam: John Benjamins. doi:10.1075/lllt.14.27rob

Sadaf, A., Newby, T. J., & Ertmer, P. A. (2012). Exploring factors that predict preservice teachers' intentions to use web 2.0 technologies using decomposed theory of planned behavior. *Journal of Research on Technology in Education, 45*(2), 171–195. doi:10.1080/15391523.2012.10782602

Stockwell, G. (2009). Teacher Education in CALL: Teaching teachers to educate themselves. *Innovation in Language Learning and Teaching, 3*(1), 99–112. doi:10.1080/17501220802655524

Stokes, A. (1997). Making a success of CALL. *English Teaching Professional, 4*, 20–21.

Taylor, S., & Todd, P. A. (1995). Understanding information technology usage: A test of competing models. *Information Systems Research, 6*(2), 144–176. doi:10.1287/isre.6.2.144

Volman, M. (2005). A variety of roles for a new type of teacher educational technology and the teaching profession. *Teaching and Teacher Education, 2*(1), 15–31. doi:10.1016/j.tate.2004.11.003

Warshauer, M. (1996). Computer-Assisted Language Learning: An Introduction. In S. Fotos (Ed.), *Multimedia language teaching* (pp. 3–20). Tokyo: Logos International.

Wiebe, G., & Kabata, K. (2010). Students' and instructors' attitudes toward the use of CALL in foreign language teaching and learning. *Computer Assisted Language Learning, 23*(3), 221–234. doi:10.1080/09588221.2010.486577

KEY TERMS AND DEFINITIONS

CALL: The use of computers and the Internet in teaching and learning a foreign language.

Prospective EFL Teachers: Student teachers who are enrolled at a 4-year degree program on English as a foreign language teacher training.

Technology Resources: The available resources on the Internet for the teachers and the learners of the target language.

Chapter 13
The Impact of Pre-service Teachers' Reflection on their Instructional Practices

Yesim Kesli Dollar
Bahcesehir University, Turkey

Enisa Mede
Bahcesehir University, Turkey

ABSTRACT

This chapter aims to investigate the impact of reflection on freshmen pre-service English teachers' classroom practices. Specifically, it explores how the participating student teachers' perceptions influenced their instructional practices as a result of participation in reflection activities. The participants of the study were ten freshmen student teachers enrolled in the English Language Teaching undergraduate program at a foundation (non-profit private) university in Turkey. Data came from the reflections of the participating student teachers about their recently-completed 15-hour field-based experience at the preschool level. As a part of this class reflection activity, the participants were prompted to keep a diary in one of their undergraduate courses and respond to a series of statements or questions related to their classroom observation tasks. They were also engaged in class discussions and were required to write their overall feedback based on their field-based experience. The findings of the study revealed that reflective activities helped the prospective student teachers identify their strengths and weaknesses related to classroom activities, use of materials (use of technology and visuals) and classroom management, leading to self-awareness about their understanding and application of teaching skills and strategies.

INRODUCTION

The importance of teacher candidates being able to develop their ability to engage in reflective practices has gained the attention of various theorists and practitioners in the field of teacher education (Fairbanks and Meritt, 1998; McDraw, et.al., 2004; Frid and Reid, 2005; Pedro, 2005; Rodman, 2010). Based on a theoretical framework derived from the works of Dewey (1919, 1933) and Schön (1983), the use of

DOI: 10.4018/978-1-4666-9471-2.ch013

reflection and reflective practice encourage pre-service teachers to actively consider and reconsider their beliefs and to think critically about their classroom practices (Rodman, 2010). As Dewey (1933) argued, reflection preceded intelligent action and is the act of active, persistent and careful consideration of any belief or supposed form of knowledge in the light of grounds that support it, and the consequence to which it leads. Emanating from Dewey's work, Shön (1983, p. 26) defined two distinct kinds of reflection: reflection-in-action which is the process that allows teachers to reshape what they are working on while they are working on it and reflection-on-action referring to thinking back on what teachers have done in order to discover how their knowing-in-action may have contributed to an unexpected outcome.

A close examination of research on the Turkish training system reveals that most studies are descriptive and there has been little empirical research. One of the possible reasons behind this problem might be the fact that many teacher education programs in Turkey provide pre-service teachers with inadequate opportunities to actively engage in designing their lesson plans, reflecting on their classroom practices and developing research-based strategies in a classroom context. In the Turkish education system, the pre-service teachers start their practicum experiences in their senior year which gives them few opportunities to develop their reflective thinking skills. Right after graduation they start teaching in a real classroom environment without having enough reflective practice, which causes feelings of frustration and burnout. Thus, particularly in Turkish teacher education programs, there is a great need to ensure that pre-service teachers are involved in continuous reflection which help them to make meaning of their teaching practices through connecting the learned theories and teaching practice experiences. In light of these observations, this chapter examines the effects of reflection and reflective activities on freshmen English pre-service teachers' instructional practices.

This chapter will highlight the following objectives:

1. Give a brief preview of pre-service teacher education programs and reflective teaching.
2. Investigate the effects of reflection and reflective activities on freshmen English pre-service teachers' instructional practices in a Turkish context.
3. Discuss the results of the study for evaluating and developing pre-service teacher education programs.
4. Provide solutions and recommendations for the existing pre-service teacher education programs.

BACKGROUND

There are many definitions of the term reflection (e.g., Goodman, 1984; Houston, 1988; Roth, 1989; Schön, 1987). One of the most widely known definitions, based on Dewey's 1904 notion, states that "the primary purpose of teacher preparation programs should be to help students reflect upon the underlying principles of practice" (Goodman, 1984; p. 9). Likewise, Grant and Zeichner (1984) claim that "reflective teaching involves a balance between thought and action; a balance between the arrogance that blindly rejects what is commonly accepted as truth and the servility that blindly receives the 'truth'" (p. 10), whereas Semerci (2007) proposes "a reflective thinking teacher always tries to train students with his/her best" (p. 1370). Finally, Crowe and Berry (2007) argue that "becoming a teacher involves learning to think like a teacher…thinking like a teacher involves developing a sensitive awareness of one's actions and a consistent focus on recognizing alternative perspectives and approaches to learning situations" (p. 32). Based on these definitions, it can be inferred that reflection is one of the most important components in teacher education programs.

Why Reflection in Teacher Education Programs?

In teacher education programs, there needs to be a shift from an apprenticeship to a reflective practice model (Calderhead, 1989). Pre-service teachers have the capacity to analyze and evaluate their practices; therefore, teacher education programs should emphasize not only the technical parts of teaching but also the relationship between theory and practice, and the importance of reflecting upon what they practice. How to reflect must be one of the required parts of the teacher educators programs; pre-service teachers need to learn to initiate new ways of thinking and reflecting because they are only provided with the theories and principles at their teacher educator programs.

When you think of a pre-service teacher in his/her first years of education, they lack the necessary skills to analyse and evaluate their own practice, they do not even know how to word their experiences or think about situations related with their teaching.

According to Richert (1992), pre-service teachers must actively engage in the process of reflection to make it become a habit in their profession. Richert also claims that reflection of their practices gives teachers the opportunity to construct knowledge about teaching and their profession. The process of reflection should not be a process for pre-service teachers only; rather, both pre-service and in-service teachers need to engage in it in order to learn from their experiences.

Reflection or reflective teaching is a central part of the teacher/learning process. Without reflection or reflective teaching, one can risk of relying on routinized teaching and problems in professional development. Mewborn (1999) states that teacher education programs should give opportunities to pre-service teachers to learn how to reflect on their personal experiences and learn how to make use of those experiences and reflections for their future teachings. It is believed that if pre-service teachers learn how to reflect on their teaching during their practice teaching process and continue doing so during the in-service years (Loughran, 2007). This will end up improving teaching, and professional development. Likewise, teacher education programs should focus on the reason why teachers employ certain instructional strategies and on how they can achieve effective teaching with professional development; that is why pre-service teachers are highly encouraged to be involved in reflective practice not only to achieve a better state of professional development but also to have a better and more positive effect on their students through their teaching.

Although several studies attempted to find out the effect of reflection and reflective practice of pre-service teachers in teacher education, the overwhelming majority of these studies have been qualitative in design, focusing on a small number of cases (Fairbanks and Meritt, 1998; McDraw, et.al., 2004; Frid and Reid, 2005; Pedro, 2005; Rodman, 2010; Robichaux and Guarino, 2012).

Teacher educators must start teaching about reflection, its importance, and how to reflect on actions before the practice teaching experiences begin. For a pre-service teacher to get used to reflecting, they need time and a lot of practice. Frid and Reid (2002) proposed that long before novice teachers start their actual teaching in their own classrooms, their teacher educators should provide them with controlled situations which will help them to improve the ability to reflect on classroom practice and teaching. Through this, educators will raise awareness in pre-service teachers of the different choices and teaching behaviours observed in them through reflection and in this way they can integrate their observations made through reflections into their future teaching.

McDraw, et al. (2004) worked with four undergraduate special education majors to observe the development of a personal philosophy of education as well as the effectiveness of reflection and its influence on teachers' beliefs, attitudes, and behaviours. They suggest that reflecting thinking should be a process offered as a component of a teacher education program. In addition, they believe that reflection is a way of developing critical thinking on education among pre-service teachers.

In their research, Fairbanks and Meritt (1998) tried to apply activity theory to the learning-to-learn experiences of four pre-service teachers. They analyzed the products of the pre-service teachers' reflective activities and observational data gathered during their year-long preparation. They looked into the intersections between context and practice. The study found that reflection on the activities and the teaching indicated the value of reflection in the teacher education program, and this affected their social identity growth. Moreover, the reflections provided them with an understanding of the people and the events they may encounter during their teaching. In brief, reflective activities helped the pre-service teachers to construct their professional identity.

Pedro's (2005) qualitative study using a descriptive and interpretive design, aimed to interpret the pre-service teachers' conceptions and understandings of reflective practice through the transcription and analysis of three individual in-depth interviews and through the examination of the pre-service teachers' reflective journals. According to the findings, the pre-service teachers understood the concept of reflection which they used as a conceptual device to help them think about their knowledge and better their teaching skills. In a parallel study, Rodman (2010) attempted to learn how the reflective engagement of pre-service teachers reinforces the application of the teaching-learning process in the classroom and enables them to construct meaning from that application. The results of this study suggested that repeated use of reflection throughout the teacher preparation experience can be useful for encouraging growth and professional development.

Robichaux and Guarino (2012) examined the hypothesis that pre-service teachers who were required to assemble portfolio assessment would promote greater scores on professional growth than the pre-service teachers who were not required to assemble a portfolio assessment. The results of the study revealed that even if pre-service teachers do not receive any formal training on how to reflect upon their teaching and are not given reflection prompts, they still appear to reflect more on issues considered important to becoming effective educators, which aids in their capacity to handle the complexities of the teaching profession.

The findings of these studies support the notion that through reflection and reflective activities, pre-service teachers have the ability to develop a better understanding of their teaching skills and practices. They point the way to how pre-service teachers should be engaged in reflective practice and how reflection can be encouraged in different pedagogical contexts.

Apart from the research studies carried out in different ESL/EFL contexts, several studies in Turkey revealed that pre-service teachers were limited in discussion and reflections on teaching practices in their teacher education courses (Çakıroğlu and Çakıroğlu, 2003; Şahin-Taşkın, 2006; Armutcu and Yaman, 2010; Hacıömeroğlu, 2010). Hacıömeroğlu (2010), for example, examined the nature of pre-service secondary teachers' instructional strategies and views about teaching and learning with regard to teaching mathematics in Turkey. The analysis of the pre-service teachers' written reflections, activities, class discussions and observations indicated that engagement in reflective activities helped the participating teachers identify their major strengths and weaknesses in their lessons, and analyze issues in teaching. As a result of reflective activities, collaboration between pre-service teachers increased which helped them to refine and revise their lessons and improve their teaching. Moreover, Armutcu and Yaman (2010) explored teacher reflection of senior ELT pre-service teachers during their practicum experience in terms of "sex and instruction types". The researchers collected the data through "Teacher Reflection

The Impact of Pre-service Teachers' Reflection

Scale and semi-structured interviews" (p.30) both at the very beginning and at the end of the practicum in a form of a pre- and a post-test. As a result of the study, it was found that both before and after the practicum experience senior ELT students' teacher reflections were high; in other words, no meaningful differences were found between the effect of gender and instruction types on teachers' teacher reflections. These findings indicate that reflection is a continuous process starting at the freshman year through senior year. Finally, Odabaşı Çimer and Çimer (2012) tried to explore and analyze the current practices of reflection in teacher education programs in Turkey. In this study, the researchers came to the conclusion that, within the teacher education community, the views regarding being an effective teacher have changed; traditional views have shifted to recognize the importance of reflection. They also conclude that if there is a demand to increase the quality of education in schools, it is important to develop reflective skills in student-teachers and make reflection part of their teaching experience and part of the teacher education programs.

MAIN FOCUS OF THIS CHAPTER

Issues, Controversies, Problems

Methodology

The qualitative methodology for this study is positioned within critical research. According to Merriam (2009), critical research is interpretive as is other forms of qualitative research which attempt to investigate a phenomenon in which participants make meaning of the world. However, unlike basic qualitative studies, critical research seeks not just to explore and understand but also to examine, challenge, and transform the perceptions of the participants about themselves and others. Thus this study examined:

1. How participants interpret their experiences within a given context,
2. How participants construct their own meaning,
3. What meaning participants attribute to their experiences as a result of their reflections,
4. What kind of effects these reflections have on the participants' instructional practices.

Participants

In this study, the participants were ten freshmen pre-service teachers (8 female and 2 male) aged 10-to-22 years who were enrolled in the English Language Teaching (ELT) undergraduate program at a private university in Turkey. All participants were full-time students of Turkish nationality. They passed the language proficiency exam before they started their freshman year at the department.

Data Collection Instruments

Data was collected from the reflections of the participating pre-service English teachers about their recently-completed 15-hour field-based experience in a private kindergarten. As a part of this class reflection activity, the participants were prompted to keep a diary in one of their undergraduate courses in which they received an observation task with specific topics: teaching activities, instructional materials, and classroom management. They were asked to make observations in English kindergarten classrooms and complete each task as a requirement of their field-based experience. After each week, the participants had a discussion session, of which the researcher kept field notes, about the observation tasks completed that week. Finally, at the end of the term, the participants were required to write their overall feedback, by responding to prompts regarding what they did throughout the semester.

Data Analysis

The data from diaries were subjected to content analysis (Strauss and Corbin, 1990). Due to the small number of the participants, the data were coded by hand. Next, the researcher identified the central themes for each set of data relating to a specific objective which were in turn identified under sub-themes. This process was carried out with the help of another researcher who was blind to the aim of the study to ensure the reliability. As for the class discussion, the notes taken by the researcher were analyzed in accordance with the categorizations obtained from the diaries. Finally, the participants' written feedback was investigated to find out how the freshmen pre-service English teacher felt during their field based experience.

Findings

Regarding the findings gathered from the diaries, the pre-service ELT teachers shared common observation points about teaching activities, use of materials and classroom management. In the diaries, the majority of the participants mentioned the same central themes and sub-themes shown in Table 1.

As can be seen in the table, due to the fact that the observed classrooms were kindergarten, the most used teaching activities are games, songs, and stories which reflect the needs of this particular age group. Since, in kindergarten, the students do not yet have literacy skills, the main activities are based on play and fun. Following are some examples in which the freshmen pre-service English teachers reflected on the teaching activities:

...they generally play games like, matching or they do painting to learn the names of things (Freshmen pre-service English teacher 1, Diary).

...they play musical chairs. It was so funny (Freshmen pre-service English teacher 1, Diary).

Table 1. Perceptions about teaching activities, use of materials and classroom management

Central Themes	Sub-Themes
Teaching activities	Games: Question game, matching game and board game Songs: Nursery rhymes Story telling
Instructional materials	Pictures and paintings I pads Smart board Flashcards
Classroom management	Teacher's action zone Teacher's role: Mothers and fathers Use of positive language Creating friendly classroom atmosphere

The Impact of Pre-service Teachers' Reflection

...the teacher sings songs together with the students (Freshmen pre-service English teacher 2, Diary).

...their teacher tells them English stories or teachers them some adjectives through stories (Freshmen pre-service English teacher 1, Diary).

Parallel to the reflections made about teaching activities, the participants also made some reflections on the use of instructional materials. For example:

...I observe use of technologies and visuals in the classroom...Children play musical chairs with the songs from an I pad...So, they generally benefit from technology when they are playing games.....There are lots of things such as the pictures of colours, numbers, animals on the walls of the classroom. Also they sometimes put the paintings that they panted themselves on the walls (Freshmen pre-service English teacher 1, Diary).

...the teacher uses the smart board to make the students practice. For example, she teaches them how to search for a specific country or play a game on their individual I pads (Freshmen pre-service English teacher 3, Diary).

...the teacher uses flashcards while presenting a new topic to the class (Freshmen pre-service English teacher 2, Diary).

Finally, the participating pre-service English teachers emphasized the role of classroom management in kindergarten through their diary reflections. They not only made some reflections on classroom management, but made further suggestions as can be seen in the following excerpts:

...actually there isn't an exact action zone for the teachers. I mean they should be able to move everywhere in the classroom. Because children are always moving, teachers should be dynamic in order to keep up with them (Freshmen pre-service English teacher 1, Diary).

...they are not just teachers but also they are in the role of mother and father. For instance, they help children to wear their clothes, to eat their meals and to go to the toilet (Freshmen pre-service English teacher 1, Diary).

...using negative or positive language is extremely effective on children. The teacher always keeps students motivated by telling them positive things such as "good job, nice work and very good example" (Freshmen pre-service English teacher 2, Diary).

...the teacher creates a friendly classroom atmosphere. She doesn't start the lesson immediately, but first, she welcomes the students, asks about their health and then starts the lesson. She knows every student names and also treats them equally (Freshmen pre-service English teacher 2, Diary).

Besides the reflections made in the diaries, the participants shared their general impressions from their observations in the classroom discussions which were noted by the researcher in field notes. Some examples of field notes gathered from the class discussions were quoted as follows:

...when they want to do something, it is really hard to prevent them or when they don't want to do something, it is again very hard to persuade them to do it. However, whatever they do, they are so forgivable. I mean, you know they are so little and cute, so, you can't get angry with them. Therefore, if someone wants to be a kindergarten teacher, s/he should be more patient and lovely that anyone else.

...it was really good to learn. I wonder what I would learn more thanks to these observations.

...I have learned that it is not easy to be a teacher. I have learned a lot and I will try to use all of them in the future.

...I think the teachers' way of teaching is very effective. I hope to follow these techniques in the future.

SOLUTIONS AND RECOMMENDATIONS

As reflection is a link between what is being done in the past and what can be done in the future, it is very helpful for pre-service teachers in terms of making the connection between theory and practice, as well as professional development.

Proposed by many researchers (Frid and Reid, 2003; McDraw, et.al. 2004; Fairbanks and Meritt, 1998; Rodman, 2010), there is a fair consensus that teacher education programs, beginning in the very first year, need to integrate reflection and reflective practice in their curriculum in order to help prospective teachers construct their professional identity. This will provide them with the opportunity to develop their personal philosophy of education with regard to their beliefs, attitudes and behaviours. As indicated in the findings of this study, engaging pre-service teachers in reflective activities at an early stage of their education raised their awareness of the importance and effectiveness of reflection into their future teaching. The earlier the reflective practice component is integrated in teacher education programs, the sooner the pre-service teachers will start establishing their personal and professional constructs for understanding teachers, students, teaching, and the learning environment.

Furthermore, in the study, the analyses of the diaries, field notes, and class discussions revealed that freshmen pre-service English teachers started to think more critically about the incidents happening in a real teaching environment. This indicates that if teacher education programs give more importance to reflection and reflective practice, it will enhance the development of critical thinking skills at early stages which will have a positive effect on their instructional practices in the future.

These experiences also facilitate the feeling of being a teacher and the capacity of dealing with the complexities in the real classroom environment. To exemplify, when the participating teachers first started the observations, they were not aware of important concepts in teaching such as teaching activities, instructional materials, and classroom management. After completion of the observation tasks, they became more aware of effective materials and activities to be implemented during language teaching and learning as well as with the efficient strategies to cope with classroom management problems in general.

To conclude, based on the findings of the study, through reflection and reflective activities, pre-service teachers develop the ability to better understand their teaching skills and practices. It is recommended that teacher education programs in Turkey should be evaluated and redesigned according to the needs of the students, teachers, administrators, parents and other stakeholders while taking into consideration the premises of reflection and reflective practice in professional development.

FUTURE RESEARCH DIRECTIONS

As an application drawn from this study, in Turkey there is a need to improve teacher education programs based on constructivist models (Armutcu and Yaman, 2010) especially in the field of English Language Teaching (ELT). Since this is a case study, more extensive research should be conducted for the generalizability of the results to explore the effectiveness of reflection in practice teaching. An interesting future research project would be to do a follow up study with the same group of pre-service students in upcoming years which will enable the researchers to monitor the impact of reflection throughout their academic studies. Another future study could focus on novice in-service English teachers to highlight what the strengths and weaknesses are in their teaching which should be reflected in teacher education programs.

CONCLUSION

This chapter tried to highlight the importance of reflection and reflective practices in pre-service teacher education programs. Especially, this chapter aimed to share the findings of a study which tried to explore the effects of reflection and reflective activities on freshmen English pre-service teachers' instructional practices in a Turkish context. The findings of the study supported that if teacher education programs integrate reflection and reflective practice into their programs, pre-service teachers will develop the ability to better understand their teaching skills and practices and critical thinking skills at early stages.

In addition, the study proposes that there is an emergent need for evaluating and developing pre-service teacher education programs. Most of the pre-service English teachers start their teaching practice right before their graduation which results in feelings of frustration and incapability as they start their teaching career after graduation. This obviously indicates that there is serious need for beginning practice teaching during the first years of teacher education programs. In order to accomplish this, all of the ELT programs in Turkey should establish a consortium to take action on improving the practicum component of current programs.

REFERENCES

Armutcu, N., & Yaman, S. (2010). ELT pre-service teachers' teacher reflection through practicum. *Procedia: Social and Behavioral Sciences*, *3*, 28–35. doi:10.1016/j.sbspro.2010.07.009

Çakıroğlu, E., & Çakıroğlu, J. (2003). Reflections on teacher education in Turkey. *European Journal of Teacher Education*, *26*, 253–265. doi:10.1080/0261976032000088774

Calderhead, J. (1987). Reflective teaching and teacher education. *Teaching and Teacher Education*, *5*(1), 43–52. doi:10.1016/0742-051X(89)90018-8

Crowe, A. R., & Berry, A. (2007). Teaching prospective teachers about learning to think like a teacher: Articulating some of our principles. In T. Russell & J. Loughran (Eds.), *Enacting a pedagogy of teacher education: Values, relationships and practices* (pp. 31–44). New York: Routledge.

Ferguson, P. (1989). A reflective approach to the methods practicum. *Journal for Teacher Education*, 36-41.

Frid, S., & Reid, J. (2002). Competency = Complexity and Connectedness: Professional portfolios as a technology for reflective practice in pre-service education. In J. Reid, & T. Brown (Eds), *Challenging futures. Changing agendas in teacher education (Proceedings of the Challenging Futures conference, Armidale, NSW)*. Retrieved from http://scs.une.edu.au/CF/Papers/editorial.htm

Goodman, J. (1984). Reflection and teacher education: A case study and theoretical analysis. *Interchange*, *15*(3), 9–26. doi:10.1007/BF01807939

Grant, C. A., & Zeichner, K. M. (1984). On becoming a reflective teacher. In C. A. Grant (Ed.), *Preparing for reflective teaching* (pp. 1–18). Toronto, ON: Allyn and Bacon.

Hacıömeroğlu, G. (2010). Preservice Teachers' Reflections on their Instructional Practices. *Proceedings of the 31st annual meeting of the North American Chapter of the International Group for the Psychology of Mathematics Education*. Atlanta, GA: Georgia State University.

Houston, W. R. (1988). Reflecting on reflection in teacher education. In H. C. Waxman, H. J. Freiberg, J. C. Vaughan, & M. Weil (Eds.), *Images of reflection in teacher education* (pp. 7–8). Reston, VA: Association of Teacher Educators.

Loughran, J. J. (2007). Enacting a pedagogy of teacher education. In T. Russell & J. Loughran (Eds.), Enacting a pedagogy of teacher education: Values, relationships and practices (pp. 1-15). New York: Routledge.

Mewborn, D. S. (1999). Reflective thinking among preservice elementary mathematics teachers. *Journal for Research in Mathematics Education*, *30*(9), 316–341. doi:10.2307/749838

Odabaşı Çimer, S. & Çimer, A. (2012). Issues around incorporating reflection in teacher education in Turkey. *Journal of Turkish Science Education, 9*(1), 17-30.

Pedro, J. Y. (2005). Reflective practice: International and multidisciplinary perspectives. *Reflective Practice*, *6*(1), 49–66.

Richert, A. E. (1992). Voice and power in teaching and learning to teach. In L. Valli (Ed.), *Reflective teacher education: Cases and critiques* (pp. 187–197). Albany: State University of New York Press.

Robichaux, R. R., & And Guarino, A. J. (2012). Enhancing preservice teachers' professionalism through daily teaching reflections. *Education Research International*, *2012*, 1–3. doi:10.1155/2012/452687

Rodman, G. J. (2010). Facilitating the teaching-learning process through the reflective engagement of pre-service teacher. *Australian Journal of Teacher Education*, *35*(2), 20–34.

Ross, D. (1989). First steps in developing a reflective approach. *Journal of Teacher Education*, *40*(2), 22–30. doi:10.1177/002248718904000205

Sahin–Taskin, C. (2006). Student teachers in the classroom: Their perceptions of teaching practice. *Educational Studies*, *32*(4), 387–398. doi:10.1080/03055690600948091

Schon, D. (1987). *Educating the reflective practitioner Toward a new design for teaching and learning in the professions.* San Francisco: Jossey Bass.

Schön, D. S. (1983). *The Reflective Practitioner.* London: Temple Smith.

Semerci, C. (2007). Developing a reflective thinking tendency scale for teachers and student teachers. *Educational Sciences: Theory and Practice, 7*(3), 1369–1376.

KEY TERMS AND DEFINITIONS

Classroom Management: A term used by teachers to describe the process of ensuring that classroom lessons run smoothly despite disruptive behavior by students.

EFL: The teaching of English to people whose first language is not English.

Instructional Practices: All approaches that a teacher may take to actively engage students in learning.

Pre-Service Teacher Education: A period of guided, supervised teaching.

Reflection: Important human activities in which people recapture their experience, think about it, mull over and evaluate it.

Teaching Activities: Implementations used by the teachers that help to enhance learning in the classroom.

Teaching Materials: A spectrum of educational materials used by the teachers in the classroom to support specific learning objectives.

Chapter 14
Exploring Prospective EFL Teachers' Beliefs about Teachers and Teaching through Metaphor Analysis

Anil Rakicioglu-Soylemez
Abant Izzet Baysal University, Turkey

Ayse Selmin Soylemez
Abant Izzet Baysal University, Turkey

Amanda Yesilbursa
Uludag University, Turkey

ABSTRACT

This study aimed to explore prospective EFL teachers' metaphors of "teachers, teaching" and "being a prospective EFL teacher" at the beginning and end of a ten-week practicum course. A total of 110 Turkish prospective EFL teachers voluntarily participated in the study. Data were collected by means of semi-structured interviews and metaphor-elicitation forms. Results lead to three major conclusions. First, the participants' prior beliefs about the role of an EFL teacher and teaching were affected by their previous experiences as language learners. Second, although the content analysis of the metaphors revealed a limited change throughout the practicum experience, the analysis of the interviews showed the dynamic nature of beliefs held by the prospective teachers. Finally, data analysis of the interviews showed that the variation in beliefs and practices mainly derived from individual experiences with the mentoring practices of the cooperating teachers and the socio-professional context of the practicum school.

INTRODUCTION

Teacher education programs face challenges in training highly motivated and competent teachers. The major aim of teacher education departments is to provide the necessary circumstances for prospective teachers (henceforth, PTs) to access professional learning opportunities. Therefore, it is important to identify the development of teaching motivations throughout the initial teacher education (ITE) experiences

DOI: 10.4018/978-1-4666-9471-2.ch014

Exploring Prospective EFL Teachers' Beliefs

of the PTs (Rots, Kelchtermans & Aelterman, 2012). A number of motivational sources for PTs to enter teaching profession are listed in the literature (see, e.g., Sinclair, 2008). Field experience in particular has a notable effect on PTs' professional learning experiences (Roness & Smith, 2010; Sinclair, 2008).

These experiences of PTs have been addressed in a number of ways in terms of data collection techniques, such as self-narratives (e.g., Dyson, 2007; Ruohotie-Lyhty, 2013), journals (e.g., Appel, 1995; Bailey, 1990; Numrich, 1996), in-depth interviews (e.g., Borg, 2006; Cheng, Cheng, & Tang, 2010) and classroom observations (e.g., Mattheoudakis, 2007). Metaphor analysis has also been widely used in mainstream and language teaching studies both internationally (see, e.g. Beijaard, Meijer, & Verloop, 2004; Ellis, 1998; Farrell, 2007) and in the Turkish context (see, e.g., Eren & Tekinarslan, 2012; Saban, Koçbeker & Saban; 2006, 2007; Saban, 2010; Yeşilbursa, 2012; Yeşilbursa & Sayar, 2014).

These studies are based on the notion of metaphor as a cognitive process, rather than the traditional view of metaphor as ornamental use of language in the literary sense (Lakoff & Johnson, 1980; Marchant, 1992). According to Lakoff and Johnson (1980), metaphor is a means of understanding new concepts with reference to familiar ones and 'is pervasive in everyday life, not just in language but in thought and action' (p. 3). Thus Lakoff and Johnson (1980) stressed the fact that our conceptual system is mainly metaphorical in nature. Given that, as Nespor (1987) pointed out 'to understand teaching from teachers' perspectives we have to understand the beliefs with which they define their work' (p. 323). Thus, metaphor analysis has the potential to provide a 'comprehensive picture which reveals how PTs envision their teaching-related future' (Eren &Tekinarslan, 2012, p. 435), we considered it to be a suitable approach to adopt in the current study.

Although PTs are one of the main participant groups of practice teaching, the extent to which they professionally benefit from the process has not been addressed to date in the researchers' knowledge in the Turkish EFL context. Thus, the current study aims to provide an in-depth understanding of prospective EFL teachers' (henceforth, in the current paper all PTs referred to will be those in the field of EFL) reflections on their professional learning throughout their field experience. In addition, it aims to attract the attention of teacher educators and other stakeholders of practice teaching to the fact that beliefs and perceptions are important in understanding the way PTs approach the profession. Although most of the studies on practice teaching in the literature focused on the problems, perceptions, beliefs and practices of PTs (e.g., Atay, 2007; Merç, 2004, 2010; Rakıcıoğlu-Söylemez, 2012; Rakıcıoğlu-Söylemez & Eröz-Tuğa, 2014; Seferoğlu, 2006), or the processes of change were labeled (Oxford, Griffiths, Longhini, Cohen, Macaro & Harris, 2014; Yuan & Lee, 2014), concepts of change in their professional learning processes have not been addressed in the EFL teacher education literature. Therefore, the present study aims to address the conceptual changes in the metaphorical descriptions of PTs, in addition to the reasons of change they propose as the agents of change.

Very recently the possible extension of beliefs through real classroom experiences has been emphasized in the international literature(e.g. Tang, Cheng & Cheng, 2013; Rusznyak & Walton, 2014) and is considered as a useful way of accessing participants' conceptions of teaching and the profession as well as tracking the process of how the conceptions develop over time. However, the dynamic nature of beliefs held by PTs has not been addressed throughout their practicum experience. Thus, the study aims to fill this gap in the extant literature. The following research questions have been formulated to this aim:

1. What are the perceptions of PTs on self, teachers and teaching before attending the practice teaching course?
2. What are the perceptions of PTs on self, teachers and teaching after attending the practice teaching course?
3. What change, if any, did they experience in their professional perceptions of self, teachers and teaching throughout the course?
4. What factors might explain such change or lack of change?

The findings of the study will offer insights into PTs' beliefs about themselves, teachers' role and the profession and practices of EFL teaching in a real school setting.

BACKGROUND

The unprecedented spread of English as a global language has been widely acknowledged by many scholars over the past four decades (e.g., Crystal, 2003; Kachru, 1986). Similar to many other countries whose official language is not English, Turkey has responded to the status of English by making adjustments to its language policy at a macro level, and to instructional implications at a micro level (see, e.g. Doğançay-Aktuna & Kızıltepe, 2005; and Kırkgöz, 2007, 2009 for more details). Briefly, with the reforms of 1998 which increased compulsory education from five to eight years by combining the primary and lower-secondary tiers, EFL was introduced into grades four and five with the aims of increasing exposure to the language. In methodological terms this reform was significant, because the concept of the communicative approach in ELT was introduced into the Ministry of National Education (MoNE) EFL curriculum for the first time (Kırkgöz, 2007). The more recent educational reforms of 2012 (see, e.g., MoNE, 2013; OECD, 2014) resulted in the separation of the single eight-year primary tier into a four-year primary tier and a four-year lower secondary tier. The consequence of this reform on ELT has been that EFL has been made part of the grade-two curriculum.

With the establishment of the Council of Higher Education (henceforth, CHE) in 1981, full responsibility for teacher education was given to the Faculties of Education, which currently offer four-year undergraduate degree programs (see, e.g., Çakıroğlu & Çakıroğlu, 2003; Grossman, 2013). At present, the only route into these programs is via the centralized two-phase University Entrance Examination (Kilimci, 2009). In order to increase the quality of teacher education, the content of which had largely been left to the preferences of the academic staff, in 1998 CHE decreed that teacher education programs for all domains (e.g., English Language Teaching, Primary School Teaching) be centrally developed (CHE, 2007). The current ELT program (CHE, 2007) requires PTs to take a number of field-specific courses (e.g., Teaching English to Young Learners) in addition to general pedagogical courses (e.g., classroom management). In the final year, there are two 10-week Practicum courses, School Practice and Teaching Practice, during which PTs are assigned to local state-run primary and secondary schools to conduct observations and teaching under the guidance of a cooperating teacher from the school and a university supervisor (Rakıcıoğlu-Söylemez, 2012). Following completion of teacher education, new teachers are appointed to state schools by means of a centralized selection examination (Yüksel, 2012).

METHODOLOGY

The study is designed as a descriptive case study in that it aims to report on a naturally occurring representation of professional learning beliefs throughout the practice teaching course. In that sense, the study aims to provide an in-depth understanding of PTs' reflections on their professional learning throughout their field experience. As Yin (2011) suggests, case study approach is suitable when contextual conditions are met and highly relevant. The study can also be considered as an opportunistic case study (Creswell, 2007) as the case was accessible because the researchers were the instructors of the course and one group of the triad members of practice teaching as university supervisors. Although a case study aims to focus on a particular aspect of a case (Creswell, 2007; Yin, 2011), the findings of the study can be compared to other contexts and experiences presented here by practitioners and researchers to make naturalistic generalizations (Stake, 2005).

The Research Context

The two field-experience courses, School Experience and Practice Teaching, provide the context of the current study. In order to complete the requirements of these courses, all PTs are appointed to selected state-run schools of Ministry of National Education (MoNE) in the city where they pursue their undergraduate studies. Therefore, the courses are twofold, one part takes place the MoNE schools for six hours a week, focusing on observation and teaching practices of the PTs; the other is a two-hour seminar once a week and offered by the university supervisors. The seminars aim to gather PTs together and share their professional experiences in the cooperating schools throughout their practice teaching.

Throughout the observations and teaching practices PTs attend the English language classes at the cooperating schools. They are assigned to prepare lesson plans, materials and incorporating necessary assessment tools to their teaching practices. During the processes of observations and teaching practices, PTs work with CTs at the cooperating schools. Therefore, they have a certain professional contact with the CTs at their last year of initial teacher education program.

Although the curriculum is provided by CHE (2007), only the responsibilities and task descriptions are provided. Thus, the content of the School Experience and Practice Teaching courses are designed by the university supervisors offering the course without a certain course outline proposed for the aforementioned courses in the initial teacher education programs (Rakıcıoğlu-Söylemez, 2012). The university supervisors' applications and theories to evaluate PT practices throughout these courses depend on the supervisors' priorities. In the current research context, the university supervisors organized the course according to CHE regulations, thus there was no intervention to design the study to collect the data.

Participants

A total of 110 PTs (female N=81, male N=29, age range 20-22 years) voluntarily participated in the study. They were all in their senior year of studies the English Language Teaching (ELT) program of a state-run university located in the Mid-Western Black Sea region of Turkey, and enrolled on the practice teaching course. Most of the participants in the study were graduates of teacher training high schools in Turkey. Therefore, the participants formed a homogeneous group in terms of their educational background and pre-service instructional experience.

The Roles of the Researchers

The potential influence of offering the course as well as collecting the data by the instructors of the course has been acknowledged. Therefore, throughout the data collection and analysis, the researchers were cautious of the importance of willingness on the part of the PTs to participate in the study and tried to observe and reflect on the effects of the researchers' presence in the study as well as participating in the participants' reflections through conducting interviews.

Data Collection

As Creswell (2007) emphasizes, the fact that case studies collect multiple sources of information (e.g. observations, interviews, audiovisual material, and documents and reports), and reports a case description and case-based themes, throughout the analysis, perspectives of the PTs were gathered from multiple data sources (see Table 1). In Table 1, the participants and valid return rate of the data collection tools were also highlighted.

As Table 1 presents, the data sources consisted of pre- and post-course metaphor forms in addition to semi-structured interviews with the PTs during the data collection procedures. Data were collected during the spring semester of 2013-2014 academic year. Data cited from the pre- and post-course metaphors and interviews are referred as Pre-M, Post-M and Int, respectively throughout the study. All PTs participated in the study were informed about their rights to participate in the study and asked to give their consent to participate. Throughout the data collection and analysis procedures, PTs were given pseudonyms to preserve their anonymity.

Data Analysis

Data were collected and analyzed on a simultaneously on-going basis. Specifically, to examine PTs' professional perceptions of selves and teaching practices, a qualitative approach was employed and the grounded theory procedures (Strauss & Corbin, 1998) based on the procedures of thematic analysis (Miles, Huberman & Saldaña, 2014). The interviews conducted with the PTs were transcribed verbatim, and the transcriptions were reviewed by the researchers for accuracy. The transcriptions of the interviews and the reflective journals as well as the metaphor forms of the PTs were read several times in order to find commonly emerging topics and themes about 'teachers, teaching and being a prospective EFL teacher' throughout the practice teaching course. The topics and themes of each data source were listed and then grouped into similar categories. Categories uncovering the change or lack of change in the perceptions of PTs were then established with reference to the conceptual framework and related literature in PTs' situated professional learning. Following the naming and labeling stage, the researchers decided on the unit of analysis by sorting the metaphors. The metaphors were compiled and categorized considering the

Table 1. Data sources of the study

	Early-M	Post-M	Int
Participants	110	119	10 (appr. 15 min)
Valid data turnout	44	81	10 (appr. 15 min.)

establishment of an inter-rater reliability analysis (*K=.90*). Finally, the data were analyzed quantitatively to elaborate more on the content and frequencies of metaphors used by the prospective EFL teachers to outline their professional learning experience during practice teaching.

During the data analysis, not every metaphor produced by the PTs was considered valid. A total of 95 metaphors were excluded from the analysis with the following qualities: plain description or no mention of a metaphor at all, mention of a metaphor but no provision of a rationale, fuzzy/hybrid metaphors or researchers' having difficulty in placing the metaphor under one clearly recognizable conceptual theme.

There were no specific hypotheses suggested due to the explorative nature of the present study. Nevertheless, previous studies provide a solid basis to predict the metaphors disposed by the PTs (e.g. Saban, Koçbeker & Saban, 2006, 2007; Seferoğlu, Korkmazgil & Ölçü, 2009; Yeşilbursa, 2012; Eren & Tekinarslan, 2012; Yeşilbursa & Sayar, 2014). The valid metaphors collected and analyzed in the data analysis were explored and examined according to their relevancy, coherency, and meaningfulness in terms of addressing the research questions of the study.

The results of the study were grouped under three main headings (see Table 2). The first stage of the analysis was the early images of the PTs with regards to the proposed concepts. In the second stage, PTs were asked to reflect on their experiences after attending the practice teaching. In order to elicit the post-images of the PTs, they were given the same data collection tool at the end of the practice teaching. Finally, interviews were transcribed and analyzed in order to address the possible changes of definitions made by the PTs.

The order of sequencing showed that before attending the practice teaching, PTs thought of their role more as an *obedient* and a directed figure when compared to the metaphors they gave after attending the course. However, after attending the practice teaching, PTs considered themselves more as an *infant* which is explained by the PTs as professional learning is a progress and they have 'a lot to learn'(Ercan, Post-M). The concepts of teachers and teaching were not examined by the PTs through significant changes. The sequencing of the objectives did not show any radical changes when the early and post images were examined. However, some of the definitions gained priority such as in the images of teachers, PTs considered teachers as *source* in their early images of third place, whereas PTs considered teachers as frustrated figures as third in their post images. In addition, PTs' definition of teaching was considered as transmitting of knowledge as priority. On the other hand, PTs defined teaching as guiding in the post images.

Table 2. Initial content analysis of the metaphors

Metaphor	Data	Themes
Being a PT	Early images	Obedient/directed, craftsperson, examiner, guide, infant
	Post images	Infant, obedient/directed, provider of knowledge, guide, bystander, craftsperson, flourishing, source, reflective, needed object
Teachers	Early images	Guide, craftsperson, source, needed object, hoper, bystander
	Post images	Guide, craftsperson, frustration, source, nurturer, tool
Teaching	Early images	Transmitting knowledge, guiding, interaction
	Post images	Guiding, transmitting knowledge, interaction, suffering, blessing

The first stage of data analysis began with the examination of PTs' early images of the given concepts (see Table 3). The metaphors given by the PTs were grouped under three headings, being a PT, teachers and teaching, respectively. The number of occurrence of the metaphors and the percentages were calculated.

As shown in Table 3, the PTs reflected on their role more as an *apprentice*, *helper* and *a little child* referring to their role as an assistant to the cooperating teacher and as someone in a progress of professional learning. The second most frequently used metaphor was *chef*. When PTs referred to their role as a *chef*, they defined their role as 'someone who is responsible for a number of duties'. Although the metaphor *chef* seems to have an active role in the process, PTs reflected on the number of duties and the extent to which they feel responsible for the teaching and learning context. PTs considered their role as *daylight* by referring to their 'existence in the classroom through bringing a new energy to the classroom'.

In the early-images of the PTs, the roles of the teachers were defined as *sun*, *earth*, *light*, *lighthouse* and *precious stone*, referring to the teachers as the sources of knowledge and learning process. When PTs reflected on the roles of the teachers, they used the metaphor *friend* to refer to the teachers 'they travel with the students together on the learning road'. The definition of teachers being *a friend on the road* provides an understanding of how PTs observe the learning process as a road, and the teachers as travel mates. PTs quote on their metaphors of teachers as *architects* assigning the roles of the teachers as they 'build-up a future'. In the early-images of teachers, PTs characterized them as playing a main role in the teaching process.

The last concept of early-images defined by the PTs was *teaching*. In order to refer to the concept of teaching, PTs refereed to teaching English in the classrooms. PTs referred to the concept of teaching as specifically teaching English in the classrooms. In the explanations of the metaphors, PTs characterized what they understand from teaching English in the current context. PTs referred to English language teaching as *teaching the world*, mostly. By relating the concept of teaching the world and teaching English, PTs conveyed that 'English is a global language and in ten years time, people who cannot speak it will be considered as illiterate' (Ali, Pre-M). Similar to teaching as *teaching the world* metaphor, PTs referred to teaching as revolution. PTs considered that 'if learning is living then teaching is revolution' (Elcin, Pre-M). PTs extended their definition of teaching as revolution stating that 'in order to have a good quality of life, everyone should learn English' (Sonay, Int.) and through teaching English, a revolutionary act of 'transforming a regular life into a qualified one' (Kenan, Int.). While defining teaching through metaphors, PTs defined teaching as *cooking* and *art* in terms its nature in 'providing a number of opportunities and a coherent context of experience' (Esra, Post-M). In defining teaching as *raining*

Table 3. Findings of the early-images

Being a PT	N	%	Teachers	N	%	Teaching	N	%
apprentice	6	13.6	sun	5	11.3	teaching the world	6	13.6
chef	5	11.3	earth	5	11.3	cooking	5	11.3
helper	5	11.3	architect	5	11.3	art	5	11.3
daylight	4	9.0	light	4	9.0	raining	4	9.0
guide	4	9.0	lighthouse	4	9.0	revolution	4	9.0
a little child	3	3.7	lighthouse	5	6.17	raining	4	9.0
magnet	3	6.8	precious stone	3	6.8	transmitting knowledge	3	6.8

Exploring Prospective EFL Teachers' Beliefs

and *seeding,* PTs addressed the nature of teaching as 'pouring water to the earth/soil to make it grow and become healthy' (Melih, Post-M). This definition of teaching was very similar to the definition of teaching as *transmitting* in terms of 'pouring information and knowledge on someone's life' (Serap, Int.).

In the second stage of data analysis, the post-images of the PTs were examined (see Table 4). The metaphors of the PTs were grouped under three headings, the frequencies and the percentages were calculated. When the data of post-images were examined, there was a consistency in the thematic analysis of the data.

As shown in Table 4, although the frequency of metaphors is the same, the content analysis of the post-images reveals that the metaphor of PTs as learners has the highest frequency of the analysis. PTs reflected on their role as a *learner* and *apprentice* by not just referring to their role as an assistant to the cooperating teacher and as someone in a progress of professional learning: They also referred to their role as a *camera* and as *an observer* to 'record the classroom events and reflect back on them' (Ayşe, Post-M.). Each role definition made by the PTs reveals a secondary role during the practice teaching experience. The second most frequently used metaphors of the post images of self were *gardener* and *producer.* Although gardener has an active role in 'collecting the seeds' (Sevim, Post-M) and 'producing a film' (Fulya, Post-M) as output of learning, PTs referred to their role as *gardener* and *producer* to reflect on 'the number of duties to accomplish' (Ezgi, Post-M) during the learning process. As PTs previously mentioned their role as a *chef* in the early images of self, in the post images, they refer to an active role to address the number of tasks to be accomplished. PTs considered their role as a *camera* and an *observer* to characterize their secondary role in the classroom during practice teaching. PTs defined their role in the classroom as 'a tool to record the events of the classroom' (Ozlem, Post-M). In addition as an observer who 'is not allowed to intervene the classroom events' (Kadir, Post-M).

In the post-images of the PTs, the roles of the teachers were defined as *sun, lighthouse,* and *compass* referring to the teachers as' the source of knowledge' and 'learning process' (Soner, Barış, Sema, Gulin, Post-M). The post-images of the PTs are similar to the ones they provided for the early-images as they considered teachers as the source of information. When PTs reflected on the roles of the teachers, they used the metaphor *tour guide* to refer to the teachers' role as they describe in the early images as *friend.* In the early-images, PTs referred to teachers by saying 'they travel with the students together on the learning road' (Kayra, Post-M) as travel mates. In the post-images, PTs reflected on the image of teacher as a *guide* rather than a travel mate. As a novel description of the teacher concept, PTs portray the teachers as *candles at its end.* With this metaphor, PTs refer to the burnout of the teachers as they

Table 4. Findings of the post-images

Being a PT	N	%	Teachers	N	%	Teaching	N	%
learner	5	6.1	tour guide	7	8.64	teaching the world	6	7.41
apprentice	5	6.1	gardener	7	8.64	watering	6	7.41
gardener	5	6.1	a candle at its ends	6	7.64	travelling	6	7.41
producer	5	6.1	sun	6	7.41	cooking	5	6.41
camera	4	4.9	chef	5	6.17	art	5	6.17
observer	3	3.7	lighthouse	5	6.17	raining	4	4.94
sun	3	3.7	compass	4	4.94	growing up a child	4	4.94

are 'energy-free' (Betul, Int.) and not 'willing to do anything new' (Emel, Post-M). According to the PTs, teachers are contended with the flow of the teaching process and resist on not bringing something new to the classroom.

The last concept of post-images defined by the PTs was teaching. PTs referred to English language teaching as *teaching the world*, mostly, as they did in the early-images. By relating the concept of teaching the world and the teaching English, PTs highlighted the importance of learning English in the global context. Similar to teaching as *teaching the world* metaphor, PTs referred to teaching as *raising a child*. PTs considered that 'learning is an onerous process and it takes a lot of time just like raising a child'. While defining teaching through metaphors in the post-images, PTs defined teaching as *cooking* and *art* as they did in the early images with similar explanations in terms its nature as a 'coherent context of experience' (Tuğba, Post-M) and a 'gradual process' (Gulcin, Post-M).

PTs reflected on their perceptions of being a PT, teachers of English and teaching profession both before and after the practice teaching experience. In terms of overall content analysis, it was observed that PTs found it difficult to reflect on their role as a prospective teacher before they attended the practice teaching. Although PTs were given the same data collection tool at the end of the practice teaching experience, it was observed that the descriptors used by the PTs to define their role increased and PTs used an increased number of secondary concepts that do not play a primary role in teaching to define their role in the practice teaching course.

Interviews

In this section, the change (or lack of change) in the beliefs of the prospective EFL teachers in terms of self, teachers and teaching will be reported. The data analyses of the interviews were conducted after completing the verbatim transcription of the interviews. The findings based on the influencing factors were examined and discussed.

Change (or Lack of Change) Throughout the Practice Teaching Course

The findings showed that some PTs reported on a stable understanding of their experience throughout the course, whereas some of the PTs reflected on the difference in their understanding of the profession which could be ascribed to a number of reasons. The influencing factors of change or lack of change were addressed by the PTs as the context of practice teaching and the independence of the PTs during practice teaching experience. The two concepts were very closely related to each other and were difficult to distinguish. In addition to the conceptual change in the professional learning processes of PTs, they considered a number of facilitating reasons for them to monitor their professional learning and impeding factors affected their understanding of the practice teaching process. By referring to the context of professional learning experience, PTs were worried about their role as they were treated as students rather than prospective teachers.

The mentors I observed were very kind and nice to me; however, [rather than a professional], they treated me like a student... It was true but they should have considered the fact that I will become a teacher soon.(Seda, Int.)

Similar to Seda's explanation of her role in the practice teaching, Ümit addressed the importance of being addressed as a prospective teacher and gaining independence as a teacher during the practice teaching experience. As she had the chance to experience to work with two teachers, she compared two different applications of cooperating teachers during their professional learning.

I figured that teaching is learned when you can find the chance to experience [practice] it...Some mentors let me practice and conduct the lesson plans that I prepared...whereas others were very strict and in control all the time [referring to not providing the chances of practicing teaching].(Ümit, Int.)

PTs, who had the chance to gain independence in the classroom, further claimed that not only PTs benefitted from the practice teaching experience. CTs were also in advantage in terms of having PTs in their classes. During the interviews, a PT, Orhan, addressed the fact that CTs learn from the currently used activities from the PTs since PTs have recently learned how to implement a number of activities and find time to prepare extra learning materials other than the course books used in the classes.

I prepared and used a number of activities, games, worksheets, and other materials to attract the attention of the students... I think my mentor really liked that because she [integrated extra materials other than the textbook] focused on grabbing the attention of the students...I think we learned a lot from each other. I think I made a positive effect on the mentor.(Orhan, Int.)

As facilitating factors of monitoring the professional learning process, PTs also considered the content of the seminar course and professional development activities organized by the university supervisors throughout the seminar. The opportunities provided for the PTs to reflect on their professional learning processes were highlighted by the PTs. In addition to reflecting and sharing the ideas with peers, PTs also addressed the role of the university supervisor and CTs as role models and sources of professional support. Therefore, significant others were addressed in the professional learning process in addition to Self-professional learning experiences.

The results of the study demonstrate potentially positive effects of practice teaching on professional learning of prospective EFL teachers. The change in the beliefs can be explained by the opportunities of reflective practices conducted throughout the practice teaching both at the university setting and at the school setting. Thus, the mutual interaction among the stakeholders of practice teaching, in addition to guidance provided both by the cooperating teachers and the university supervisor play an important role in the professional learning processes of the PTs.

Dynamic Nature of Belief Systems

Although the exact change or lack of change cannot be clearly observed through elicited metaphors and interviews, a certain development and modification of professional ideas is observed in the data analysis. The content analysis of the interviews showed that the variation in beliefs and practices mainly derived from PTs' individual experiences with the mentoring practices of the mentors. In addition, the socio-professional context provided for the PTs within the school context also played an important role in PTs ways of practicing their ways of becoming an EFL teacher. As Ayşe suggests in the following quote, PTs should get the chance of building relationships with everyone involved in the process in order to consider themselves that they are actually practicing to become an EFL teacher.

I believe that an English language teacher should [get to know his/her students and] build up a strong relationship to engage the students. (Ayse, Int.)

When PTs professional learning experiences were considered, the real teaching experience cannot be replaced with the macro teachings they conduct for certain courses at the university. As Birol suggested

Language teaching is different from knowing a language. The microteachings [in the department] were not that effective when compared to the real classroom experience. We got answers from our peers [during the microteachings at the university courses] whereas in the real classroom, getting the students talk was quite difficult (Birol, Int.)

Through their experiences in the practice teaching, PTs find the chance to live the real teaching experience. As they experience the reality shock in real teaching contexts, they realize the need to modify their beliefs (Rakıcıoğlu-Söylemez & Eröz-Tuğa, 2014). Therefore, through experiencing difficulties as well as the joyful experience of teaching, PTs make adaptations and modifications in their beliefs. As it is directly stated, 'at the beginning of the practicum, I thought I could handle 10-year-old kids in the classroom… because I am good with kids… but teaching was different…I had difficulty in classroom management' (Esra, Int.).

DISCUSSION

Although the content analysis of the metaphors revealed a limited change throughout the practicum experience, the analysis of the interviews displayed the dynamic nature of belief systems throughout the practice teaching experience. In addition to the difficulty of addressing belief change in a short amount of time (Borg, 2006; Yuan & Lee, 2014), the modifications and adaptations in the professional learning beliefs could depend on a number of reasons. As Yuan and Lee (2014) suggested, prospective teachers' personal motivation as a prospective professional and the socio-cultural factors play an important role in the process of professional learning. In addition, professional motivation of the PTs is reported as having a considerable impact on the future work experiences and continuing professional development involvement (Eren, &Tekinarslan, 2012). Considering the complexity of PTs' belief change related to self, significant others and the profession, it is very important to cater prospective EFL teachers' beliefs at the initial stages of teacher education (Darling Hammond, 2014; Manuel & Hughes, 2006; Seferoğlu, et al. 2009; Yuan & Lee, 2014). Otherwise, the aims of the teacher training program might not be well understood by the PTs and may not accomplish its aims the way it is planned to prepare prospective teachers for the profession.

The current study demonstrates the extent to which beliefs of PTs are not considered as stable or subject to drastic changes. However, beliefs held by the PTs are 'open to change and development' (Yuan & Lee, 2014, p. 8). The results of the study corroborates with the claim that significant modifications and developments do take place in PTs' professional learning beliefs through the practice teaching experience (Borg, 2006; 2011). In addition, drawing on socio-professional perspectives, a number of influencing and impeding factors can be identified which contribute to the processes of PTs' belief adaptation and modification during practice teaching. First of all, through actively participating in the socio-professional context of the school, PTs find the opportunities to take part in a variety of professional learning activi-

Exploring Prospective EFL Teachers' Beliefs

ties (e.g. classroom observation, grading students' work, preparing assessment tools). The professional learning activities provide effective professional learning context for the PTs to expand their beliefs about EFL teaching and becoming a language teacher (Johnson, 2006). As PTs reflected on their professional learning experiences to test out their time management skills, the more opportunities they find to practice their teaching skills, the more they adapt their beliefs about classroom implementations. Therefore as a second factor of providing the necessary socio-professional context for the PTs, CTs also play an influential role in their developing PTs' beliefs about teaching.

In terms of content analysis of the metaphors, the findings showed both consistencies and displayed novel results for the literature. Specifically, the metaphors to refer to the role of the teacher as a guide is consistent with the results of the studies reported in the literature (e.g. Saban et al., 2007; Farrell, 2011; Thomas & Beauchamp, 2011). However, unlike the studies conducted with the practicing teachers, the flexibility of teaching practices (e.g. Thomas & Beauchamp, 2011; Yeşilbursa, 2012), the nurturing nature of teaching practices (Farrell, 2011; Thomas & Beauchamp, 2011; Yeşilbursa, 2012), and the authority of teachers (e.g. Saban et al., 2007; Seferoğlu et al., 2009) were not addressed by the PTs in the current study. However, the exhaustion of the teachers have been observed and reported on by the PTs by using the metaphor 'candle at its ends'. The aspect of frustration and considering teachers as hamsters were also addressed in the literature (e.g. Thomas & Beauchamp, 2011; Yeşilbursa, 2012). Although the findings of the current study show that the metaphors provided by the PTs could be categorized under certain concepts, as Seferoğlu et al. (2009) and Oktay and Vancı-Osam (2013) claimed, the differences among the reflections of the participants were observed throughout the data analysis.

SOLUTIONS AND RECOMMENDATIONS

PTs' cognitions about their previous experiences regarding the roles of teachers and teaching practices should be examined and addressed in initial teacher training programs. Teacher educators should guide PTs to become aware of their unexamined preconceptions about teaching and becoming EFL teachers in order to consider the ways those beliefs influence their teaching and approaches to teaching. Given the strong relationship between beliefs (Verbinska, 2014), attitudes and practice, teacher beliefs are important in understanding teachers' way of thinking and their professional growth.

Foreign language teacher education departments mainly focus on providing the context of professional learning for the prospective teachers. However, the context of professional learning not only requires teacher educators to convey the necessary theoretical foundations of learning and teaching a foreign language but also to provide the necessary opportunities for PTs to reflect on their professional development processes. Thus, metaphors are an alternative platform for PTs to examine their beliefs about language learning and teaching. The metaphorical analysis of the beliefs could provide the chance for PTs to form their professional identities. The present study, therefore, creates the opportunity for the current and future PTs studying at the current EFL teacher education program to construct and reflect on their beliefs throughout their professional learning experience within their initial teacher training program (Saban, 2010). The metaphorical representations of the professional learning processes guide not only teacher educators but also PTs in terms of examining, understanding and modifying the preconceived professional beliefs regarding language learning and teaching. As an alternative, PTs could be asked to reflect on the professional learning theories through analyzing the metaphors they provide for reflection. In examining their professional learning theories, PTs will have the chance to put the theoretical foundations into application through developing professional awareness on their personalized practices.

In addition, PTs could be asked to reflect on the perceived and idealized conceptions of the profession and reflect on the differences of their personal considerations. Through examining the differences in idealized and actual conceptions of the professional learning processes, PTs could have the chance to enhance their progress in the professional learning processes.

LIMITATIONS AND DIRECTIONS FOR FUTURE RESEARCH

The study was limited to one EFL teacher education program in a non-native teacher education setting. Therefore, more participants are needed in order to reach a coherent understanding of the socio-cultural underpinnings of the PTs in the current initial teacher education setting. It may also be worthwhile to investigate the epistemological reasoning of PTs in terms of perceived and idealized understandings of the proposed professional concepts, which was beyond the scope of the current study. The study examined the changes and possible development in the awareness of the PTs throughout their practice teaching experience; however it did not consider any possible changes in teaching behavior. Therefore, future studies focusing on the change in PTs' teaching behavior through observations will display a more coherent and in-depth understanding of PTs' teaching practices.

CONCLUSION

The present study provides an example of asking PTs to reflect on their professional learning experiences through metaphors. The data analysis provides an important insight into the professional learning experiences of the PTs during their contact with real teaching contexts. The metaphor analysis conducted in the study indicated a move from the early images of language teaching to a post-image nature as PTs progress in the practice teaching. As Yuan and Lee (2014) and Borg (2006) pointed out, beliefs about learning and teaching do not change in a short amount of time, but modifications and developments might be observed. Therefore, the professional learning processes of the PTs tend to tie beliefs, experiences and professional needs. Thus, the professional awareness to be raised throughout the initial teacher education of the PTs will guide them to adapt and modify their beliefs about EFL teaching (Yeşilbursa, 2012).

Considering the number of cases presented in the study, the findings may not be generalized to a number of foreign language teacher education programs across the globe. Despite this fact, the findings of the study add to the foreign language teacher education literature by providing insights of the prospective EFL teachers' professional learning experiences during their practice teaching.

REFERENCES

Appel, J. (1995). *Diary of a language teacher*. Oxford: Heinemann.

Atay, D. (2007). Beginning teacher efficacy and the practicum in an EFL context. *Teacher Development*, *11*(2), 203–219. doi:10.1080/13664530701414720

Bailey, K. M. (1990). The use of diary studies in teacher education programs. In J. C. Richards & D. Nunan (Eds.), *Second language teacher education* (pp. 215–226). Cambridge: Cambridge University Press.

Beijaard, D., Meijer, P. C., & Verloop, N. (2004). Reconsidering research on teachers' professional identity. *Teaching and Teacher Education, 20*(2), 107–128. doi:10.1016/j.tate.2003.07.001

Borg, S. (2006). *Teacher cognition and language education: Research and practice*. London: Continuum.

Borg, S. (2011). Language teacher education. In J. Simpson (Ed.), *The Routledge Handbook of Applied Linguistics* (pp. 215–228). London: Routledge.

Çakıroğlu, E., & Çakıroğlu, J. (2003). Reflections on teacher education in Turkey. *European Journal of Teacher Education, 26*(2), 253–264. doi:10.1080/0261976032000088774

Cheng, M. M. H., Cheng, A. Y. N., & Tang, S. Y. F. (2010). Closing the gap between the theory and practice of teaching: Implications for teacher education programmes in Hong Kong. *Journal of Education for Teaching, 36*(1), 91–104. doi:10.1080/02607470903462222

Council of Higher Education (CHE). (2007). *Öğretmen yetiştirme ve eğitim fakülteleri (1982-2007)* [Teacher education and faculties of education (1982-2007)]. Ankara, Turkey: Council of Higher Education.

Creswell, J. W. (2007). *Qualitative inquiry and research design: Choosing among five approaches* (2nd ed.). Thousand Oaks, CA: Sage.

Crystal, D. (2003). *English as a global language*. New York, NY: Cambridge University Press. doi:10.1017/CBO9780511486999

Darling-Hammond, L. (2014). Strengthening clinical preparation: The holy grail of teacher education. *Peabody Journal of Education: Issues of Leadership, Policy, and Organizations, 89*(4), 547–561. doi:10.1080/0161956X.2014.939009

Doğançay-Aktuna, S., & Kızıltepe, Z. (2005). English in Turkey. *World Englishes, 24*(2), 253–265. doi:10.1111/j.1467-971X.2005.00408.x

Dyson, M. (2007). My story in a profession of stories: Auto ethnography – an empowering methodology for educators. *Australian Journal of Teacher Education, 32*(1), 36–48. doi:10.14221/ajte.2007v32n1.3

Ellis, R. (1998). Discourse control and the acquisition-rich classroom. In W. Renandya & G. Jacobs (Eds.), *Learners and language learning* (pp. 145–171). Singapore: SEAMEO.

Eren, A. (2014). 'Not only satisfied and responsible, but also hopeful': Prospective teachers' career choice satisfaction, hope, and personal responsibility. *Cambridge Journal of Education*, 1–18. doi:10.1080/0305764X.2014.930417

Eren, A., & Tekinarslan, E. (2012). Prospective teachers' metaphors: Teacher, teaching, learning, instructional material and evaluation concepts. *International Journal of Social Science. &. Education, 3*(2), 435–445.

Farrell, T. S. C. (2007). *Reflective language teaching: From research to practice*. London: Continuum.

Farrell, T. S. C. (2011). Exploring the professional role identities of experienced ESL teachers through reflective practice. *System, 39*(1), 54–62. doi:10.1016/j.system.2011.01.012

Grossman, G. (2013). Developing social capital through national education: the transformation of teacher education in Turkey. In I. R. Haslam, M. S. Khine, & I. M. Saleh (Eds.), *Large scale reform and social capital building*. New York, NY: Routledge.

Johnson, K. E. (2006). The sociocultural turn and its challenges for second language teacher education. *TESOL Quarterly, 40*(1), 235–257. doi:10.2307/40264518

Kachru, B. B. (1986). *The alchemy of English: The spread, functions, and models of non-native English*. Oxford, NY: Pergamon Press.

Kilimci, S. (2009). Teacher training in some EU countries and Turkey: How similar are they? *Procedia: Social and Behavioral Sciences, 1*(1), 1975–1980. doi:10.1016/j.sbspro.2009.01.347

Kırkgöz, Y. (2007). English language teaching in Turkey: Policy changes and their implementations. *RELC Journal, 38*(2), 216–228. doi:10.1177/0033688207079696

Kırkgöz, Y. (2009). Globalization and English language policy in Turkey. *Educational Policy, 23*(5), 663–684. doi:10.1177/0895904808316319

Lakoff, G., & Johnson, M. (1980/2003). Afterword 2003. In G. Lakoff & M. Johnson (Eds.), *Metaphors we live by*. Chicago: University of Chicago Press.

Manuel, J., & Hughes, J. (2006). 'It has always been my dream': Exploring pre-service teachers' motivations for choosing to teach. *Teacher Development, 10*(1), 5–24. doi:10.1080/13664530600587311

Marchant, G. (1992). 'A teacher is like a ... Using simile lists to explore personal metaphors'. *Language and Education, 6*(1), 33–45. doi:10.1080/09500789209541323

Mattheoudakis, M. (2007). Tracking changes in pre-service EFL teacher beliefs in Greece: A longitudinal study. *Teaching and Teacher Education, 23*(8), 1272–1288. doi:10.1016/j.tate.2006.06.001

Merç, A. (2004). *Reflections of PTs throughout their teaching practicum: What has been good? What has gone wrong? What has changed?* [Unpublished MA Thesis]. Anadolu University, Eskişehir, Turkey.

Merç, A. (2010). Self-reported problems of pre-service EFL teachers throughout their practicum. *Anadolu University Journal of Social Sciences, 10*(2), 199–226.

Miles, B. M., Huberman, A. M., & Saldaña, J. (2014). *Qualitative data analysis: A methods sourcebook* (3rd ed.). Washington, DC: Sage Publications.

Ministry of National Education [MoNE]. (2013). *National education statistics: Formal education: 2012-2013*. MoNE: Ankara.

Nespor, J. (1987). The role of beliefs in the practice of teaching. *Journal of Curriculum Studies, 19*(4), 317–328. doi:10.1080/0022027870190403

Numrich, C. (1996). On becoming a language teacher: Insights from diary studies. *TESOL Quarterly*, *30*(1), 131–153. doi:10.2307/3587610

Oktay, Y. B., & Vancı-Osam, Ü. (2013). Viewing foreign language teachers' roles through the eyes of teachers and students. *Hacettepe University Journal of Education*, *44*, 249–261.

Organization for Economic Co-operation and Development. [OECD] (2014). *Turkey: Overview of the education system (EAG 2014)*. Retrieved from http://gpseducation.oecd.org/CountryProfile?primaryCountry=TUR&treshold=10&topic=EO

Oxford, R. L., Griffiths, C., Longhini, A., Cohen, A. D., Macaro, E., & Harris, V. (2014). Experts' personal metaphors and similes about language learning strategies. *System*, *43*, 11–29. doi:10.1016/j.system.2014.01.001

Rakıcıoğlu-Söylemez, A. (2012). *An exploratory case study of pre-service EFL teachers' sense of efficacy beliefs and perceptions of mentoring practices during practice teaching* [Unpublished Doctoral Dissertation]. Middle East Technical University, Ankara, Turkey.

Rakıcıoğlu-Söylemez, A., & Eröz-Tuğa, B. (2014). Mentoring expectations and experiences of prospective and cooperating teachers during practice teaching. *Australian Journal of Teacher Education*, *39*(10), 146–168.

Roness, D., & Smith, K. (2010). Stability in motivation during teacher education. *Journal of Education for Teaching*, *36*(2), 169–185. doi:10.1080/02607471003651706

Rots, I., Kelchtermans, G., & Aelterman, A. (2012). Learning (not) to become a teacher: A qualitative analysis of the job entrance issue. *Teaching and Teacher Education*, *28*(1), 1–10. doi:10.1016/j.tate.2011.08.008

Ruohotie-Lyhty, M. (2013). Struggling for a professional identity: Two newly qualified language teachers' identity narratives during the first years at work. *Teaching and Teacher Education*, *30*, 120–129. doi:10.1016/j.tate.2012.11.002

Rusznyak, L., & Walton, E. (2014). Affordances and limitations of a special school practicum as a means to prepare pre-service teachers for inclusive education. *International Journal of Inclusive Education*, *18*(9), 957–974. doi:10.1080/13603116.2013.872203

Saban, A. (2006). Functions of metaphor in teaching and teacher education: A review essay. *Teaching Education*, *17*(4), 299–315. doi:10.1080/10476210601017386

Saban, A. (2010). Prospective teachers' metaphorical conceptualizations of learner. *Teaching and Teacher Education*, *26*(2), 290–305. doi:10.1016/j.tate.2009.03.017

Saban, A., Koçbeker, B. N., & Saban, A. (2006). An investigation of the concept of teacher among prospective teachers through metaphor analysis. *Educational Sciences: Theory and Practice*, *6*(2), 509–522.

Saban, A., Koçbeker, B. N., & Saban, A. (2007). Prospective teachers' conceptions of teaching and learning revealed through metaphor analysis. *Learning and Instruction*, *17*(2), 123–139. doi:10.1016/j.learninstruc.2007.01.003

Seferoğlu, G. (2006). Teacher candidates' reflections on some components of a pre-service English teacher education programme in Turkey. *Journal of Education for Teaching, 32*(4), 369–378. doi:10.1080/02607470600981953

Seferoğlu, G., Korkmazgil, S., & Ölçü, Z. (2009). Gaining insights into teachers' ways of thinking via metaphors. *Educational Studies, 35*(3), 323–335. doi:10.1080/03055690802648135

Sinclair, C. (2008). Initial and changing student teacher motivation and commitment to teaching. *Asia-Pacific Journal of Teacher Education, 36*(2), 79–104. doi:10.1080/13598660801971658

Stake, R. (2005). Qualitative case studies. In N. K. Denzin & Y. S. Lincoln (Eds.), *The Sage handbook of qualitative research* (pp. 433–466). Thousand Oaks, CA: Sage.

Strauss, A., & Corbin, J. (1998). *Basics of qualitative research: Techniques and procedures for developing grounded theory* (2nd ed.). Thousand Oaks, CA: Sage.

Tang, S. Y. F., Cheng, M. M. H., & Cheng, A. Y. N. (2013). Shifts in teaching motivation and sense of self as teacher. *Educational Review, 66*(4), 465-481.

Thomas, L., & Beauchamp, C. (2011). Understanding new teachers' professional identities through metaphor. *Teaching and Teacher Education, 27*(4), 762–769. doi:10.1016/j.tate.2010.12.007

Verbinska, D. (2014). Stability and variability in pre-service language teachers' beliefs. In M. Pawlak, J. Bielak, & A. Mystkowska-Wiertelak (Eds.), *Classroom-oriented research* (pp. 33–53). Berlin: Springer. doi:10.1007/978-3-319-00188-3_3

Yeşilbursa, A. (2012). Using metaphor to explore the professional role identities of higher education English language instructors. *Procedia: Social and Behavioral Sciences, 46*, 468–472. doi:10.1016/j.sbspro.2012.05.143

Yeşilbursa, A., & Sayar, E. (2014). *EFL teachers' professional identity: A metaphor analysis*. Saarbrücken: LAP Lambert Academic Publishing.

Yin, R. K. (2011). *Qualitative research from start to finish*. New York, NY: The Guilford Press.

Yuan, R., & Lee, I. (2014). Understanding language teacher educators' professional experiences: An exploratory study in Hong Kong. *The Asia-Pacific Education Researcher, 23*(1), 143–149. doi:10.1007/s40299-013-0117-6

Yüksel, İ. (2012). The current developments in teacher education in Turkey on the threshold of European Union. *International Journal of Humanities and Social Science, 2*(8), 49–56.

KEY TERMS AND DEFINITIONS

Practice Teaching: 10-week course in which PTs spend time in the schools of MoNE observing, teaching and practice in the real teaching contexts.

Prospective EFL Teacher: Student teacher enrolled in a four-year degree program specializing in English Language Teaching.

Teachers: Professionals who are performing the teaching action in schools during the practice teaching context.

Teaching Self: Student teachers' role as a prospective teacher in the teaching practice context.

Teaching: PTs' beliefs about the purposes and actions of teaching and reflection on the concept as a profession.

Related References

To continue our tradition of advancing knowledge management and discovery research, we have compiled a list of recommended IGI Global readings. These references will provide additional information and guidance to further enrich your knowledge and assist you with your own research and future publications.

Abril, R. M. (2011). The quality attribution in data, information and knowledge. In D. Schwartz & D. Te'eni (Eds.), *Encyclopedia of knowledge management* (2nd ed., pp. 1343–1354). Hershey, PA: Information Science Reference; doi:10.4018/978-1-59904-931-1.ch129

Abufardeh, S. (2013). KM and global software engineering (GSE). In S. Saeed & I. Alsmadi (Eds.), *Knowledge-based processes in software development* (pp. 12–34). Hershey, PA: Information Science Reference; doi:10.4018/978-1-4666-4229-4.ch002

Aggestam, L., Backlund, P., & Persson, A. (2010). Supporting knowledge evaluation to increase quality in electronic knowledge repositories. [IJKM]. *International Journal of Knowledge Management*, 6(1), 23–43. doi:10.4018/jkm.2010103002

Aggestam, L., Backlund, P., & Persson, A. (2012). Supporting knowledge evaluation to increase quality in electronic knowledge repositories. In M. Jennex (Ed.), *Conceptual models and outcomes of advancing knowledge management: New technologies* (pp. 24–44). Hershey, PA: Information Science Reference; doi:10.4018/978-1-4666-0035-5.ch002

Aiken, P., Gillenson, M., Zhang, X., & Rafner, D. (2011). Data management and data administration: Assessing 25 years of practice. [JDM]. *Journal of Database Management*, 22(3), 24–45. doi:10.4018/jdm.2011070102

Akabawi, S., & Hodeeb, H. (2013). Implementing business intelligence in the dynamic beverages sales and distribution environment. In M. Khosrow-Pour (Ed.), *Cases on performance measurement and productivity improvement: Technology integration and maturity* (pp. 194–221). Hershey, PA: Business Science Reference; doi:10.4018/978-1-4666-2618-8.ch010

Al-Busaidi, K. A. (2011). A social and technical investigation of knowledge utilization from a repository knowledge management system. In M. Al-Shammari (Ed.), *Knowledge management in emerging economies: Social, organizational and cultural implementation* (pp. 122–139). Hershey, PA: Information Science Reference; doi:10.4018/978-1-61692-886-5.ch007

Related References

Al-Busaidi, K. A. (2012). The impact of supporting organizational knowledge management through a corporate portal on employees and business processes. In M. Jennex (Ed.), *Conceptual models and outcomes of advancing knowledge management: New technologies* (pp. 208–229). Hershey, PA: Information Science Reference; doi:10.4018/978-1-4666-0035-5.ch011

Alaraifi, A., Molla, A., & Deng, H. (2013). An empirical analysis of antecedents to the assimilation of sensor information systems in data centers. [IJITSA]. *International Journal of Information Technologies and Systems Approach, 6*(1), 57–77. doi:10.4018/jitsa.2013010104

Alguezaui, S., & Filieri, R. (2010). Social capital: Knowledge and technological innovation. In P. López Sáez, G. Castro, J. Navas López, & M. Delgado Verde (Eds.), *Intellectual capital and technological innovation: Knowledge-based theory and practice* (pp. 271–296). Hershey, PA: Information Science Reference; doi:10.4018/978-1-61520-875-3.ch013

Alhashem, A., & Shaqrah, A. A. (2012). Exploring the relationship between organizational memory and business innovation. [IJKBO]. *International Journal of Knowledge-Based Organizations, 2*(3), 32–46. doi:10.4018/ijkbo.2012070102

Allan, M. B., Korolis, A. A., & Griffith, T. L. (2011). Reaching for the moon: Expanding transactive memory's reach with wikis and tagging. In M. Jennex (Ed.), *Global aspects and cultural perspectives on knowledge management: Emerging dimensions* (pp. 144–156). Hershey, PA: Information Science Reference; doi:10.4018/978-1-60960-555-1.ch010

Alsmadi, I., & Alda, S. (2013). Knowledge management and semantic web services. In S. Saeed & I. Alsmadi (Eds.), *Knowledge-based processes in software development* (pp. 35–48). Hershey, PA: Information Science Reference; doi:10.4018/978-1-4666-4229-4.ch003

Alstete, J. W., & Meyer, J. P. (2011). Expanding the model of competitive business strategy for knowledge-based organizations. [IJKBO]. *International Journal of Knowledge-Based Organizations, 1*(4), 16–31. doi:10.4018/ijkbo.2011100102

Alstete, J. W., & Meyer, J. P. (2013). Expanding the model of competitive business strategy for knowledge-based organizations. In J. Wang (Ed.), *Intelligence methods and systems advancements for knowledge-based business* (pp. 132–148). Hershey, PA: Information Science Reference; doi:10.4018/978-1-4666-1873-2.ch008

Alves da Silva, N. S., Alvarez, I. M., & Rogerson, S. (2011). Glocality, diversity and ethics of distributed knowledge in higher education. In G. Morais da Costa (Ed.), *Ethical issues and social dilemmas in knowledge management: Organizational innovation* (pp. 131–159). Hershey, PA: Information Science Reference; doi:10.4018/978-1-61520-873-9.ch009

Anantatmula, V. S., & Kanungo, S. (2011). Strategies for successful implementation of KM in a university setting. In M. Jennex & S. Smolnik (Eds.), *Strategies for knowledge management success: Exploring organizational efficacy* (pp. 262–276). Hershey, PA: Information Science Reference; doi:10.4018/978-1-60566-709-6.ch014

Andreu, R., & Sieber, S. (2011). External and internal knowledge in organizations. In D. Schwartz & D. Te'eni (Eds.), *Encyclopedia of knowledge management* (2nd ed., pp. 298–307). Hershey, PA: Information Science Reference; doi:10.4018/978-1-59904-931-1.ch029

Andriessen, D. (2011). Metaphor use in knowledge management. In D. Schwartz & D. Te'eni (Eds.), *Encyclopedia of knowledge management* (2nd ed., pp. 1118–1124). Hershey, PA: Information Science Reference; doi:10.4018/978-1-59904-931-1.ch107

Angelopoulos, S., Kitsios, F., & Moustakis, V. (2012). Transformation of management in the public sector: Exploring the strategic frameworks of e-government. In T. Papadopoulos & P. Kanellis (Eds.), *Public sector reform using information technologies: Transforming policy into practice* (pp. 44–58). Hershey, PA: Information Science Reference; doi:10.4018/978-1-60960-839-2.ch003

Anselma, L., Bottrighi, A., Molino, G., Montani, S., Terenziani, P., & Torchio, M. (2013). Supporting knowledge-based decision making in the medical context: The GLARE approach. In J. Wang (Ed.), *Intelligence methods and systems advancements for knowledge-based business* (pp. 24–42). Hershey, PA: Information Science Reference; doi:10.4018/978-1-4666-1873-2.ch002

Arh, T., Dimovski, V., & Blažic, B. J. (2011). ICT and web 2.0 technologies as a determinant of business performance. In M. Al-Mutairi & L. Mohammed (Eds.), *Cases on ICT utilization, practice and solutions: Tools for managing day-to-day issues* (pp. 59–77). Hershey, PA: Information Science Reference; doi:10.4018/978-1-60960-015-0.ch005

Ariely, G. (2011). Operational knowledge management in the military. In D. Schwartz & D. Te'eni (Eds.), *Encyclopedia of knowledge management* (2nd ed., pp. 1250–1260). Hershey, PA: Information Science Reference; doi:10.4018/978-1-59904-931-1.ch119

Assefa, T., Garfield, M., & Meshesha, M. (2014). Enabling factors for knowledge sharing among employees in the workplace. In Y. Al-Bastaki & A. Shajera (Eds.), *Building a competitive public sector with knowledge management strategy* (pp. 246–271). Hershey, PA: Business Science Reference; doi:10.4018/978-1-4666-4434-2.ch011

Assudani, R. H. (2011). Negotiating knowledge gaps in dispersed knowledge work. [IJKBO]. *International Journal of Knowledge-Based Organizations*, *1*(3), 1–21. doi:10.4018/ijkbo.2011070101

Assudani, R. H. (2013). Negotiating knowledge gaps in dispersed knowledge work. In J. Wang (Ed.), *Intelligence methods and systems advancements for knowledge-based business* (pp. 75–96). Hershey, PA: Information Science Reference; doi:10.4018/978-1-4666-1873-2.ch005

Atkins, R. (2011). Supply chain knowledge integration in emerging economies. In M. Al-Shammari (Ed.), *Knowledge management in emerging economies: Social, organizational and cultural implementation* (pp. 104–121). Hershey, PA: Information Science Reference; doi:10.4018/978-1-61692-886-5.ch006

Aung, Z., & Nyunt, K. K. (2014). Constructive knowledge management model and information retrieval methods for software engineering. In *Software design and development: Concepts, methodologies, tools, and applications* (pp. 253–269). Hershey, PA: Information Science Reference; doi:10.4018/978-1-4666-4301-7.ch014

Aziz, M. W., Mohamad, R., & Jawawi, D. N. (2013). Ontology-based service description, discovery, and matching in distributed embedded real-time systems. In M. Nazir Ahmad, R. Colomb, & M. Abdullah (Eds.), *Ontology-based applications for enterprise systems and knowledge management* (pp. 178–190). Hershey, PA: Information Science Reference; doi:10.4018/978-1-4666-1993-7.ch010

Related References

Badia, A. (2011). Knowledge management and intelligence work: A promising combination. In D. Schwartz & D. Te'eni (Eds.), *Encyclopedia of knowledge management* (2nd ed., pp. 612–623). Hershey, PA: Information Science Reference; doi:10.4018/978-1-59904-931-1.ch059

Badr, K. B., & Ahmad, M. N. (2013). Managing lessons learned: A comparative study of lessons learned systems. In M. Nazir Ahmad, R. Colomb, & M. Abdullah (Eds.), *Ontology-based applications for enterprise systems and knowledge management* (pp. 224–245). Hershey, PA: Information Science Reference; doi:10.4018/978-1-4666-1993-7.ch013

Bakshi, K. (2014). Technologies for big data. In W. Hu & N. Kaabouch (Eds.), *Big data management, technologies, and applications* (pp. 1–22). Hershey, PA: Information Science Reference; doi:10.4018/978-1-4666-4699-5.ch001

Ballou, D. P., Belardo, S., & Pazer, H. L. (2012). A project staffing model to enhance the effectiveness of knowledge transfer in the requirements planning phase for multi-project environments. In M. Jennex (Ed.), *Conceptual models and outcomes of advancing knowledge management: New technologies* (pp. 77–98). Hershey, PA: Information Science Reference; doi:10.4018/978-1-4666-0035-5.ch005

Baporikar, N. (2011). Knowledge management and entrepreneurship cases in India. In M. Al-Shammari (Ed.), *Knowledge management in emerging economies: Social, organizational and cultural implementation* (pp. 325–346). Hershey, PA: Information Science Reference; doi:10.4018/978-1-61692-886-5.ch020

Baporikar, N. (2014). Knowledge management initiatives in Indian public sector. In Y. Al-Bastaki & A. Shajera (Eds.), *Building a competitive public sector with knowledge management strategy* (pp. 53–89). Hershey, PA: Business Science Reference; doi:10.4018/978-1-4666-4434-2.ch002

Baporikar, N. (2014). Organizational barriers and facilitators in embedding knowledge strategy. In M. Chilton & J. Bloodgood (Eds.), *Knowledge management and competitive advantage: Issues and potential solutions* (pp. 149–173). Hershey, PA: Information Science Reference; doi:10.4018/978-1-4666-4679-7.ch009

Barioni, M. C., Kaster, D. D., Razente, H. L., Traina, A. J., & Júnior, C. T. (2011). Querying multimedia data by similarity in relational DBMS. In L. Yan & Z. Ma (Eds.), *Advanced database query systems: Techniques, applications and technologies* (pp. 323–359). Hershey, PA: Information Science Reference; doi:10.4018/978-1-60960-475-2.ch014

Baroni de Carvalho, R., & Tavares Ferreira, M. A. (2011). Knowledge management software. In D. Schwartz & D. Te'eni (Eds.), *Encyclopedia of knowledge management* (2nd ed., pp. 738–749). Hershey, PA: Information Science Reference; doi:10.4018/978-1-59904-931-1.ch072

Barroso, A. C., Ricciardi, R. I., & Junior, J. A. (2012). Web 2.0 and project management: Reviewing the change path and discussing a few cases. In I. Boughzala & A. Dudezert (Eds.), *Knowledge management 2.0: Organizational models and enterprise strategies* (pp. 164–189). Hershey, PA: Information Science Reference; doi:10.4018/978-1-61350-195-5.ch009

Baskaran, V., Naguib, R., Guergachi, A., Bali, R., & Arochen, H. (2011). Does knowledge management really work? A case study in the breast cancer screening domain. In A. Eardley & L. Uden (Eds.), *Innovative knowledge management: Concepts for organizational creativity and collaborative design* (pp. 177–189). Hershey, PA: Information Science Reference; doi:10.4018/978-1-60566-701-0.ch010

Bebensee, T., Helms, R., & Spruit, M. (2012). Exploring the impact of web 2.0 on knowledge management. In I. Boughzala & A. Dudezert (Eds.), *Knowledge management 2.0: Organizational models and enterprise strategies* (pp. 17–43). Hershey, PA: Information Science Reference; doi:10.4018/978-1-61350-195-5.ch002

Becerra-Fernandez, I., & Sabherwal, R. (2011). The role of information and communication technologies in knowledge management: A classification of knowledge management systems. In D. Schwartz & D. Te'eni (Eds.), *Encyclopedia of knowledge management* (2nd ed., pp. 1410–1418). Hershey, PA: Information Science Reference; doi:10.4018/978-1-59904-931-1.ch134

Benbya, H. (2013). Valuing knowledge-based initiatives: What we know and what we don't know. In M. Jennex (Ed.), *Dynamic models for knowledge-driven organizations* (pp. 1–15). Hershey, PA: Business Science Reference; doi:10.4018/978-1-4666-2485-6.ch001

Berends, H., van der Bij, H., & Weggeman, M. (2011). Knowledge integration. In D. Schwartz & D. Te'eni (Eds.), *Encyclopedia of knowledge management* (2nd ed., pp. 581–590). Hershey, PA: Information Science Reference; doi:10.4018/978-1-59904-931-1.ch056

Berger, H., & Beynon-Davies, P. (2011). Knowledge-based diffusion in practice: A case study experience. In A. Eardley & L. Uden (Eds.), *Innovative knowledge management: Concepts for organizational creativity and collaborative design* (pp. 40–55). Hershey, PA: Information Science Reference; doi:10.4018/978-1-60566-701-0.ch003

Berio, G., Di Leva, A., Harzallah, M., & Sacco, G. M. (2012). Competence management over social networks through dynamic taxonomies. In I. Boughzala & A. Dudezert (Eds.), *Knowledge management 2.0: Organizational models and enterprise strategies* (pp. 103–120). Hershey, PA: Information Science Reference; doi:10.4018/978-1-61350-195-5.ch006

Bhatt, S., Chaudhary, S., & Bhise, M. (2013). Migration of data between cloud and non-cloud datastores. In A. Ionita, M. Litoiu, & G. Lewis (Eds.), *Migrating legacy applications: Challenges in service oriented architecture and cloud computing environments* (pp. 206–225). Hershey, PA: Information Science Reference; doi:10.4018/978-1-4666-2488-7.ch009

Bloodgood, J. M., Chilton, M. A., & Bloodgood, T. C. (2014). The effect of knowledge transfer motivation, receiver capability, and motivation on organizational performance. In M. Chilton & J. Bloodgood (Eds.), *Knowledge management and competitive advantage: Issues and potential solutions* (pp. 232–242). Hershey, PA: Information Science Reference; doi:10.4018/978-1-4666-4679-7.ch013

Boersma, K., & Kingma, S. (2011). Organizational learning facilitation with intranet (2.0): A sociocultural approach. In D. Schwartz & D. Te'eni (Eds.), *Encyclopedia of knowledge management* (2nd ed., pp. 1280–1289). Hershey, PA: Information Science Reference; doi:10.4018/978-1-59904-931-1.ch122

Bond, P. L. (2010). Toward a living systems framework for unifying technology and knowledge management, organizational, cultural and economic change. In D. Harorimana (Ed.), *Cultural implications of knowledge sharing, management and transfer: Identifying competitive advantage* (pp. 108–132). Hershey, PA: Information Science Reference; doi:10.4018/978-1-60566-790-4.ch006

Related References

Bordogna, G., Bucci, F., Carrara, P., Pepe, M., & Rampini, A. (2011). Flexible querying of imperfect temporal metadata in spatial data infrastructures. In L. Yan & Z. Ma (Eds.), *Advanced database query systems: Techniques, applications and technologies* (pp. 140–159). Hershey, PA: Information Science Reference; doi:10.4018/978-1-60960-475-2.ch006

Boughzala, I. (2012). Collaboration 2.0 through the new organization (2.0) transformation. In I. Boughzala & A. Dudezert (Eds.), *Knowledge management 2.0: Organizational models and enterprise strategies* (pp. 1–16). Hershey, PA: Information Science Reference; doi:10.4018/978-1-61350-195-5.ch001

Bratianu, C. (2011). A new perspective of the intellectual capital dynamics in organizations. In B. Vallejo-Alonso, A. Rodriguez-Castellanos, & G. Arregui-Ayastuy (Eds.), *Identifying, measuring, and valuing knowledge-based intangible assets: New perspectives* (pp. 1–21). Hershey, PA: Business Science Reference; doi:10.4018/978-1-60960-054-9.ch001

Bratianu, C. (2011). Universities as knowledge-intensive learning organizations. In A. Eardley & L. Uden (Eds.), *Innovative knowledge management: Concepts for organizational creativity and collaborative design* (pp. 1–17). Hershey, PA: Information Science Reference; doi:10.4018/978-1-60566-701-0.ch001

Breu, K., Ward, J., & Murray, P. (2000). Success factors in leveraging the corporate information and knowledge resource through intranets. In Y. Malhotra (Ed.), *Knowledge management and virtual organizations* (pp. 306–320). Hershey, PA: Idea Group Publishing; doi:10.4018/978-1-930708-65-5.ch016

Briones-Peñalver, A., & Poças-Rascão, J. (2014). Information technologies (ICT), network organizations, and information systems for business cooperation: A focus on organization and strategic knowledge management. In G. Jamil, A. Malheiro, & F. Ribeiro (Eds.), *Rethinking the conceptual base for new practical applications in information value and quality* (pp. 324–348). Hershey, PA: Information Science Reference; doi:10.4018/978-1-4666-4562-2.ch015

Brock, J. K., & Zhou, Y. J. (2011). MNE knowledge management across borders and ICT. In D. Schwartz & D. Te'eni (Eds.), *Encyclopedia of knowledge management* (2nd ed., pp. 1136–1148). Hershey, PA: Information Science Reference; doi:10.4018/978-1-59904-931-1.ch109

Brunet-Thornton, R., & Bureš, V. (2011). Meeting Czech knowledge management challenges head-on: KM-Be.At-It. In M. Al-Shammari (Ed.), *Knowledge management in emerging economies: Social, organizational and cultural implementation* (pp. 20–46). Hershey, PA: Information Science Reference; doi:10.4018/978-1-61692-886-5.ch002

Bucher, T., & Dinter, B. (2012). Situational method engineering to support process-oriented information logistics: Identification of development situations. [JDM]. *Journal of Database Management, 23*(1), 31–48. doi:10.4018/jdm.2012010102

Burstein, F., & Linger, H. (2011). Task-based knowledge management approach. In D. Schwartz & D. Te'eni (Eds.), *Encyclopedia of knowledge management* (2nd ed., pp. 1479–1489). Hershey, PA: Information Science Reference; doi:10.4018/978-1-59904-931-1.ch141

Butler, T. (2011). Anti-foundational knowledge management. In D. Schwartz & D. Te'eni (Eds.), *Encyclopedia of knowledge management* (2nd ed., pp. 1–11). Hershey, PA: Information Science Reference; doi:10.4018/978-1-59904-931-1.ch001

Butler, T., & Murphy, C. (2011). Work and knowledge. In D. Schwartz & D. Te'eni (Eds.), *Encyclopedia of knowledge management* (2nd ed., pp. 1556–1566). Hershey, PA: Information Science Reference; doi:10.4018/978-1-59904-931-1.ch148

Cabrilo, S., & Grubic-Nesic, L. (2013). The role of creativity, innovation, and invention in knowledge management. In S. Buckley & M. Jakovljevic (Eds.), *Knowledge management innovations for interdisciplinary education: Organizational applications* (pp. 207–232). Hershey, PA: Information Science Reference; doi:10.4018/978-1-4666-1969-2.ch011

Cabrita, M. D., Machado, V. C., & Grilo, A. (2010). Intellectual capital: How knowledge creates value. In E. O'Brien, S. Clifford, & M. Southern (Eds.), *Knowledge management for process, organizational and marketing innovation: Tools and methods* (pp. 237–252). Hershey, PA: Information Science Reference; doi:10.4018/978-1-61520-829-6.ch015

Cagliero, L., & Fiori, A. (2013). Knowledge discovery from online communities. In *Data mining: Concepts, methodologies, tools, and applications* (pp. 1230–1252). Hershey, PA: Information Science Reference; doi:10.4018/978-1-4666-2455-9.ch063

Camisón-Zornoza, C., & Boronat-Navarro, M. (2010). Linking exploration and exploitation capabilities with the process of knowledge development and with organizational facilitators. In M. Russ (Ed.), *Knowledge management strategies for business development* (pp. 159–179). Hershey, PA: Business Science Reference; doi:10.4018/978-1-60566-348-7.ch008

Carneiro, A. (2010). Change knowledge management: Transforming a ghost community into a real asset. In E. O'Brien, S. Clifford, & M. Southern (Eds.), *Knowledge management for process, organizational and marketing innovation: Tools and methods* (pp. 120–132). Hershey, PA: Information Science Reference; doi:10.4018/978-1-61520-829-6.ch007

Carrillo, F. J. (2010). Knowledge-based value generation. In K. Metaxiotis, F. Carrillo, & T. Yigitcanlar (Eds.), *Knowledge-based development for cities and societies: Integrated multi-level approaches* (pp. 1–16). Hershey, PA: Information Science Reference; doi:10.4018/978-1-61520-721-3.ch001

Cartelli, A. (2012). Frameworks for the benchmarking of digital and knowledge management best practice in SME and organizations. In A. Cartelli (Ed.), *Current trends and future practices for digital literacy and competence* (pp. 166–175). Hershey, PA: Information Science Reference; doi:10.4018/978-1-4666-0903-7.ch015

Castellano, G., Fanelli, A. M., & Torsello, M. A. (2010). Soft computing techniques in content-based multimedia information retrieval. In K. Anbumani & R. Nedunchezhian (Eds.), *Soft computing applications for database technologies: Techniques and issues* (pp. 170–192). Hershey, PA: Information Science Reference; doi:10.4018/978-1-60566-814-7.ch010

Chalkiti, K., & Carson, D. (2010). Knowledge cultures, competitive advantage and staff turnover in hospitality in Australia's northern territory. In D. Harorimana (Ed.), *Cultural implications of knowledge sharing, management and transfer: Identifying competitive advantage* (pp. 203–229). Hershey, PA: Information Science Reference; doi:10.4018/978-1-60566-790-4.ch010

Related References

Chang, W., & Li, S. (2011). Deploying knowledge management in R&D workspaces. In A. Eardley & L. Uden (Eds.), *Innovative knowledge management: Concepts for organizational creativity and collaborative design* (pp. 56–76). Hershey, PA: Information Science Reference; doi:10.4018/978-1-60566-701-0.ch004

Chawla, D., & Joshi, H. (2013). Impact of knowledge management dimensions on learning organization: Comparison across business excellence awarded and non-awarded indian organizations. In M. Jennex (Ed.), *Dynamic models for knowledge-driven organizations* (pp. 145–162). Hershey, PA: Business Science Reference; doi:10.4018/978-1-4666-2485-6.ch008

Chen, E. (2012). Web 2.0 social networking technologies and strategies for knowledge management. In I. Boughzala & A. Dudezert (Eds.), *Knowledge management 2.0: Organizational models and enterprise strategies* (pp. 84–102). Hershey, PA: Information Science Reference; doi:10.4018/978-1-61350-195-5.ch005

Chihara, K., & Nakamori, Y. (2013). Clarification of abilities and qualities of knowledge coordinators: The case of regional revitalization projects. In G. Yang (Ed.), *Multidisciplinary studies in knowledge and systems science* (pp. 1–17). Hershey, PA: Information Science Reference; doi:10.4018/978-1-4666-3998-0.ch001

Christidis, K., Papailiou, N., Apostolou, D., & Mentzas, G. (2011). Semantic interfaces for personal and social knowledge work. [IJKBO]. *International Journal of Knowledge-Based Organizations*, *1*(1), 61–77. doi:10.4018/ijkbo.2011010104

Christidis, K., Papailiou, N., Apostolou, D., & Mentzas, G. (2013). Semantic interfaces for personal and social knowledge work. In J. Wang (Ed.), *Intelligence methods and systems advancements for knowledge-based business* (pp. 213–230). Hershey, PA: Information Science Reference; doi:10.4018/978-1-4666-1873-2.ch012

Chua, C. E., Storey, V. C., & Chiang, R. H. (2012). Knowledge representation: A conceptual modeling approach. [JDM]. *Journal of Database Management*, *23*(1), 1–30. doi:10.4018/jdm.2012010101

Clinton, M. S., Merritt, K. L., & Murray, S. R. (2011). Facilitating knowledge transfer and the achievement of competitive advantage with corporate universities: An exploratory model based on media richness and type of knowledge to be transferred. In M. Jennex (Ed.), *Global aspects and cultural perspectives on knowledge management: Emerging dimensions* (pp. 329–345). Hershey, PA: Information Science Reference; doi:10.4018/978-1-60960-555-1.ch020

Colomb, R. M. (2013). Representation of action is a primary requirement in ontologies for interoperating information systems. In M. Nazir Ahmad, R. Colomb, & M. Abdullah (Eds.), *Ontology-based applications for enterprise systems and knowledge management* (pp. 68–76). Hershey, PA: Information Science Reference; doi:10.4018/978-1-4666-1993-7.ch004

Colucci, S., Di Noia, T., Di Sciascio, E., Donini, F. M., & Mongiello, M. (2011). Description logic-based resource retrieval. In D. Schwartz & D. Te'eni (Eds.), *Encyclopedia of knowledge management* (2nd ed., pp. 185–197). Hershey, PA: Information Science Reference; doi:10.4018/978-1-59904-931-1.ch018

Connell, N. A. (2011). Organisational storytelling. In D. Schwartz & D. Te'eni (Eds.), *Encyclopedia of knowledge management* (2nd ed., pp. 1261–1269). Hershey, PA: Information Science Reference; doi:10.4018/978-1-59904-931-1.ch120

Cooper, L. P., & Rober, M. B. (2012). Moving wikis behind the firewall: Intrapedias and work-wikis. In I. Boughzala & A. Dudezert (Eds.), *Knowledge Management 2.0: Organizational Models and Enterprise Strategies* (pp. 44–63). Hershey, PA: Information Science Reference; doi:10.4018/978-1-61350-195-5. ch003

Corallo, A., De Maggio, M., & Margherita, A. (2011). Knowledge democracy as the new mantra in product innovation: A framework of processes and competencies. In A. Eardley & L. Uden (Eds.), *Innovative knowledge management: Concepts for organizational creativity and collaborative design* (pp. 141–156). Hershey, PA: Information Science Reference; doi:10.4018/978-1-60566-701-0.ch008

Costa, G. (2011). Knowledge worker fair compensation: Ethical issues and social dilemmas. In G. Morais da Costa (Ed.), *Ethical issues and social dilemmas in knowledge management: Organizational innovation* (pp. 215–231). Hershey, PA: Information Science Reference; doi:10.4018/978-1-61520-873-9.ch013

Costello, R. (2014). Evaluating e-learning from an end user perspective. In M. Pańkowska (Ed.), *Frameworks of IT prosumption for business development* (pp. 259–283). Hershey, PA: Business Science Reference; doi:10.4018/978-1-4666-4313-0.ch017

Crasso, M., Zunino, A., & Campo, M. (2013). A survey of approaches to web service discovery in service-oriented architectures. In K. Siau (Ed.), *Innovations in database design, web applications, and information systems management* (pp. 107–138). Hershey, PA: Information Science Reference; doi:10.4018/978-1-4666-2044-5.ch005

Croasdell, D., & Wang, Y. K. (2011). Virtue-nets. In D. Schwartz & D. Te'eni (Eds.), *Encyclopedia of knowledge management* (2nd ed., pp. 1545–1555). Hershey, PA: Information Science Reference; doi:10.4018/978-1-59904-931-1.ch147

Cucchiara, S., Ligorio, M. B., & Fujita, N. (2014). Understanding online discourse strategies for knowledge building through social network analysis. In H. Lim & F. Sudweeks (Eds.), *Innovative methods and technologies for electronic discourse analysis* (pp. 42–62). Hershey, PA: Information Science Reference; doi:10.4018/978-1-4666-4426-7.ch003

Cudanov, M., & Kirchner, K. (2011). Knowledge management in high-growth companies: A case study in Serbia. In M. Al-Shammari (Ed.), *Knowledge management in emerging economies: Social, organizational and cultural implementation* (pp. 227–248). Hershey, PA: Information Science Reference; doi:10.4018/978-1-61692-886-5.ch014

Cuel, R., Bouquet, P., & Bonifacio, M. (2011). Distributed knowledge management. In D. Schwartz & D. Te'eni (Eds.), *Encyclopedia of knowledge management* (2nd ed., pp. 198–208). Hershey, PA: Information Science Reference; doi:10.4018/978-1-59904-931-1.ch019

Daidj, N. (2012). The evolution of KM practices: The case of the Renault-Nissan international strategic alliance. In I. Boughzala & A. Dudezert (Eds.), *Knowledge management 2.0: Organizational models and enterprise strategies* (pp. 190–213). Hershey, PA: Information Science Reference; doi:10.4018/978-1-61350-195-5.ch010

Related References

Daniel, B. K., Zapata-Rivera, J., & McCalla, G. I. (2010). A Bayesian belief network methodology for modeling social systems in virtual communities: Opportunities for database technologies. In K. Anbumani & R. Nedunchezhian (Eds.), *Soft computing applications for database technologies: Techniques and issues* (pp. 125–152). Hershey, PA: Information Science Reference; doi:10.4018/978-1-60566-814-7.ch008

Darchen, S., & Tremblay, D. (2010). Attracting and retaining knowledge workers: The impact of quality of place in the case of Montreal. In K. Metaxiotis, F. Carrillo, & T. Yigitcanlar (Eds.), *Knowledge-based development for cities and societies: Integrated multi-level approaches* (pp. 42–58). Hershey, PA: Information Science Reference; doi:10.4018/978-1-61520-721-3.ch003

Davenport, D. L., & Hosapple, C. W. (2011). Knowledge organizations. In D. Schwartz & D. Te'eni (Eds.), *Encyclopedia of knowledge management* (2nd ed., pp. 822–832). Hershey, PA: Information Science Reference; doi:10.4018/978-1-59904-931-1.ch079

Davenport, D. L., & Hosapple, C. W. (2011). Social capital knowledge. In D. Schwartz & D. Te'eni (Eds.), *Encyclopedia of knowledge management* (2nd ed., pp. 1448–1459). Hershey, PA: Information Science Reference; doi:10.4018/978-1-59904-931-1.ch138

De Maggio, M., Del Vecchio, P., Elia, G., & Grippa, F. (2011). An ICT-based network of competence centres for developing intellectual capital in the Mediterranean area. In A. Al Ajeeli & Y. Al-Bastaki (Eds.), *Handbook of research on e-services in the public sector: E-government strategies and advancements* (pp. 164–181). Hershey, PA: Information Science Reference; doi:10.4018/978-1-61520-789-3.ch014

Dehuri, S., Patra, M. R., Misra, B., & Jagadev, A. (2013). Intelligent techniques in recommendation systems: Contextual advancements and new methods (pp. 1-350). doi:10.4018/978-1-4666-2542-6

Delbaere, M., Di Zhang, D., Bruning, E. R., & Sivaramakrishnan, S. (2014). Knowledge management and the roles it plays in achieving superior performance. In M. Chilton & J. Bloodgood (Eds.), *Knowledge management and competitive advantage: Issues and potential solutions* (pp. 90–108). Hershey, PA: Information Science Reference; doi:10.4018/978-1-4666-4679-7.ch006

Delgado-Verde, M., & Cruz-González, J. (2010). An intellectual capital-based view of technological innovation. In P. López Sáez, G. Castro, J. Navas López, & M. Delgado Verde (Eds.), *Intellectual capital and technological innovation: Knowledge-based theory and practice* (pp. 166–193). Hershey, PA: Information Science Reference; doi:10.4018/978-1-61520-875-3.ch008

Deltour, F., Plé, L., & Roussel, C. S. (2012). Knowledge sharing in the age of web 2.0: A social capital perspective. In I. Boughzala & A. Dudezert (Eds.), *Knowledge management 2.0: Organizational models and enterprise strategies* (pp. 122–141). Hershey, PA: Information Science Reference; doi:10.4018/978-1-61350-195-5.ch007

Derballa, V., & Pousttchi, K. (2011). Mobile technology for knowledge management. In D. Schwartz & D. Te'eni (Eds.), *Encyclopedia of knowledge management* (2nd ed., pp. 1158–1166). Hershey, PA: Information Science Reference; doi:10.4018/978-1-59904-931-1.ch111

Dieng-Kuntz, R. (2011). Corporate semantic webs. In D. Schwartz & D. Te'eni (Eds.), *Encyclopedia of knowledge management* (2nd ed., pp. 131–149). Hershey, PA: Information Science Reference; doi:10.4018/978-1-59904-931-1.ch014

Diosteanu, A., Stellato, A., & Turbati, A. (2012). SODA: A service oriented data acquisition framework. In M. Pazienza & A. Stellato (Eds.), *Semi-automatic ontology development: Processes and resources* (pp. 48–77). Hershey, PA: Information Science Reference; doi:10.4018/978-1-4666-0188-8.ch003

Donate-Manzanares, M. J., Guadamillas-Gómez, F., & Sánchez de Pablo, J. D. (2010). Strategic alliances and knowledge management strategies: A case study. In M. Russ (Ed.), *Knowledge management strategies for business development* (pp. 240–260). Hershey, PA: Business Science Reference; doi:10.4018/978-1-60566-348-7.ch011

Donnet, T., Keast, R., & Pickernell, D. (2010). Up the junction? Exploiting knowledge-based development through supply chain and SME cluster interactions. In K. Metaxiotis, F. Carrillo, & T. Yigitcanlar (Eds.), *Knowledge-based development for cities and societies: Integrated multi-level approaches* (pp. 179–195). Hershey, PA: Information Science Reference; doi:10.4018/978-1-61520-721-3.ch011

Douglas, I. (2011). Organizational needs analysis and knowledge management. In D. Schwartz & D. Te'eni (Eds.), *Encyclopedia of knowledge management* (2nd ed., pp. 1290–1297). Hershey, PA: Information Science Reference; doi:10.4018/978-1-59904-931-1.ch123

Edvardsson, I. R., & Oskarsson, G. K. (2013). Outsourcing in knowledge-based service firms. In J. Wang (Ed.), *Intelligence methods and systems advancements for knowledge-based business* (pp. 97–113). Hershey, PA: Information Science Reference; doi:10.4018/978-1-4666-1873-2.ch006

Elenurm, T. (2013). Knowledge management and innovative learning. In S. Buckley & M. Jakovljevic (Eds.), *Knowledge management innovations for interdisciplinary education: Organizational applications* (pp. 108–131). Hershey, PA: Information Science Reference; doi:10.4018/978-1-4666-1969-2.ch006

Eppler, M. J., & Burkhard, R. A. (2011). Knowledge visualization. In D. Schwartz & D. Te'eni (Eds.), *Encyclopedia of knowledge management* (2nd ed., pp. 987–999). Hershey, PA: Information Science Reference; doi:10.4018/978-1-59904-931-1.ch094

Ergazakis, K., Metaxiotis, K., & Ergazakis, E. (2011). Exploring paths towards knowledge cities developments: A research agenda. In D. Schwartz & D. Te'eni (Eds.), *Encyclopedia of knowledge management* (2nd ed., pp. 288–297). Hershey, PA: Information Science Reference; doi:10.4018/978-1-59904-931-1.ch028

Eri, Z. D., Abdullah, R., Jabar, M. A., Murad, M. A., & Talib, A. M. (2013). Ontology-based virtual communities model for the knowledge management system environment: Ontology design. In M. Nazir Ahmad, R. Colomb, & M. Abdullah (Eds.), *Ontology-based applications for enterprise systems and knowledge management* (pp. 343–360). Hershey, PA: Information Science Reference; doi:10.4018/978-1-4666-1993-7.ch019

Erickson, G. S. (2014). Government as a partner in knowledge management: Lessons from the US freedom of information act. In Y. Al-Bastaki & A. Shajera (Eds.), *Building a competitive public sector with knowledge management strategy* (pp. 90–103). Hershey, PA: Business Science Reference; doi:10.4018/978-1-4666-4434-2.ch003

Erickson, G. S., & Rothberg, H. N. (2011). Assessing knowledge management needs: A strategic approach to developing knowledge. [IJKM]. *International Journal of Knowledge Management*, 7(3), 1–10. doi:10.4018/jkm.2011070101

Related References

Erickson, G. S., & Rothberg, H. N. (2011). Assessing knowledge management needs: A strategic approach to developing knowledge. [IJKM]. *International Journal of Knowledge Management, 7*(3), 1–10. doi:10.4018/jkm.2011070101

Erickson, G. S., & Rothberg, H. N. (2011). Protecting knowledge assets. In D. Schwartz & D. Te'eni (Eds.), *Encyclopedia of knowledge management* (2nd ed., pp. 1336–1342). Hershey, PA: Information Science Reference; doi:10.4018/978-1-59904-931-1.ch128

Erickson, G. S., & Rothberg, H. N. (2013). Assessing knowledge management needs: A strategic approach to developing knowledge. In M. Jennex (Ed.), *Dynamic models for knowledge-driven organizations* (pp. 180–189). Hershey, PA: Business Science Reference; doi:10.4018/978-1-4666-2485-6.ch010

Evermann, J., & Wand, Y. (2011). Ontology based object-oriented domain modeling: Representing behavior. In K. Siau (Ed.), *Theoretical and practical advances in information systems development: Emerging trends and approaches* (pp. 37–60). Hershey, PA: Information Science Reference; doi:10.4018/978-1-60960-521-6.ch003

Fadel, K. J., Durcikova, A., & Cha, H. S. (2011). An experiment of information elaboration in mediated knowledge transfer. In M. Jennex (Ed.), *Global aspects and cultural perspectives on knowledge management: Emerging dimensions* (pp. 311–328). Hershey, PA: Information Science Reference; doi:10.4018/978-1-60960-555-1.ch019

Fazel-Zarandi, M., Fox, M. S., & Yu, E. (2013). Ontologies in expertise finding systems: Modeling, analysis, and design. In M. Nazir Ahmad, R. Colomb, & M. Abdullah (Eds.), *Ontology-based applications for enterprise systems and knowledge management* (pp. 158–177). Hershey, PA: Information Science Reference; doi:10.4018/978-1-4666-1993-7.ch009

Ferri, F., & Grifoni, P. (2011). Sketching in knowledge creation and management. In D. Schwartz & D. Te'eni (Eds.), *Encyclopedia of knowledge management* (2nd ed., pp. 1438–1447). Hershey, PA: Information Science Reference; doi:10.4018/978-1-59904-931-1.ch137

Filho, C. G., Baroni de Carvalho, R., & Jamil, G. L. (2011). Market knowledge management, innovation and product performance: Survey in medium and large Brazilian industrial firms. In M. Jennex & S. Smolnik (Eds.), *Strategies for knowledge management success: Exploring organizational efficacy* (pp. 32–50). Hershey, PA: Information Science Reference; doi:10.4018/978-1-60566-709-6.ch003

Fink, D., & Disterer, G. (2011). Knowledge management in professional service firms. In D. Schwartz & D. Te'eni (Eds.), *Encyclopedia of knowledge management* (2nd ed., pp. 650–659). Hershey, PA: Information Science Reference; doi:10.4018/978-1-59904-931-1.ch063

Fink, K. (2011). Process model for knowledge potential measurement in SMEs. In M. Jennex & S. Smolnik (Eds.), *Strategies for knowledge management success: Exploring organizational efficacy* (pp. 91–105). Hershey, PA: Information Science Reference; doi:10.4018/978-1-60566-709-6.ch006

Fink, K., & Ploder, C. (2011). Knowledge management toolkit for SMEs. In M. Jennex (Ed.), *Global aspects and cultural perspectives on knowledge management: Emerging dimensions* (pp. 49–63). Hershey, PA: Information Science Reference; doi:10.4018/978-1-60960-555-1.ch004

Flynn, R., & Marshall, V. (2014). The four levers for change in knowledge management implementation. In Y. Al-Bastaki & A. Shajera (Eds.), *Building a competitive public sector with knowledge management strategy* (pp. 227–245). Hershey, PA: Business Science Reference; doi:10.4018/978-1-4666-4434-2.ch010

Fortier, J., & Kassel, G. (2011). Organizational semantic webs. In D. Schwartz & D. Te'eni (Eds.), *Encyclopedia of knowledge management* (2nd ed., pp. 1298–1307). Hershey, PA: Information Science Reference; doi:10.4018/978-1-59904-931-1.ch124

Framinan, J. M., & Molina, J. M. (2010). An overview of enterprise resource planning for intelligent enterprises. In *Business information systems: Concepts, methodologies, tools and applications* (pp. 60–68). Hershey, PA: Business Science Reference; doi:10.4018/978-1-61520-969-9.ch005

Franco, M., Di Virgilio, F., & Di Pietro, L. (2014). Management of group knowledge and the role of E-WOM for business organizations. In M. Chilton & J. Bloodgood (Eds.), *Knowledge management and competitive advantage: Issues and potential solutions* (pp. 71–89). Hershey, PA: Information Science Reference; doi:10.4018/978-1-4666-4679-7.ch005

Franke, U. J. (2000). The knowledge-based view (KBV) of the virtual web, the virtual corporation and the net-broker. In Y. Malhotra (Ed.), *Knowledge management and virtual organizations* (pp. 20–42). Hershey, PA: Idea Group Publishing; doi:10.4018/978-1-930708-65-5.ch002

Freivalds, D., & Lush, B. (2012). Thinking inside the grid: Selecting a discovery system through the RFP process. In M. Popp & D. Dallis (Eds.), *Planning and implementing resource discovery tools in academic libraries* (pp. 104–121). Hershey, PA: Information Science Reference; doi:10.4018/978-1-4666-1821-3.ch007

Frieß, M. R., Groh, G., Reinhardt, M., Forster, F., & Schlichter, J. (2012). Context-aware creativity support for corporate open innovation. [IJKBO]. *International Journal of Knowledge-Based Organizations*, 2(1), 38–55. doi:10.4018/ijkbo.2012010103

Fuller, C. M., & Wilson, R. L. (2011). Extracting knowledge from neural networks. In D. Schwartz & D. Te'eni (Eds.), *Encyclopedia of knowledge management* (2nd ed., pp. 320–330). Hershey, PA: Information Science Reference; doi:10.4018/978-1-59904-931-1.ch031

Furquim, T. D., & do Amaral, S. A. (2011). Knowledge management practices in brazilian software organizations: The case of SERPRO. In M. Al-Shammari (Ed.), *Knowledge management in emerging economies: Social, organizational and cultural implementation* (pp. 213–226). Hershey, PA: Information Science Reference; doi:10.4018/978-1-61692-886-5.ch013

Gaál, Z., Szabó, L., Obermayer-Kovács, N., Kovács, Z., & Csepregi, A. (2011). Knowledge management profile: An innovative approach to map knowledge management practice. In A. Eardley & L. Uden (Eds.), *Innovative knowledge management: Concepts for organizational creativity and collaborative design* (pp. 253–263). Hershey, PA: Information Science Reference; doi:10.4018/978-1-60566-701-0.ch016

Ganguly, A., Mostashari, A., & Mansouri, M. (2013). Measuring knowledge management/knowledge sharing (KM/KS) efficiency and effectiveness in enterprise networks. In M. Jennex (Ed.), *Dynamic models for knowledge-driven organizations* (pp. 318–336). Hershey, PA: Business Science Reference; doi:10.4018/978-1-4666-2485-6.ch019

Related References

Gaumand, C., Chapdaniel, A., & Dudezert, A. (2012). Strategic knowledge management system framework for supply chain at an intra-organizational level. In I. Boughzala & A. Dudezert (Eds.), *Knowledge management 2.0: Organizational models and enterprise strategies* (pp. 142–163). Hershey, PA: Information Science Reference; doi:10.4018/978-1-61350-195-5.ch008

Ghazali, R., & Zakaria, N. H. (2013). Knowledge management processes in enterprise systems: A systematic literature review. In M. Nazir Ahmad, R. Colomb, & M. Abdullah (Eds.), *Ontology-based applications for enterprise systems and knowledge management* (pp. 1–24). Hershey, PA: Information Science Reference; doi:10.4018/978-1-4666-1993-7.ch001

Ghosh, B. (2011). Cross-cultural knowledge management practices to support offshore outsourcing. In M. Al-Shammari (Ed.), *Knowledge management in emerging economies: Social, organizational and cultural implementation* (pp. 249–260). Hershey, PA: Information Science Reference; doi:10.4018/978-1-61692-886-5.ch015

Gohil, U., Carrillo, P., Ruikar, K., & Anumba, C. (2013). Development of a business process model for a project-based service organisation. [IJKBO]. *International Journal of Knowledge-Based Organizations*, *3*(1), 37–56. doi:10.4018/ijkbo.2013010103

Goldsmith, R. E., & Pillai, K. G. (2011). Knowledge calibration and knowledge management. In D. Schwartz & D. Te'eni (Eds.), *Encyclopedia of knowledge management* (2nd ed., pp. 497–505). Hershey, PA: Information Science Reference; doi:10.4018/978-1-59904-931-1.ch048

Gomes de Andrade, F., & Baptista, C. D. (2013). An ontology-based approach to support information discovery in spatial data infrastructures. In C. Rückemann (Ed.), *Integrated information and computing systems for natural, spatial, and social sciences* (pp. 369–387). Hershey, PA: Information Science Reference; doi:10.4018/978-1-4666-2190-9.ch018

Gonçalo, C. R., & Jacques, E. J. (2010). Best practices of knowledge strategy in hospitals: A contextual perspective based on the implementation of medical protocols. In D. Harorimana (Ed.), *Cultural implications of knowledge sharing, management and transfer: Identifying competitive advantage* (pp. 180–202). Hershey, PA: Information Science Reference; doi:10.4018/978-1-60566-790-4.ch009

Górniak-Kocikowska, K. (2011). Knowledge management and democracy: A critical review of some moral issues and social dilemmas. In G. Morais da Costa (Ed.), *Ethical issues and social dilemmas in knowledge management: Organizational innovation* (pp. 28–44). Hershey, PA: Information Science Reference; doi:10.4018/978-1-61520-873-9.ch003

Gottschalk, P. (2014). Police knowledge management strategy. In M. Chilton & J. Bloodgood (Eds.), *Knowledge management and competitive advantage: Issues and potential solutions* (pp. 202–220). Hershey, PA: Information Science Reference; doi:10.4018/978-1-4666-4679-7.ch011

Goudos, S. K., Peristeras, V., & Tarabanis, K. (2010). Application of semantic web technology in e-business: Case studies in public domain data knowledge representation. In *Business information systems: Concepts, methodologies, tools and applications* (pp. 1223–1233). Hershey, PA: Business Science Reference; doi:10.4018/978-1-61520-969-9.ch075

Govindarajan, M., & Chandrasekaran, R. (2012). A hybrid multilayer perceptron neural network for direct marketing. [IJKBO]. *International Journal of Knowledge-Based Organizations, 2*(3), 63–73. doi:10.4018/ijkbo.2012070104

Grant, J., & Minker, J. (2011). Logic and knowledge bases. In D. Schwartz & D. Te'eni (Eds.), *Encyclopedia of knowledge management* (2nd ed., pp. 1022–1033). Hershey, PA: Information Science Reference; doi:10.4018/978-1-59904-931-1.ch097

Green, A. (2011). Engineering business reasoning, analytics and intelligence network (E-BRAIN): A new approach to intangible asset valuation based on Einstein's perspective. In B. Vallejo-Alonso, A. Rodriguez-Castellanos, & G. Arregui-Ayastuy (Eds.), *Identifying, measuring, and valuing knowledge-based intangible assets: New perspectives* (pp. 232–253). Hershey, PA: Business Science Reference; doi:10.4018/978-1-60960-054-9.ch011

Greenaway, K. E., & Vuong, D. C. (2010). Taking charities seriously: A call for focused knowledge management research. [IJKM]. *International Journal of Knowledge Management, 6*(4), 87–97. doi:10.4018/jkm.2010100105

Greenaway, K. E., & Vuong, D. C. (2012). Taking charities seriously: A call for focused knowledge management research. In M. Jennex (Ed.), *Conceptual models and outcomes of advancing knowledge management: New technologies* (pp. 333–344). Hershey, PA: Information Science Reference; doi:10.4018/978-1-4666-0035-5.ch017

Gunjal, B., Gaitanou, P., & Yasin, S. (2012). Social networks and knowledge management: An explorative study in library systems. In I. Boughzala & A. Dudezert (Eds.), *Knowledge management 2.0: Organizational models and enterprise strategies* (pp. 64–83). Hershey, PA: Information Science Reference; doi:10.4018/978-1-61350-195-5.ch004

Habhab-Rave, S. (2010). Knowledge management in SMEs: A mixture of innovation, marketing and ICT: Analysis of two case studies. In E. O'Brien, S. Clifford, & M. Southern (Eds.), *Knowledge management for process, organizational and marketing innovation: Tools and methods* (pp. 183–194). Hershey, PA: Information Science Reference; doi:10.4018/978-1-61520-829-6.ch011

Habicht, H., Möslein, K. M., & Reichwald, R. (2012). Open innovation maturity. [IJKBO]. *International Journal of Knowledge-Based Organizations, 2*(1), 92–111. doi:10.4018/ijkbo.2012010106

Hamburg, I., & Hall, T. (2010). Readiness for knowledge management, methods and environments for innovation. In E. O'Brien, S. Clifford, & M. Southern (Eds.), *Knowledge management for process, organizational and marketing innovation: Tools and methods* (pp. 1–15). Hershey, PA: Information Science Reference; doi:10.4018/978-1-61520-829-6.ch001

Hamza, S. E. (2011). Capturing tacit knowledge from transient workers: Improving the organizational competitiveness. In M. Jennex (Ed.), *Global aspects and cultural perspectives on knowledge management: Emerging dimensions* (pp. 172–188). Hershey, PA: Information Science Reference; doi:10.4018/978-1-60960-555-1.ch012

Related References

Harorimana, D. (2010). Knowledge, culture, and cultural impact on knowledge management: Some lessons for researchers and practitioners. In D. Harorimana (Ed.), *Cultural implications of knowledge sharing, management and transfer: Identifying competitive advantage* (pp. 48–59). Hershey, PA: Information Science Reference; doi:10.4018/978-1-60566-790-4.ch003

Hasan, H. (2011). Formal and emergent standards in KM. In D. Schwartz & D. Te'eni (Eds.), *Encyclopedia of knowledge management* (2nd ed., pp. 331–342). Hershey, PA: Information Science Reference; doi:10.4018/978-1-59904-931-1.ch032

He, G., Xue, G., Yu, K., & Yao, S. (2013). Business process modeling: Analysis and evaluation. In Z. Lu (Ed.), *Design, performance, and analysis of innovative information retrieval* (pp. 382–393). Hershey, PA: Information Science Reference; doi:10.4018/978-1-4666-1975-3.ch027

Heiman, B. A., & Hurmelinna-Laukkanen, P. (2010). Problem finding and solving: A knowledge-based view of managing innovation. In P. López Sáez, G. Castro, J. Navas López, & M. Delgado Verde (Eds.), *Intellectual capital and technological innovation: Knowledge-based theory and practice* (pp. 105–130). Hershey, PA: Information Science Reference; doi:10.4018/978-1-61520-875-3.ch005

Hendriks, P. H. (2011). Organizational structure. In D. Schwartz & D. Te'eni (Eds.), *Encyclopedia of knowledge management* (2nd ed., pp. 1308–1318). Hershey, PA: Information Science Reference; doi:10.4018/978-1-59904-931-1.ch125

Hercheui, M. D. (2012). KMS for fostering behavior change: A case study on Microsoft Hohm. In I. Boughzala & A. Dudezert (Eds.), *Knowledge management 2.0: Organizational models and enterprise strategies* (pp. 214–232). Hershey, PA: Information Science Reference; doi:10.4018/978-1-61350-195-5.ch011

Hipkin, I. (2011). Perceptions of factors influencing knowledge-based technology management in conflict areas. In M. Al-Shammari (Ed.), *Knowledge management in emerging economies: Social, organizational and cultural implementation* (pp. 294–307). Hershey, PA: Information Science Reference; doi:10.4018/978-1-61692-886-5.ch018

Hofer, F. (2011). Knowledge transfer between academia and industry. In D. Schwartz & D. Te'eni (Eds.), *Encyclopedia of knowledge management* (2nd ed., pp. 977–986). Hershey, PA: Information Science Reference; doi:10.4018/978-1-59904-931-1.ch093

Holjevac, I. A., Crnjar, K., & Hrgovic, A. V. (2013). Knowledge management and quality in Croatian tourism. In S. Buckley & M. Jakovljevic (Eds.), *Knowledge management innovations for interdisciplinary education: Organizational applications* (pp. 178–192). Hershey, PA: Information Science Reference; doi:10.4018/978-1-4666-1969-2.ch009

Holsapple, C. W., & Joshi, K. D. (2011). Knowledge management ontology. In D. Schwartz & D. Te'eni (Eds.), *Encyclopedia of knowledge management* (2nd ed., pp. 704–711). Hershey, PA: Information Science Reference; doi:10.4018/978-1-59904-931-1.ch068

Holsapple, C. W., & Oh, J. (2014). Reactive and proactive dynamic capabilities: Using the knowledge chain theory of competitiveness. In M. Chilton & J. Bloodgood (Eds.), *Knowledge management and competitive advantage: Issues and potential solutions* (pp. 1–19). Hershey, PA: Information Science Reference; doi:10.4018/978-1-4666-4679-7.ch001

Huang, A., Xiao, J., & Wang, S. (2013). A combined forecast method integrating contextual knowledge. In G. Yang (Ed.), *Multidisciplinary studies in knowledge and systems science* (pp. 274–290). Hershey, PA: Information Science Reference; doi:10.4018/978-1-4666-3998-0.ch019

Huff, C. (2011). What does knowledge have to do with ethics? In G. Morais da Costa (Ed.), *Ethical issues and social dilemmas in knowledge management: Organizational innovation* (pp. 17–27). Hershey, PA: Information Science Reference; doi:10.4018/978-1-61520-873-9.ch002

Hürster, W., Wilbois, T., & Chaves, F. (2010). An integrated systems approach for early warning and risk management systems. [IJITSA]. *International Journal of Information Technologies and Systems Approach, 3*(2), 46–56. doi:10.4018/jitsa.2010070104

Iyer, S. R., Sharda, R., Biros, D., Lucca, J., & Shimp, U. (2011). Organization of lessons learned knowledge: A taxonomy and implementation. In M. Jennex (Ed.), *Global aspects and cultural perspectives on knowledge management: Emerging dimensions* (pp. 190–209). Hershey, PA: Information Science Reference; doi:10.4018/978-1-60960-555-1.ch013

Jacobson, C. M. (2011). Knowledge sharing between individuals. In D. Schwartz & D. Te'eni (Eds.), *Encyclopedia of knowledge management* (2nd ed., pp. 924–934). Hershey, PA: Information Science Reference; doi:10.4018/978-1-59904-931-1.ch088

Jakovljevic, M. (2013). A conceptual model of creativity, invention, and innovation (MCII) for entrepreneurial engineers. In S. Buckley & M. Jakovljevic (Eds.), *Knowledge management innovations for interdisciplinary education: Organizational applications* (pp. 66–87). Hershey, PA: Information Science Reference; doi:10.4018/978-1-4666-1969-2.ch004

Jasimuddin, S. M., Connell, N., & Klein, J. H. (2011). Understanding organizational memory. In D. Schwartz & D. Te'eni (Eds.), *Encyclopedia of knowledge management* (2nd ed., pp. 1536–1544). Hershey, PA: Information Science Reference; doi:10.4018/978-1-59904-931-1.ch146

Jennex, M. E. (2010). Do organizational memory and information technology interact to affect organizational information needs and provision? In *Ubiquitous developments in knowledge management: Integrations and trends* (pp. 1–20). Hershey, PA: Information Science Reference; doi:10.4018/978-1-60566-954-0

Jennex, M. E. (2010). Knowledge sharing model of 24-hour knowledge factory. In *Ubiquitous developments in knowledge management: Integrations and trends* (pp. 141–154). Hershey, PA: Information Science Reference; doi:10.4018/978-1-60566-954-0

Jennex, M. E. (2010). Operationalizing knowledge sharing for informers. In *Ubiquitous developments in knowledge management: Integrations and trends* (pp. 319–340). Hershey, PA: Information Science Reference; doi:10.4018/978-1-60566-954-0

Jennex, M. E. (2010). Qualitative pre-processing for semantic search of unstructured knowledge. In *Ubiquitous developments in knowledge management: Integrations and trends* (pp. 252–263). Hershey, PA: Information Science Reference; doi:10.4018/978-1-60566-954-0

Jennex, M. E. (2010). A specialized evaluation and comparison of sample data mining software. In *Ubiquitous developments in knowledge management: Integrations and trends* (pp. 300–318). Hershey, PA: Information Science Reference; doi:10.4018/978-1-60566-954-0

Related References

Jennex, M. E. (2010). Using soft systems methodology to reveal socio-technical barriers to knowledge sharing and management: A case study from the UK national health service. In *Ubiquitous developments in knowledge management: Integrations and trends* (pp. 215–235). Hershey, PA: Information Science Reference; doi:10.4018/978-1-60566-954-0

Jennex, M. E. (2011). Knowledge management success models. In D. Schwartz & D. Te'eni (Eds.), *Encyclopedia of knowledge management* (2nd ed., pp. 763–771). Hershey, PA: Information Science Reference; doi:10.4018/978-1-59904-931-1.ch074

Jennex, M. E., & Olfman, L. (2011). A model of knowledge management success. In M. Jennex & S. Smolnik (Eds.), *Strategies for knowledge management success: Exploring organizational efficacy* (pp. 14–31). Hershey, PA: Information Science Reference; doi:10.4018/978-1-60566-709-6.ch002

Jennex, M. E., Smolnik, S., & Croasdell, D. (2011). Towards a consensus knowledge management success definition. In M. Jennex & S. Smolnik (Eds.), *Strategies for knowledge management success: Exploring organizational efficacy* (pp. 1–13). Hershey, PA: Information Science Reference; doi:10.4018/978-1-60566-709-6.ch001

Jewels, T. (2013). Teaching enterprise information systems in the United Arab Emirates. In F. Albadri (Ed.), *Information systems applications in the Arab education sector* (pp. 322–337). Hershey, PA: Information Science Reference; doi:10.4018/978-1-4666-1984-5.ch022

Jolly, R., & Wakeland, W. (2011). Using agent based simulation and game theory analysis to study knowledge flow in organizations: The KMscape. In M. Jennex (Ed.), *Global aspects and cultural perspectives on knowledge management: Emerging dimensions* (pp. 19–29). Hershey, PA: Information Science Reference; doi:10.4018/978-1-60960-555-1.ch002

Joshi, S. (2014). Web 2.0 and its implications on globally competitive business model. In M. Pańkowska (Ed.), *Frameworks of IT prosumption for business development* (pp. 86–101). Hershey, PA: Business Science Reference; doi:10.4018/978-1-4666-4313-0.ch007

Judge, R. (2011). A simulation system for evaluating knowledge management system (KMS) implementation strategies in small to mid-size enterprises (SME). In M. Jennex (Ed.), *Global aspects and cultural perspectives on knowledge management: Emerging dimensions* (pp. 92–112). Hershey, PA: Information Science Reference; doi:10.4018/978-1-60960-555-1.ch007

Kalid, K. S. (2011). Transfer knowledge using stories: A Malaysian university case study. In M. Al-Shammari (Ed.), *Knowledge management in emerging economies: Social, organizational and cultural implementation* (pp. 186–198). Hershey, PA: Information Science Reference; doi:10.4018/978-1-61692-886-5.ch011

Kamau, C. (2010). Strategising impression management in corporations: Cultural knowledge as capital. In D. Harorimana (Ed.), *Cultural implications of knowledge sharing, management and transfer: Identifying competitive advantage* (pp. 60–83). Hershey, PA: Information Science Reference; doi:10.4018/978-1-60566-790-4.ch004

Kamthan, P., & Fancott, T. (2011). A knowledge management model for patterns. In D. Schwartz & D. Te'eni (Eds.), *Encyclopedia of knowledge management* (2nd ed., pp. 694–703). Hershey, PA: Information Science Reference; doi:10.4018/978-1-59904-931-1.ch067

Kamthan, P., & Pai, H. (2011). Knowledge representation in pattern management. In D. Schwartz & D. Te'eni (Eds.), *Encyclopedia of knowledge management* (2nd ed., pp. 893–904). Hershey, PA: Information Science Reference; doi:10.4018/978-1-59904-931-1.ch085

Kane, G. C., Schwaig, K. S., & Storey, V. C. (2011). Information privacy: Understanding how firms behave online. In K. Siau (Ed.), *Theoretical and practical advances in information systems development: Emerging trends and approaches* (pp. 81–100). Hershey, PA: Information Science Reference; doi:10.4018/978-1-60960-521-6.ch005

Kankanhalli, A., Tan, B. C., & Wei, K. (2011). Knowledge producers and consumers. In D. Schwartz & D. Te'eni (Eds.), *Encyclopedia of knowledge management* (2nd ed., pp. 867–877). Hershey, PA: Information Science Reference; doi:10.4018/978-1-59904-931-1.ch083

Karagiannis, D., Woitsch, R., & Hrgovcic, V. (2010). Industrialisation of the knowledge work: The knowledge conveyer belt approach. In E. O'Brien, S. Clifford, & M. Southern (Eds.), *Knowledge management for process, organizational and marketing innovation: Tools and methods* (pp. 79–94). Hershey, PA: Information Science Reference; doi:10.4018/978-1-61520-829-6.ch005

Karlsson, F., & Ågerfalk, P. J. (2011). Towards structured flexibility in information systems development: Devising a method for method configuration. In K. Siau (Ed.), *Theoretical and practical advances in information systems development: Emerging trends and approaches* (pp. 214–238). Hershey, PA: Information Science Reference; doi:10.4018/978-1-60960-521-6.ch010

Karna, A., Singh, R., & Verma, S. (2010). Knowledge management for an effective sales and marketing function. In M. Russ (Ed.), *Knowledge management strategies for business development* (pp. 324–337). Hershey, PA: Business Science Reference; doi:10.4018/978-1-60566-348-7.ch015

Kassim, A. M., & Cheah, Y. (2013). SEMblog: An ontology-based semantic blogging tool for knowledge identification, organization, and reuse. In M. Nazir Ahmad, R. Colomb, & M. Abdullah (Eds.), *Ontology-based applications for enterprise systems and knowledge management* (pp. 210–223). Hershey, PA: Information Science Reference; doi:10.4018/978-1-4666-1993-7.ch012

Kayakutlu, G. (2010). Knowledge worker profile: A framework to clarify expectations. In K. Metaxiotis, F. Carrillo, & T. Yigitcanlar (Eds.), *Knowledge-based development for cities and societies: Integrated multi-level approaches* (pp. 162–178). Hershey, PA: Information Science Reference; doi:10.4018/978-1-61520-721-3.ch010

Kettunen, J., & Chaudhuri, M. R. (2011). Knowledge management to promote organizational change in India. In M. Al-Shammari (Ed.), *Knowledge management in emerging economies: Social, organizational and cultural implementation* (pp. 308–324). Hershey, PA: Information Science Reference; doi:10.4018/978-1-61692-886-5.ch019

Khalil, O. E., & Seleim, A. (2012). Culture and knowledge transfer capacity: A cross-national study. In M. Jennex (Ed.), *Conceptual models and outcomes of advancing knowledge management: New technologies* (pp. 305–332). Hershey, PA: Information Science Reference; doi:10.4018/978-1-4666-0035-5.ch016

Related References

Khasawneh, R., & Alazzam, A. (2014). Towards customer knowledge management (CKM): Where knowledge and customer meet. In M. Chilton & J. Bloodgood (Eds.), *Knowledge management and competitive advantage: Issues and potential solutions* (pp. 109–121). Hershey, PA: Information Science Reference; doi:10.4018/978-1-4666-4679-7.ch007

Kim, J. (2014). Big data sharing among academics. In W. Hu & N. Kaabouch (Eds.), *Big data management, technologies, and applications* (pp. 177–194). Hershey, PA: Information Science Reference; doi:10.4018/978-1-4666-4699-5.ch008

Kim, S., Felan, J., & Kang, M. H. (2011). An ontological approach to enterprise knowledge modeling in a shipping company. [IJKM]. *International Journal of Knowledge Management*, 7(4), 70–84. doi:10.4018/jkm.2011100105

Kim, S., Felan, J., & Kang, M. H. (2013). An ontological approach to enterprise knowledge modeling in a shipping company. In M. Jennex (Ed.), *Dynamic models for knowledge-driven organizations* (pp. 351–363). Hershey, PA: Business Science Reference; doi:10.4018/978-1-4666-2485-6.ch021

King, W. R. (2011). Knowledge transfer. In D. Schwartz & D. Te'eni (Eds.), *Encyclopedia of knowledge management* (2nd ed., pp. 967–976). Hershey, PA: Information Science Reference; doi:10.4018/978-1-59904-931-1.ch092

Kivijärvi, H., Piirainen, K., & Tuominen, M. (2010). Sustaining organizational innovativeness: Advancing knowledge sharing during the scenario process. [IJKM]. *International Journal of Knowledge Management*, 6(2), 22–39. doi:10.4018/jkm.2010040102

Kivijärvi, H., Piirainen, K., & Tuominen, M. (2012). Sustaining organizational innovativeness: Advancing knowledge sharing during the scenario process. In M. Jennex (Ed.), *Conceptual models and outcomes of advancing knowledge management: New technologies* (pp. 99–117). Hershey, PA: Information Science Reference; doi:10.4018/978-1-4666-0035-5.ch006

Knyazhansky, M., & Plotkin, T. (2012). Knowledge bases over algebraic models: Some notes about informational equivalence. [IJKM]. *International Journal of Knowledge Management*, 8(1), 22–39. doi:10.4018/jkm.2012010102

Kong, E. (2014). The role of social intelligence in acquiring external knowledge for human capital development, organisational learning, and innovation. In M. Chilton & J. Bloodgood (Eds.), *Knowledge management and competitive advantage: Issues and potential solutions* (pp. 53–70). Hershey, PA: Information Science Reference; doi:10.4018/978-1-4666-4679-7.ch004

Kor, A., & Orange, G. (2011). A survey of epistemology and its implications on an organisational information and knowledge management model. In A. Eardley & L. Uden (Eds.), *Innovative knowledge management: Concepts for organizational creativity and collaborative design* (pp. 95–124). Hershey, PA: Information Science Reference; doi:10.4018/978-1-60566-701-0.ch006

Kostrzewa, A., Laaksoharju, M., & Kavathatzopoulos, I. (2011). Management of moral knowledge and ethical processes in organizations. In G. Morais da Costa (Ed.), *Ethical issues and social dilemmas in knowledge management: Organizational innovation* (pp. 199–214). Hershey, PA: Information Science Reference; doi:10.4018/978-1-61520-873-9.ch012

Kraaijenbrink, J., & Wijnhoven, F. (2011). External knowledge integration. In D. Schwartz & D. Te'eni (Eds.), *Encyclopedia of knowledge management* (2nd ed., pp. 308–319). Hershey, PA: Information Science Reference; doi:10.4018/978-1-59904-931-1.ch030

Kraft, T. A., & Steenkamp, A. L. (2012). A holistic approach for understanding project management. In F. Stowell (Ed.), *Systems approach applications for developments in information technology* (pp. 25–39). Hershey, PA: Information Science Reference; doi:10.4018/978-1-4666-1562-5.ch003

Kulkarni, U., & Freeze, R. (2011). Measuring knowledge management capabilities. In D. Schwartz & D. Te'eni (Eds.), *Encyclopedia of knowledge management* (2nd ed., pp. 1090–1100). Hershey, PA: Information Science Reference; doi:10.4018/978-1-59904-931-1.ch104

Kumar, A. S., Alrabea, A., & Sekhar, P. C. (2013). Temporal association rule mining in large databases. In *Data mining: Concepts, methodologies, tools, and applications* (pp. 586–602). Hershey, PA: Information Science Reference; doi:10.4018/978-1-4666-2455-9.ch029

Laihonen, H., & Koivuaho, M. (2011). Knowledge flow audit: indentifying, measuring and managing knowledge asset dynamics. In B. Vallejo-Alonso, A. Rodriguez-Castellanos, & G. Arregui-Ayastuy (Eds.), *Identifying, measuring, and valuing knowledge-based intangible assets: New perspectives* (pp. 22–42). Hershey, PA: Business Science Reference; doi:10.4018/978-1-60960-054-9.ch002

Land, F., Amjad, U., & Nolas, S. (2011). Knowledge management processes. In D. Schwartz & D. Te'eni (Eds.), *Encyclopedia of knowledge management* (2nd ed., pp. 719–727). Hershey, PA: Information Science Reference; doi:10.4018/978-1-59904-931-1.ch070

Lavanderos, L. P., & Fiol, E. S. (2011). Production cognitive capital as a measurement of intellectual capital. In B. Vallejo-Alonso, A. Rodriguez-Castellanos, & G. Arregui-Ayastuy (Eds.), *Identifying, measuring, and valuing knowledge-based intangible assets: New perspectives* (pp. 112–132). Hershey, PA: Business Science Reference; doi:10.4018/978-1-60960-054-9.ch006

Lavoué, É., George, S., & Prévôt, P. (2011). A knowledge management tool for the interconnection of communities of practice. [IJKM]. *International Journal of Knowledge Management*, 7(1), 55–76. doi:10.4018/jkm.2011010104

Lee, H., Chan, K., & Tsui, E. (2013). Knowledge mining Wikipedia: An ontological approach. In G. Yang (Ed.), *Multidisciplinary studies in knowledge and systems science* (pp. 52–62). Hershey, PA: Information Science Reference; doi:10.4018/978-1-4666-3998-0.ch005

Leung, N. K. (2011). A re-distributed knowledge management framework in help desk. In D. Schwartz & D. Te'eni (Eds.), *Encyclopedia of knowledge management* (2nd ed., pp. 1374–1381). Hershey, PA: Information Science Reference; doi:10.4018/978-1-59904-931-1.ch131

Li, Y., Guo, H., & Wang, S. (2010). A multiple-bits watermark for relational data. In K. Siau & J. Erickson (Eds.), *Principle advancements in database management technologies: New applications and frameworks* (pp. 1–22). Hershey, PA: Information Science Reference; doi:10.4018/978-1-60566-904-5.ch001

Related References

Lin, C. Y. (2013). Intellectual capital explains a country's resilience to financial crisis: A resource-based view. In P. Ordóñez de Pablos, R. Tennyson, & J. Zhao (Eds.), *Intellectual capital strategy management for knowledge-based organizations* (pp. 52–75). Hershey, PA: Business Science Reference; doi:10.4018/978-1-4666-3655-2.ch005

Lin, Y., & Dalkir, K. (2012). Factors affecting KM implementation in the Chinese community. In M. Jennex (Ed.), *Conceptual models and outcomes of advancing knowledge management: New technologies* (pp. 1–23). Hershey, PA: Information Science Reference; doi:10.4018/978-1-4666-0035-5.ch001

Lindsey, K. L. (2011). Barriers to knowledge sharing. In D. Schwartz & D. Te'eni (Eds.), *Encyclopedia of knowledge management* (2nd ed., pp. 49–61). Hershey, PA: Information Science Reference; doi:10.4018/978-1-59904-931-1.ch006

Liu, K., Tan, H. B., & Chen, X. (2013). Aiding maintenance of database applications through extracting attribute dependency graph. [JDM]. *Journal of Database Management, 24*(1), 20–35. doi:10.4018/jdm.2013010102

Liu, K., Tan, H. B., & Chen, X. (2013). Automated insertion of exception handling for key and referential constraints. [JDM]. *Journal of Database Management, 24*(1), 1–19. doi:10.4018/jdm.2013010101

Locuratolo, E., & Palomäki, J. (2013). Ontology for database preservation. In M. Nazir Ahmad, R. Colomb, & M. Abdullah (Eds.), *Ontology-based applications for enterprise systems and knowledge management* (pp. 141–157). Hershey, PA: Information Science Reference; doi:10.4018/978-1-4666-1993-7.ch008

López-Nicolás, C., & Meroño-Cerdán, Á. L. (2010). A model for knowledge management and intellectual capital audits. In M. Russ (Ed.), *Knowledge management strategies for business development* (pp. 115–131). Hershey, PA: Business Science Reference; doi:10.4018/978-1-60566-348-7.ch006

Luck, D. (2010). The implications of the development and implementation of CRM for knowledge management. In M. Russ (Ed.), *Knowledge management strategies for business development* (pp. 338–352). Hershey, PA: Business Science Reference; doi:10.4018/978-1-60566-348-7.ch016

Lukovic, I., Ivancevic, V., Celikovic, M., & Aleksic, S. (2014). DSLs in action with model based approaches to information system development. In *Software design and development: Concepts, methodologies, tools, and applications* (pp. 596–626). Hershey, PA: Information Science Reference; doi:10.4018/978-1-4666-4301-7.ch029

Luna-Reyes, L. F., & Gil-Garcia, J. R. (2012). Government and inter-organizational collaboration as strategies for administrative reform in Mexico. In T. Papadopoulos & P. Kanellis (Eds.), *Public sector reform using information technologies: Transforming policy into practice* (pp. 79–101). Hershey, PA: Information Science Reference; doi:10.4018/978-1-60960-839-2.ch005

Lungu, C. I., Caraiani, C., & Dascalu, C. (2013). Sustainable intellectual capital: The inference of corporate social responsibility within intellectual capital. In P. Ordóñez de Pablos, R. Tennyson, & J. Zhao (Eds.), *Intellectual capital strategy management for knowledge-based organizations* (pp. 156–173). Hershey, PA: Business Science Reference; doi:10.4018/978-1-4666-3655-2.ch009

Ma, Z. M. (2011). Engineering design knowledge management. In D. Schwartz & D. Te'eni (Eds.), *Encyclopedia of knowledge management* (2nd ed., pp. 263–269). Hershey, PA: Information Science Reference; doi:10.4018/978-1-59904-931-1.ch025

Maier, R., & Hadrich, T. (2011). Knowledge management systems. In D. Schwartz & D. Te'eni (Eds.), *Encyclopedia of knowledge management* (2nd ed., pp. 779–790). Hershey, PA: Information Science Reference; doi:10.4018/978-1-59904-931-1.ch076

Maria, E. D., & Micelli, S. (2010). SMEs and competitive advantage: A mix of innovation, marketing and ICT—The case of "made in Italy". In M. Russ (Ed.), *Knowledge management strategies for business development* (pp. 310–323). Hershey, PA: Business Science Reference; doi:10.4018/978-1-60566-348-7.ch014

Mariano, S., & Simionato, N. (2010). Where are we looking? A practical approach to managing knowledge captured from eye-tracking experiments: The experience of gulf air. In E. O'Brien, S. Clifford, & M. Southern (Eds.), *Knowledge management for process, organizational and marketing innovation: Tools and methods* (pp. 216–227). Hershey, PA: Information Science Reference; doi:10.4018/978-1-61520-829-6.ch013

Marques, M. B. (2014). The value of information and information services in knowledge society. In G. Jamil, A. Malheiro, & F. Ribeiro (Eds.), *Rethinking the conceptual base for new practical applications in information value and quality* (pp. 134–161). Hershey, PA: Information Science Reference; doi:10.4018/978-1-4666-4562-2.ch007

Masrom, M., Mahmood, N. H., & Al-Araimi, A. A. (2014). Exploring knowledge types and knowledge protection in organizations. In M. Chilton & J. Bloodgood (Eds.), *Knowledge management and competitive advantage: Issues and potential solutions* (pp. 271–280). Hershey, PA: Information Science Reference; doi:10.4018/978-1-4666-4679-7.ch016

Masterson, F. (2013). Knowledge management in practice: Using wikis to facilitate project-based learning. In S. Buckley & M. Jakovljevic (Eds.), *Knowledge management innovations for interdisciplinary education: Organizational applications* (pp. 385–401). Hershey, PA: Information Science Reference; doi:10.4018/978-1-4666-1969-2.ch019

Mattmann, C. A., Hart, A., Cinquini, L., Lazio, J., Khudikyan, S., & Jones, D. ... Robnett, J. (2014). Scalable data mining, archiving, and big data management for the next generation astronomical telescopes. In W. Hu, & N. Kaabouch (Eds.) Big data management, technologies, and applications (pp. 196-221). Hershey, PA: Information Science Reference. doi:10.4018/978-1-4666-4699-5.ch009

Maule, R. W. (2011). Military knowledge management. In D. Schwartz & D. Te'eni (Eds.), *Encyclopedia of knowledge management* (2nd ed., pp. 1125–1135). Hershey, PA: Information Science Reference; doi:10.4018/978-1-59904-931-1.ch108

Mavridis, I. (2011). Deploying privacy improved RBAC in web information systems. [IJITSA]. *International Journal of Information Technologies and Systems Approach, 4*(2), 70–87. doi:10.4018/jitsa.2011070105

Mavridis, I. (2012). Deploying privacy improved RBAC in web information systems. In F. Stowell (Ed.), *Systems approach applications for developments in information technology* (pp. 298–315). Hershey, PA: Information Science Reference; doi:10.4018/978-1-4666-1562-5.ch020

Related References

McLaughlin, S. (2011). Assessing the impact of knowledge transfer mechanisms on supply chain performance. In M. Jennex (Ed.), *Global aspects and cultural perspectives on knowledge management: Emerging dimensions* (pp. 157–171). Hershey, PA: Information Science Reference; doi:10.4018/978-1-60960-555-1.ch011

Medina, J. M., & Spinola, M. D. (2011). Understanding the behavior of knowledge management pathways: The case of small manufacturers of footwear in Peru and Brazil. In M. Al-Shammari (Ed.), *Knowledge management in emerging economies: Social, organizational and cultural implementation* (pp. 261–271). Hershey, PA: Information Science Reference; doi:10.4018/978-1-61692-886-5.ch016

Meloche, J. A., Hasan, H., Willis, D., Pfaff, C. C., & Qi, Y. (2011). Cocreating corporate knowledge with a wiki. In M. Jennex (Ed.), *Global aspects and cultural perspectives on knowledge management: Emerging dimensions* (pp. 126–143). Hershey, PA: Information Science Reference; doi:10.4018/978-1-60960-555-1.ch009

Melzer, S. (2013). On the relationship between ontology-based and holistic representations in a knowledge management system. In M. Nazir Ahmad, R. Colomb, & M. Abdullah (Eds.), *Ontology-based applications for enterprise systems and knowledge management* (pp. 292–323). Hershey, PA: Information Science Reference; doi:10.4018/978-1-4666-1993-7.ch017

Mendes, E., & Baker, S. (2013). Using knowledge management and aggregation techniques to improve web effort estimation. In S. Saeed & I. Alsmadi (Eds.), *Knowledge-based processes in software development* (pp. 64–85). Hershey, PA: Information Science Reference; doi:10.4018/978-1-4666-4229-4.ch005

Metaxiotis, K. (2011). Healthcare knowledge management. In D. Schwartz & D. Te'eni (Eds.), *Encyclopedia of knowledge management* (2nd ed., pp. 366–375). Hershey, PA: Information Science Reference; doi:10.4018/978-1-59904-931-1.ch035

Mikolajuk, Z. (2013). Community-based development of knowledge products. In M. Jennex (Ed.), *Dynamic models for knowledge-driven organizations* (pp. 268–281). Hershey, PA: Business Science Reference; doi:10.4018/978-1-4666-2485-6.ch016

Mischo, W. H., Schlembach, M. C., Bishoff, J., & German, E. M. (2012). User search activities within an academic library gateway: Implications for web-scale discovery systems. In M. Popp & D. Dallis (Eds.), *Planning and implementing resource discovery tools in academic libraries* (pp. 153–173). Hershey, PA: Information Science Reference; doi:10.4018/978-1-4666-1821-3.ch010

Mishra, B., & Shukla, K. K. (2014). Data mining techniques for software quality prediction. In *Software design and development: Concepts, methodologies, tools, and applications* (pp. 401–428). Hershey, PA: Information Science Reference; doi:10.4018/978-1-4666-4301-7.ch021

Moffett, S., Walker, T., & McAdam, R. (2014). Best value and performance management inspired change within UK councils: A knowledge management perspective. In Y. Al-Bastaki & A. Shajera (Eds.), *Building a competitive public sector with knowledge management strategy* (pp. 199–226). Hershey, PA: Business Science Reference; doi:10.4018/978-1-4666-4434-2.ch009

Mueller, C. E., & Bradley, K. D. (2011). Utilizing the Rasch model to develop and evaluate items for the tacit knowledge inventory for superintendents (TKIS). In M. Jennex (Ed.), *Global aspects and cultural perspectives on knowledge management: Emerging dimensions* (pp. 264–284). Hershey, PA: Information Science Reference; doi:10.4018/978-1-60960-555-1.ch017

Muhammed, S., Doll, W. J., & Deng, X. (2011). Impact of knowledge management practices on task knowledge: An individual level study. [IJKM]. *International Journal of Knowledge Management*, 7(4), 1–21. doi:10.4018/jkm.2011100101

Muhammed, S., Doll, W. J., & Deng, X. (2011). Measuring knowledge management outcomes at the individual level: Towards a tool for research on organizational culture. In M. Jennex (Ed.), *Global aspects and cultural perspectives on knowledge management: Emerging dimensions* (pp. 1–18). Hershey, PA: Information Science Reference; doi:10.4018/978-1-60960-555-1.ch001

Muhammed, S., Doll, W. J., & Deng, X. (2013). Impact of knowledge management practices on task knowledge: An individual level study. In M. Jennex (Ed.), *Dynamic models for knowledge-driven organizations* (pp. 282–301). Hershey, PA: Business Science Reference; doi:10.4018/978-1-4666-2485-6.ch017

Murata, K. (2011). Knowledge creation and sharing in Japanese organisations: A socio-cultural perspective on ba. In G. Morais da Costa (Ed.), *Ethical issues and social dilemmas in knowledge management: Organizational innovation* (pp. 1–16). Hershey, PA: Information Science Reference; doi:10.4018/978-1-61520-873-9.ch001

Murphy, P. (2013). Systems of communication: Information, explanation, and imagination. In G. Yang (Ed.), *Multidisciplinary studies in knowledge and systems science* (pp. 63–78). Hershey, PA: Information Science Reference; doi:10.4018/978-1-4666-3998-0.ch006

Nach, H. (2013). Structuring knowledge for enterprise resource planning implementation through an ontology. In M. Nazir Ahmad, R. Colomb, & M. Abdullah (Eds.), *Ontology-based applications for enterprise systems and knowledge management* (pp. 25–42). Hershey, PA: Information Science Reference; doi:10.4018/978-1-4666-1993-7.ch002

Nah, F. F., Hong, W., Chen, L., & Lee, H. (2010). Information search patterns in e-commerce product comparison services. [JDM]. *Journal of Database Management*, 21(2), 26–40. doi:10.4018/jdm.2010040102

Nah, F. F., Hong, W., Chen, L., & Lee, H. (2012). Information search patterns in e-commerce product comparison services. In K. Siau (Ed.), *Cross-disciplinary models and applications of database management: Advancing approaches* (pp. 131–145). Hershey, PA: Information Science Reference; doi:10.4018/978-1-61350-471-0.ch006

Natarajan, R., & Shekar, B. (2011). Knowledge patterns in databases. In D. Schwartz & D. Te'eni (Eds.), *Encyclopedia of knowledge management* (2nd ed., pp. 842–852). Hershey, PA: Information Science Reference; doi:10.4018/978-1-59904-931-1.ch081

Nelson, R. E., & Hsu, H. S. (2011). A social network perspective on knowledge management. In D. Schwartz & D. Te'eni (Eds.), *Encyclopedia of knowledge management* (2nd ed., pp. 1470–1478). Hershey, PA: Information Science Reference; doi:10.4018/978-1-59904-931-1.ch140

Related References

Neto, R. C., & Souza, R. R. (2010). Knowledge management as an organizational process: From a theoretical framework to implementation guidelines. In E. O'Brien, S. Clifford, & M. Southern (Eds.), *Knowledge management for process, organizational and marketing innovation: Tools and methods* (pp. 16–35). Hershey, PA: Information Science Reference; doi:10.4018/978-1-61520-829-6.ch002

Newell, S. (2011). Understanding innovation processes. In D. Schwartz & D. Te'eni (Eds.), *Encyclopedia of knowledge management* (2nd ed., pp. 1525–1535). Hershey, PA: Information Science Reference; doi:10.4018/978-1-59904-931-1.ch145

Nikabadi, M. S., & Zamanloo, S. (2012). A multidimensional structure for describing the influence of supply chain strategies, business strategies, and knowledge management strategies on knowledge sharing in supply chain. [IJKM]. *International Journal of Knowledge Management, 8*(4), 50–70. doi:10.4018/jkm.2012100103

Nissen, M. (2014). Cyberspace and cloud knowledge. In *Harnessing dynamic knowledge principles in the technology-driven world* (pp. 193–204). Hershey, PA: Information Science Reference; doi:10.4018/978-1-4666-4727-5.ch012

Nissen, M. (2014). Social media knowledge. In *Harnessing dynamic knowledge principles in the technology-driven world* (pp. 219–227). Hershey, PA: Information Science Reference; doi:10.4018/978-1-4666-4727-5.ch014

Nissen, M. E. (2014). Harnessing knowledge power for competitive advantage. In M. Chilton & J. Bloodgood (Eds.), *Knowledge management and competitive advantage: Issues and potential solutions* (pp. 20–34). Hershey, PA: Information Science Reference; doi:10.4018/978-1-4666-4679-7.ch002

Nissen, M. E., & Levitt, R. E. (2011). Knowledge management research through computational experimentation. In D. Schwartz & D. Te'eni (Eds.), *Encyclopedia of knowledge management* (2nd ed., pp. 728–737). Hershey, PA: Information Science Reference; doi:10.4018/978-1-59904-931-1.ch071

Nisula, A. (2014). Developing organizational renewal capability in the municipal (city) organization. In Y. Al-Bastaki & A. Shajera (Eds.), *Building a competitive public sector with knowledge management strategy* (pp. 151–172). Hershey, PA: Business Science Reference; doi:10.4018/978-1-4666-4434-2.ch007

Niu, B., Martin, P., & Powley, W. (2011). Towards autonomic workload management in DBMSs. In K. Siau (Ed.), *Theoretical and practical advances in information systems development: Emerging trends and approaches* (pp. 154–173). Hershey, PA: Information Science Reference; doi:10.4018/978-1-60960-521-6.ch008

Nobre, F. S., & Walker, D. S. (2011). A dynamic ability-based view of the organization. [IJKM]. *International Journal of Knowledge Management, 7*(2), 86–101. doi:10.4018/jkm.2011040105

O'Brien, J. (2014). Lessons from the private sector: A framework to be adopted in the public sector. In Y. Al-Bastaki & A. Shajera (Eds.), *Building a competitive public sector with knowledge management strategy* (pp. 173–198). Hershey, PA: Business Science Reference; doi:10.4018/978-1-4666-4434-2.ch008

Omari, A. (2013). Supporting companies management and improving their productivity through mining customers transactions. In *Data mining: Concepts, methodologies, tools, and applications* (pp. 1519–1533). Hershey, PA: Information Science Reference; doi:10.4018/978-1-4666-2455-9.ch079

Onwubiko, C. (2014). Modelling situation awareness information and system requirements for the mission using goal-oriented task analysis approach. In *Software design and development: Concepts, methodologies, tools, and applications* (pp. 460–478). Hershey, PA: Information Science Reference; doi:10.4018/978-1-4666-4301-7.ch023

Orth, A., Smolnik, S., & Jennex, M. E. (2011). The relevance of integration for knowledge management success: Towards conceptual and empirical evidence. In M. Jennex & S. Smolnik (Eds.), *Strategies for knowledge management success: Exploring organizational efficacy* (pp. 238–261). Hershey, PA: Information Science Reference; doi:10.4018/978-1-60566-709-6.ch013

Othman, A. K., & Abdullah, H. S. (2011). The influence of emotional intelligence on tacit knowledge sharing in service organizations. In M. Al-Shammari (Ed.), *Knowledge management in emerging economies: Social, organizational and cultural implementation* (pp. 171–185). Hershey, PA: Information Science Reference; doi:10.4018/978-1-61692-886-5.ch010

Pagallo, U. (2011). The trouble with digital copies: A short KM phenomenology. In G. Morais da Costa (Ed.), *Ethical issues and social dilemmas in knowledge management: Organizational innovation* (pp. 97–112). Hershey, PA: Information Science Reference; doi:10.4018/978-1-61520-873-9.ch007

Palte, R., Hertlein, M., Smolnik, S., & Riempp, G. (2013). The effects of a KM strategy on KM performance in professional services firms. In M. Jennex (Ed.), *Dynamic models for knowledge-driven organizations* (pp. 16–35). Hershey, PA: Business Science Reference; doi:10.4018/978-1-4666-2485-6.ch002

Pańkowska, M. (2014). Information technology prosumption acceptance by business information system consultants. In M. Pańkowska (Ed.), *Frameworks of IT prosumption for business development* (pp. 119–141). Hershey, PA: Business Science Reference; doi:10.4018/978-1-4666-4313-0.ch009

Pankowski, T. (2011). Pattern-based schema mapping and query answering in peer-to-peer XML data integration system. In L. Yan & Z. Ma (Eds.), *Advanced database query systems: Techniques, applications and technologies* (pp. 221–246). Hershey, PA: Information Science Reference; doi:10.4018/978-1-60960-475-2.ch009

Papoutsakis, H. (2010). New product development based on knowledge creation and technology education. In E. O'Brien, S. Clifford, & M. Southern (Eds.), *Knowledge management for process, organizational and marketing innovation: Tools and methods* (pp. 148–163). Hershey, PA: Information Science Reference; doi:10.4018/978-1-61520-829-6.ch009

Paquette, S. (2011). Applying knowledge management in the environmental and climate change sciences. In D. Schwartz & D. Te'eni (Eds.), *Encyclopedia of knowledge management* (2nd ed., pp. 20–26). Hershey, PA: Information Science Reference; doi:10.4018/978-1-59904-931-1.ch003

Paquette, S. (2011). Customer knowledge management. In D. Schwartz & D. Te'eni (Eds.), *Encyclopedia of knowledge management* (2nd ed., pp. 175–184). Hershey, PA: Information Science Reference; doi:10.4018/978-1-59904-931-1.ch017

Parker, K. R., & Nitse, P. S. (2011). Competitive intelligence gathering. In D. Schwartz & D. Te'eni (Eds.), *Encyclopedia of knowledge management* (2nd ed., pp. 103–111). Hershey, PA: Information Science Reference; doi:10.4018/978-1-59904-931-1.ch011

Related References

Páscoa, C., & Tribolet, J. (2014). Maintaining organizational viability and performance: The organizational configuration map. In G. Jamil, A. Malheiro, & F. Ribeiro (Eds.), *Rethinking the conceptual base for new practical applications in information value and quality* (pp. 266–283). Hershey, PA: Information Science Reference; doi:10.4018/978-1-4666-4562-2.ch012

Paukert, M., Niederée, C., & Hemmje, M. (2011). Knowledge in innovation processes. In D. Schwartz & D. Te'eni (Eds.), *Encyclopedia of knowledge management* (2nd ed., pp. 570–580). Hershey, PA: Information Science Reference; doi:10.4018/978-1-59904-931-1.ch055

Pawlak, P. (2011). Global "knowledge management" in humanist perspective. In G. Morais da Costa (Ed.), Ethical issues and social dilemmas in knowledge management: Organizational innovation (pp. 45-62). Hershey, PA: Information Science Reference. doi:10.4018/978-1-61520-873-9.ch004

Perry, M. (2013). Strategic knowledge management: A university application. In S. Buckley & M. Jakovljevic (Eds.), *Knowledge management innovations for interdisciplinary education: Organizational applications* (pp. 132–144). Hershey, PA: Information Science Reference; doi:10.4018/978-1-4666-1969-2.ch007

Pessoa, C. R., Silva, U. P., & Cruz, C. H. (2014). Information management in industrial areas: A knowledge management view. In G. Jamil, A. Malheiro, & F. Ribeiro (Eds.), *Rethinking the conceptual base for new practical applications in information value and quality* (pp. 378–395). Hershey, PA: Information Science Reference; doi:10.4018/978-1-4666-4562-2.ch017

Peter, H., & Greenidge, C. (2011). An ontology-based extraction framework for a semantic web application. [IJKBO]. *International Journal of Knowledge-Based Organizations, 1*(3), 56–71. doi:10.4018/ijkbo.2011070104

Peter, H., & Greenidge, C. (2013). An ontology-based extraction framework for a semantic web application. In J. Wang (Ed.), *Intelligence methods and systems advancements for knowledge-based business* (pp. 231–246). Hershey, PA: Information Science Reference; doi:10.4018/978-1-4666-1873-2.ch013

Pham, Q. T., & Hara, Y. (2011). KM approach for improving the labor productivity of Vietnamese enterprise. [IJKM]. *International Journal of Knowledge Management, 7*(3), 27–42. doi:10.4018/jkm.2011070103

Pham, Q. T., & Hara, Y. (2013). KM approach for improving the labor productivity of Vietnamese enterprise. In M. Jennex (Ed.), *Dynamic models for knowledge-driven organizations* (pp. 206–219). Hershey, PA: Business Science Reference; doi:10.4018/978-1-4666-2485-6.ch012

Philpott, E., & Beaumont-Kerridge, J. (2010). Overcoming reticence to aid knowledge creation between universities and business: A case reviewed. In D. Harorimana (Ed.), *Cultural implications of knowledge sharing, management and transfer: Identifying competitive advantage* (pp. 355–368). Hershey, PA: Information Science Reference; doi:10.4018/978-1-60566-790-4.ch016

Pike, S., & Roos, G. (2011). Measuring and valuing knowledge-based intangible assets: Real business uses. In B. Vallejo-Alonso, A. Rodriguez-Castellanos, & G. Arregui-Ayastuy (Eds.), *Identifying, measuring, and valuing knowledge-based intangible assets: New perspectives* (pp. 268–293). Hershey, PA: Business Science Reference; doi:10.4018/978-1-60960-054-9.ch013

Pineda, J. L., Zapata, L. E., & Ramírez, J. (2010). Strengthening knowledge transfer between the university and enterprise: A conceptual model for collaboration. In D. Harorimana (Ed.), *Cultural implications of knowledge sharing, management and transfer: Identifying competitive advantage* (pp. 134–151). Hershey, PA: Information Science Reference; doi:10.4018/978-1-60566-790-4.ch007

Platonov, V., & Bergman, J. (2013). Cross-border cooperative network in the perspective of innovation dynamics. In J. Wang (Ed.), *Intelligence methods and systems advancements for knowledge-based business* (pp. 150–169). Hershey, PA: Information Science Reference; doi:10.4018/978-1-4666-1873-2.ch009

Poels, G. (2013). Understanding business domain models: The effect of recognizing resource-event-agent conceptual modeling structures. In K. Siau (Ed.), *Innovations in database design, web applications, and information systems management* (pp. 72–106). Hershey, PA: Information Science Reference; doi:10.4018/978-1-4666-2044-5.ch004

Poels, G., Decreus, K., Roelens, B., & Snoeck, M. (2013). Investigating goal-oriented requirements engineering for business processes. [JDM]. *Journal of Database Management*, 24(2), 35–71. doi:10.4018/jdm.2013040103

Pomares-Quimbaya, A., & Torres-Moreno, M. E. (2013). Knowledge management processes supported by ontology technologies. In M. Nazir Ahmad, R. Colomb, & M. Abdullah (Eds.), *Ontology-based applications for enterprise systems and knowledge management* (pp. 125–140). Hershey, PA: Information Science Reference; doi:10.4018/978-1-4666-1993-7.ch007

Ponis, S. T., Vagenas, G., & Koronis, E. (2010). Exploring the knowledge management landscape: A critical review of existing knowledge management frameworks. In D. Harorimana (Ed.), *Cultural implications of knowledge sharing, management and transfer: Identifying competitive advantage* (pp. 1–25). Hershey, PA: Information Science Reference; doi:10.4018/978-1-60566-790-4.ch001

Powers, S. M., & Salmon, C. (2010). Management of learning space. In D. Wu (Ed.), *Temporal structures in individual time management: Practices to enhance calendar tool design* (pp. 210–219). Hershey, PA: Business Science Reference; doi:10.4018/978-1-60566-776-8.ch015

Pretorius, A. B., & Coetzee, F. P. (2011). Model of a knowledge management support system for choosing intellectual capital assessment methods. In B. Vallejo-Alonso, A. Rodriguez-Castellanos, & G. Arregui-Ayastuy (Eds.), *Identifying, measuring, and valuing knowledge-based intangible assets: New perspectives* (pp. 336–359). Hershey, PA: Business Science Reference; doi:10.4018/978-1-60960-054-9.ch016

Pullinger, D. (2011). Mobilizing knowledge in the UK public sector: Current issues and discourse. In G. Morais da Costa (Ed.), *Ethical issues and social dilemmas in knowledge management: Organizational innovation* (pp. 232–249). Hershey, PA: Information Science Reference; doi:10.4018/978-1-61520-873-9.ch014

Rabaey, M. (2013). Complex adaptive systems thinking approach for intelligence base in support of intellectual capital management. In P. Ordóñez de Pablos, R. Tennyson, & J. Zhao (Eds.), *Intellectual capital strategy management for knowledge-based organizations* (pp. 122–141). Hershey, PA: Business Science Reference; doi:10.4018/978-1-4666-3655-2.ch007

Related References

Rabaey, M., & Mercken, R. (2013). Framework of knowledge and intelligence base: From intelligence to service. In *Data mining: Concepts, methodologies, tools, and applications* (pp. 474–502). Hershey, PA: Information Science Reference; doi:10.4018/978-1-4666-2455-9.ch023

Radziwill, N. M., & DuPlain, R. F. (2010). Quality and continuous improvement in knowledge management. In M. Russ (Ed.), *Knowledge management strategies for business development* (pp. 353–363). Hershey, PA: Business Science Reference; doi:10.4018/978-1-60566-348-7.ch017

Rahman, B. A., Saad, N. M., & Harun, M. S. (2010). Knowledge management orientation and business performance: The Malaysian manufacturing and service industries perspective. In K. Metaxiotis, F. Carrillo, & T. Yigitcanlar (Eds.), *Knowledge-based development for cities and societies: Integrated multi-level approaches* (pp. 315–328). Hershey, PA: Information Science Reference; doi:10.4018/978-1-61520-721-3.ch019

Randles, T. J., Blades, C. D., & Fadlalla, A. (2012). The knowledge spectrum. [IJKM]. *International Journal of Knowledge Management*, 8(2), 65–78. doi:10.4018/jkm.2012040104

Real, J. C., Leal, A., & Roldan, J. L. (2011). Measuring organizational learning as a multidimensional construct. In D. Schwartz & D. Te'eni (Eds.), *Encyclopedia of knowledge management* (2nd ed., pp. 1101–1109). Hershey, PA: Information Science Reference; doi:10.4018/978-1-59904-931-1.ch105

Rech, J., & Bogner, C. (2010). Qualitative analysis of semantically enabled knowledge management systems in agile software engineering. [IJKM]. *International Journal of Knowledge Management*, 6(2), 66–85. doi:10.4018/jkm.2010040104

Rech, J., & Bogner, C. (2012). Qualitative analysis of semantically enabled knowledge management systems in agile software engineering. In M. Jennex (Ed.), *Conceptual models and outcomes of advancing knowledge management: New technologies* (pp. 144–164). Hershey, PA: Information Science Reference; doi:10.4018/978-1-4666-0035-5.ch008

Reis, R. S., & Curzi, Y. (2011). Knowledge integration in the creative process of globally distributed teams. In M. Al-Shammari (Ed.), *Knowledge management in emerging economies: Social, organizational and cultural implementation* (pp. 47–65). Hershey, PA: Information Science Reference; doi:10.4018/978-1-61692-886-5.ch003

Remli, M. A., & Deris, S. (2013). An approach for biological data integration and knowledge retrieval based on ontology, semantic web services composition, and AI planning. In M. Nazir Ahmad, R. Colomb, & M. Abdullah (Eds.), *Ontology-based applications for enterprise systems and knowledge management* (pp. 324–342). Hershey, PA: Information Science Reference; doi:10.4018/978-1-4666-1993-7.ch018

Reychav, I., Stein, E. W., Weisberg, J., & Glezer, C. (2012). The role of knowledge sharing in raising the task innovativeness of systems analysts. [IJKM]. *International Journal of Knowledge Management*, 8(2), 1–22. doi:10.4018/jkm.2012040101

Reychav, I., & Weisberg, J. (2011). Human capital in knowledge creation, management, and utilization. In D. Schwartz & D. Te'eni (Eds.), *Encyclopedia of knowledge management* (2nd ed., pp. 389–401). Hershey, PA: Information Science Reference; doi:10.4018/978-1-59904-931-1.ch037

Rhoads, E., O'Sullivan, K. J., & Stankosky, M. (2011). An evaluation of factors that influence the success of knowledge management practices in US federal agencies. In M. Jennex & S. Smolnik (Eds.), *Strategies for knowledge management success: Exploring organizational efficacy* (pp. 74–90). Hershey, PA: Information Science Reference; doi:10.4018/978-1-60566-709-6.ch005

Ribière, V. M. (2011). The effect of organizational trust on the success of codification and personalization KM approaches. In M. Jennex & S. Smolnik (Eds.), *Strategies for knowledge management success: Exploring organizational efficacy* (pp. 192–212). Hershey, PA: Information Science Reference; doi:10.4018/978-1-60566-709-6.ch011

Ribière, V. M., & Román, J. A. (2011). Knowledge flow. In D. Schwartz & D. Te'eni (Eds.), *Encyclopedia of knowledge management* (2nd ed., pp. 549–559). Hershey, PA: Information Science Reference; doi:10.4018/978-1-59904-931-1.ch053

Ricceri, F., Guthrie, J., & Coyte, R. (2010). The management of knowledge resources within private organisations: Some European "better practice" illustrations. In E. O'Brien, S. Clifford, & M. Southern (Eds.), *Knowledge management for process, organizational and marketing innovation: Tools and methods* (pp. 36–61). Hershey, PA: Information Science Reference; doi:10.4018/978-1-61520-829-6.ch003

Riss, U. V. (2011). Pattern-based task management as means of organizational knowledge maturing. [IJKBO]. *International Journal of Knowledge-Based Organizations*, *1*(1), 20–41. doi:10.4018/ijkbo.2011010102

Riss, U. V. (2013). Pattern-based task management as means of organizational knowledge maturing. In J. Wang (Ed.), *Intelligence methods and systems advancements for knowledge-based business* (pp. 1–23). Hershey, PA: Information Science Reference; doi:10.4018/978-1-4666-1873-2.ch001

Roos, G. (2013). The role of intellectual capital in business model innovation: An empirical study. In P. Ordóñez de Pablos, R. Tennyson, & J. Zhao (Eds.), *Intellectual capital strategy management for knowledge-based organizations* (pp. 76–121). Hershey, PA: Business Science Reference; doi:10.4018/978-1-4666-3655-2.ch006

Rothberg, H. N., & Klingenberg, B. (2010). Learning before doing: A theoretical perspective and practical lessons from a failed cross-border knowledge transfer initiative. In D. Harorimana (Ed.), *Cultural implications of knowledge sharing, management and transfer: Identifying competitive advantage* (pp. 277–294). Hershey, PA: Information Science Reference; doi:10.4018/978-1-60566-790-4.ch013

Ruano-Mayoral, M., Colomo-Palacios, R., García-Crespo, Á., & Gómez-Berbís, J. M. (2012). Software project managers under the team software process: A study of competences based on literature. In J. Wang (Ed.), *Project management techniques and innovations in information technology* (pp. 115–126). Hershey, PA: Information Science Reference; doi:10.4018/978-1-4666-0930-3.ch007

Russell, S. (2010). Knowledge management and project management in 3D: A virtual world extension. In E. O'Brien, S. Clifford, & M. Southern (Eds.), *Knowledge management for process, organizational and marketing innovation: Tools and methods* (pp. 62–78). Hershey, PA: Information Science Reference; doi:10.4018/978-1-61520-829-6.ch004

Related References

Ryan, G., & Shinnick, E. (2011). Knowledge and intellectual property rights: An economics perspective. In D. Schwartz & D. Te'eni (Eds.), *Encyclopedia of knowledge management* (2nd ed., pp. 489–496). Hershey, PA: Information Science Reference; doi:10.4018/978-1-59904-931-1.ch047

Sabetzadeh, F., & Tsui, E. (2013). Delivering knowledge services in the cloud. In G. Yang (Ed.), *Multidisciplinary studies in knowledge and systems science* (pp. 247–254). Hershey, PA: Information Science Reference; doi:10.4018/978-1-4666-3998-0.ch017

Sáenz, J., & Aramburu, N. (2011). Organizational conditions as catalysts for successful people-focused knowledge sharing initiatives: An empirical study. [IJKBO]. *International Journal of Knowledge-Based Organizations*, *1*(2), 39–56. doi:10.4018/ijkbo.2011040103

Sáenz, J., & Aramburu, N. (2013). Organizational conditions as catalysts for successful people-focused knowledge sharing initiatives: An empirical study. In J. Wang (Ed.), *Intelligence methods and systems advancements for knowledge-based business* (pp. 263–280). Hershey, PA: Information Science Reference; doi:10.4018/978-1-4666-1873-2.ch015

Sakr, S., & Al-Naymat, G. (2011). Relational techniques for storing and querying RDF data: An overview. In L. Yan & Z. Ma (Eds.), *Advanced database query systems: Techniques, applications and technologies* (pp. 269–285). Hershey, PA: Information Science Reference; doi:10.4018/978-1-60960-475-2.ch011

Salem, P. J. (2013). The use of mixed methods in organizational communication research. In M. Bocarnea, R. Reynolds, & J. Baker (Eds.), *Online instruments, data collection, and electronic measurements: Organizational advancements* (pp. 24–39). Hershey, PA: Information Science Reference; doi:10.4018/978-1-4666-2172-5.ch002

Salisbury, M. (2011). A framework for managing the life cycle of knowledge in global organizations. In M. Jennex (Ed.), *Global aspects and cultural perspectives on knowledge management: Emerging dimensions* (pp. 64–80). Hershey, PA: Information Science Reference; doi:10.4018/978-1-60960-555-1.ch005

Salleh, K. (2014). Drivers, benefits, and challenges of knowledge management in electronic government: Preliminary examination. In Y. Al-Bastaki & A. Shajera (Eds.), *Building a competitive public sector with knowledge management strategy* (pp. 135–150). Hershey, PA: Business Science Reference; doi:10.4018/978-1-4666-4434-2.ch006

Salleh, K., Ikhsan, S. O., & Ahmad, S. N. (2011). Knowledge management enablers and knowledge sharing process: A case study of public sector accounting organization in Malaysia. In M. Al-Shammari (Ed.), *Knowledge management in emerging economies: Social, organizational and cultural implementation* (pp. 199–211). Hershey, PA: Information Science Reference; doi:10.4018/978-1-61692-886-5.ch012

Saunders, C. (2011). Knowledge sharing in legal practice. In D. Schwartz & D. Te'eni (Eds.), *Encyclopedia of knowledge management* (2nd ed., pp. 935–945). Hershey, PA: Information Science Reference; doi:10.4018/978-1-59904-931-1.ch089

Scarso, E., & Bolisani, E. (2011). Knowledge intermediation. In D. Schwartz & D. Te'eni (Eds.), *Encyclopedia of knowledge management* (2nd ed., pp. 601–611). Hershey, PA: Information Science Reference; doi:10.4018/978-1-59904-931-1.ch058

Scarso, E., & Bolisani, E. (2011). Managing professions for knowledge management. [IJKM]. *International Journal of Knowledge Management, 7*(3), 61–75. doi:10.4018/jkm.2011070105

Scarso, E., & Bolisani, E. (2013). Managing professions for knowledge management. In M. Jennex (Ed.), *Dynamic models for knowledge-driven organizations* (pp. 238–253). Hershey, PA: Business Science Reference; doi:10.4018/978-1-4666-2485-6.ch014

Scarso, E., Bolisani, E., & Padova, A. (2011). The complex issue of measuring KM performance: Lessons from the practice. In B. Vallejo-Alonso, A. Rodriguez-Castellanos, & G. Arregui-Ayastuy (Eds.), *Identifying, measuring, and valuing knowledge-based intangible assets: New perspectives* (pp. 208–230). Hershey, PA: Business Science Reference; doi:10.4018/978-1-60960-054-9.ch010

Schumann, C., & Tittmann, C. (2010). Potentials for externalizing and measuring of tacit knowledge within knowledge nodes in the context of knowledge networks. In D. Harorimana (Ed.), *Cultural implications of knowledge sharing, management and transfer: Identifying competitive advantage* (pp. 84–107). Hershey, PA: Information Science Reference; doi:10.4018/978-1-60566-790-4.ch005

Schwartz, D. (2011). An Aristotelian view of knowledge for knowledge management. In D. Schwartz & D. Te'eni (Eds.), *Encyclopedia of knowledge management* (2nd ed., pp. 39–48). Hershey, PA: Information Science Reference; doi:10.4018/978-1-59904-931-1.ch005

Senaratne, S., & Victoria, M. F. (2014). Building a supportive culture for sustained organisational learning in public sectors. In Y. Al-Bastaki & A. Shajera (Eds.), *Building a competitive public sector with knowledge management strategy* (pp. 118–134). Hershey, PA: Business Science Reference; doi:10.4018/978-1-4666-4434-2.ch005

Shah, A., Singhera, Z., & Ahsan, S. (2011). Web services for bioinformatics. In M. Al-Mutairi & L. Mohammed (Eds.), *Cases on ICT utilization, practice and solutions: Tools for managing day-to-day issues* (pp. 28–46). Hershey, PA: Information Science Reference; doi:10.4018/978-1-60960-015-0.ch003

Shajera, A., & Al-Bastaki, Y. (2014). Organisational readiness for knowledge management: Bahrain public sector case study. In Y. Al-Bastaki & A. Shajera (Eds.), *Building a competitive public sector with knowledge management strategy* (pp. 104–117). Hershey, PA: Business Science Reference; doi:10.4018/978-1-4666-4434-2.ch004

Sharma, A. K., Goswami, A., & Gupta, D. (2011). An extended relational model & SQL for fuzzy multidatabases. In L. Yan & Z. Ma (Eds.), *Advanced database query systems: Techniques, applications and technologies* (pp. 185–219). Hershey, PA: Information Science Reference; doi:10.4018/978-1-60960-475-2.ch008

Sharma, R., Banati, H., & Bedi, P. (2012). Building socially-aware e-learning systems through knowledge management. [IJKM]. *International Journal of Knowledge Management, 8*(3), 1–26. doi:10.4018/jkm.2012070101

Sharma, R. S., Chandrasekar, G., & Vaitheeswaran, B. (2012). A knowledge framework for development: Empirical investigation of 30 societies. In M. Jennex (Ed.), *Conceptual models and outcomes of advancing knowledge management: New technologies* (pp. 244–265). Hershey, PA: Information Science Reference; doi:10.4018/978-1-4666-0035-5.ch013

Shaw, D. (2011). Mapping group knowledge. In D. Schwartz & D. Te'eni (Eds.), *Encyclopedia of knowledge management* (2nd ed., pp. 1072–1081). Hershey, PA: Information Science Reference; doi:10.4018/978-1-59904-931-1.ch102

Sheluhin, O. I., & Atayero, A. A. (2013). Principles of modeling in information communication systems and networks. In A. Atayero & O. Sheluhin (Eds.), *Integrated models for information communication systems and networks: Design and development* (pp. 1–15). Hershey, PA: Information Science Reference; doi:10.4018/978-1-4666-2208-1.ch001

Sheluhin, O. I., & Garmashev, A. V. (2013). Numerical methods of multifractal analysis in information communication systems and networks. In A. Atayero & O. Sheluhin (Eds.), *Integrated models for information communication systems and networks: Design and development* (pp. 16–46). Hershey, PA: Information Science Reference; doi:10.4018/978-1-4666-2208-1.ch002

Siau, K., Long, Y., & Ling, M. (2010). Toward a unified model of information systems development success. [JDM]. *Journal of Database Management, 21*(1), 80–101. doi:10.4018/jdm.2010112304

Siau, K., Long, Y., & Ling, M. (2012). Toward a unified model of information systems development success. In K. Siau (Ed.), *Cross-disciplinary models and applications of database management: Advancing approaches* (pp. 80–102). Hershey, PA: Information Science Reference; doi:10.4018/978-1-61350-471-0.ch004

Simard, A. J., & Jourdeuil, P. (2014). Knowledge manageability: A new paradigm. In Y. Al-Bastaki & A. Shajera (Eds.), *Building a competitive public sector with knowledge management strategy* (pp. 1–52). Hershey, PA: Business Science Reference; doi:10.4018/978-1-4666-4434-2.ch001

Simonette, M. J., & Spina, E. (2014). Enabling IT innovation through soft systems engineering. In M. Pańkowska (Ed.), *Frameworks of IT prosumption for business development* (pp. 64–72). Hershey, PA: Business Science Reference; doi:10.4018/978-1-4666-4313-0.ch005

Sivaramakrishnan, S., Delbaere, M., Zhang, D., & Bruning, E. (2012). Critical success factors and outcomes of market knowledge management: A conceptual model and empirical evidence. In M. Jennex (Ed.), *Conceptual models and outcomes of advancing knowledge management: New technologies* (pp. 165–185). Hershey, PA: Information Science Reference; doi:10.4018/978-1-4666-0035-5.ch009

Small, C. T., & Sage, A. P. (2010). A complex adaptive systems-based enterprise knowledge sharing model. In D. Paradice (Ed.), *Emerging systems approaches in information technologies: Concepts, theories, and applications* (pp. 137–155). Hershey, PA: Information Science Reference; doi:10.4018/978-1-60566-976-2.ch009

Smedlund, A. (2011). Social network structures for explicit, tacit and potential knowledge. In M. Jennex (Ed.), *Global aspects and cultural perspectives on knowledge management: Emerging dimensions* (pp. 81–90). Hershey, PA: Information Science Reference; doi:10.4018/978-1-60960-555-1.ch006

Smith, A. D. (2013). Competitive uses of information and knowledge management tools: Case study of supplier-side management. [IJKBO]. *International Journal of Knowledge-Based Organizations, 3*(1), 71–87. doi:10.4018/ijkbo.2013010105

Smith, P., & Coakes, E. (2011). Exploiting KM in support of innovation and change. In A. Eardley & L. Uden (Eds.), *Innovative knowledge management: Concepts for organizational creativity and collaborative design* (pp. 242–252). Hershey, PA: Information Science Reference; doi:10.4018/978-1-60566-701-0.ch015

Smith, T. A., Mills, A. M., & Dion, P. (2010). Linking business strategy and knowledge management capabilities for organizational effectiveness. [IJKM]. *International Journal of Knowledge Management*, 6(3), 22–43. doi:10.4018/jkm.2010070102

Smith, T. A., Mills, A. M., & Dion, P. (2012). Linking business strategy and knowledge management capabilities for organizational effectiveness. In M. Jennex (Ed.), *Conceptual models and outcomes of advancing knowledge management: New technologies* (pp. 186–207). Hershey, PA: Information Science Reference; doi:10.4018/978-1-4666-0035-5.ch010

Smuts, H., van der Merwe, A., & Loock, M. (2011). Key characteristics relevant for selecting knowledge management software tools. In A. Eardley & L. Uden (Eds.), *Innovative knowledge management: Concepts for organizational creativity and collaborative design* (pp. 18–39). Hershey, PA: Information Science Reference; doi:10.4018/978-1-60566-701-0.ch002

Soffer, P., & Kaner, M. (2013). Complementing business process verification by validity analysis: A theoretical and empirical evaluation. In K. Siau (Ed.), *Innovations in database design, web applications, and information systems management* (pp. 265–288). Hershey, PA: Information Science Reference; doi:10.4018/978-1-4666-2044-5.ch010

Soffer, P., Kaner, M., & Wand, Y. (2012). Assigning ontological meaning to workflow nets. In K. Siau (Ed.), *Cross-disciplinary models and applications of database management: Advancing approaches* (pp. 209–244). Hershey, PA: Information Science Reference; doi:10.4018/978-1-61350-471-0.ch009

Sohrabi, B., Raeesi, I., & Khanlari, A. (2010). Intellectual capital components, measurement and management: A literature survey of concepts and measures. In P. López Sáez, G. Castro, J. Navas López, & M. Delgado Verde (Eds.), *Intellectual capital and technological innovation: Knowledge-based theory and practice* (pp. 1–38). Hershey, PA: Information Science Reference; doi:10.4018/978-1-61520-875-3.ch001

Sohrabi, B., Raeesi, I., Khanlari, A., & Forouzandeh, S. (2011). A comprehensive model for assessing the organizational readiness of knowledge management. In M. Jennex (Ed.), *Global aspects and cultural perspectives on knowledge management: Emerging dimensions* (pp. 30–48). Hershey, PA: Information Science Reference; doi:10.4018/978-1-60960-555-1.ch003

Sparrow, J. (2011). Knowledge management in small and medium sized enterprises. In D. Schwartz & D. Te'eni (Eds.), *Encyclopedia of knowledge management* (2nd ed., pp. 671–681). Hershey, PA: Information Science Reference; doi:10.4018/978-1-59904-931-1.ch065

Stam, C. D. (2011). Making sense of knowledge productivity. In B. Vallejo-Alonso, A. Rodriguez-Castellanos, & G. Arregui-Ayastuy (Eds.), *Identifying, measuring, and valuing knowledge-based intangible assets: New perspectives* (pp. 133–155). Hershey, PA: Business Science Reference; doi:10.4018/978-1-60960-054-9.ch007

Related References

Stamkopoulos, K., Pitoura, E., Vassiliadis, P., & Zarras, A. (2012). Accelerating web service workflow execution via intelligent allocation of services to servers. In K. Siau (Ed.), *Cross-disciplinary models and applications of database management: Advancing approaches* (pp. 385–416). Hershey, PA: Information Science Reference; doi:10.4018/978-1-61350-471-0.ch016

Sterling, L. (2011). Applying agents within knowledge management. In D. Schwartz & D. Te'eni (Eds.), *Encyclopedia of knowledge management* (2nd ed., pp. 12–19). Hershey, PA: Information Science Reference; doi:10.4018/978-1-59904-931-1.ch002

Su, S., & Chiong, R. (2011). Business intelligence. In D. Schwartz & D. Te'eni (Eds.), *Encyclopedia of knowledge management* (2nd ed., pp. 72–80). Hershey, PA: Information Science Reference; doi:10.4018/978-1-59904-931-1.ch008

Su, W. B., Li, X., & Chow, C. W. (2012). Exploring the extent and impediments of knowledge sharing in Chinese business enterprise. In M. Jennex (Ed.), *Conceptual models and outcomes of advancing knowledge management: New technologies* (pp. 266–290). Hershey, PA: Information Science Reference; doi:10.4018/978-1-4666-0035-5.ch014

Subramanian, D. V., & Geetha, A. (2012). Application of multi-dimensional metric model, database, and WAM for KM system evaluation. [IJKM]. *International Journal of Knowledge Management*, 8(4), 1–21. doi:10.4018/jkm.2012100101

Surendran, A., & Samuel, P. (2013). Knowledge-based code clone approach in embedded and real-time systems. In S. Saeed & I. Alsmadi (Eds.), *Knowledge-based processes in software development* (pp. 49–62). Hershey, PA: Information Science Reference; doi:10.4018/978-1-4666-4229-4.ch004

Takahashi, Y. (2011). The importance of balancing knowledge protection and knowledge interchange. In G. Morais da Costa (Ed.), *Ethical issues and social dilemmas in knowledge management: Organizational innovation* (pp. 180–198). Hershey, PA: Information Science Reference; doi:10.4018/978-1-61520-873-9.ch011

Talet, A. N., Alhawari, S., & Alryalat, H. (2012). The outcome of knowledge process for customers of Jordanian companies on the achievement of customer knowledge retention. In M. Jennex (Ed.), *Conceptual models and outcomes of advancing knowledge management: New technologies* (pp. 45–61). Hershey, PA: Information Science Reference; doi:10.4018/978-1-4666-0035-5.ch003

Talet, A. N., Alhawari, S., Mansour, E., & Alryalat, H. (2011). The practice of Jordanian business to attain customer knowledge acquisition. [IJKM]. *International Journal of Knowledge Management*, 7(2), 49–67. doi:10.4018/jkm.2011040103

Tanner, K. (2011). The role of emotional capital in organisational KM. In D. Schwartz & D. Te'eni (Eds.), *Encyclopedia of knowledge management* (2nd ed., pp. 1396–1409). Hershey, PA: Information Science Reference; doi:10.4018/978-1-59904-931-1.ch133

Tauber, D., & Schwartz, D. G. (2011). Integrating knowledge management with the systems analysis process. In D. Schwartz & D. Te'eni (Eds.), *Encyclopedia of knowledge management* (2nd ed., pp. 431–441). Hershey, PA: Information Science Reference; doi:10.4018/978-1-59904-931-1.ch041

Tavana, M., Busch, T. E., & Davis, E. L. (2011). Modeling operational robustness and resiliency with high-level Petri nets. [IJKBO]. *International Journal of Knowledge-Based Organizations, 1*(2), 17–38. doi:10.4018/ijkbo.2011040102

Taxén, L. (2010). Aligning business and knowledge strategies: A practical approach for aligning business and knowledge strategies. In M. Russ (Ed.), *Knowledge management strategies for business development* (pp. 277–308). Hershey, PA: Business Science Reference; doi:10.4018/978-1-60566-348-7.ch013

Te'eni, D. (2011). Knowledge for communicating knowledge. In D. Schwartz & D. Te'eni (Eds.), *Encyclopedia of knowledge management* (2nd ed., pp. 560–569). Hershey, PA: Information Science Reference; doi:10.4018/978-1-59904-931-1.ch054

Toiviainen, H., & Kerosuo, H. (2013). Development curriculum for knowledge-based organizations: Lessons from a learning network. [IJKBO]. *International Journal of Knowledge-Based Organizations, 3*(3), 1–18. doi:10.4018/ijkbo.2013070101

Tran, B. (2014). The human element of the knowledge worker: Identifying, managing, and protecting the intellectual capital within knowledge management. In M. Chilton & J. Bloodgood (Eds.), *Knowledge management and competitive advantage: Issues and potential solutions* (pp. 281–303). Hershey, PA: Information Science Reference; doi:10.4018/978-1-4666-4679-7.ch017

Tsamoura, E., Gounaris, A., & Manolopoulos, Y. (2011). Optimal service ordering in decentralized queries over web services. [IJKBO]. *International Journal of Knowledge-Based Organizations, 1*(2), 1–16. doi:10.4018/ijkbo.2011040101

Tsamoura, E., Gounaris, A., & Manolopoulos, Y. (2013). Optimal service ordering in decentralized queries over web services. In J. Wang (Ed.), *Intelligence methods and systems advancements for knowledge-based business* (pp. 43–58). Hershey, PA: Information Science Reference; doi:10.4018/978-1-4666-1873-2.ch003

Tull, J. (2013). Slow knowledge: The case for savouring learning and innovation. In S. Buckley & M. Jakovljevic (Eds.), *Knowledge management innovations for interdisciplinary education: Organizational applications* (pp. 274–297). Hershey, PA: Information Science Reference; doi:10.4018/978-1-4666-1969-2.ch014

Turner, G., & Minonne, C. (2013). Effective knowledge management through measurement. In S. Buckley & M. Jakovljevic (Eds.), *Knowledge management innovations for interdisciplinary education: Organizational applications* (pp. 145–176). Hershey, PA: Information Science Reference; doi:10.4018/978-1-4666-1969-2.ch008

Uden, L., & Eardley, A. (2011). Knowledge sharing in the learning process: Experience with problem-based learning. In A. Eardley & L. Uden (Eds.), *Innovative knowledge management: Concepts for organizational creativity and collaborative design* (pp. 215–229). Hershey, PA: Information Science Reference; doi:10.4018/978-1-60566-701-0.ch013

Upadhyaya, S., Rao, H. R., & Padmanabhan, G. (2011). Secure knowledge management. In D. Schwartz & D. Te'eni (Eds.), *Encyclopedia of knowledge management* (2nd ed., pp. 1429–1437). Hershey, PA: Information Science Reference; doi:10.4018/978-1-59904-931-1.ch136

Urbancová, H., & Königová, M. (2013). The influence of the application of business continuity management, knowledge management, and knowledge continuity management on the innovation in organizations. In S. Buckley & M. Jakovljevic (Eds.), *Knowledge management innovations for interdisciplinary education: Organizational applications* (pp. 254–273). Hershey, PA: Information Science Reference; doi:10.4018/978-1-4666-1969-2.ch013

Van Canh, T., & Zyngier, S. (2014). Using ERG theory as a lens to understand the sharing of academic tacit knowledge: Problems and issues in developing countries – Perspectives from Vietnam. In M. Chilton & J. Bloodgood (Eds.), *Knowledge management and competitive advantage: Issues and potential solutions* (pp. 174–201). Hershey, PA: Information Science Reference; doi:10.4018/978-1-4666-4679-7.ch010

Vat, K. H. (2011). Knowledge synthesis framework. In D. Schwartz & D. Te'eni (Eds.), *Encyclopedia of knowledge management* (2nd ed., pp. 955–966). Hershey, PA: Information Science Reference; doi:10.4018/978-1-59904-931-1.ch091

Vert, S. (2012). Extensions of web browsers useful to knowledge workers. In C. Jouis, I. Biskri, J. Ganascia, & M. Roux (Eds.), *Next generation search engines: Advanced models for information retrieval* (pp. 239–273). Hershey, PA: Information Science Reference; doi:10.4018/978-1-4666-0330-1.ch011

Wagner, L., & Van Belle, J. (2011). Web mining for strategic competitive intelligence: South African experiences and a practical methodology. In M. Al-Shammari (Ed.), *Knowledge management in emerging economies: Social, organizational and cultural implementation* (pp. 1–19). Hershey, PA: Information Science Reference; doi:10.4018/978-1-61692-886-5.ch001

Wautelet, Y., Schinckus, C., & Kolp, M. (2010). Towards knowledge evolution in software engineering: An epistemological approach. [IJITSA]. *International Journal of Information Technologies and Systems Approach*, *3*(1), 21–40. doi:10.4018/jitsa.2010100202

Weiß, S., Makolm, J., Ipsmiller, D., & Egger, N. (2011). DYONIPOS: Proactive knowledge supply. In M. Jennex & S. Smolnik (Eds.), *Strategies for knowledge management success: Exploring organizational efficacy* (pp. 277–287). Hershey, PA: Information Science Reference; doi:10.4018/978-1-60566-709-6.ch015

Welschen, J., Todorova, N., & Mills, A. M. (2012). An investigation of the impact of intrinsic motivation on organizational knowledge sharing. [IJKM]. *International Journal of Knowledge Management*, *8*(2), 23–42. doi:10.4018/jkm.2012040102

Wickramasinghe, N. (2011). Knowledge creation. In D. Schwartz & D. Te'eni (Eds.), *Encyclopedia of knowledge management* (2nd ed., pp. 527–538). Hershey, PA: Information Science Reference; doi:10.4018/978-1-59904-931-1.ch051

Wickramasinghe, N. (2011). Knowledge management: The key to delivering superior healthcare solutions. In A. Eardley & L. Uden (Eds.), *Innovative knowledge management: Concepts for organizational creativity and collaborative design* (pp. 190–203). Hershey, PA: Information Science Reference; doi:10.4018/978-1-60566-701-0.ch011

Wijnhoven, F. (2011). Operational knowledge management. In D. Schwartz & D. Te'eni (Eds.), *Encyclopedia of knowledge management* (2nd ed., pp. 1237–1249). Hershey, PA: Information Science Reference; doi:10.4018/978-1-59904-931-1.ch118

Williams, R. (2011). A Knowledge Process Cycle. In D. Schwartz & D. Te'eni (Eds.), *Encyclopedia of knowledge management* (2nd ed., pp. 853–866). Hershey, PA: Information Science Reference; doi:10.4018/978-1-59904-931-1.ch082

Wilson, R. L., Rosen, P. A., & Al-Ahmadi, M. S. (2011). Knowledge structure and data mining techniques. In D. Schwartz & D. Te'eni (Eds.), *Encyclopedia of knowledge management* (2nd ed., pp. 946–954). Hershey, PA: Information Science Reference; doi:10.4018/978-1-59904-931-1.ch090

Wimmer, H., Yoon, V., & Rada, R. (2013). Integrating knowledge sources: An ontological approach. [IJKM]. *International Journal of Knowledge Management*, 9(1), 60–75. doi:10.4018/jkm.2013010104

Woods, S., Poteet, S. R., Kao, A., & Quach, L. (2011). Knowledge dissemination in portals. In D. Schwartz & D. Te'eni (Eds.), *Encyclopedia of knowledge management* (2nd ed., pp. 539–548). Hershey, PA: Information Science Reference; doi:10.4018/978-1-59904-931-1.ch052

Worden, D. (2010). Agile alignment of enterprise execution capabilities with strategy. In M. Russ (Ed.), *Knowledge management strategies for business development* (pp. 45–62). Hershey, PA: Business Science Reference; doi:10.4018/978-1-60566-348-7.ch003

Wu, D. (2010). Who are effective time managers? Bivariate correlation analysis and hypotheses testing. In D. Wu (Ed.), *Temporal structures in individual time management: Practices to enhance calendar tool design* (pp. 116–138). Hershey, PA: Business Science Reference; doi:10.4018/978-1-60566-776-8.ch009

Wu, J., Du, H., Li, X., & Li, P. (2010). Creating and delivering a successful knowledge management strategy. In M. Russ (Ed.), *Knowledge management strategies for business development* (pp. 261–276). Hershey, PA: Business Science Reference; doi:10.4018/978-1-60566-348-7.ch012

Wu, J., Liu, N., & Xuan, Z. (2013). Simulation on knowledge transfer processes from the perspectives of individual's mentality and behavior. In G. Yang (Ed.), *Multidisciplinary studies in knowledge and systems science* (pp. 233–246). Hershey, PA: Information Science Reference; doi:10.4018/978-1-4666-3998-0.ch016

Wu, J., Wang, S., & Pan, D. (2013). Evaluation of technological influence power of enterprises through the enterprise citation network. In G. Yang (Ed.), *Multidisciplinary studies in knowledge and systems science* (pp. 34–44). Hershey, PA: Information Science Reference; doi:10.4018/978-1-4666-3998-0.ch003

Wu, S. T. (2011). Innovation in new technology and knowledge management: Comparative case studies of its evolution during a quarter century of change. In A. Eardley & L. Uden (Eds.), *Innovative knowledge management: Concepts for organizational creativity and collaborative design* (pp. 77–93). Hershey, PA: Information Science Reference; doi:10.4018/978-1-60566-701-0.ch005

Xiao, L., & Pei, Y. (2013). A task context aware physical distribution knowledge service system. In G. Yang (Ed.), *Multidisciplinary studies in knowledge and systems science* (pp. 18–33). Hershey, PA: Information Science Reference; doi:10.4018/978-1-4666-3998-0.ch002

Xu, D., & Wang, H. (2011). Integration of knowledge management and e-learning. In D. Schwartz & D. Te'eni (Eds.), *Encyclopedia of knowledge management* (2nd ed., pp. 442–451). Hershey, PA: Information Science Reference; doi:10.4018/978-1-59904-931-1.ch042

Related References

Yaniv, E., & Schwartz, D. G. (2011). Organizational attention. In D. Schwartz & D. Te'eni (Eds.), *Encyclopedia of knowledge management* (2nd ed., pp. 1270–1279). Hershey, PA: Information Science Reference; doi:10.4018/978-1-59904-931-1.ch121

Yeung, C. L., Cheung, C. F., Wang, W. M., & Tsui, E. (2013). A study of organizational narrative simulation for decision support. In G. Yang (Ed.), *Multidisciplinary studies in knowledge and systems science* (pp. 179–192). Hershey, PA: Information Science Reference; doi:10.4018/978-1-4666-3998-0.ch013

Yigitcanlar, T. (2013). Moving towards a knowledge city? Brisbane's experience in knowledge-based urban development. In J. Wang (Ed.), *Intelligence methods and systems advancements for knowledge-based business* (pp. 114–131). Hershey, PA: Information Science Reference; doi:10.4018/978-1-4666-1873-2.ch007

Yigitcanlar, T., & Martinez-Fernandez, C. (2010). Making space and place for knowledge production: Socio-spatial development of knowledge community precincts. In K. Metaxiotis, F. Carrillo, & T. Yigitcanlar (Eds.), *Knowledge-based development for cities and societies: Integrated multi-level approaches* (pp. 99–117). Hershey, PA: Information Science Reference; doi:10.4018/978-1-61520-721-3.ch006

Yıldırım, A. A., Özdoğan, C., & Watson, D. (2014). Parallel data reduction techniques for big datasets. In W. Hu & N. Kaabouch (Eds.), *Big data management, technologies, and applications* (pp. 72–93). Hershey, PA: Information Science Reference; doi:10.4018/978-1-4666-4699-5.ch004

Yoon, K. S. (2012). Measuring the influence of expertise and epistemic engagement to the practice of knowledge management. [IJKM]. *International Journal of Knowledge Management*, 8(1), 40–70. doi:10.4018/jkm.2012010103

Yusof, Z. M., & Ismail, M. B. (2011). Factors affecting knowledge sharing practice in Malaysia: A preliminary overview. In M. Al-Shammari (Ed.), *Knowledge management in emerging economies: Social, organizational and cultural implementation* (pp. 157–170). Hershey, PA: Information Science Reference; doi:10.4018/978-1-61692-886-5.ch009

Zapata-Cantú, L., Ramírez, J., & Pineda, J. L. (2011). HRM adaptation to knowledge management initiatives: Three Mexican cases. In M. Al-Shammari (Ed.), *Knowledge management in emerging economies: Social, organizational and cultural implementation* (pp. 273–293). Hershey, PA: Information Science Reference; doi:10.4018/978-1-61692-886-5.ch017

Zarri, G. P. (2011). Knowledge representation. In D. Schwartz & D. Te'eni (Eds.), *Encyclopedia of knowledge management* (2nd ed., pp. 878–892). Hershey, PA: Information Science Reference; doi:10.4018/978-1-59904-931-1.ch084

Zarri, G. P. (2011). RDF and OWL for knowledge management. In D. Schwartz & D. Te'eni (Eds.), *Encyclopedia of knowledge management* (2nd ed., pp. 1355–1373). Hershey, PA: Information Science Reference; doi:10.4018/978-1-59904-931-1.ch130

Zhang, Y., Wang, Y., Colucci, W., & Wang, Z. (2013). The paradigm shift in organizational research. In J. Wang (Ed.), *Intelligence methods and systems advancements for knowledge-based business* (pp. 60–74). Hershey, PA: Information Science Reference; doi:10.4018/978-1-4666-1873-2.ch004

Zhang, Z. J. (2011). Managing customer knowledge with social software. In D. Schwartz & D. Te'eni (Eds.), *Encyclopedia of knowledge management* (2nd ed., pp. 1046–1053). Hershey, PA: Information Science Reference; doi:10.4018/978-1-59904-931-1.ch099

Zyngier, S. (2011). Governance of knowledge management. In D. Schwartz & D. Te'eni (Eds.), *Encyclopedia of knowledge management* (2nd ed., pp. 354–365). Hershey, PA: Information Science Reference; doi:10.4018/978-1-59904-931-1.ch034

Zyngier, S. (2011). Knowledge management: Realizing value through governance. [IJKM]. *International Journal of Knowledge Management*, 7(1), 35–54. doi:10.4018/jkm.2011010103

Zyngier, S. (2013). Knowledge management: Realizing value through governance. In M. Jennex (Ed.), *Dynamic models for knowledge-driven organizations* (pp. 36–55). Hershey, PA: Business Science Reference; doi:10.4018/978-1-4666-2485-6.ch003

Compilation of References

Patel, M., & Powell-Davies, P. (Eds.). (2009). Access English: English Bilingual Education Symposium. Jakarta: British Council; Retrieved from http://www.teachingenglish.org.uk/sites/teacheng/files/download-accessenglish-publications-ebe-proceedings.pdf

Abel, S. K., & Lederman, N. G. (2007). *Handbook of research in science education*. New Jersey: Erlbaum.

Abrams, L. M. (2007). Implications of high-stakes testing for the use of formative classroom assessment. In H. McMillan (Ed.), *Formative assessment classroom: Theory into practice* (pp. 70–98). NY: Teachers College Press.

Achieve, (May, 2008). The Building Blocks for Success: Higher level math for all students. National Research Council Retrieved from: http://www.achieve.org/files/BuildingBlocksofSuccess.pdf

ACT. (2011). ACT Profile Report: Graduating Class 2011 National. Retrieved from http://www.act.org/newsroom/data/2011/pdf/profile/National2011.pdf

Ajzen, I. (1991). The theory of planned behavior. *Organizational Behavior and Human Decision Processes*, *50*(2), 179–211. doi:10.1016/0749-5978(91)90020-T

Akkus, R., Gunel, M., & Hand, B. (2007). Comparing an inquiry based approach known as the Science Writing Heuristic to traditional science teaching practices: Are there differences? *International Journal of Science Education*, *29*(14), 1745–1765. doi:10.1080/09500690601075629

Al-Daami, K. K., & Wallace, G. (2007). Curriculum reform in a global context: A study of teachers in Jordan. *Journal of Curriculum Studies*, *39*(3), 339–360. doi:10.1080/00220270601057790

Alexander, P. A., & Murphy, P. K. (1998). The research base for APA's learner-centered psychological principles. In N. M. Lambert & B. L. McCombs (Eds.), *Issues in school reform: A sampler of psychological perspectives on learner-centered schools* (pp. 33–60). Washington, DC: American Psychological Association; doi:10.1037/10258-001

Alkin, M. C. (1976). Evaluation: Who needs it? Who cares? *Studies in Educational Evaluation*, *1*(3), 201–212. doi:10.1016/0191-491X(75)90023-1

Angelle, P. S., & DeHart, C. A. (2011). Teacher Perceptions of Teacher Leadership: Examining Differences by Experience, Degree, and Position. *NASSP Bulletin*, *95*(2), 141–160. doi:10.1177/0192636511415397

Appel, J. (1995). *Diary of a language teacher*. Oxford: Heinemann.

Arli, E. E. (2014). *Argumantasyon Tabanli Bilim Ogrenme (ATBO) Yaklasiminin uygulandigi ilkogretim fen ve teknoloji siniflarinda ogrencilerin arguman olusturmadaki degisim ve gelisimlerinin yazili metinler uzerinden incelenmesi*. (Unpublished master thesis). Ataturk University.

Arli, E. E., & Gunel, M. (2012). *Akademik basari duzeyleri dusuk ogrencilerin fen kavramlarini ogrenmelerinin desteklenmesi: Argumantasyon tabanli bilim ogrenme uygulamalari*. Paper presented at the 10th Annual Meeting of National Science and Mathematics Education Conference (UFBMEK), Nigde.

Arli, E. E., & Gunel, M. (2014). *Dezavantajli ogrencilerin egitiminde dusunme becerileri odakli fen egitimi yaklasimi: mevsimlik tarim iscisi ogrenci orneklemi*. Paper presented at the 11th Annual Best Practices in Education Conference (EIOK), Istanbul, Turkey.

Armutcu, N., & Yaman, S. (2010). ELT pre-service teachers' teacher reflection through practicum. *Procedia: Social and Behavioral Sciences, 3*, 28–35. doi:10.1016/j.sbspro.2010.07.009

Atay, D. (2006). Teachers' professional development: Partnerships in research. *TESL-EJ, 10*(2), 1–14.

Atay, D. (2007). Beginning teacher efficacy and the practicum in an EFL context. *Teacher Development, 11*(2), 203–219. doi:10.1080/13664530701414720

Atherton, J. (1999). Resistance to Learning: A discussion based on participants in in-service professional training programmes. *Journal of Vocational Education and Training, 51*(1), 77–90. doi:10.1080/13636829900200070

Auhl, G. & Daniel, G.R. (2014).Preparing pre-service teachers for the profession: creating spaces for transformative practice. *Journal of Education for Teaching: International Research and Pedagogy, 40*(4), 377-390.

Avalos, B. (2011). Teacher professional development in teaching and teacher education over ten years. *Teaching and Teacher Education, 27*(1), 10–20. doi:10.1016/j.tate.2010.08.007

Avery, Z. K., & Reeve, E. M. (2013). Developing effective STEM professional development programs. *Journal of Technology in Education, 25*(1), 55–69.

Bailey, K. M. (1990). The use of diary studies in teacher education programs. In J. C. Richards & D. Nunan (Eds.), *Second language teacher education* (pp. 215–226). Cambridge: Cambridge University Press.

Ball, D. L., & Cohen, D. K. (1999). Developing practices, developing practitioners: Toward a practice-based theory of professional development. In G. Sykes & L. Darling-Hammonds (Eds.), *Teaching as the learning profession: Handbook of policy and practice* (pp. 30–32). San Francisco, CA: Jossey-Bass.

Ball, D. L., Thames, M. H., & Phelps, G. (2008). Content knowledge for teaching: What makes it special? *Journal of Teacher Education, 59*(5), 389–407. doi:10.1177/0022487108324554

Bandura, A. (1986). *Social foundations of thought and action: A social cognitive theory*. Englewood Cliffs, NJ: Prentice-Hall.

Bandura, A. (1988). Organizational Application of Social Cognitive Theory. *Australian Journal of Management, 13*(2), 275–302. doi:10.1177/031289628801300210

Bandura, A. (1997). *Self-efficacy: The exercise of control*. New York: W.H. Freeman and Company.

Barman, C. (1996). How do students really view science and scientists? *Science and Children*, 30–33.

Barman, C. (1997). Students' views of scientists and science: Results from a national study. *Science and Children, 35*(1), 18–23.

Barmby, P., Kind, P., & Jones, K. (2008). Examining Changing Attitudes in Secondary School Science. *International Journal of Science Education, 30*(8), 1075–1093. doi:10.1080/09500690701344966

Bashturkmen, H. (2010). *Developing courses in ESP*. New York: Palgrave Macmillan.

Baumard, P. (1999). *Tacit knowledge in organisations*. London: Sage.

Compilation of References

Beijaard, D., Meijer, P. C., & Verloop, N. (2004). Reconsidering research on teachers' professional identity. *Teaching and Teacher Education*, *20*(2), 107–128. doi:10.1016/j.tate.2003.07.001

Bennett, J., & Hogarth, S. (2009). "Would you want to talk to a scientist at a party?": High school students' attitude to school science and to science. *International Journal of Science Education*, *31*(14), 1975–1998. doi:10.1080/09500690802425581

Black, P., Harrison, C., Lee, C., Marshall, B., & Wiliam, D. (2004). Working inside the black box: Assessment for learning in the classroom. *Phi Delta Kappan*, *86*(1), 8–21. doi:10.1177/003172170408600105

Black, P., & Wiliam, D. (1998). Assessment and classroom learning. *Assessment in Education: Principles, Policy & Practice*, *5*(1), 7–71. doi:10.1080/0969595980050102

Blake, R. (2005). Bimodal CMC: The glue of language learning at a distance. *CALICO Journal*, *22*, 497–511.

Borg, S. (1999). Studying teacher cognition in second language grammar teaching. *System*, *27*(1), 19–31. doi:10.1016/S0346-251X(98)00047-5

Borg, S. (2006). *Teacher cognition and language education: Research and practice*. London: Continuum.

Borg, S. (2006). *Teacher cognition and language Education: Research and practice*. London: Continuum.

Borg, S. (2009). Language teacher cognition. In A. Burns & J. C. Richards (Eds.), *The Cambridge guide to second language teacher education* (pp. 163–171). New York: Cambridge University Press.

Borg, S. (2011). Language teacher education. In J. Simpson (Ed.), *The Routledge Handbook of Applied Linguistics* (pp. 215–228). London: Routledge.

Borko, H. (2004, November01). Professional development and teacher learning: Mapping the terrain. *Educational Researcher*, *33*(8), 3–15. doi:10.3102/0013189X033008003

Bozdin, A., & Gehringer, M. (2001). Breaking science stereotypes: Can meeting actual scientists change students' perceptions of scientists? *Science and Children*, *38*, 24–27.

Brown, J. D. (1995). *The elements of language curriculum: A systematic approach to program development*. Boston: Heinle & Heinle Publishers.

Brown, J. D. (1997). Computers in language testing: Present research and some future directions. *Language Learning & Technology*, *1*(1), 44–59.

Buck, G., Plano, C. V., Leslie-Pelecky, D., Lu, Y., & Cerda-Lizarraga, P. (2007). Examining the cognitive processes used by adolescent girls and women scientists in identifying science role models: A feminist approach. *Science Education.*, *92*(4), 688–707. doi:10.1002/sce.20257

Buczynski, S., & Hansen, C. B. (2010). Impact of professional development on teacher practice: Uncovering connections. *Teaching and Teacher Education*, *26*(3), 599–607. doi:10.1016/j.tate.2009.09.006

Budak, Y., & Demirel, O. (2003). In-service training needs for teachers. *Educational Administration in Theory and Practice*, *33*(1), 62–81.

Bullough, R. V., & Gitlin, A. (1995). *Becoming a student of teaching: Methodologies for exploring self and school context*. New York: Garland.

Bush, R. N. (1984). Effective staff development in making schools more effective: *Proceedings of three state conferences*. San Francisco, CA: Far West Laboratory.

Byars-Winston, A. (2014). Toward a framework for multicultural STEM-focused career interventions. *The Career Development Quarterly, 62*(4), 340–357. doi:10.1002/j.2161-0045.2014.00087.x PMID:25750480

Bybee, R., & Loucks-Horsley, S. (2000). Advancing technology education: The role of professional development. *Technology Teacher, 60*(2), 31–36.

CADRE. (the Community for Advancing Discovery Research in Education). (2011). Preparing and supporting STEM educators. Retrieved from http://successfulstemeducation.org/sites/successfulstemeducation.org/files/Preparing%20Supporting%20STEM%20Educators_FINAL.pdf

Caglayan, N., Yesildag-Hasancebi, F., Tanriverdi, K., & Gunel, M. (2013). *Implementation of the argumentation based science inquiry approach to the targets of electricity unit*. Paper presented at the 1st International Conference on Immersion Approaches to Argument-based Inquiry (ABI) for Science Classrooms, Busan, Korea.

Çakıroğlu, E., & Çakıroğlu, J. (2003). Reflections on teacher education in Turkey. *European Journal of Teacher Education, 26*, 253–265. doi:10.1080/0261976032000088774

Calderhead, J. (1987). Reflective teaching and teacher education. *Teaching and Teacher Education, 5*(1), 43–52. doi:10.1016/0742-051X(89)90018-8

Carlson, S. 2002. Wired to the Hilt: Saint Joseph's University stakes its future on a $ 30 million bet. *The Chronicle of Higher Education: Information Technology*. Retrieved from http://chronicle.com/free/v48/i29/29a03301.htm

Carr, W., & Kemmis, S. (1986). *Becoming critical: Education, knowledge and action research*. Basingstoke: Falmer Press.

Catelli, L. A. (1995). Action research and collaborative inquiry in a school-university partnership. *Action in Teacher Education, 265*(4), 25–38. doi:10.1080/01626620.1995.10463216

Center for Public Education. (2005). Teacher Quality and Student Achievement: Research Review. Retrieved from www.centerforpubliceducation.org/Main-Menu/Staffingstudents/Teacher-quality-and-student-achievement-Research-review.html

Chambers, D. W. (1983). Stereotypic images of the scientist: The Draw-a-Scientist Test. *Science Education, 67*(2), 255–265. doi:10.1002/sce.3730670213

Chapelle, C. (2001). *Computer applications in second language acquisition: Foundations for teaching, testing, and research*. Cambridge: Cambridge University Press. doi:10.1017/CBO9781139524681

Chapelle, C. (2006). Foreword. In P. Hubbard & M. Levy (Eds.), *Teacher education in CALL*. Amsterdam: John Benjamins. doi:10.1075/lllt.14.01cha

Cheng, M., Cheng, A., & Tang, S. (2010). Closing the gap between the theory and practice of teaching: Implications for teacher education programmes in Hong Kong. *Journal of Education for Teaching: International Research and Pedagogies, 36*(1), 91–104. doi:10.1080/02607470903462222

Chen, X. (2013). *STEM Attrition: College Students' Paths Into and Out of STEM Fields (NCES 2014-001)*. Washington, DC: National Center for Education Statistics, Institute of Education Sciences, U.S. Department of Education.

Cikmaz, A. (2014). *Examining two Turkish Teachers' Questionning Patterns in Secondary School Science Classrooms*. (Unpublished master thesis). University of Iowa, Iowa City, IA.

Clark, L. M., DePiper, J. N., Frank, T. J., Nishio, M., & Capmbell, P. F. et al. (2014). Teacher. characteristics associated with mathematics teachers' beliefs and awareness of their students' mathematical dispositions. *Journal for Research in Mathematics Education, 45*(2), 246–284. doi:10.5951/jresematheduc.45.2.0246

Cohen, D. K. (1988). Teaching practice: Plus a change. In P. W. Jackson (Ed.), *Contributing to educational change: Perspectives on research and practice* (pp. 27–84). Berkeley, CA: McCutchan.

Cohen, D. K., & Hill, H. (2001). *Learning policy: When state education reform works*. New Haven, CT: Yale University Press. doi:10.12987/yale/9780300089479.001.0001

Cohen, D. K., & Hill, H. C. (2000). Instructional policy and classroom performance: The mathematics reform in California. *Teachers College Record*, *102*(2), 294–343. doi:10.1111/0161-4681.00057

Common Core state Standards Initiative (2010). Common Core State Standards for Mathematics. Retrieved from: http://corestandards.org

Costley, C. & Stephenson, J. (2005). The Impact of Workplace Doctorates – a review of 10 case studies at Middlesex University. Proceedings of *AERA conference*.

Costley, C., & Lester, S. (2010). Work-based doctorates: Professional extension at the highest levels. *Studies in Higher Education*, *37*(3), 257–269. doi:10.1080/03075079.2010.503344

Council of Higher Education (CHE). (2007). *Öğretmen yetiştirme ve eğitim fakülteleri (1982-2007)* [Teacher education and faculties of education (1982-2007)]. Ankara, Turkey: Council of Higher Education.

Council of Higher Education (Turkey)) & World Bank. (1998). School-Faculty Partnership, Ankara: YÖK.

Creswell, J. W. (2007). *Qualitative inquiry and research design: Choosing among five approaches* (2nd ed.). Thousand Oaks, CA: Sage.

Crowe, A. R., & Berry, A. (2007). Teaching prospective teachers about learning to think like a teacher: Articulating some of our principles. In T. Russell & J. Loughran (Eds.), *Enacting a pedagogy of teacher education: Values, relationships and practices* (pp. 31–44). New York: Routledge.

Crystal, D. (2003). *English as a global language*. New York, NY: Cambridge University Press. doi:10.1017/CBO9780511486999

Cuban, L. (2001). *Oversold & Underused: Computers in the Classroom. Harvard*. University Press.

Cunningham, C. M., Lachapelle, C. P., & Keenan, K. (2010). Elementary teachers' changing ideas about STEM and STEM pedagogy through interaction with a pedagogically supportive STEM curriculum. Paper presented at the P-12 Engineering and Design Education Research Summit, Seaside, OR.

Darling-Hammond, L., & Ball, D. L. 1997. Teaching for high standards: What policymakers need to know and be able to do. *National Educational Goals Panel*. Retrieved from http://www.negp.gov/Reports/highstds.htm

Darling-Hammond, L. (1999).*Teacher Quality and Student Achievement: A Review of State Policy Evidence*. Seattle, WA: Center for the Study of Teaching and Policy, University of Washington.

Darling-Hammond, L. (2014). Strengthening clinical preparation: The holy grail of teacher education. *Peabody Journal of Education: Issues of Leadership, Policy, and Organizations*, *89*(4), 547–561. doi:10.1080/0161956X.2014.939009

Darling-Hammond, L., & Bransford, J. (Eds.). (2005). *Preparing teachers for a changing world: What teachers should learn and be able to do*. San Francisco: Jossey Bass.

Darling-Hammond, L., Chung Wei, R., Andree, A., & Richardson, N. (2009). *Professional learning in the learning profession: A status report on teacher development in the United States and abroad*. Oxford, OH: National Staff Development Council.

Darling-Hammond, L., & McLaughlin, M. (1995). Policies That Support Professional Development in an Era of Reform. *Phi Delta Kappan, 76*(8), 597–604.

Darling-Hammond, L., Wei, R. C., Andree, A., Richardson, N., & Orphanos, S. (2009). *Professional learning in the learning profession: A status report on teacher professional development in the United States and abroad.* Washington, D.C.: National Staff Development Council.

Demir, M., Yesildag-Hasancebi, F., & Gunel, M. (2013). *Unit Preparation Process in The Applications of Argumentation Based Inquiry Approach.* Paper presented at the 1st International Conference on Immersion Approaches to Argument-based Inquiry (ABI) for Science Classrooms, Busan, Korea.

Denzin, N. K., & Lincoln, Y. S. (Eds.). (2000). Collecting and interpreting qualitative materials. 2nd Edition. Place: SAGE Publications.

Department of Health. (2000). *The NHS Plan: A plan for investment. A plan for reforms.* London: The Stationery Office.

Department of Health. (2001). *Working Together, Learning Together: A framework for lifelong learning in the NHS.* London: The Stationery Office.

Department of Health. (2004). *The NHS Improvement Plan: putting people at the heart of public services.* London: The Stationery Office.

Desimone, L. (2009). How can we best measure teachers' professional development and its effects on teachers and students? *Educational Researcher, 38*(3), 181–199. doi:10.3102/0013189X08331140

Dewey, J. (1933). *How we think.* Lexington, MA: D.C. Heath.

Dexter, S. L., Anderson, R. E., & Becker, H. J. (1999). Teachers' views of computers as catalysts for changes in their teaching practice. *Journal of research on computing in education, 31*(3), 221-239.

Diaconu, D., Radigan, J., Suskavcevic, M., & Nichol, C. (2012). A multi-year study of the impact of the Rice model professional development on elementary teachers. *International Journal of Science Education, 34*(6), 855–877. doi:10.1080/09500693.2011.642019

Dijkstra, P., Kuyper, H., van der Werf, G., Buunk, A. P., & van der Zee, Y. G. (2008). Social comparison in the classroom: A review. *Review of Educational Research, 78*(4), 828–879. doi:10.3102/0034654308321210

Dillman, D. A., Smyth, J. D., & Christian, L. M. (2014). *Internet, Phone, Mail, and Mixed-Mode Surveys: The Tailored Design Method* (4th ed.). Wiley.

Directorate-General for Teacher Training and Development. (2014). 2013 In-Service Training Activity Report. Ankara, Turkey: Author.

Doğançay-Aktuna, S., & Kızıltepe, Z. (2005). English in Turkey. *World Englishes, 24*(2), 253–265. doi:10.1111/j.1467-971X.2005.00408.x

Dörnyei, Z. (2010). *Questionnaires in second language research: Construction, administration, and processing.* London: Routledge.

Driver, R., Asoko, H., Leach, J., Mortimer, E., & Scott, P. (1994). Constructing scientific knowledge in the classroom. *Educational Researcher, 23*(7), 5–12. doi:10.3102/0013189X023007005

Dudley-Evans, T., & St John, M. J. (1998). *Developments in English for specific purposes: A multi-disciplinary approach.* Cambridge: Cambridge University Press.

Duffy, F. M. (2004). *Moving upward together: Creating strategic alignment to sustain systemic school improvement*. Lanham, MD: Scarecrow Education.

Duran, M., Fossum R. (2010). Technology Integration into Teacher Preparation: Part 1—Current Practice and Theoretical Grounding for Pedagogical Renewal. *Ahi Evran Üniversitesi Egitim Fakültesi Dergisi,Cilt 11,Sayı 2,Agustos, Sayfa 209-228*

Dyson, M. (2007). My story in a profession of stories: Auto ethnography – an empowering methodology for educators. *Australian Journal of Teacher Education, 32*(1), 36–48. doi:10.14221/ajte.2007v32n1.3

Eliahoo, R. (2011). Dilemmas in measuring the impact of subject-specific mentoring on mentees' learners in the lifelong learning sector. *Practitioner Research in Higher Education, 5*(1), 39–47.

Elliot, J. (1991). *Action research for educational change*. Buckingham, UK: Open University Press.

Ellis, R. (1998). Discourse control and the acquisition-rich classroom. In W. Renandya & G. Jacobs (Eds.), *Learners and language learning* (pp. 145–171). Singapore: SEAMEO.

Ennis, R. H., Millman, J., & Thomko, T. N. (2005). *Cornell Critical Thinking Tests Level X & Level Z Manual*. The Critical Thinking Co.

Eren, A. (2014). 'Not only satisfied and responsible, but also hopeful': Prospective teachers' career choice satisfaction, hope, and personal responsibility. *Cambridge Journal of Education*, 1–18. doi:10.1080/0305764X.2014.930417

Eren, A., & Tekinarslan, E. (2012). Prospective teachers' metaphors: Teacher, teaching, learning, instructional material and evaluation concepts. *International Journal of Social Science. &. Education, 3*(2), 435–445.

Evans, M. O. (1992). An estimate of race and gender role-model effects in teaching high school. *The Journal of Economic Education, 23*(3), 209–217. doi:10.1080/00220485.1992.10844754

Evans, T. P. (1986). Guidelines for effective science teacher inservice education programs: Perspectives from research. In B. S. Spector (Ed.), *A guide to inservice science teacher education: Research into practice* (pp. 13–56). Columbus, OH: Association for the Education of Teachers in Science and SMEAC Information Reference Center.

Ezzy, D. (2002). *Qualitative analysis: Practice and innovation*. London: Routledge.

Farell, T. S. C. (2008). Here is the book, go and teach: ELT practicum support. *RELC Journal, 39*(2), 226–241. doi:10.1177/0033688208092186

Farrell, T. S. C. (1999). The reflective assignment: Unlocking pre-service teachers' beliefs on grammar teaching. *RELC Journal, 30*(2), 1–17. doi:10.1177/003368829903000201

Farrell, T. S. C. (2003). Learning to teach English language during the first year: Personal influences and challenges. *Teaching and Teacher Education, 19*(1), 95–111. doi:10.1016/S0742-051X(02)00088-4

Farrell, T. S. C. (2007). *Reflective language teaching: From research to practice*. London: Continuum Press.

Farrell, T. S. C. (2011). Exploring the professional role identities of experienced ESL teachers through reflective practice. *System, 39*(1), 54–62. doi:10.1016/j.system.2011.01.012

Fell, A., Flint, K., & Haines, I. (2011). *Professional Doctorates in the UK*. London: UK Council for Graduate Education.

Fereday, J., & Muir-Cochrane, E. (2008). Demonstrating rigor using thematic analysis: A hybrid approach of inductive and deductive coding and theme development. *International Journal of Qualitative Methods, 5*(1), 80–92.

Ferguson, P. (1989). A reflective approach to the methods practicum. *Journal for Teacher Education*, 36-41.

Finson, K. D. (2002). A multicultural comparison of draw-a-scientist test drawings of eighth graders. Paper presented at the Annual International Conference of the Association of Educators of Teachers of Science; Charlotte, NC.

Finson, K. D., & Enochs, L. G. (1987). Student attitudes toward science-technology-society resulting from visitation to a science-technology museum. *Journal of Research in Science Teaching*, *24*(7), 593–609. doi:10.1002/tea.3660240702

Fishman, B., Marx, R., Best, S., & Tal, R. (2003). Linking teacher and student learning to improve professional development in systemic reform. *Teaching and Teacher Education*, *19*(6), 643–665. doi:10.1016/S0742-051X(03)00059-3

Flick, L. (1990). Scientist in Residence program: Improving children's images of science and scientists. *School Science and Mathematics*, *90*(3), 204–214. doi:10.1111/j.1949-8594.1990.tb15536.x

Fok, S., Chan, K., Sin, K., Ng, A. H., &Yeung, A. S. (2005). *In-Service Teacher Training Needs in Hong Kong*. Paper presented at the Annual Meeting of the Australian Association for Research in Education, Sydney, Australia.

Fort, D. C., & Varney, H. L. (1989). How students see scientists: Mostly male, mostly white, mostly benevolent. *Science and Children*, *26*(8), 8–13.

Freeman, D., & Johnson, K. E. (1998). Reconceptualizing the knowledge-base of language teacher education. *TESOL Quarterly*, *32*(3), 397–417. doi:10.2307/3588114

Frid, S., & Reid, J. (2002). Competency = Complexity and Connectedness: Professional portfolios as a technology for reflective practice in pre-service education. In J. Reid, & T. Brown (Eds), *Challenging futures. Changing agendas in teacher education (Proceedings of the Challenging Futures conference, Armidale, NSW)*. Retrieved from http://scs.une.edu.au/CF/Papers/editorial.htm

Fuchs, L. S., & Fuchs, D. (1986). Effects of Systematic Formative Evaluation: A Meta-Analysis. *Exceptional Children*, *53*(3), 199–208. PMID:3792417

Fullan, M. (2001).The meaning of educational change. In M. Fullan (Ed.), *The New Meaning of Educational Change*. London: Routledge.

Fulp, S. L. (2002). *2000 National Survey of Science and Mathematics Education: Status of elementary school science teaching*. Chapel Hill, NC: Horizon Research.

Fulton, J., Kuit, J., Sanders, G., & Smith, P. (2012a). The role of the Professional Doctorate in developing professional practice. *Journal of Nursing Management*, *20*(1), 130–139. doi:10.1111/j.1365-2834.2011.01345.x PMID:22229909

Fulton, J., Kuit, J., Sanders, G., & Smith, P. (2012b). *The Professional Doctorate: A Practical Guide for Students and Supervisors*. London: Palgrave.

Garcia, M. R., & Arias, F. V. (2000). A comparative study in motivation and learning through print-oriented and computer-oriented tests. *Computer Assisted Language Learning*, *13*(4-5), 457–465. doi:10.1076/0958-8221(200012)13:4-5;1-E;FT457

Garet, M., Birman, B., Porter, A., Desimone, L., Herman, R., & Suk Yoon, K. (1999). *Designing effective professional development: Lessons from the Eisenhower program*. Washington, DC: U.S. Department of Education.

Garet, M., Porter, A., Desimone, L., Briman, B., & Yoon, K. (2001). What makes professional development effective? Analysis of a national sample of teachers. *American Educational Research Journal*, *38*(4), 915–945. doi:10.3102/00028312038004915

Gebhard, J. (2009). The practicum. In A. Burns & J. C. Richards (Eds.), *The Cambridge guide to second language teacher education* (pp. 250–258). New York: Cambridge University Press.

Gokdere, M., & Cepni, S. (2004). A study on the assessment of the in-service needs of the science teachers of gifted students: A case for science art center. *Gazi University Journal of Gazi Educational Faculty, 24*(2), 1–14.

Gokdere, M., & Kuçuk, M. (2003). Science education of gifted students at intellectual area; a case for science art centers. *Educational Sciences: Theory and Practice, 3*(1), 101–124.

Goldschmidt, P., & Phelps, G. (2009). Does teacher professional development affect content and pedagogical knowledge: How much and for how long? *Economics of Education Review, 29*(3), 432–439. doi:10.1016/j.econedurev.2009.10.002

Gonen, S., & Kocakaya, S. (2006). An evaluation of high school physics teachers' oppinions about in-service education. *Pamukkale University Journal of Educational Faculty, 19*(1), 37–44.

Goodman, J. (1984). Reflection and teacher education: A case study and theoretical analysis. *Interchange, 15*(3), 9–26. doi:10.1007/BF01807939

Goodnough, K. (2003). Facilitating action research in the context of science education: Reflections of a university researcher. *Educational Action Research, 11*(1), 41–64. doi:10.1080/09650790300200203

Gordon, S. P. (2004). *Professional development for school improvement: Empowering Learning Communities*. New York: Pearson.

Gottfried, M. A., & Williams, D. N. (2013). STEM Club Participation and STEM Schooling Outcomes. *Education Policy Analysis Archives, 21*(79), 1–23.

Graddol, D. (2006). English next. London: British Council; Retrieved from http://englishagenda.britishcouncil.org/publications/english-next

Grant, C. A., & Zeichner, K. M. (1984). On becoming a reflective teacher. In C. A. Grant (Ed.), *Preparing for reflective teaching* (pp. 1–18). Toronto, ON: Allyn and Bacon.

Greene, J. C., Caracelli, V. J., & Graham, W. F. (1989). Toward a conceptual framework for mixed-method evaluation designs. *Educational Evaluation and Policy Analysis, 11*(3), 255–274. doi:10.3102/01623737011003255

Greyling, F. C. 2007. *The why and how of technology-assisted learning: Authentic professional development for higher education practitioners* [Unpublished doctoral thesis]. University of Johannesburg, Johannesburg.

Grimberg, I. B., Mohammed, E., & Hand, B. (2004). *A grade six case study of cognitive involvement and attitudes towards scientific inquiry using the SWH*. Paper presented at the International Conference of the Association for Educators of Teachers of Science, Nashville, TN.

Grossman, G. (2013). Developing social capital through national education: the transformation of teacher education in Turkey. In I. R. Haslam, M. S. Khine, & I. M. Saleh (Eds.), *Large scale reform and social capital building*. New York, NY: Routledge.

Guba, E. G., & Lincoln, Y. S. (1989). Epistemological and methodological bases for naturalistic inquiry. *Educational Communication and Technology, 30*(4), 233–252.

Gultekin, M., Cubukcu, Z., & Dal, S. (2010). In-service training needs of the primary school teachers regarding education-teaching. *Selcuk University Journal of Ahmet Kelesoglu Educational Faculty, 29*, 131–152.

Gunel, M. (2013). *The relationship between science teaching and critical thinking skills: Where does the teacher stand for?* Paper presented at the First African Conferences on Research in Chemistry Education, Addis Ababa, Ethiopia.

Gunel, M. (2013a). *Problems faced and strategies developed by teachers implementing inquiry based science teaching approaches*. Paper presented at the 1st International Conference on Immersion Approaches to Argument-based Inquiry (ABI) for Science Classrooms, Busan, Korea.

Gunel, M. (2013b). *Structuring, organizing and implementing longitudinal professional development project focusing on argumentation based science inquiry; a case of Turkish research setting*. Paper presented at the 1st International Conference on Immersion Approaches to Argument-based Inquiry (ABI) for Science Classrooms, Busan, Korea.

Gunel, M., & Tanriverdi, K. (2012). *Boylamsal arastirma projesi: Hizmetici egitim ve sinifici uygulamalarinin, ogretmen pedagojisine, ogrenci akademik basarisina, dusunme becerilerine etkisinin arastirilmasi*. Paper presented at the 10th Annual Meeting of National Science and Mathematics Education Conference (UFBMEK), Nigde.

Gunel, M., Akkus, R., & Ozer-Keskin, M. (2011). *Implementing the argumentation based science learning approach in middle school setting through professional development programs and investigating the impact of the approach on teachers' pedagogy and students' academic achievements, skills and perceptions toward science*. Paper presented at the annual meeting of the European Science Education Research Association (ESERA), Lyon, France.

Gunel, M., Akkus, R., Ozer-Keskin, M., & Keskin-Samanci, N. (2012). *The effect of the SWH implementation in Turkish school system: results from a scale up research project*. Paper presented at the Annual Meeting of the National Association for Research in Science Teaching (NARST), Indianapolis, IN.

Gunel, M., Akkus, R., Ozer-Keskin, M., & Keskin-Samanci, N. (2013). *Improving students' conceptual understanding of science through argument based science inquiry implementations: a case of nationwide professional development project*. Paper presented at the 1st International Conference on Immersion Approaches to Argument-based Inquiry (ABI) for Science Classrooms, Busan, Korea.

Gunel, M., Akkus, R., Ozer-Keskin, M., & Keskin-Samanci, N. (2014). *Enhancing students' critical thinking skills through argument based inquiry: results from a scale up research project in Turkey*. Paper presented at the Annual Meeting of the National Association for Research in Science Teaching (NARST), Pittsburgh, PA.

Gunel, M., Yesildag-Hasancebi, F., Keskin-Samanci, N., Demir, M., Ozgur, S., Gundogan, F., & Akbay, Y. (2012). *Ogretirken Ogrenen Ogretmenler: Profesyonel Degisim ve Gelisim*. Paper presented at the 10th Annual Meeting of National Science and Mathematics Education Conference (UFBMEK), Nigde.

Gunel, M., & Tanriverdi, K. (2014). In-service teacher training from international and national perspectives: The retention and loss of institutional and academic memories. *Education & Science*, *39*(175), 73–94.

Guskey, T. R. (2000). *Evaluating Professional Development*. Thousand Oaks, CA: Corvin.

Guskey, T. R. (2002). Professional development and teacher change, *Teachers and teaching. Theory into Practice*, *8*(4), 381–391.

Guskey, T. R. (2014). Planning professional learning. *Educational Leadership*, 11–16.

Guthrie, J. (2009). The Case for a Modern Doctorate of Education Degree (Ed.D): Multipurpose Education Doctorates No Longer Appropriate. Peabody Journal of Education, 84(1), 3-8.

Hacıömeroğlu, G. (2010). Preservice Teachers' Reflections on their Instructional Practices. *Proceedings of the 31st annual meeting of the North American Chapter of the International Group for the Psychology of Mathematics Education*. Atlanta, GA:Georgia State University.

Hadacek, S., & Carpenter, D. (1998). Student Perceptions of Nursing Doctorates: Similarities and Differences. *Journal of Professional Nursing*, *14*(1), 14–21. doi:10.1016/S8755-7223(98)80008-2 PMID:9473900

Hand, B. (2009). Negotiating Science: The Critical Role of Argument in Student Inquiry, Grades 5-10. Portsmouth, NH: Heinemann.

Hand, B. (2008). *Science Inquiry, Argument and Language: A Case for the Science Writing Heuristic*. Rotterdam, The Netherlands: Sense Publishers.

Hand, B., & Keys, C. (1999). Inquiry investigation: A new approach to laboratory reports. *Science Teacher (Normal, Ill.)*, *66*, 27–29.

Hand, B., & Treagust, D. F. (1995). Development of a constructivist model for teacher inservice. *Australian Journal of Teacher Education*, *20*(2), 28–38. doi:10.14221/ajte.1995v20n2.4

Hanover Research. (2011). K-12 STEM education overview. Retrieved from http://www.hanoverresearch.com/wp-content/uploads/2011/12/K-12-STEM-Education-Overview-Membership.pdf

Hanushek, E. A., & Rivkin, S. G. (2004). *How to improve the supply of high-quality teachers* (pp. 7–25). Brookings Papers on Education Policy doi:10.1353/pep.2004.0001

Hascher, T., Cocard, Y., & Moser, P. (2004). Forget about theory - practice is all? Student teachers' learning in practicum. *Teachers and Teaching: Theory and Practice*, *10*(6), 623–637. doi:10.1080/1354060042000304800

Hawley, W., & Valli, L. (2000). Learner-centered professional development. *Phi Delta Kappan Research Bulletin*. Retrieved from http://tlcliteracy.org/images/downloads/Professional_Development/learner_centered_pro.pdf

Hawley, W. D., & Valli, L. (2000). *Learner-centered professional development. Research Bulletin, No. 27*. Phi Delta Kappa Center for Evaluation, Development, and Research.

Haycock, K. (1998). Good teaching matters…a lot. *Thinking K-16*, *3*(2), 1-14.

Hayes, R. Q., Whalen, S. K., & Cannon, B. (2009). *2008–2009 CSRDE stem retention report*. Norman: Center for Institutional Data Exchange and Analysis, University of Oklahoma.

Heck, D. J., Banilower, E. R., Weiss, I. R., & Rosenberg, S. L. (2008). Studying the effects of professional development: The case of the NSF's local systemic change through teacher enhancement initiative. *Journal for Research in Mathematics Education*, *39*(2), 113–152.

Heritage, M. (2007). Formative assessment: What do teachers need to know and do? *Phi Delta Kappan*, *89*(2), 140–145. doi:10.1177/003172170708900210

Herreid, C. F., & Schiller, N. A. (2013). Case studies and the flipped classroom. *Journal of College Science Teaching*, *42*(5), 62–66.

Herrington, J., & Oliver, R. (2000). An instructional design framework for authentic learning environments. *Educational Technology Research and Development*, *48*(3), 23–48. doi:10.1007/BF02319856

Higgins, J., & Parsons, R. (2009). A successful professional development model in mathematics: A system-wide New Zealand case. *Journal of Teacher Education*, *60*(3), 231–242. doi:10.1177/0022487109336894

Hodijah, I. S. (2012). Towards the understanding of bilingual education: The views of teaching other subjects through English (TOSTE) at international Standard schools (ISS). *Asia-Pacific Collaborative Education Journal*, *8*(1), 79–88.

Hohenshell, L. M., & Hand, B. (2006). Writing-to learn strategies in secondary school cell biology: A mixed method study. *International Journal of Science Education*, *28*(2-3), 261–289. doi:10.1080/09500690500336965

Houston, W. R. (1988). Reflecting on reflection in teacher education. In H. C. Waxman, H. J. Freiberg, J. C. Vaughan, & M. Weil (Eds.), *Images of reflection in teacher education* (pp. 7–8). Reston, VA: Association of Teacher Educators.

Hoy, W. K., & Miskel, C. G. (2008). *Educational administration: Theory, research and practice* (8th ed.). Boston: McGraw-Hill.

Hsu, M., Cardella, M., & Purzer, S. (2010). Assessing elementary teachers' design knowledge before and after introduction of a design process model. Paper presented at American Society for Engineering Education 2010 annual conference.

Huang, D., Lee, S., & Lim, K. Y. T. (2012). Authenticity in learning for the twenty-first century: Bridging the formal and the informal. *Educational Technology Research and Development*, *60*(6), 1071–1091. doi:10.1007/s11423-012-9272-3

Huang, H. M. (2002). Towards constructivism for adult learners in online learning environment. *British Journal of Educational Technology*, *33*(1), 27–37. doi:10.1111/1467-8535.00236

Hubbard, P. (2004). Learner training for effective use of CALL. In S. Fotos & C. Browne (Eds.), *New perspectives on CALL for second language classrooms* (pp. 45–68). Mahwah, NJ: Lawrence Erlbaum.

Hudson, P. (2009). Learning to teach science using English as the medium of instruction. *Eurasian Journal of Mathematics, Science and Technology Education*, *5*(2), 165-170. Retrieved from http://www.ejmste.com/v5n2/eurasia_v5n2_hudson.pdf

Huhta, M., Vogt, K., & Tulkki, H. (2013). *Needs analysis for language course design: A holistic approach to ESP*. Cambridge: Cambridge University Press.

Hutchinson, T. (1987). *English for specific purposes*. Cambridge: Cambridge University Press. doi:10.1017/CBO9780511733031

Hutson, H. M. (1981). Inservice best practices: The learning of general education. *Journal of Research and Development in Education*, *14*(3), 1–10.

Ingels, S. J., Pratt, D. J., Rogers, J. E., Siegel, P. H., & Stutts, E. S. (2004). *Education Longitudinal Study of 2002: Base-Year Data File User's Manual (NCES 2004-405)*. Washington, DC: National Center for Education Statistics, Institute of Education Sciences, U.S. Department of Education.

Jamieson, J., Chapelle, C. A., & Preiss, S. (2005). CALL Evaluation by developers, a teacher, and students. *CALICO Journal*, *23*(1), 93–138.

Johnson, K. E. (1994). The emerging beliefs and instructional practices of pre-service ESL teachers. *Teaching and Teacher Education*, *10*, 439–452. doi:10.1016/0742-051X(94)90024-8

Johnson, K. E. (1999). *Understanding language teaching: Reasoning in action*. Boston: Heinle and Heinle.

Johnson, K. E. (2006). The sociocultural turn and its challenges for second language teacher education. *TESOL Quarterly*, *40*(1), 235–257. doi:10.2307/40264518

Jordan, R. R. (1997). *English for academic purposes: A guide and resource book for teachers*. Cambridge: Cambridge University Press. doi:10.1017/CBO9780511733062

Junor-Clarke, P. A., & Fournillier, J. B. (2012). Action research, pedagogy, and activity theory: Tools facilitating two instructors' interpretations of the professional development of four preservice teachers. *Teaching and Teacher Education*, *28*(5), 649–660. doi:10.1016/j.tate.2012.01.013

Kachru, B. B. (1986). *The alchemy of English: The spread, functions, and models of non-native English*. Oxford, NY: Pergamon Press.

Kafai, Y. B., & Gilliland-Swetland, A. J. (2000). The use of historical materials in elementary science classrooms. *Science Education*, *85*(4), 349–367. doi:10.1002/sce.1014

Kanli, U., & Yagbasan, R. (2001). In-service teacher training summer courses for physics teachers. *Gazi University Journal of Gazi Educational Faculty*, *21*(3), 39–46.

Karplus, R. (1970). *Science curriculum improvement study-a program report*. Berkley: Educational Products Information Exchange Institute.

Keller, J. M. (1987). Development and use of the ARCS model of instructional design. *Journal of Instructional Development*, *10*(3), 2–10. doi:10.1007/BF02905780

Keller, J. M., & Suzuki, K. (1988). Use of the ARCS motivation model in courseware design. In *D. H. Jonassen (ED.) Instructional designs for microcomputer courseware*. Hillsdale, NJ: Lawrence Erlbaum.

Keller, J. M., & Suzuki, K. (2004). Learner Motivation and E-Learning Design: A Multinationally Validated Process. *Journal of Educational Media*, *29*(3), 229–239. doi:10.1080/1358165042000283084

Kelly, P. (2006). What is teacher learning? A socio-cultural perspective. *Oxford Review of Education*, *32*(4), 505–519. doi:10.1080/03054980600884227

Kemmis, S. (1998). Action research. In J. Keeves (Ed.), *Educational Research, Methodology, and Measurement: An International Handbook* (pp. 42–49). New York: Pergamon.

Kennedy, M. (1998). *The Relevance of Content in Inservice Teacher Education*. San Diego, CA: American Educational Research Association.

Kessler, G. (2006). Assessing CALL teacher training: What are we doing and what could we do better? In P. Hubbard & M. Levy (Eds.), *Teacher education in CALL*. Amsterdam: John Benjamins. doi:10.1075/lllt.14.05kes

Keys, C., Hand, B., Prain, V., & Collins, S. (1999). Using the science writing heuristic as a tool for learning from laboratory investigations in secondary science. *Journal of Research in Science Teaching*, *36*(10), 1065–1084. doi:10.1002/(SICI)1098-2736(199912)36:10<1065::AID-TEA2>3.0.CO;2-I

Kılıçkaya, F., & Krajka, J. (2010). Comparative usefulness of online and traditional vocabulary learning. *Turkish Online Journal of Educational Technology*, *9*(2), 55–63.

Kılıçkaya, F., & Krajka, J. (2012). Can the use of web-based comic strip creation tool facilitate EFL learners' grammar and sentence writing? *British Journal of Educational Technology*, *43*(6), E161–E165. doi:10.1111/j.1467-8535.2012.01298.x

Kılıçkaya, F., & Seferoğlu, G. (2013). The impact of CALL instruction on English language teachers' use of technology in language teaching. *Journal of Second and Multiple Language Acquisition*, *1*(1), 20–38.

Kilimci, S. (2009). Teacher training in some EU countries and Turkey: How similar are they? *Procedia: Social and Behavioral Sciences*, *1*(1), 1975–1980. doi:10.1016/j.sbspro.2009.01.347

Kırkgöz, Y. (2007). English language teaching in Turkey: Policy changes and their implementations. *RELC Journal*, *38*(2), 216–228. doi:10.1177/0033688207079696

Kırkgöz, Y. (2009). Globalization and English language policy in Turkey. *Educational Policy*, *23*(5), 663–684. doi:10.1177/0895904808316319

Kırkgöz, Y. (2014). A school-university collaborative action research teacher development programme: A case of six Turkish novice teachers of English. *The Asian EFL Journal Professional Teaching Articles*, *71*, 31–56.

Klein, B. S. (2001). *Guidelines for effective elementary science teacher inservice education*. Journal of Elementary Science Education, 13(2), 29–40. doi:10.1007/BF03176218

Knapp, M. S., McCaffrey, T., & Swanson, J. (2003, April). District Support for Professional Learning: What Research Says and Has Yet to Establish. Paper presented at the Annual Meeting of the American Education Research Association, Chicago, April 21-25.

Knight, P., Tait, J., & Yorke, M. (2007). The professional learning of teachers in higher education. *Studies in Higher Education, 31*(3), 319–339. doi:10.1080/03075070600680786

Knowles, M. (1980). The modern practice of adult education: From pedagogy to andragogy (2nd ed.). Englewood Cliffs, NJ: Prentice Hall/Cambridge.

Koellner, K., Colsman, M., & Risley, R. (2011). Multidimensional Assessment. *Teaching Exceptional Children, 44*(2), 48–56.

Kolb, D. A. (1984). *Experiential Learning: Experience as the Source of Learning and Development*. Englewood Cliffs, NJ: Prentice Hall.

Koufaris, M. (2002). Applying the Technology Acceptance Model and Flow Theory to Online Consumer Behavior. *Information Systems Research, 13*(2), 205–223. doi:10.1287/isre.13.2.205.83

Kuhn, T. S. (1972). *The structure of scientific revolutions* (2nd ed.). Chicago: University Press.

Labaree, D. F. (2000). On the nature of teaching and teacher education: Difficult practices that look easy. *Journal of Teacher Education, 51*(3), 228–233. doi:10.1177/0022487100051003011

Lakoff, G., & Johnson, M. (1980/2003). Afterword 2003. In G. Lakoff & M. Johnson (Eds.), *Metaphors we live by*. Chicago: University of Chicago Press.

Lee, M.-C. (2010). Explaining and Predicting Users' Continuance Intention toward E-Learning: An Extension of the Expectation–Confirmation Model. *Computers & Education, 54*(2), 506–516. doi:10.1016/j.compedu.2009.09.002

Leshem, S., & Bar-Hama, R. (2008, July). Evaluating teaching practice. *ELT Journal, 62*(3), 257–265. doi:10.1093/elt/ccm020

Lester, S. (2004). Conceptualising the Practitioner Doctorate. *Studies in Higher Education, 29*(6), 757–770. doi:10.1080/0307507042000287249

Levin, B. B., & Rock, T. C. (2003). The effects of collaborative action research on preservice and experienced teacher partners in professional development schools. *Journal of Teacher Education, 54*(2), 135–149. doi:10.1177/0022487102250287

Levy, M., & Stockwell, G. (2006). *CALL dimensions: Options and issues in computer assisted language learning*. Mahwah, NJ: Lawrence Erlbaum.

Little, J. W. (1998). Seductive Images and Organizational Realities in Professional Development. In A. Lieberman (Ed.), *Rethinking School Improvement*. New York: Teachers College Press.

Lock, J. V. (2006). A new image: Online Communities to Facilitate Teacher Professional Development. *Journal of Technology and Teacher Education, 14*(4), 663–678.

Lombardi, M. (2007). Authentic learning for the 21st century: An overview. Retrieved from http://net.educause.edu/ir/library/pdf/ELI3009.pdf

Compilation of References

Long, M. H. (Ed.). (2005). *Second language needs analysis*. Cambridge: Cambridge University Press. doi:10.1017/CBO9780511667299

Loucks-Horsey, S., Stiles, K., & Hewson, P. (1996). *Principles of effective professional development for mathematics and science education: A synthesis of standards*. Madison, WI: University of Wisconsin at Madison, National Institute for Science Education.

Loucks-Horsley, S. (1995). Professional development and the learner centered school. *Theory into Practice*, *34*(4), 265–271. doi:10.1080/00405849509543690

Loucks-Horsley, S., Stiles, K. E., Mundry, S., Love, N., & Hewson, P. W. (2010). *Designing professional development for teachers of science and mathematics* (3rd ed.). Thousand Oaks, CA: Corwin Press.

Loughran, J. J. (2007). Enacting a pedagogy of teacher education. In T. Russell & J. Loughran (Eds.), Enacting a pedagogy of teacher education: Values, relationships and practices (pp. 1-15). New York: Routledge.

Low, E., Chong, S., & Ellis, M. (2014). Teachers' English communication skills: Using IELTS to measure competence of graduates from a Singaporean teacher education program. *Australian Journal of Teacher Education*, *39*(10).

Luft, J. A. (2001). Changing inquiry practices and beliefs: The impact of an inquiry-based professional development programme on beginning and experienced secondary science teachers. *International Journal of Science Education*, *23*(5), 517–534. doi:10.1080/09500690121307

Malfroy, J. (2005). Doctoral Supervision, workplace research, and changing pedagogic practices. *Higher Education Research & Development*, *24*(2), 165–178. doi:10.1080/07294360500062961

Manuel, J., & Hughes, J. (2006). 'It has always been my dream': Exploring pre-service teachers' motivations for choosing to teach. *Teacher Development*, *10*(1), 5–24. doi:10.1080/13664530600587311

Marchant, G. (1992). 'A teacher is like a ... Using simile lists to explore personal metaphors'. *Language and Education*, *6*(1), 33–45. doi:10.1080/09500789209541323

Martin, C. S., & Polly, D. (2015). Using the AMC Anywhere web-based assessment system to examine primary students' understanding of number sense. In D. Polly (Ed.), *Cases on Technology Integration in Mathematics Education* (pp. 366–377). Hershey, PA: IGI Global; doi:10.4018/978-1-4666-6497-5.ch018

Marzano, R. J. (2003). *What works in schools: Translating research into action*. Alexandria, VA: Association for Supervision and Curriculum Development.

Masuum, T. N. R. T. M., Maarof, N., Zakaria, E., & Yamat, H. (2012). Content-based instruction needs and challenges in diversified literacy context. *US-China Foreign Language*, *10*(3), 999–1004.

Mattheoudakis, M. (2007). Tracking changes in pre-service EFL teacher beliefs in Greece: A longitudinal study. *Teaching and Teacher Education*, *23*(8), 1272–1288. doi:10.1016/j.tate.2006.06.001

McCann, T. M., Alan, C. J., & Gail, A. (2012). *Teaching matters Most, A School Leader's Guide to improving classroom instruction*. Thousand Oaks, CA: Corwin Sage.

McDermott, L. C., & DeWater, L. S. (2000). The need for special science courses for teachers: two perspectives. In J. Minstrell & E. H. van Zee (Eds.), *Inquiring into inquiry science learning and teaching*. Washington, DC: American Association for the Advancement of Science.

McDonald, M. (2003). *The integration of social justice: Reshaping teacher education*. (Unpublished doctoral dissertation). Stanford University.

McGee, J. R., Wang, C., & Polly, D. (2013). Guiding teachers in the use of a standards-based mathematics curriculum: Perceptions and subsequent instructional practices after an intensive professional development program. *School Science and Mathematics*, *113*(1), 16–28. doi:10.1111/j.1949-8594.2012.00172.x

McKernan, J. (1991). *Curriculum action research. A handbook of methods and resources for the reflective practitioner*. London: Kogan Page.

Mead, M., & Metraux, R. (1957). The image of the scientist amongst high school students. In B. Barbar & W. Hirsch (Eds.), The Sociology of Science, 38-61. Lewes, England: Falmer Press.

Means, B., Confrey, J., House, A., & Bhanot, R. (2008). STEM high schools: Specialized science technology engineering and mathematics secondary schools in the U.S. (Bill and Melinda Gates Foundation Report). Retrieved from http://www.hsalliance.org/stem/index.asp

MEB. (2008). *Öğretmen yeterlikleri: Öğretmenlik mesleği genel ve özel alan yeterlikleri* [Teacher Competencies: General and specific field competencies of teaching profession]. Ankara: Devlet Kitapları Müdürlüğü.

Meijer, P., Zanting, A., & Verloop, N. (2002). How can student teachers elicit experienced teachers' practical knowledge? Tools, suggestions, and significance. *Journal of Teacher Education*, *53*(5), 406–419. doi:10.1177/002248702237395

Merç, A. (2004). *Reflections of PTs throughout their teaching practicum: What has been good? What has gone wrong? What has changed?* [Unpublished MA Thesis]. Anadolu University, Eskişehir, Turkey.

Merç, A. (2010). Self-reported problems of pre-service EFL teachers throughout their practicum. *Anadolu University Journal of Social Sciences*, *10*(2), 199–226.

Merriam, S. B. (2009). *Qualitative research: A guide to design and implementation*. San Francisco: John Wiley and Sons.

Mewborn, D. S. (1999). Reflective thinking among preservice elementary mathematics teachers. *Journal for Research in Mathematics Education*, *30*(9), 316–341. doi:10.2307/749838

Miaoulis, I. (2009). *Engineering the K-12 curriculum for technological innovation*. USA Today's Engineer Online.

Miles, B. M., Huberman, A. M., & Saldaña, J. (2014). *Qualitative data analysis: A methods sourcebook* (3rd ed.). Washington, DC: Sage Publications.

Millar, R., & Osborne, J. (1998). *Beyond 2000: Science education for the future*. London: Nuffield Seminar Series: Interim Report V3.

Millar, R., Osborne, J., & Nott, M. (1998). Science education for the future. *The School Science Review*, *80*(291), 19–25.

Ministry of National Education [MoNE]. (2013). *National education statistics: Formal education: 2012-2013*. MoNE: Ankara.

Mishra, P., & Koehler, M. (2006). Technological pedagogical content knowledge: A framework for teacher knowledge. *Teachers College Record*, *108*(6), 1017–1054.

Mitchell, S. N., Reilly, R. C., & Logue, M. E. (2009). Benefits of collaborative action research for the beginning teacher. *Teaching and Teacher Education*, *25*(2), 344–349. doi:10.1016/j.tate.2008.06.008

Moakler, M. W. Jr, & Kim, M. M. (2014). College Major Choice in STEM: Revisiting Confidence and Demographic Factors. *The Career Development Quarterly*, *62*(2), 128–142. doi:10.1002/j.2161-0045.2014.00075.x

MoNE. (2008). *Teacher competencies: general and specific areas competencies for the teaching profession*. Ankara, Turkey: The Directorate of State Books.

Munby, J. (1978). *Communicative syllabus design: A sociolinguistic model for defining the content of purpose-specific language programmers*. Cambridge: Cambridge University Press.

Mutlu-Pehlivan, N., Yesildag-Hasancebi, F., Tanriverdi, K., & Gunel, M. (2013). *Dusunen, tartisan, uygulayan ogrenciler icin ATBO uygulamasi: Alan bilgisi ve bilim ogrenme sureci ogrenme surecleriende ogretmen yaklasimlari*. Paper presented at the 10th Annual Best Practices in Education Conference (EIOK), Istanbul, Turkey.

Myles, J., Cheng, L., & Wang, H. (2006). Teaching in elementary school: Perceptions of foreign-trained teacher candidates on their teaching practicum. *Teaching and Teacher Education, 22*(2), 233–245. doi:10.1016/j.tate.2005.09.001

NAS/NAE. (2007). *Rising above the gathering storm: Energizing and employing America for a brighter economic future*. Washington, D. C.: National Academies Press.

National Academy of Engineering. (2004). NAE Annual Report 2004. Retrieved from https://www.nae.edu/File.aspx?id=43371

National Academy of Engineering. (2009). *Engineering in K-12 education: Understanding the status and improving the prospects*. Washington, DC: National Academies Press.

National Council for Teachers of Mathematics. (2014). *Principles to Action*. Reston, VA: Author.

National Mathematics Advisory Panel. (2008). *Foundations for Success*. Washington, DC: U.S. Department of Education.

National Research Council (NRC). (1996). *National science education standards*. Washington, DC: Academic Press.

National Research Council (NRC). (2012). *A Framework for K-12 science education. Practices, Crosscutting Concepts, and core ideas*. Washington, D.C.: National Academy Press.

National Research Council. (2000). *Inquiry and the National Science Education Standards: a guide for teaching and learning*. Washington, DC: National Academy Press.

National Research Council. (2011). *Expanding Underrepresented Minority Participation: America's Science and Technology Talent at the Crossroads*. Washington, DC: National Academies Press.

National Science Board. (2004). *Science and engineering indicators 2004*. Arlington, VA: National Science Board.

National Science Board. (2007). *National Action Plan for Addressing the Critical Needs of the U.S. Science, Technology, Engineering, and Mathematics Education System*. Arlington, VA: National Science Foundation.

National Science Board. (2008). *Science and engineering indicators 2008*. Arlington, VA: National Science Foundation.

National Science Board. (2010). *Science & Engineering Indicators 2010*. Arlington, VA: National Science Foundation.

Nation, I. S. P., & Macalister, J. (2009). *Language curriculum design*. New York, London: Routledge.

Nespor, J. (1987). The role of beliefs in the practice of teaching. *Journal of Curriculum Studies, 19*(4), 317–328. doi:10.1080/0022027870190403

Newmann, F. M., & Wehlage, G. G. (1993). Five standards for authentic instruction. *Educational Leadership, 50*(7), 8–12.

Nguyen, D. H. (2013, March 25). *Bilingual education in Vietnam: Success and challenges*. CambridgeEducational Leadership Seminar; Ho Chi Mihn City. Retrieved from http://www.cambridgeassessment.org.uk/Images/137032-dr-dong-hai-nguyen-presentation-slides-.pdf

Noe, R. A. (1988). An investigation of the determinants of successful assigned mentoring relationship. *Personnel Psychology, 41*(1), 457–479. doi:10.1111/j.1744-6570.1988.tb00638.x

Norton-Meier, L., Hand, B., Günel, M., & Akkuş, R. (2009). *Teaching in the service of learning: A 3–year mixed methods study of embedding authentic language and science practices within elementary science classrooms.* Paper Presented at Annual Meeting of American Educational Research, AERA Annual Conference, San Diego, CA.

Nuhoğlu, H. (2008). The development of an attitude scale for science and technology course. *Elementary Education Online, 7*(3), 627–638.

Numrich, C. (1996). On becoming a language teacher: Insights from diary studies. *TESOL Quarterly, 30*(1), 131–153. doi:10.2307/3587610

Nye, B., Konstantopoulos, S., & Hedges, L. V. (2004). How large are teacher effects? *Educational Evaluation and Policy Analysis, 26*(3), 237–257. doi:10.3102/01623737026003237

Odabaşı Çimer, S. & Çimer, A. (2012). Issues around incorporating reflection in teacher education in Turkey. *Journal of Turkish Science Education, 9*(1), 17-30.

Oktay, Y. B., & Vancı-Osam, Ü. (2013). Viewing foreign language teachers' roles through the eyes of teachers and students. *Hacettepe University Journal of Education, 44*, 249–261.

Olesen, H. S. (2001). Professional Identity as Learning Processes in Life Histories. *Journal of Workplace Learning, 13*(7/8), 290–297. doi:10.1108/13665620110411076

Onen, F., Mertoğlu, H., Saka, M., & Gürdal, A. (2009). The effects of in-service training on teachers' knowledge about teaching methods and techniques: OPYEP Case. *Ahi Evran University Journal of Educational Faculty, 10*(3), 9–23.

Organization for Economic Co-operation and Development. [OECD] (2014). *Turkey: Overview of the education system (EAG 2014).* Retrieved from http://gpseducation.oecd.org/CountryProfile?primaryCountry=TUR&treshold=10&topic=EO

Orhun, E. (2002). Information and Communication Technologies in Education. In E.P.A. Orhun M., & Kommers (Ed.), Ege Üniversitesi: İzmir.

Othman, J., & Mohd Saat, R. (2009). Challenges of using English as a medium of instruction: Pre-service science teachers' perspective. *The Asia-Pacific Education Researcher, 18*(2), 307–316.

Overbaugh, R., & Lu, R. (2008). The impact of a NCLB-EETT funded professional development program on teacher self- efficacy and resultant implementation. *Journal of Research on Technology in Education, 41*(1), 43–62. doi:10.1080/15391523.2008.10782522

Oxford, R. L., Griffiths, C., Longhini, A., Cohen, A. D., Macaro, E., & Harris, V. (2014). Experts' personal metaphors and similes about language learning strategies. *System, 43*, 11–29. doi:10.1016/j.system.2014.01.001

Ozgur, S., Tanriverdi, K., Gunel, M., & Porikli, A. B. (2012). *Cevre ve mufredat entegrasyonu: canlilar ve hayat unitesinde deniz kestaneleri etkinligi.* Paper presented at the 10th Annual Meeting of National Science and Mathematics Education Conference (UFBMEK), Nigde.

Parsad, B., Lewis, L., & Farris, E. (2001). *Teacher preparation and professional development. 2000 (NCES Publication No. 2001-088).* Washington: D.C. National Center for Educational Statistics.

Patton, M. Q. (2015). *Qualitative Research & Evaluation Methods* (4th ed.). Thousand Oaks, CA: Sage.

Pedro, J. Y. (2005). Reflective practice: International and multidisciplinary perspectives. *Reflective Practice, 6*(1), 49–66.

Petraglia, J. (1998). *The rhetoric and technology of authenticity in education.* Mahwah, NJ: Lawrence Erlbaum.

Compilation of References

Polly, D., Martin, C. S., Wang, C., Lambert, R. G., & Pugalee, D. K. (under review). Primary grades teachers' instructional decisions while participating in mathematics formative assessment professional development.

Polly, D., Wang, C., Martin, C. S., Lambert, R. G., Pugalee, D. K., Stephan, M., & Ringer, C. (2014, April). Examining the influence of professional development on primary students' mathematical achievement. Paper presented at the 2014 Annual Meeting of the American Educational Research Association. Philadelphia, PA.

Polly, D. (2006). Participants' focus in a learner-centered technology-rich mathematics professional development program. *The Mathematics Educator*, *16*(1), 14–21.

Polly, D. (2011). Examining teachers' enactment of technological pedagogical and content knowledge (TPACK) in their mathematics teaching after technology integration professional development. *Journal of Computers in Mathematics and Science Teaching*, *30*(1), 37–59.

Polly, D. (2011). Teachers' learning while constructing technology-based instructional resources. *British Journal of Educational Technology*, *42*(6), 950–961. doi:10.1111/j.1467-8535.2010.01161.x

Polly, D., & Hannafin, M. J. (2010). Reexamining technology's role in learner-centered professional development. *Educational Technology Research and Development*, *58*(5), 557–571. doi:10.1007/s11423-009-9146-5

Polly, D., & Hannafin, M. J. (2011). Examining how learner-centered professional development influences teachers' espoused and enacted practices. *The Journal of Educational Research*, *104*(2), 120–130. doi:10.1080/00220671003636737

Polly, D., McGee, J. R., & Martin, C. S. (2010). Employing technology-rich mathematical tasks to develop teachers' technological, pedagogical, and content knowledge (TPACK). *Journal of Computers in Mathematics and Science Teaching*, *29*(4), 455–472.

Polly, D., McGee, J. R., Wang, C., Martin, C. S., Lambert, R. G., & Pugalee, D. K. (in press). Linking professional development, teacher outcomes, and student achievement: The case of a learner-centered mathematics program for elementary school teachers. *International Journal of Educational Research*.

Polly, D., & Mims, C. (2009). Designing professional development to support teachers' TPACK and integration of Web 2.0 technologies. In T. T. Kidd & I. Chen (Eds.), *Wired for Learning: Web 2.0 Guide for Educators* (pp. 301–316).

Polly, D., & Orrill, C. H. (2012). Developing technological pedagogical and content knowledge (TPACK) through professional development focused on technology-rich mathematics tasks. *Meridian*, *15*, •••. Retrieved from http://ced.ncsu.edu/meridian/index.php/meridian/article/view/44/43

Polly, D., Wang, C., McGee, J. R., Lambert, R. G., Martin, C. S., & Pugalee, D. K. (2014). Examining the influence of a curriculum-based elementary mathematics professional development program. *Journal of Research in Childhood Education*, *28*(3), 327–343. doi:10.1080/02568543.2014.913276

Porter, A., Garet, M., Deimone, L., Yoon, K., & Birman, B. (2000). *Does professional development change teaching practice? Results from a three year study*. Washington, D.C.: US Department of Education.

Posner, G. J., Strike, K. A., Hewson, P. W., & Gertzog, W. A. (1982). Accommodation of a scientific conception: Toward a theory of conceptual change. *Science Education*, *66*(2), 211–227. doi:10.1002/sce.3730660207

Potter, S. L., & Rockinson-Szapkiw, A. J. (2012). Technology integration for instructional improvement: The impact of professional development. *Performance Improvement*, *51*(2), 22–27. doi:10.1002/pfi.21246

Puentedura, R. (2012). SAMR Model (Image). Retrieved from http://hippasus.com/rrpweblog

Puentedura, R. R. (2012). The SAMR model: Background and exemplars.

Quinn, D. M. (2003). Legal Issues in Educational Technology: Implications for School Leaders. *Educational Administration Quarterly, 39*(2), 187–207. doi:10.1177/0013161X03251152

Ragins, B. R., & Kram, K. E. (2007). The roots and meaning of mentoring. In B. R. Ragins & K. E. Kram (Eds.), *The handbook of mentoring at work*. London: Sage Publications Ltd.

Rakıcıoğlu-Söylemez, A. (2012). *An exploratory case study of pre-service EFL teachers' sense of efficacy beliefs and perceptions of mentoring practices during practice teaching* [Unpublished Doctoral Dissertation]. Middle East Technical University, Ankara, Turkey.

Rakıcıoğlu-Söylemez, A., & Eröz-Tuğa, B. (2014). Mentoring expectations and experiences of prospective and cooperating teachers during practice teaching. *Australian Journal of Teacher Education, 39*(10), 146–168.

Research Now. (2012). Math Relevance to U.S. middle school students: A survey commissioned by Raytheon Company. Retrieved from http://www.raytheon.com/newsroom/rtnwcm/groups/corporate/documents/content/rtn12_studentsmth_results.pdf

Richardson, K. (1998). *Developing Number Concepts: Counting, Comparing, and Pattern*. New York: Dale Seymour.

Richardson, K. (2012). *How Children Learn Number Concepts: A Guide to the Critical Learning Phases*. Bellingham, WA: Math Perspectives.

Richardson, V., & Placier, P. (2001). Teacher change. In V. Richardson (Ed.), *Handbook of Research on Teaching* (4th ed.; pp. 905–947). Washington, DC: American Educational Research Association.

Richert, A. E. (1992). Voice and power in teaching and learning to teach. In L. Valli (Ed.), *Reflective teacher education: Cases and critiques* (pp. 187–197). Albany: State University of New York Press.

Riegle-Crumb, C., & Grodsky, E. (2010). Racial ethnic differences at the intersection of math course-taking and achievement. *Sociology of Education, 83*(3), 248–270. doi:10.1177/0038040710375689

Rivkin, S. G., Hanushek, E. A., & Kain, J. F. (2005). Teachers, schools, and academic achievement. *Econometrica, 79*(2), 417–458. doi:10.1111/j.1468-0262.2005.00584.x

Robb, T. (2006). Helping teachers to help themselves. In P. Hubbard & M. Levy (Eds.), *Teacher education in CALL*. Amsterdam: John Benjamins. doi:10.1075/lllt.14.27rob

Robichaux, R. R., & And Guarino, A. J. (2012). Enhancing preservice teachers' professionalism through daily teaching reflections. *Education Research International, 2012*, 1–3. doi:10.1155/2012/452687

Rodman, G. J. (2010). Facilitating the teaching-learning process through the reflective engagement of pre-service teacher. *Australian Journal of Teacher Education, 35*(2), 20–34.

Roness, D., & Smith, K. (2010). Stability in motivation during teacher education. *Journal of Education for Teaching, 36*(2), 169–185. doi:10.1080/02607471003651706

Rosen, L. (2012). STEM gets a boost from Business: Business leaders are partnering with elementary schools to help increase students' interest and achievement in STEM. Retrieved from https://www.naesp.org/book/export/html/4708

Ross, D. (1989). First steps in developing a reflective approach. *Journal of Teacher Education, 40*(2), 22–30. doi:10.1177/002248718904000205

Rots, I., Kelchtermans, G., & Aelterman, A. (2012). Learning (not) to become a teacher: A qualitative analysis of the job entrance issue. *Teaching and Teacher Education, 28*(1), 1–10. doi:10.1016/j.tate.2011.08.008

Rozelle, J., & Wilson, S. (2012). Opening the black box of field experiences: How cooperating teachers' beliefs and practices shape student teachers' beliefs and practices. *Teaching and Teacher Education, 28*(8), 1196–1205. doi:10.1016/j.tate.2012.07.008

Rubba, P. A. (1985). Chemistry teachers inservice needs: Are they unique? *Journal of Chemical Education, 58*(5), 430–431. doi:10.1021/ed058p430

Rudd, J., Greenbowe, T., Hand, B., & Legg, M. (2001). *Using the science writing heuristic to promote conceptual understanding of equilibrium*. Paper presented at the 221st National Meeting of the American Chemical Society, San Diego CA.

Ruohotie-Lyhty, M. (2013). Struggling for a professional identity: Two newly qualified language teachers' identity narratives during the first years at work. *Teaching and Teacher Education, 30*, 120–129. doi:10.1016/j.tate.2012.11.002

Rusznyak, L., & Walton, E. (2014). Affordances and limitations of a special school practicum as a means to prepare pre-service teachers for inclusive education. *International Journal of Inclusive Education, 18*(9), 957–974. doi:10.1080/13603116.2013.872203

Saban, A. (2006). Functions of metaphor in teaching and teacher education: A review essay. *Teaching Education, 17*(4), 299–315. doi:10.1080/10476210601017386

Saban, A. (2010). Prospective teachers' metaphorical conceptualizations of learner. *Teaching and Teacher Education, 26*(2), 290–305. doi:10.1016/j.tate.2009.03.017

Saban, A., Koçbeker, B. N., & Saban, A. (2006). An investigation of the concept of teacher among prospective teachers through metaphor analysis. *Educational Sciences: Theory and Practice, 6*(2), 509–522.

Saban, A., Koçbeker, B. N., & Saban, A. (2007). Prospective teachers' conceptions of teaching and learning revealed through metaphor analysis. *Learning and Instruction, 17*(2), 123–139. doi:10.1016/j.learninstruc.2007.01.003

Sadaf, A., Newby, T. J., & Ertmer, P. A. (2012). Exploring factors that predict preservice teachers' intentions to use web 2.0 technologies using decomposed theory of planned behavior. *Journal of Research on Technology in Education, 45*(2), 171–195. doi:10.1080/15391523.2012.10782602

Sahin–Taskin, C. (2006). Student teachers in the classroom: Their perceptions of teaching practice. *Educational Studies, 32*(4), 387–398. doi:10.1080/03055690600948091

Sanders, G., Kuit, J., Smith, P., Fulton, J. & Curtis, H. (2011). Identity, reflection and developmental networks as processes in professional doctorate development. *Work Based Learning e-Journal, 2*(1), 113-134.

Sanders, G. (2010). Towards a Model of Multi-organisational Work-based Learning: Developmental networks as a mechanism for tacit knowledge transfer and exploration of professional identity. *Learning and Teaching in Higher Education, 4*(1), 51–68.

Sanders, G., Kuit, J., Smith, P., & Fulton, J. (2012). Hidden Voices: Searching for Authenticity in Professional Doctorate Candidates.*Third International conference on Professional Doctorates*, UK Council for Graduate Education.

Schibeci, R. A., & Sorenson, I. (1983). Elementary school children's perceptions of scientists. *School Science and Mathematics, 83*(1), 14–19. doi:10.1111/j.1949-8594.1983.tb10087.x

Schon, D. (1987). *Educating the reflective practitioner Toward a new design for teaching and learning in the professions*. San Francisco: Jossey Bass.

Schön, D. S. (1983). *The Reflective Practitioner*. London: Temple Smith.

Seferoğlu, G. (2006). Teacher candidates' reflections on some components of a pre-service English teacher education programme in Turkey. *Journal of Education for Teaching, 32*(4), 369–378. doi:10.1080/02607470600981953

Seferoğlu, G., Korkmazgil, S., & Ölçü, Z. (2009). Gaining insights into teachers' ways of thinking via metaphors. *Educational Studies, 35*(3), 323–335. doi:10.1080/03055690802648135

Seferoğlu, S. S. (2004). Öğretmen yeterlikleri ve mesleki gelişim.[Teacher competencies and professional development]. *Bilim ve Aklın Aydınlığında Eğitim, 58*, 40–45.

Semerci, C. (2007). Developing a reflective thinking tendency scale for teachers and student teachers. *Educational Sciences: Theory and Practice, 7*(3), 1369–1376.

Sherin, M. G., & Drake, C. (2009). Curriculum strategy framework: Investigating patterns in teachers' use of a reform-based mathematics curriculum. *Journal of Curriculum Studies, 41*(4), 467–500. doi:10.1080/00220270802696115

Shulman, L. S. (1986). Those who understand: Knowledge growth in teaching. *Educational Researcher, 15*(2), 4–14. doi:10.3102/0013189X015002004

Simon, M. A., & Schifter, D. (1987). *Teacher education from a constructivist perspective: The educational leaders in mathematics project*. Washington, DC: National Science Foundation (TEI-8552391).

Simon, M. (1995). Reconstructing mathematics pedagogy from a constructivist perspective. *Journal for Research in Mathematics Education, 26*(2), 114–145. doi:10.2307/749205

Sinclair, C. (2008). Initial and changing student teacher motivation and commitment to teaching. *Asia-Pacific Journal of Teacher Education, 36*(2), 79–104. doi:10.1080/13598660801971658

Slick, S. (1998). The university supervisor: A disenfranchised outsider. *Teaching and Teacher Education, 14*(8), 821–834. doi:10.1016/S0742-051X(98)00028-6

Smith, P., Curtis, H., Sanders, G., Kuit, J. & Fulton, J. (2011). Student perceptions of the professional doctorate. *Work Based Learning e-Journal, 2*(1), 135-154.

Smith, P., Walker-Gleaves, C., Fulton, J., & Candlish, C. (2009a). Developing Inter-Professional Communities of Practice within the context of a Professional Doctorate Programme. Proceedings of Higher Education Academy conference, Manchester.

Smith, K. A., & Welliver, P. (2006). The development of a science process assessment for fourth-grade students. *Journal of Research in Science Teaching, 27*(8), 727–738. doi:10.1002/tea.3660270803

Smith, P., Walker-Gleaves, C., Fulton, J., & Candlish, C. (2009b). The Professional Doctorate within the context of Leadership Development Strategies.*First International conference on Professional Doctorates*, UK Council for Graduate Education.

Snape, P., & Fox-Turnbull, W. (2013). Perspectives of authenticity: Implementation in technology education. *International Journal of Technology and Design Education, 23*(1), 51–68. doi:10.1007/s10798-011-9168-2

Stake, R. (2005). Qualitative case studies. In N. K. Denzin & Y. S. Lincoln (Eds.), *The Sage handbook of qualitative research* (pp. 433–466). Thousand Oaks, CA: Sage.

State Planning Organization. (n.d.). *The study of socio-economic development ranking of the provinces*. Retrieved from http://www.dpt.gov.tr/DPT.portal

Stein, M. K., Smith, M. S., & Silver, E. A. (1999). The development of professional developers: Learning to assist teachers in new settings in new ways. *Harvard Educational Review, 69*(3), 237–269. doi:10.17763/haer.69.3.h2267130727v6878

Stemler, S. (2001). An overview of content analysis. *Practical Assessment, Research & Evaluation, 7*(17). Retrieved from http://PAREonline. net/getvn.asp? v=7 &n=17

Stipek, D. J., Givvin, K. B., Salmon, J. M., & MacGyvers, V. L. (2001). Teachers' beliefs and practices related to mathematics instruction. *Teaching and Teacher Education, 17*(2), 213–226. doi:10.1016/S0742-051X(00)00052-4

Stockwell, G. (2009). Teacher Education in CALL: Teaching teachers to educate themselves. *Innovation in Language Learning and Teaching, 3*(1), 99–112. doi:10.1080/17501220802655524

Stokes, A. (1997). Making a success of CALL. *English Teaching Professional, 4*, 20–21.

Strauss, A., & Corbin, J. (1998). Basics of qualitative research: Procedures and techniques for developing grounded theory. Thousand Oaks, CA: Sage.

Strauss, A., & Corbin, J. (1998). *Basics of qualitative research: Techniques and procedures for developing grounded theory* (2nd ed.). Thousand Oaks, CA: Sage.

Strobel, J., Wang, J., Weber, N. R., & Dyehouse, M. (2013). The role of authenticity in design-based learning environments: The case of engineering education. *Computers & Education, 64*, 143–152. doi:10.1016/j.compedu.2012.11.026

Stuart, C., & Thurlow, D. (2000). Making it their own: Preservice teachers' experiences, beliefs, and classroom practice. *Journal of Teacher Education, 51*(2), 113–121. doi:10.1177/002248710005100205

Sun, Y., & Strobel, J. (2013). Elementary engineering education (EEE) adoption and expertise development framework: An inductive and deductive study. *Journal of Pre-College Engineering Education Research, 3*(1), 32–52.

Sun, Y., & Strobel, J. (2014). From knowing-about to knowing-to: Development of engineering PCK by elementary teachers through perceived learning and implementing difficulties. *American Journal of Engineering Education, 5*(1), 41–60.

Supovitz, J. A., Mayers, D. P., & Kahle, J. B. (2000). Promoting inquiry-based instructional practice: The longitudinal impact of professional development in the context of systemic reform. *Educational Policy, 14*(3), 331–356. doi:10.1177/0895904800014003001

Supovitz, J. A., & Turner, H. M. (2000). The effects of professional development on science teaching practices and classroom culture. *Journal of Research in Science Teaching, 37*(9), 963–980. doi:10.1002/1098-2736(200011)37:9<963::AID-TEA6>3.0.CO;2-0

Swan, M. (2006). Designing and using research instruments to describe the beliefs and practices of mathematics teachers. *Research in Education, 75*(-1), 58–70. doi:10.7227/RIE.75.5

Tang, S. Y. F., Cheng, M. M. H., & Cheng, A. Y. N. (2013). Shifts in teaching motivation and sense of self as teacher. *Educational Review, 66*(4), 465-481.

Tang, S. Y. F. (2004). The dynamics of school-based learning in initial teacher education. *Research Papers in Education, 19*(2), 185–204. doi:10.1080/02671520410001695425

Tanriverdi, K., & Gunel, M. (2012). *Ogretmen pedagojisinde kritik sorun: Degisime karsi direnc*. Paper presented at the 10th Annual Meeting of National Science and Mathematics Education Conference (UFBMEK), Nigde.

Tanriverdi, K., Gunel, M., Asci, O., & Ocak, A. (2013). *365 day in-service training*. Paper presented at the 1st International Conference on Immersion Approaches to Argument-based Inquiry (ABI) for Science Classrooms, Busan, Korea.

Taylor, A. (2007). Learning to Become Researching Professionals: The case of the Doctorate of Education. *International Journal of Teaching and Learning in Higher Education, 19*(2), 154–166.

Taylor, S., & Todd, P. A. (1995). Understanding information technology usage: A test of competing models. *Information Systems Research*, *6*(2), 144–176. doi:10.1287/isre.6.2.144

TERC. (2008). *Investigations in Number, Data, and Space* (2nd ed.). Saddle River, NJ: Pearson.

Thair, M., & Treagust, D. F. (2003). A brief history of a science teacher professional development initiative in Indonesia and the implications for centralised teacher development. *International Journal of Educational Development*, *23*(2), 201–213. doi:10.1016/S0738-0593(02)00014-7

The Holmes Group. (1996). *Tomorrow's teachers: A report of the Holmes Group*. East Lansing, MI: The Holmes Group.

Thomas, L., & Beauchamp, C. (2011). Understanding new teachers' professional identities through metaphor. *Teaching and Teacher Education*, *27*(4), 762–769. doi:10.1016/j.tate.2010.12.007

Thompson, J., Smith, P. & Cooper, B. (2012). An autoethnographic study of the impact of reflection and doctoral study on practice. *Work Based Learning e-Journal*, *2*(2), 1-12.

Tinto, V. (1993). *Leaving college: rethinking the causes and cures of student attrition* (2nd ed.). Chicago, London: University of Chicago Press.

Tlhoaele, M. J., & Van Ryneveld, L. (2008). What's in it for me? An analysis of the need for credit-bearing professional development modules on the topic of elearning. *SAJHE*, *22*(6), 1279–1291.

Tsui, B. M. (2003). *Understanding expertise in teaching: Case studies of second language teachers*. Cambridge: Cambridge University Press. doi:10.1017/CBO9781139524698

uentedura, R. (2012). SAMR Model (Image). Retrieved from http://hippasus.com/rrpweblog

UKCGE. (2010). *Professional Doctorate Awards in the UK*. London: UK Council for Graduate Education.

United States Department of Education. (2008). Foundations for Success: The Final Report of the National Mathematics Advisory Panel. Retrieved from http://www2.ed.gov/about/bdscomm/list/mathpanel/report/final-report.pdf

Usher, E. L., & Pajares, F.Timms Study Usher. (2008). Sources of self-efficacy in school: Critical review of the literatures and future directions. *Review of Educational Research*, *78*(4), 751–796. doi:10.3102/0034654308321456

Van Driel, J. H., Beijaard, D., & Verloop, N. (2001). Professional development and reform in science education: The role of teachers' practical knowledge. *Journal of Research in Science Teaching*, *38*(2), 137–158. doi:10.1002/1098-2736(200102)38:2<137::AID-TEA1001>3.0.CO;2-U

Van Driel, J. H., Verloop, N., & de Vos, W. (1998). Developing science teachers' pedagogical content knowledge. *Journal of Research in Science Teaching*, *35*(6), 673–695. doi:10.1002/(SICI)1098-2736(199808)35:6<673::AID-TEA5>3.0.CO;2-J

Vann, C. B. (2013). Pioneering a new path for STEM education. *Industrial Engineer*, *45*(5), 30–33.

Verbinska, D. (2014). Stability and variability in pre-service language teachers' beliefs. In M. Pawlak, J. Bielak, & A. Mystkowska-Wiertelak (Eds.), *Classroom-oriented research* (pp. 33–53). Berlin: Springer. doi:10.1007/978-3-319-00188-3_3

Volman, M. (2005). A variety of roles for a new type of teacher educational technology and the teaching profession. *Teaching and Teacher Education*, *2*(1), 15–31. doi:10.1016/j.tate.2004.11.003

Vygotsky, L. S. (1978). *Mind and society: The development of higher mental processes*. Cambridge, MA: Harvard University Press.

Compilation of References

Vygotsky, L. S. (1978). *Mind in society: The development of higher psychological processes* (M. Cole, V. John-Steiner, S. Scribner, & E. Souberman, Trans. & Eds.). Cambridge, MA: Harvard University Press.

Wallance, C., Yang, E.-M., Hand, B., & Hohenshell, L. (2001). *Using a science writing heuristic to enhance learning from laboratory activities in seventh grade science: Quantitative and qualitative outcomes.* Paper presented at the annual meeting of the National Association for Research in Science Teaching, St. Louis, MO.

Wang, C., Polly, D., Lambert, R. G., Pugalee, D. K., & Evans, A. (2014, February). Examining the influence of elementary mathematics professional development on formative assessment of teachers. Presentation given at the Annual Meeting of the North Carolina Association for Research in Education: Greensboro, NC.

Wang, C., Polly, D., Lehew, A., Pugalee, D., Lambert, R., & Martin, C. S. (2013). Supporting teachers' enactment of elementary school student-centered mathematics pedagogies: The evaluation of a curriculum-focused professional development program. *New Waves - Educational.*[PubMed]. *Research for Development*, *16*(1), 76–91. Retrieved from http://www.caerda.org/journal/index.php/newwaves/article/view/97/46 PMID:23154410

Warshauer, M. (1996). Computer-Assisted Language Learning: An Introduction. In S. Fotos (Ed.), *Multimedia language teaching* (pp. 3–20). Tokyo: Logos International.

Weick, K. E., & Sutcliffe, K. M. (2006). Mindfulness and the Quality of Organisational Attention. *Organization Science*, *17*(4), 514–524. doi:10.1287/orsc.1060.0196

Wellington, J., & Osborne, J. (2001). *Language and literacy in science education.* Philadelphia, PA: Open University Press.

Wiebe, G., & Kabata, K. (2010). Students' and instructors' attitudes toward the use of CALL in foreign language teaching and learning. *Computer Assisted Language Learning*, *23*(3), 221–234. doi:10.1080/09588221.2010.486577

Wiggins, G., & McTighe, J. (2005). *Understanding by design* (2nd ed.). Alexandria, VA: Association for Supervision & Curriculum Development.

Wiliam, D. (2007b). What does research say the benefits of formative assessment are? National Council of Teachers of Mathematics Research Brief. Retrieved from http://www.nctm.org/uploadedFiles/Research_News_and_Advocacy/Research/Clips_and_Briefs/Research_brief_05_-_Formative_Assessment.pdf

Wiliam, D. (2007a). Keeping learning on track: Formative assessment and the regulation of learning. In F. K. Lester (Ed.), *Second Handbook of Mathematics Teaching and Learning* (pp. 1053–1098). Greenwich, CT: Information Age Publishing.

Wiliam, D., & Thompson, M. (2007). Integrating assessment with instruction: what will it take to make it work? In C. A. Dwyer (Ed.), *The future of assessment: shaping teaching and learning* (pp. 53–82). Mahwah, NJ: Lawrence Erlbaum Associates.

William, D. (2010). An integrative summary of the research literature and implications for a new theory of formative assessment. In H. Andrade & G. Cizek (Eds.), *Handbook of formative assessment* (pp. 18–40). New York, NY: Routledge.

Williams, J. (2009). Beyond the practicum experience. *ELT Journal*, *63*(1), 68–77. doi:10.1093/elt/ccn012

Wilson, S. M. (2011). Effective STEM teacher preparation, induction, and professional development. Paper presented at the National Research Counci's Workshop on Successful STEM Education in K–12 Schools, Washington, DC.

Windschitd, M. (2002). Framing constructivism in practice as the negotiation of dilemmas: An analysis of the conceptual, pedagogical, cultural and political challenges facing teachers. *Review of Educational Research*, *72*(2), 131–175. doi:10.3102/00346543072002131

Work, A. P. A. Group of the Board of Educational Affairs (1997). Learner-centered psychological principles: A framework for school reform and redesign. Washington, DC.

Yahaya, M. F., Noor, M. A., Mokhtar, A. A., Rawian, R. B., Othman, M. B., & Jusoff, K. (2009). Teaching of mathematics and science in English: The teachers' voices. *English Language Teaching*, *2*(2), 141–147. doi:10.5539/elt.v2n2p141

Yasar, S., Baker, D., Robinson-Kurpius, S., Krause, S., & Roberts, C. (2006). Development of a survey to assess K–12 teachers' perception of Engineers and familiarity with teaching design, engineering, and technology. *The Journal of Engineering Education*, *95*(3), 205–216. doi:10.1002/j.2168-9830.2006.tb00893.x

Yeşilbursa, A. (2012). Using metaphor to explore the professional role identities of higher education English language instructors. *Procedia: Social and Behavioral Sciences*, *46*, 468–472. doi:10.1016/j.sbspro.2012.05.143

Yeşilbursa, A., & Sayar, E. (2014). *EFL teachers' professional identity: A metaphor analysis.* Saarbrücken: LAP Lambert Academic Publishing.

Yesildag-Hasancebi, F. (2014). *Argumantasyon Tabanli Bilim Ogrenme Yaklasiminin (ATBO) Ogrencilerin Fen Basarilari, Arguman Olusturma Becerileri ve Grup İci Etkilesimleri Uzerine Etkisi.* (Unpublished PhD thesis). Ataturk University.

Yesildag-Hasancebi, F., & Gunel, M. (2013). Effect of the argumentation based inquiry approach on disadvantaged students' science achievement. *Elementary Education Online*, *12*(4), 1056–1073.

Yesildag-Hasancebi, F., & Gunel, M. (2014). Delving into the effect of argumentation based inquiry approach on learning science from multiple perspectives. *Journal of Research in Education and Society*, *1*(1), 23–44.

Yin, R. K. (2003). *Case study research: Design and method.* Thousand Oaks, CA: Sage.

Yin, R. K. (2011). *Qualitative research from start to finish.* New York, NY: The Guilford Press.

Yoon, K. S., Duncan, T., Lee, S. W. Y., Scarloss, B., & Shapley, K. (2007). Reviewing the evidence on how teacher professional development affects student achievement (Vol. 033). Washington, DC: US Department of Education.

Yoon, K. S., Duncan, T., Lee, S. W.-Y., Scarloss, B., & Shapley, K. (2007). Reviewing the evidence on how teacher professional development affects student achievement (Issues & Answers Report, REL 2007–No. 033). Washington, DC: U.S. Department of Education; Retrieved from http://ies.ed.gov/ncee/edlabs

Youngs, P. (2013). *Using teacher evaluation reform and professional development to support Common Core assessments.* Washington, D.C.: Center for American Progress.

Yuan, R., & Lee, I. (2014). Pre-service teachers' changing beliefs in the teaching practicum: Three cases in an EFL context. *System*, *44*, 1–12. doi:10.1016/j.system.2014.02.002

Yuan, R., & Lee, I. (2014). Understanding language teacher educators' professional experiences: An exploratory study in Hong Kong. *The Asia-Pacific Education Researcher*, *23*(1), 143–149. doi:10.1007/s40299-013-0117-6

Yüksel, İ. (2012). The current developments in teacher education in Turkey on the threshold of European Union. *International Journal of Humanities and Social Science*, *2*(8), 49–56.

Zeichner, K. M. (1990). Changing directions in the practicum: Looking ahead to the 1990's. *Journal of Education for Teaching*, *16*(2), 105–132. doi:10.1080/0260747900160201

Zeldin, A. L., & Pajares, F. (2000). Against the odds: Self-efficacy beliefs of women in mathematical, scientific and technological careers. *American Educational Research Journal*, *37*(1), 215–246. doi:10.3102/00028312037001215

Zemke, R., & Zemke, S. (1995). Adult Learning: What Do We Know For Sure? *Training (New York, N.Y.)*, *32*(6), 31–40.

Zepeda, S. J. (1999). *Staff Development Practices That Promote Leadership in Learning Communities.* Larchmont, NY: Eye on Education.

About the Contributors

Kenan Dikilitas is currently an Assistant Professor at department of English language teaching at Hasan Kalyoncu University, Gaziantep, Turkey. He completed his PhD in ELT at Yeditepe University, Istanbul. He has published articles and edited books on teacher research as a professional development strategy. He has also conducted teacher research projects and has given hands-on workshops on how to do educational research across Turkey and overseas. His teacher training experience primarily includes supporting teacher research for professional development. His primary research interests are language teacher education, educational research, research into language teaching and learning, and linguistics for teaching pedagogy. He is one of the committee members of IATEFL ReSIG.

* * *

Sedat Akayoglu graduated from the Department of English Language and Literature, Hacettepe University in 2002 and he completed his MA degree at Abant Izzet Baysal University. He moved to Ankara and started to work at Middle East Technical University in 2007 and he completed his PhD Degree at the same university. Currently, he is working as an assistant professor at AIBU.

Patricia Dickenson is Lead Faculty of Teacher Education at National University in San Jose. She completed her doctoral work at the University of Southern California in Educational Psychology. Her research focuses on the sociocultural aspects of motivation, engagement, and instruction, within mathematics, technology and standard-based teaching practices of Latino English learners. Dr. Dickenson began teaching for the Los Angeles Unified School District. She has taught elementary, middle and high school. In addition to classroom teaching Dr. Dickenson was a Mathematics Coach. She believes strongly in the use of alternative assessments such as performance based tasks, project-based learning and authentic assessment to measure students knowledge and skills. Dr. Dickenson has worked as a teacher trainer and consultant for Princeton Review and Harcourt Publishing. She has taught courses in Teacher Education at University of California Santa Cruz, University of Southern California and University of Phoenix. Dr. Dickenson Website: www.doctorofed.com Twitter: @techteacherprep.

Yesim Kesli Dollar is an assistant professor and chair of the Department of Foreign Language Education at Bahcesehir University, Turkey. Dr. Kesli Dollar holds a BA degree in ELT from Middle East Technical University, Turkey; a MA and a Ph.D. degree in English Language Education from Cukurova University, Turkey, and a second MA degree in Applied Linguistics from Texas Tech University, USA.

Some of Dr. Kesli Dollar's professional interests include SLA, language teacher education (pre-service and in-service), teaching English to young learners, curriculum evaluation and design, use of technology in language education.

Donna Farland-Smith is an Associate Professor of Science Education in the School of Teaching & Learning at The Ohio State University. Her research focuses on middle school girls' attitudes and perceptions of scientists who are working 'side-by-side' with scientists as well as the characteristics of scientists that most positively affect the girl's perception of scientists. She previously taught science to all grades K-12.

John Fulton is Principal Lecturer in Nursing at University of Sunderland UK.

Murat Gunel is Professor at the Department of Primary Education, TED University. His research interest areas include argumentation based science inquiry, improving critical thinking skills, professional development for teachers, non-traditional writing in science, improving students' understanding of science with multi modal representations.

Alastair Irons is Associate Professor of Computing at University of Sunderland UK.

Melike Özer Keskin is Associate Professor at the Department of Biology Education, Gazi University. Her research interests include biology education, socioscientific issues, argumentation based inquiry and bioethics education.

Yasemin Kırkgöz works as a professor at the ELT Department of Çukurova University, Turkey. She completed her MA and PhD at Aston University, England. Previously, she has been a vice director and director of the Centre for Foreign Languages, curriculum coordinator, and teacher trainer. Her main research interests include foreign language education policy and its implementation, curriculum renewal, innovation management, teaching EAP/ESP in higher education, and the use of technology in education. She has published on these topics in international journals, and has reviewed several books. Yasemin has also received the IATEFL award for her work on Initiating and Managing the Process of Curriculum Innovation from the IATEFL's Leadership and Management Special Interest Group in 2013.

Richard Lambert is a Professor in the Department of Educational Leadership at the Univesrity of North Carolina at Charlotte. He has served as the external evaluator of multiple professional development grants and state-wide initiatives.

Christie Martin is an assistant professor in the Instruction and Teacher Education Department at the University of South Carolina in Columbia. Her research interests include content area writing, digital literacy, and evaluation of professional development.

About the Contributors

Enisa Mede is an Assistant Professor and the MA TEFL Program Coordinator of the Department of Foreign Language Education at Bahcesehir University, Istanbul, Turkey. She holds a BA degree from Bogazici University, Department of Foreign Language Education; and an MA and a PhD degree from Yeditepe University, Department of Foreign Language Education. Her chief research interests are program design and evaluation, early bilingualism, intercultural competency and language transfer.

Judith Montgomery has been the director of the Monterey Bay Area Math Project (MBAMP) since 1998. MBAMP is housed in the Mathematics Department and is the University of California Santa Cruz Mathematics project. MBAMP's primary purpose is to deliver Professional Development (PD) in mathematics to k-12 teachers, while mentoring teachers to become teacher leaders. MBAMP uses a teachers-teaching-teachers model for all PD.

İbrahim Nişanci graduated from the English Language Teaching Department, Hacettepe University in 2004. Since then he has been teaching English in different countries; Kosovo, Bosnia, and Iraq. He is currently teaching at ELT Department of Ishik University in Erbil. He has written his M.A. thesis on use of songs in language teaching. He is doing his PhD on English Language Teaching at Canakkale Onsekiz Mart University. His interest areas are developing materials from authentic videos and songs, ESP, and language teacher education.

Emsal Ates Özdemir holds a BA degree in English Language and Literature from Hacettepe University and holds MA in English Language Teaching from Mersin University. She has been teaching English for 17 years. Emsal has completed her PhD studies on "The use of technology in English Language Teaching" at Çukurova University. Constructivist learning theory, computer assisted language learning, moodle learning management system and the use of Web 2.0 technologies, Google Apps and IOS apps are among her interests. She is also a certified Google Education Trainer.

Drew Polly is an associate professor in the Department of Reading and Elementary Education at the University of North Carolina at Charlotte. His research agenda focuses on examining how to support the implementation of technology and standards-based pedagogies.

David Pugalee is the Director of the Center of Science, Technology, Engineering, and Mathematics (STEM) Education and a Professor in the Department of Middle Grades, Secondary, and K-12 Education at the University of North Carolina at Charlotte. His research interests focus on supporting research-based pedagogies in mathematics and incorporating writing in mathematics classrooms.

Reenay R. H. Rogers holds a Master's degree in secondary science education and a Ph. D. in instructional leadership with an emphasis in instructional technology from The University of Alabama. She is an assistant professor at The University of West Alabama. Dr. Rogers currently serves as a co-director for Project Engage, a STEM grant from the U. S. Department of Education, the chair of the Department of Instructional Leadership and Support, and was recently named Director of Assessment and Evaluation for the College of Education. Research interests include online education, technology integration, and STEM education.

Linda van Ryneveld believes that it is not what you teach, but what your students learn that matters. As such she is passionate about creating learning environments that are authentic and real, and prepare the learners for their future employment. She believes that learners, who take courses that are fun and inspirational, are more motivated to spend time on task. Linda van Ryneveld joined the University of Pretoria in March 2013 in the position of Director: Teaching and Learning, Faculty of Veterinary Science at the Onderstepoort campus. From 2008 to early 2013 she was the Director for Curriculum Development and Support at the Tshwane University of Technology. Previously, she was a Deputy Director in the Directorate for Teaching and Learning with Technology at the same institution. Linda van Ryneveld was awarded a Doctorate degree in Computer-Integrated Education by the University of Pretoria in 2004 and an Associate Professorship in 2013. Linda loves living life to the fullest and appreciates humour, passion and a zeal for life in others. Her current interests include all types of learning (including mobile learning), instructional and curriculum design, open educational resources, educational games and simulations, assessment, student hand-held response devices (clickers), learning theories, recognition of prior learning, faculty/staff and professional development, cost-effective web-based applications for teaching and learning and gender issues.

Nilay Keskin Samanci is Assistant Professor at the Department of Primary Education, Gazi University. Her research interests include bioethics education, argumentation based inquiry and socioscientific issues.

Gail Sanders is Professor of Management Education and Development. She is programme leader for the University of Sunderland Professional Doctorate and leader of the 'Leadership and Professional Practice' research cluster in the Faculty of Business and Law.

Peter Smith is Emeritus Professor of Computing. He joined the University as an undergraduate student in 1975 and received his Doctorate in 1981. Since then he has held several teaching, research and management positions at the University, including Dean, and Chair of the University Research Degrees Committee. He has published over 250 papers, and supervised and examined over 100 doctoral candidates at Universities in the UK, Europe and Hong Kong. Peter is a Fellow of the British Computer Society and the Higher Education Academy. He has published extensively on a range of subjects including computing, management, and doctoral studies, particularly in relation to Professional Doctorates.

Anil S. Rakicioglu Soylemez is an instructor at Abant İzzet Baysal University. Her major research interests include teacher education, mentoring practices and practice teaching.

Ayse Selmin Soylemez is an instructor at Abant İzzet Baysal University. Her major research interests include teaching English to young learners, materials evaluation and teacher education.

Yan Sun is an Assistant Professor of Instructional Technology at the University of West Alabama (UWA). She received her Ph.D. in Learning, Design, and Technology from Purdue University and worked as a Postdoctoral researcher at Texas A&M University before joining UWA. Her research interests revolve around K-12 STEM education and technology integration.

About the Contributors

Ece Zehir Topkaya is a lecturer at Çanakkale Onsekiz Mart University, Faculty of Education, ELT Department. She teaches several courses at undergraduate and graduate levels. Her research interests include teacher education, program evaluation, psychology of learning.

Amanda Yesilbursa is an associate professor at Uludag University. Her major research interests include teacher education and reflective teaching.

Chuang Wang is an associate professor of educational research at the University of North Carolina at Charlotte. His research interests include self-efficacy beliefs and self-regulatory behaviors of students studying English as a second language and mathematics. He teaches educational research courses and provides program evaluation services to federal- and state-funded grants. He has published 6 books, 10 book chapters, and 62 journal articles. Of the 78 publications, 45 were in the areas of reading or mathematics and were related to factors such as student, teacher, principal, superintendent, and community characteristics. He also had more than 40 paper presentations at national and international academic conferences.

Jodie Winship holds a Ph. D. from Capella University. She currently is an Assistant Professor in Special Education and serves as the Department Chair for Curriculum and Instruction at the University of West Alabama. Dr. Winship has also served as the principal investigator on Project Bloom, a STEM grant for recruiting first generation black American STEM students. Dr. Winship's research interests include assistive technologies, students with special needs, and STEM education.

Index

A

Action Research 11, 14, 16, 129, 176-178, 180, 184, 189-190, 194
AMC Anywhere 35-42, 44-48, 141-145
Authentic Learning 74, 77-78, 90, 132

B

Blended Learning 115, 119

C

CALL 38, 76, 129, 133, 168, 195-201, 204-206, 208
Capacity Building 126-128
classroom activities 34, 189, 209
Classroom Management 54, 116, 154, 159, 181-183, 185-186, 189-190, 209, 213-216, 219, 222, 230
classroom observation 141, 181, 188, 209, 231
Collaborative Action Research 176-178, 189-190, 194
Common Core 94, 138-139
conceptual understanding 93-94, 142
Content Knowledge 74, 76-77, 80, 84-85, 90, 93, 106, 110, 116, 124, 139, 141, 145, 151

D

Dilemma 126, 178, 180, 182, 184, 186, 194
Doctorate 1-2, 4-14, 16, 21, 134

E

Educational Technology 115-116, 118-119, 126-127, 129, 134-136
EFL 179, 190, 195-196, 198, 200, 205-206, 208, 212, 219-222, 224-225, 228-232, 236
English as a Foreign Language (EFL) 195

F

Fidelity 32-33, 35-48, 141, 143
flexibility 5, 29, 39, 45, 103, 231
Formative Assessment 32-37, 41, 44, 46-48, 127, 141-142, 145

H

Higher Education 9-10, 115, 126-128, 133-136, 205, 222
Hutchinson and Waters 153, 157-158, 168, 170-171

I

Instructional Practices 37, 46, 91, 145, 209-210, 216-217, 219

K

K-12 STEM Education 74-77, 80, 84

L

Learner-Centered Professional Development 34, 137-139, 143-144, 146

M

Mathematics 22, 32-39, 43-44, 47-48, 53, 60, 73, 75-76, 83, 91-99, 101, 103, 105-106, 112, 137-142, 144, 146, 150-152, 154, 171, 212
Mathematics Education 103, 105, 137
Mathematics Professional Development 32-34, 91, 94, 96, 98, 101, 106, 137, 139
Mentor 17-18, 21-22, 24-25, 28-29, 96, 176-180, 182-184, 186, 189, 194, 229
metaphors 220, 224-232

Index

N

Needs Analysis 130, 149-150, 152-157, 170
Non-Native 149-150, 154, 158, 167, 170, 232
Number Sense 34, 36, 45, 47, 141-143

P

Partners@Work 128-136
pedagogical change 57
Pedagogical Content Knowledge 74, 76, 116, 124, 139
Pedagogy 17, 27, 33-35, 57-59, 63, 65, 76, 78, 84, 94, 105, 112, 116-117, 137, 139, 150, 153
personal transformation 14
Practice Teaching 198, 205, 211, 217, 221, 223-225, 227-230, 232, 236-237
Practicum 176-183, 185-186, 188-190, 194, 210, 212-213, 217, 220-222, 230
Pre-Service Teacher Education 217, 219
Productive Language Skills 149, 170
Professional Development 5, 32-38, 40-48, 52-58, 61, 63, 66, 73-82, 84-85, 90-99, 101-106, 109, 111-113, 115-118, 120, 122, 126-129, 133-146, 165, 176-178, 180-181, 189-190, 194, 198, 211-212, 216, 229-231
Professional Development (PD) 37, 105-106, 142
Professional development programme 57-58, 61, 128-129, 136, 176, 178, 180
Professional Doctorate 1-2, 4-10, 12-14, 16
professional learning 34-35, 48, 113, 139, 145, 180, 190, 196, 205, 220-221, 223-232
Prospective EFL Teacher 220, 224, 236
Prospective EFL Teachers 195-196, 200, 205-206, 208, 220-221, 225, 228-230, 232

R

Receptive Language Skills 170
Reflection 1, 8-13, 16, 24, 33-34, 36, 38-39, 41, 43, 45, 48, 56, 63, 132, 178, 180-181, 183, 185, 187, 189-190, 194, 205, 210-213, 216-217, 219, 231, 237
reflective practice 2-4, 7, 12-14, 84, 210-212, 216-217

S

Scaffolding 63, 77, 81, 90
science education 17-18, 22, 26, 29, 56, 60
self-awareness 209
Self-efficacy Beliefs 78, 81, 85
Social Constructivist Theory 90
Staff Development 10, 92, 128, 135
Stakeholders 34, 66, 132-134, 149, 151, 155-157, 159, 167-168, 170, 178, 196, 216, 221, 229
STEM Content Knowledge 74, 76-77, 80, 84-85
STEM teacher 73-75
Student-centered pedagogies 141
Subject Teachers 149-168, 170-171

T

Target Needs 149, 153, 157-158, 167-168, 170-171
Teacher Education 54, 150-151, 154, 171, 176-179, 184, 188-191, 194-200, 205-206, 209-213, 216-217, 219-223, 230-232
Teacher Knowledge 94, 116
Teacher Leaders 91, 96-101, 103-106, 109-110, 112-113
Teacher Learning 34, 61, 94-95, 106, 139, 144-146, 176
Teacher Training 55-56, 61, 63, 103, 117, 122-123, 150, 154, 168, 170-171, 177, 197-198, 205, 208, 223, 230-231
Teaching Activities 136, 213-216, 219
Teaching Materials 219
Teaching Self 237
Technology 6, 19, 37, 53, 55, 57, 59-60, 73, 76, 83, 115-119, 121-123, 126-130, 132-136, 139, 149-150, 176, 196-199, 201-206, 208-209, 215
Technology Resources 202, 208
thinking skills 52, 59-61, 63-65, 210, 216-217
Trainee Teacher 176-178, 180, 186, 190, 194

U

use of materials 209, 214

311

IRMA — Information Resources Management Association

Become an IRMA Member

Members of the **Information Resources Management Association (IRMA)** understand the importance of community within their field of study. The Information Resources Management Association is an ideal venue through which professionals, students, and academicians can convene and share the latest industry innovations and scholarly research that is changing the field of information science and technology. Become a member today and enjoy the benefits of membership as well as the opportunity to collaborate and network with fellow experts in the field.

IRMA Membership Benefits:

- **One FREE Journal Subscription**
- **30% Off Additional Journal Subscriptions**
- **20% Off Book Purchases**

- Updates on the latest events and research on Information Resources Management through the IRMA-L listserv.
- Updates on new open access and downloadable content added to Research IRM.
- A copy of the Information Technology Management Newsletter twice a year.
- A certificate of membership.

IRMA Membership $195

Scan code to visit irma-international.org and begin by selecting your free journal subscription.

Membership is good for one full year.

www.irma-international.org